# REMAKING
# "FAMILY"
## COMMUNICATIVELY

# LIFESPAN
# COMMUNICATION

*Children, Families, and Aging*

Thomas J. Socha
GENERAL EDITOR

Vol. 1

---

The Lifespan Communication series
is part of the Peter Lang Media and Communication list.
Every volume is peer reviewed and meets
the highest quality standards for content and production.

---

**PETER LANG**
New York • Bern • Frankfurt • Berlin
Brussels • Vienna • Oxford • Warsaw

# REMAKING "FAMILY" COMMUNICATIVELY

EDITED BY **LESLIE A. BAXTER**

PETER LANG
New York • Bern • Frankfurt • Berlin
Brussels • Vienna • Oxford • Warsaw

Library of Congress Cataloging-in-Publication Data

Remaking family communicatively / edited by Leslie A. Baxter.
pages cm. — (Lifespan communication : children, families, and aging; vol. 1)
Includes bibliographical references and index.
1. Communication in families. 2. Sexual minorities' families. 3. Single-parent families.
4. Families. I. Baxter, Leslie A., editor of compilation.
HQ734.R353   306.85—dc23   2014019172
ISBN 978-1-4331-2047-3 (hardcover)
ISBN 978-1-4331-2046-6 (paperback)
ISBN 978-1-4539-1399-4 (e-book)
ISSN 2166-6466


Bibliographic information published by **Die Deutsche Nationalbibliothek.**
**Die Deutsche Nationalbibliothek** lists this publication in the "Deutsche
Nationalbibliografie"; detailed bibliographic data are available
on the Internet at http://dnb.d-nb.de/.

© 2014 Peter Lang Publishing, Inc., New York
29 Broadway, 18th floor, New York, NY 10006
www.peterlang.com

# Contents

# Remaking "Family" Communicatively

THOMAS J. SOCHA, OLD DOMINON UNIVERSITY

*Remaking "Family" Communicatively* represents a signficant development in the history of ideas about family communication. Since the early days of family communication studies in the 1980s, family communication scholars have labored to develop inclusive ways to think about and conceptualize "families." Most writers of family communication textbooks, for example, have created definitions of "family" using inclusive language and often lengthy prose to create a big tent. Similarly, those who follow the family communication research literature have also seen sincere efforts towards inclusivity, but, to date, mostly have been reading about communication in human systems populated by people cast in roles using familiar historic language. This volume offers a clarion call to all those who study, teach, and live family communication: "families" are discursively dynamic and evolve. That is, borrowing a line from an old TV commercial, today's families both are, and are not, like our "fathers'" Oldsmobiles. Professor Leslie Baxter and her authors collectively paint a wonderful portrait of the current state of conceptualizing the "family" in "family" communication that not only will inform contemporary societal discursive struggles with meanings of familial terms, but will become a much-cited work in the future.

Like this volume, the book series, *Lifespan Communication: Children, Families and Aging,* invites communication scholars to view communication through a panoramic lens—from first words to final conversations—a comprehensive communication vista that brings children, adolescents, adults, and those in later life as well as lifespan groups such as the family into focus. By viewing communication panoramically it is also my hope that communication scholars and educators will incorporate into their work the widely accepted idea that communication develops, that is, it has a starting point and a developmental arc; changing as we change over time. And further, that developmental communication arcs are historically contextualized. As infants we begin our communication education in unique historical contexts that shape our early communication learning as well as the foundations of our communication values. Children born in 2014, for example, will begin their communication learning in a time where humans are seeking to remake themselves to fit a rapidly changing and increasingly digitally mediated landscape. Of course adults caring for children—circa-2014—who, following this volume, could have been born anytime between the 1930's to the late 1990's—have experienced vastly different developmental communication arcs, but yet must discursively span the generations, pass along their communciation knowledge and values, as well as teach children how to communicate effectively within the current historical context. Historically contextualized lifespan thinking also raises important new questions such as what is to be passed along from one generation to the next as "timeless" communciation knowledge and practices? Or in contemporary digital parlance, what is to become memetic, that is, analogous to genetic information, what survives to become the communication inheritance of future generations?

It is my hope that *Remaking "Family" Communicatively*, and all of the books published in the *Lifespan Communication: Children, Families, and Aging* series will offer the communication field new understandings and deeper appreciation of the complexities of all forms of communciation as it develops across the lifespan as well as raise important questions about communication for current and future generations to study.

—Thomas J. Socha

# PART ONE

# Introductory Framings

# CHAPTER ONE

# Introduction to the Volume

LESLIE A. BAXTER

---

The goal ... should be to recognize the variety within which households can come—
the diversity of domestic relations, the inventiveness of human connection, and
not the singling out of one form of relation ... over all others.
—J. JACK HALBERSTAM, *GAGA FEMINISM* (P. 111)

The demographic data speak loudly: the modern family—the nuclear family form consisting of a husband-wife pair who raise their biological offspring in a shared household—is not the numerical norm among households. The 2010 U.S. Census was the first in the history of the census to report that households headed by a husband-wife pair dipped below the 50% point (U.S. Census Bureau, 2012, April). Households in which a husband-and-wife pair lived with their "own children" dropped to 20.2%, whereas all other household forms showed percentage increases from the 2000 Census: heterosexual couples without their own children, single-parent households, single householders living with relatives other than their own children, same-sex partner households, cohabiting opposite-sex partner households, and households headed by an adult living either alone or with non-related others. Actually, the number of husband-wife households with their own biological children is lower than this percentage. The U.S. Census Report includes as "own children" "biological, adopted, and stepchildren of the householder who are under 18" (p. 4). Of the approximately 74 million children under age 18, about 29% live with a single parent, 2.1% are adopted, 3.8% are stepchildren, 7.9% live with a grandparent, 2.2% live with another relative (usually an aunt or uncle), and 1.8% live with a nonrelative. These demographic data document a myriad of family forms that collectively are referred to as *post-nuclear families*, *nontraditional families*, *alternative families*, or *postmodern families*, and they enact what Stacey (1990) describes as the "unpredictable, often incongruous, and contested character of contemporary family practices" (p. 5) of the contemporary American family.

## The Contested Nature of "Family"

To some, the demographic portrait is reason for alarm: a nostalgic mourning for the decline in "family." However, as family historian Stephanie Coontz (1992), among others, has observed, this call to return to what is viewed as the "natural" nuclear family structure is based more on myth than on evidence of what family structure actually was like in pre-industrial America. More broadly, scholars of the history of the European family have concurred, observing that a view of the nuclear family as the natural family form is more myth than reality (e.g., Kertzer, 1991; Shorter, 1975).

The mourning of some imagined "natural" family of the historic past documents the omnipresence of a dominant ideology of "family" in which the nuclear family is valued as the natural family form. But, as the cultural critic Pierre Bourdieu (1996) has observed,

> The dominant, legitimate definition of the normal family (which may be explicit, as it is in law, or implicit, in for example, the family questionnaires used by the state statistical agencies) is based on a constellation of words ... which, while seeming to describe social reality, in fact construct it. ... A number of the groups that are called "families" in the present-day USA have absolutely no resemblance to [the] dominant definition, and ... in most modern societies the nuclear family is a minority experience. ... The new forms of family bonds that are being invented before our eyes remind us that this family, which we are led to regard as *natural* because it presents itself with the self-evidence of what "has always been that way," is a recent invention, and is perhaps fast disappearing. (p. 19)

"Family," in other words, is not a natural state of social bonding but a cultural creation. Unfortunately, what is commonly accepted as "natural" becomes a standard against which alternatives are judged as "unnatural," a deviation from what is "normal," and thus subject to a judgment of inferiority or illegitimacy. As Bourdieu continued,

> Every time we use a classificatory concept like "family," we are making both a description and a prescription, which is not perceived as such because it is (more or less) universally accepted and goes without saying. We tacitly admit that the reality to

which we give the name "family," and which we place in the category of "real" families, is a family in reality. (p. 20)

Familial arrangements that depart from the ideological "gold standard" of the nuclear family face a burden of legitimation, or what Kathleen Galvin refers to in the next chapter as the burden of discourse dependence.

But not so fast, you might be thinking. Apart from a general claim that many people bemoan the demographics in which the nuclear family appears to be on the decline, what evidence can be presented to support the claim that the ideology of the nuclear family is still alive and well in contemporary Western societies, the U.S. in particular? We can think metaphorically of the ideology of the nuclear family as a stool with three legs: co-residence, heterosexual marriage, and shared genes. These three ideological "legs" are inscribed in public policy, the attitudes of typical Americans, and even in the practices of social scientists who study families.

Let's start at the public policy level with the U.S. Census Report (U.S. Census, 2012, April), with which I began this introduction. All three ideological legs through which the nuclear family is supported as the preferred norm seep into the very statistical fabric of this census undertaking.

First, this document, and the census practices that produced it, privileges shared residence as the portal of entry into the American family: "A 'household' includes all of the people who occupy a housing unit" (U.S. Census, 2012, April p. 4). One person in each household is designated by the census participant as the "householder," usually "the person, or one of the persons, in whose name the home is being purchased or rented" (p. 4). In the ideology of the nuclear family, this identified householder is often the male head of household in a heterosexual married couple. All other household members are linked through association to this householder, and a family represents a particular kind of social arrangement: "A family consists of a householder and one or more other people living in the same household who are related to the householder by birth, marriage, or adoption" (p. 4).

The requirement of shared residence clearly instantiates one anchor of the metaphorical stool of the traditional family unit. However, as Stacey (1990, p. 6) so eloquently expressed, for many individuals "family" "is a locus not of residence but of meaning and relationships." When shared residence is invoked as a necessary criterion of "family," certain social arrangements are dis-allowed as families. For example, a nonresidential parent with whom the children live for only a minority of their time does not count as a family because the majority of the time is spent with the residential parent. Similarly, stepfamilies in which the stepchild lives with the nonresidential parent and his or her new spouse for only part of the year are not included as a family form because the child does not reside in the household for a majority of the year. Additionally, persons who think of their extended family as their "family" cannot be recognized as an official family unless all of the extended family members reside in the same household. Persons who think of their family as their close social network consisting of established bonds of affection and support—voluntary kin—are also precluded from family status, as well, unless they share a residence as a requisite condition. Such statistical invisibility makes it challenging for family policy to work on behalf of many types of families that do not share a residency, because their presence in the society cannot be statistically documented.

Although shared residence is a necessary condition for family status according to the U.S. Census Bureau, it is not sufficient. The definition of a family described above requires a relationship of marriage, legal adoption, or birth (blood). The U.S. Census Report (U.S. Census, 2012, April) is clear in privileging not just the institution of marriage, but a heterosexual, husband-wife marriage. In what can only be described as a stunning categorization feat, same-sex spousal households, the report informs the reader, are included in the category "same-sex unmarried partner households" (p. 4). Their status as a family is contingent on the presence of another person who is related to the householder (e.g., a biological or adopted child of the householder). Cohabiting heterosexual partners, in the absence of the presence of another person related to the householder, are also counted as a "nonfamily household," as are households consisting of persons who live with others with whom they are unrelated (p. 4). The U.S. Census Bureau allows female and male householders, "no spouse present" (p. 4), to count as family households so long as they contain their "own children" or other persons with whom they are related by blood or law (e.g., a parent or a sibling). In short, a heterosexual husband-wife pair automatically qualifies for family status, but other social arrangements are eligible for family status only if a third party related by law or birth resides with the primary householder.

Family status can also be earned on the basis of birth, not simply law, according to the U.S. Census Bureau (2012, April). The criterion of birth, of course, privileges a biogenetic conception of the family and the role of biological reproduction. Reported subcategories within the supra-category of "family households" are subdivided according to the presence or absence of "own children" under 18 years of age. Of course, the focus on children disadvantages households without children, by choice or circumstance, unless they are a heterosexual, husband-wife pair.

Statistical exclusion from family status does not distribute equally across racial/ethnic backgrounds. The ideological "gold standard" of families—the household consisting of a husband, wife, and their own children—captures 32% of Asian American households but only 13% of Black or African American households. Single parents with "own children" represent 20% of Black or African American households but only 7% of White, non-Hispanic households. Cohabiting pairs (including same-sex spouses; see above discussion) reflect 11% of American Indian/Alaska Native households but only 4% of Asian American households. The implication is self-evident: racial/ethnic groups in the U.S. do not live in the ideologically preferred modern family structure to the same extent (and no group has a majority of its households described as a nuclear family), positioning members of some groups more than others to face larger discursive burdens of legitimacy.

The significance of government policy cannot be underestimated, because it is the locus of institutionalized legitimation and access to resources. As Butler (2002) astutely observed, "The failure to secure state recognition for one's intimate arrangements can only be experienced as a form of derealization" (p. 26). Invisibility as a "real family," in other words, implicates psychological and material disenfranchisement.

If we move beyond the institutionalization of shared residency, heterosexual marriage, and biological ties displayed in the U.S. Census Report (U.S. Census, 2012, April) to consider attitudes of typical Americans, we see the same pattern of privilege: the ideological "gold standard" of the nuclear family is still idealized, despite its diminished demographic presence. In his classic ethnographic study of American attitudes and beliefs about kinship, Schneider (1980) noted that American conceptions of the ideal family are organized by two core constituent elements: blood (through reproduction) and law (through marriage). He argued that these two elements are both rooted in sexual intercourse between a man and a woman: "The members of the family are defined in terms of sexual intercourse as a reproductive act, stressing the sexual relationship between husband and wife and the biological identity between parent and child, and between siblings" (p. 52). The institution of marriage formally recognizes the husband-wife union, and in turn legitimizes legal relationships that are formed through marriage: the various kinds of in-laws (parent, siblings, aunts/uncles). Of course, these two criteria become fuzzier the further removed they are from the nuclear family: is a third cousin twice removed regarded as "family"? Schneider argued that at the outer boundaries of blood and law, people introduce a third criterion to organize family status: emotional closeness. Thus, that third cousin who is twice removed could count as family if the persons experience some emotional solidarity with one another.

Although Schneider's work is now dated, it is amazingly current in describing current American attitudes about "family." The Pew Research Center (Morin, 2011) recently conducted a survey about American attitudes toward changes in family structure among a national, representative sample of 2,691 adults. Respondents were asked to judge seven trends in family structure as good, bad, or of no consequence for society, five of which are relevant to this volume:

more unmarried couples raising children, more gay and lesbian couples raising children, more single women having children without a male partner to help raise them, more people living together without getting married, and more women not ever having children (the two other trends included were mothers of young children working outside the home and people of different races marrying each other). About a third (31%) of participants was categorized as *Accepters*, disproportionately reporting that the trends were of no consequence or even good for society. A similar share of the respondents (32%), the *Rejecters*, indicated that the trends were bad for society. The remainder (37%) was categorized as *Skeptics*, expressing more reservations than the Accepters but not as uniformly negative as the Rejecters. Demographic differences differentiated the groups: Accepters were more likely to be women, Hispanics, East Coast residents, and those who rarely attended religious services. Rejecters were more likely to be Whites, older adults, Republicans, married, and religiously observant. Young people, Democrats and Independents, and minorities were disproportionately more likely to be Skeptics. Overall, relatively small percentages of any group regarded any of the trends as "a good thing for society" (p. 3). Thus, even the group that most embraced change—the Accepters—might better be described as merely less skeptical and negative than the other two groups. More telling were respondent answers to questions posed about the ideal family. Although the "gold standard" of a husband-and-wife married couple with children is the ideal, about 85–90% of members from the three groups regarded a childless heterosexual married couple as a family. Respondents ranged across groups from 74–96% in regarding a single parent with children as a family. A majority of the Accepters (96%) and the Skeptics (86%) regarded an unmarried heterosexual couple with children as a family, compared to only 55% of the Rejecters. A majority of the Accepters and the Skeptics (with percentages of 84% and 75%, respectively) also regarded a same-sex couple with children as a family, compared to only 31% of the Rejecters. Whereas a majority of the Accepters regarded a same-sex couple without children and an unmarried heterosexual couple without children as a family (68% and 60%, respectively) the majority of the other two groups reported that neither configuration was a family. The results of this public opinion survey suggest that the criteria of blood (represented by the presence of biological children) and heterosexual marriage are still significant features of the contemporary American attitude with respect to who counts as a "family." Clearly "family" is conceived on a sliding scale; if a given household unit has both heterosexual marriage and biological children, it is regarded as more of a family than households that have one but not both of these core features, and household units that lack both of these elements—same-sex couples without children—are perceived as least like a family.

Research by scholars in family studies, including family communication, supports the pattern captured by the Pew Research Center (Morin, 2011). A number of studies have relied on study participant assessments of family status associated with a variety of different family structures. In 1990, Trost (1990) asked a Swedish sample to provide judgments of family status for various hypothetical family constellations, finding that the two-parent with child constellation was most frequently regarded as a family. Subsequent replications of this classic study with U.S. samples (Baxter et al., 2009; Ford, 1994) document the stability of privilege accorded the nuclear family. In particular, Baxter and her colleagues (2009) presented study participants with 23 different family scenarios designed to vary systematically with respect to several core structural features (e.g., presence vs. absence of marriage). The study also manipulated perceptions of the quantity of communication between family members. Participants were asked to indicate the extent to which each scenario was a family. Although a perception of greater communication among the scenario members increased the perception of family status across all family structures, systematic differences in perception emerged based on structural feature. Results indicated that the presence of children, intactness (as opposed to separation and divorce), co-residence, marriage, heterosexuality (but only in the absence of children), and nonfictive status (i.e., the presence of some tie legitimated through blood or law) increased perceptions of family status. Highest family status was associated with the nuclear family scenario. To test of the importance accorded to a biogenetic link between parents and children, Holtzman (2008) asked her participants to respond to a hypothetical scenario of mistaken identity in which a mix-up at the hospital sent the wrong child home with parents. The study determined whether participants privileged biology over affection in the parent-child relationship. Although they experienced some ambivalence, participants still favored the sanctity of the biological bond overall.

Several studies have examined developmental differences in a child's conception of family (e.g., Gilby & Pederson, 1982; Newman, Roberts, & Syre, 1993; Nixon, Greene, & Hogan, 2006; Powell, Wiltcher, Wedemeyer, & Claypool, 1981). Overall, this body of work suggests that children develop cognitively in ways that internalize society's norms of "family." Rigg and Pryor (2007), for example, asked children ages 9–13 to determine whether certain social constellations of people were a family. Study participants were most likely to define a married couple with children as family. However, the researchers also found that participants were quite inclusive overall. The researchers contrasted the outcomes of this study with one conducted with older adolescents (Anyan & Pryor, 2002), in which the older sample was less inclusive and used more stringent blood and law criteria of family status.

Members of nontraditional or alternative families perceive that they are stigmatized and misunderstood, facing challenges beyond those faced by nuclear families. Many of the chapters in this volume discuss this work, and I will not repeat a discussion of that research here. I will, however, provide a very personal account that provides a taste of what marginalized family status feels like. I am the single parent of an adopted daughter. One of the colleges to which my child applied found our financial aid application inadequate. First, the forms did not have a box that captured adequately our family status; marking "single" (from among the other two choices of "married" and "divorced") didn't suffice, as it turned out. "Single" parental status, it seems, still required me to have a nonresidential father complete financial forms before our financial aid package could be determined. I wrote "not applicable" on all of these forms for the nonresidential father, indicating that I had adopted my daughter from a foreign country when she was a baby and that there was, in fact, no nonresidential father who could provide financial assistance. The financial aid office replied by informing me that they couldn't accept my application as it stood, asking me to document further that there was no additional income from the nonresidential father, perhaps through a testimonial by a minister or other respected person familiar with our family. I experienced that request for outside verification from a credible source as suspicion that my application lacked full disclosure. I felt that our family configuration was invisible—impossible for others to imagine. At that point, I complained and fortunately was heard. I share this personal experience because it nicely illustrates the additional discursive burden that accompanies family forms situated outside what is commonly understood as normative. In the end, our family was treated fairly by this financial aid office, but I had to work extra hard to bring this about. This example perhaps seems inconsequential, but it documents the everyday nature of lived experience outside the normative nuclear family. It underscores what Galvin describes in the next chapter as the external boundary management work that alternative family members face as they seek to gain legitimacy for their family by outsiders.

Scholars of family communication have, in part, contributed to a reproduction of the ideology of the nuclear family by devoting the bulk of their research attention to married heterosexual couples and parent interactions with their "own children"; invisibility is a consequence of unstudied or under-studied families. In their portrait of family communication research over the 1990–2009 period, Stamp and Shue (2013) reported that the most frequently studied context was the "married couple." Related contexts such as "husbands," "wives," and "first marriage families" further implicate the marital dyad. "Children," "parent-child," and related terms implicate the centrality of children in researcher attention to the family. In an examination of over one thousand studies from the interdisciplinary area of family studies, Fingerman and Hay (2002) identified a similar abundance of work on marriage and parent-child relationships. Schneider's (1980) criteria of blood (through reproduction) and law (through marriage) appear to be central to contemporary research on the family. Furthermore, when alternative families are investigated, they are often studied in comparison to the "gold standard" of the traditional family, implying that the latter is the baseline against which all difference should be assessed (Pahl & Spencer, 2010).

## "Family" as a Communicative Accomplishment

Although researchers still appear to privilege the traditional family as the object of study, several family scholars have opened the conceptual door in ways that are potentially helpful in understanding post-nuclear families from a communication perspective. In particular, three basic conceptual approaches to defining the family have emerged in family studies (Koerner & Fitzpatrick, 2013; Segrin & Flora, 2011; Wamboldt & Reiss, 1989). The *structural* approach emphasizes the presence or absence of particular family members or roles; this definition tends to favor legally institutionalized forms of family, especially the nuclear family. The second approach, the *psychosocial task*, defines a family according to the accomplishment of certain tasks together, such as maintaining a household, raising children, and providing financial security for fellow family members. Although this definition potentially is more encompassing of a variety of family forms, it tends to privilege co-residence and child-bearing/raising as the most valued tasks, thereby contributing in the end to the value attached to the nuclear family. The third approach, the *transactional*, focuses on "a sense of family identity with emotional ties and a shared experience of a history and a future" (Koerner & Fitzpatrick, p. 129) that flows from interaction over time. This third conceptual approach is not bound by either institutional or functional constraints, instead emphasizing the affectional bonds that create a feeling of family. Certainly, all three of these definitional criteria can apply to a given family; an emotionally close nuclear family that functions effectively meets all definitions at once. But not all nuclear families are functional or have a shared identity of emotional closeness. Some social groups feel like a family, although they lack structural institutionalization and enactment of all of the functions commonly associated with a family. Other social groups could enact basic functions such as child rearing but without institutionalization or emotional closeness. Certainly, structural approaches have dominated in family studies, including family communication, and the focus on the nuclear family evidences this approach.

Psychosocial task (i.e., functional) and transactional (identity-based and affection-based) approaches implicate communication most directly and thus are of greatest relevance to the contributors of this volume. Put simply, both of these approaches share a view of the family as constructed or produced through the communicative actions of their members. Families are the result of what we *do*—the product of our everyday communicative accomplishments of functioning and feeling like a family (e.g., Medved, 2004; Nelson, 2006). Butler (2002) eloquently captured the essence of a functional approach to family, defining family as a set of practices "that emerge to address fundamental forms of human dependency, which may include birth, child-rearing, relations of emotional dependency and support, generational ties, illness, dying, and death (to name a few)" (p. 15). The litmus test of family status from a functional perspective is the "walks like a duck, talks like a duck, is a duck" approach; if a social group functions like a family, then it is a family, regardless of its institutionalized structure. Similarly, a transactional approach to family also emphasizes family-as-doing. However, unlike a functional approach, the emphasis is less on instrumental tasks that are enacted and more on the bonds of identity and affection that emerge over time through interaction. The litmus test of family status from a transactional approach is whether the members of a social group feel like a family. Both functional and transactional approaches emphasize communication, the former for its task capacities and the latter for its socioemotional capacities. Both of these approaches share a view that the family is a process of communicative enactment and performance.

From the perspective of functional and transactional approaches, a society's preference for the nuclear family structure can be understood as a sedimentation of certain functions, affections, and identities that cultural members allow and favor. It is not "natural" but rather an ideological product. The nuclear family has become sedimented as the idealized family structure because it privileges sexual reproduction and child-rearing above all other functions and legitimates above all other kinds of affection that between heterosexual partners and parents and their own children. Legitimated family forms are thus the result of the everyday communicative actions of "family" members, as they ongoingly reproduce the status quo or construct alternative meanings of "family" with respect to allowed functions, affections, and identities. Post-nuclear families, taking a variety of forms, increase the palette of the allowable with respect to functions, affections, and identities of legitimate families.

## The Present Volume

This volume represents recent scholarship by family communication scholars to understand, functionally and transactionally, how alternative families are constructed communicatively. In contrast to existing books on family communication, in which chapters or paragraphs on selected post-nuclear family forms are introduced as "add-on" counterpoint to an emphasis on nuclear families, I wanted to produce a book that gathered together as many alternatives to the nuclear family as we could identify that had amassed sufficient research to warrant a whole chapter. I wanted to produce a volume in which each alternative family form was considered on its own terms, rather than in comparison to the nuclear family. Certainly, the volume does not exhaust all of the kinds of family that are lived daily in these postmodern times. For example, foster care families or families developed through reproductive technologies receive mention in some of the chapters but await more scholarly attention by communication researchers to justify their own chapters. I also wanted to stretch beyond the boundaries of U.S. society, a challenging enterprise for family communication scholars who disproportionately focus on families in the U.S. Although anthropologists of kinship have been describing for quite some time the various forms of kinship in non-Western societies, this book is not envisioned as a comparative study of the family. Rather, the organizing question for the book focuses on resistance, reconstruction, and resilience: how is it that alternatives to the traditional family are constructed and sustained through communicative practices?

The word "remaking" in the title of the book is intended at both macro and micro levels. At the macro level, the various chapters in the book document a variety of family forms that collectively contribute to the proportional decline in the nuclear family unit, a description of which opened this chapter. But a risk in organizing a book by family form is the ease with which these categories can be seen as stable and discrete. If one were to follow a given family through time with a micro-level analysis, a more dynamic portrait would emerge in which family members float in and out of various family forms. Using myself as an example, in my lifetime I have been a member of a nuclear family, a commuter marriage family, an extended family, a single-parent biological family, a stepfamily, a single-parent adoptive family, and several fictive kin families. My suspicion is that the contributors to, and readers of, this volume could report similar fluidity in their lived experiences of family. The military family, discussed in Chapter Twelve by Erin Sahlstein Parcell, nicely illustrates the fluidity of family forms, as family members move in and out of deployments and re-entries to co-present family life. In short, individuals remake their own families across the lifespan and thereby constitute the family forms that demographers study at the societal, or macro, level.

The post-nuclear family forms highlighted in this book manifest varying degrees of blood and law. The stepfamily combines blood (biological offspring of a residential parent) with the legal bond of remarriage between adults. The adopted family supplants a biological parent-child relationship with a legal one. Single-parent families suspend the legal institution of marriage but retain a biological/legal parent-child relationship. Same-sex partnerships challenge the institution of heterosexual marriage. Grandfamilies—grandparents who serve as the primary parent—retain a legal or biological link to the child. Childless families retain marriage. Deployed military families and commuter marriage families suspend shared residence but retain some legal/biological bond among family members. Hindu marriages of urban India retain the legal institution of marriage but construct it along affectional lines. Diasporic families abandon the shared residence of the extended family unit in the face of geographic separation across nations. Fictive, or voluntary, kin typically suspend legal, biological, and perhaps even shared-residence features in envisioning family in new ways. Clearly, if we accept Galvin's argument in the next chapter, members of these various family forms assume different discursive burdens depending on their claims to the legitimated anchors of co-residence, heterosexual marriage, and biological reproduction—those three "legs" of the dominant ideology of family discussed above. None of the family forms described in the volume meets the ideological "gold standard" of the nuclear family, and in this sense they all represent a remaking of the family in profound ways.

The book is organized into four parts. Part I, "Introductory Framings" consists of this opening introductory chapter and two conceptual/theoretical chapters. In Chapter Two, Kathleen Galvin discusses her concept of discourse dependence, an important historical construct in anchoring efforts by family communication scholars to expand beyond studying marriages and biological parent-child relationships to give visibility to a variety of alternative ways of doing family. In Chapter Three, I follow up on Galvin's important conceptual work in discourse dependence to consider ways to theoretically explain and understand how discourse dependence is communicatively enacted. Several theories are mentioned throughout this book, and this chapter is an attempt to put the spotlight directly on selected theoretical issues that can illuminate discourse dependence. Three central theoretical issues (the three R's of the chapter's title) are emphasized: Remaking (the need to study communication in its own right), Resistance (the need to examine how stigma/marginalization are resisted), and Resilience (the need to study the factors that contribute to family success and well-being).

Parts II, III, and IV of the book organize chapters devoted, respectively, to communicative remakings of "family" that move beyond traditional marriage, beyond biological ties, and beyond shared residence. Several of the chapters could easily fit in more than one of these sections of the book. Stepfamilies, for example, typically contain two households—that of the residential parent and that of the nonresidential parent—and could just as easily have been placed in the last section of the book in which co-residence is suspended. However, given that much of the research focuses on the non-biological relationships in stepfamilies, especially the stepparent-stepchild, I decided to locate the stepfamily chapter in the section of the book devoted to remaking "family" beyond biological ties. Because biological linkages are given rather than voluntary, I decided to place the chapter on voluntary kin relations in Part III of the book, but voluntary kin members also challenge the institution of marriage and often co-residence, as well. Many single parents and gay/lesbian pairs adopt children. And so on, as we contemplate the many permutations of the post-nuclear family.

Part II of the book, "Remaking 'Family' Beyond Traditional Marriage," contains four chapters that cohere around communicative challenges to traditional marriage as requisite to family status. In Chapter Four, Pamela Lannutti takes up the political dispute that is highly visible in U.S. society—whether gays and lesbians should be granted legal rights to marry. Lannutti presents a complex picture, addressing, in part, the fissure within the gay/lesbian community on this issue. The institution of marriage is steeped in heteronormativity, patriarchy, and sexual reproduction, and one issue of concern is whether legitimation of same-sex marriages co-opts the critique of that institution. Chapter Five, by Tamara Afifi, Shardé Davis, and Anne Merrill, examines how single-parent families create a sense of "family" through their communicative practices with one another. Many, but certainly not all, single-parent families are the product of divorce, and many might transition into stepfamily status. But other single-parent families do not fit this pattern at all. Regardless, single-parent families face unique challenges. The chapter emphasizes the communicative practices of resilience that characterize many of these families. Chapter Six, by Melissa Alemán, pursues grandfamilies in which at least one grandparent is the primary caregiver of a grandchild. This family form is different from a multi-generational family unit in which at least one parent resides with children and the children's grandparents; grandfamilies are missing parents. Last, Chapter Seven, by Devika Chawla, pushes our sensibilities out of the U.S. to examine urban India. Although the institution of heterosexual marriage is central to Indian ideology of the family, it is the arranged marriage that is privileged: a conception of marriage in which a given husband-wife pair is integrally woven together in an extended family web headed by the husband's parents. Chawla considers how urban Indian women communicatively perform an alternative understanding of their arranged marriages, one that emphasizes romantic love.

Part III, "Remaking 'Family' beyond Biological Ties," consists of four chapters that challenge in one way or another the sanctity accorded to biological reproduction and biological children in constituting "family." Keli Steuber examines childless families in Chapter Eight. She considers the extraordinary pressure to reproduce experienced by many infertile heterosexual couples, and the pressures experienced by couples who make the voluntary choice to remain childfree. The ideology of the nuclear family is evident in both kinds of experiences. In Chapter Nine, Elizabeth Suter reviews the growing communication research on the adopted family—whether the child is adopted domestically through private adoption or the public child welfare system of foster care, or through transnational adoption. In both kinds of adoption, transracial families are often constructed in visible adoptions. Adoption typically is conceived as a triangle of relationships consisting of the adopted child, the birth mother and other blood relations, and the adoptive family. Chapter Ten, by Paul Schrodt, reviews the now fairly extensive communication research on stepfamilies. Stepfamilies experience a range of challenges, and as a result, remarried partners in stepfamily configurations face, as a group, a high divorce rate (National Stepfamily Resource Center, 2013). Schrodt examines the communicative practices that are related to stepfamily resilience or decline. Finally, Dawn Braithwaite and Rebecca DiVerniero examine so-called fictive or voluntary kin in Chapter Eleven. They demonstrate that the voluntary family is not a unitary type but instead is a mix of several functional types, each with their own unique communicative challenges.

Part IV, "Remaking 'Family" beyond Shared Households," consists of three chapters that challenge in one way or another the requisite of co-residence for family status. In Chapter Twelve, Erin Sahlstein Parcell examines the unique communicative challenges and practices of resilience faced by military families who have at least one deployed family member. In contrast to military deployment, which usually unfolds for fixed time periods of time, Karla Bergen addresses in Chapter Thirteen more permanent long-distance families: the so-called commuter family in which adults have separate residences. The challenges of long distance are highlighted in both of these chapters, but these two family forms are enacted somewhat differently, as well. The final chapter in the volume, Chapter Fourteen by Chitra Akkoor, moves us beyond U.S. borders in a consideration of diasporic families. Although the U.S. is populated with many diasporic families, the diasporic family experience is a global one, and Akkoor's chapter emphasizes the global problems faced by families who immigrate to Western societies that privilege the nuclear family instead of the extended family unit.

References are assembled at the end of the volume for the convenience of the reader interested in a reference compendium of classic and recent work on family remakings.

# CHAPTER TWO

# Blood, Law, and Discourse

## Constructing and Managing Family Identity

KATHLEEN M. GALVIN

*The family tree by the year 2033 will be rooted as deeply as ever in America's social landscape, but it will be sprouting some odd branches.*
—(U.S. NEWS & WORLD REPORT, AS QUOTED IN STACEY, 1990, P. 3)

"Family" emerged as a highly contested term during the last quarter of the 20th century. It remains so today. Around the dawn of the 21st century, numerous scholars and journalists addressed these changes. Controversial family scholar Judith Stacey claimed that "Voting with their hearts and deeds rather than their words and creeds, the vast majority of Americans have been actively remaking their family lives, and their expectations about family life as well" (1996, p. 9). Sociologist Andrew Cherlin (2009a) depicted contemporary family life as "a bewildering set of alternatives" (p. 8), arguing that these variations impacted everyday life. To the shock of many longtime readers, in 2002 the Sunday *New York Times'* wedding announcements section included commitment ceremonies between same-sex partners for the first time. Concurrently, many K-12 schools expanded the options for who may attend "school conferences," previously known as "parent-teacher conferences." Today the concept of family remains in flux as fewer families are formed solely through law and biology than was the case in the past century.

Discourse—that is, language use—now serves as the third leg of the "definitional family stool" due to its increasing importance in family identity construction, maintenance and deconstruction. An examination of contemporary families created and/or recreated through blood, law, and discourse reveals that discourse plays an increasingly significant role in constructing family identity when the cultural indicators of blood and/or law are less salient or absent. Over the past four decades, as increasing numbers of families confronted challenges to their identity, members found themselves engaging outsiders or each other in discourse designed to establish, and re-establish, their familial identities.

Discourse contributes to the creation of family identity both implicitly and explicitly. It undergirds the everyday lives of all families as it instantiates members' identity for outsiders and, frequently, even for insiders. As the family formation process shifts farther away from legal and biological ties, members find themselves enacting a wide range of discourse strategies to create, maintain, reconfigure and/or disconfirm their overall family identity and/or specific relational ties. Currently family identity serves as a commonplace subject of conversation between and among outsiders and insiders. Outsiders sometimes challenge, directly or indirectly, the validity of a familial claim when members bear little resemblance to each other; variations, such as age differences or skin color, call family membership into question. Conversely, even insiders express curiosity or concern regarding their own or another's familial status.

When a familial claim is challenged, family members' use of discourse strategies supports their ability to create and maintain their identity as a social group and to establish and reinforce family meanings. Members engage in communicative strategies to create, maintain and reinforce their own or other members' family identity. These strategies include such discourse practices as: telling family birth stories, participating in special family rituals, managing family identity secrets, developing unique family terminology, establishing communication rules about discussing identity, and creating family histories to share with each other and/or outsiders. Such implicit and explicit strategies serve to enhance family members' cohesion while signaling members' connections to outsiders.

In recent decades, family researchers across multiple disciplines have acknowledged the role of interactional effort or, more specifically, the role of discourse in constructing family identity (Gordon, 2009, Holstein & Gubrium, 1999; Nelson, 2006, Tannen, 2007). Everyday discourse plays a continuous role in managing family identity, even for members sharing full blood and/or legal ties. For members of families formed outside of full bloodlines and legal ties, conscious strategic discourse assumes an increasingly significant role in constructing or deconstructing familial identity. Therefore, the role of discourse in constructing and maintaining contemporary family identity warrants far greater attention than it has received to date.

Currently, increasing numbers of family communication scholars engage in the active exploration of "how the meanings surrounding individual and relationship identities are constructed through language use" (Baxter, 2011, p. 2). This essay addresses the processes involved in discursively constructing, maintaining, reconfiguring, and disconfirming family identity. To appreciate fully this ongoing discursive familial evolution, some elaborated background is in order before returning to the discussion of family interaction and identity.

# A Brief Historical Overview

Family history varies significantly across countries and cultures. American history privileges sentimental depictions of middle and upper class marriages and two-parent families. Although images of the tightly knit extended family and the biological nuclear family remain firmly embedded in hallowed memory, because this family form thrived during much of the 20th century, complex relational ties characterized American family life from the first settlers to the present. According to noted family historian Stephanie Coontz (1999b), "there has never been a single family model in the United States and that change has been a constant feature of every kind of family" (p. xii).

## Status of the Family

Early American history depicts significant variations in family forms as countless immigrants and pioneers struck out alone, or in pairs, creating some type of family form within the communities they founded or joined. Only in the late 19th century did Americans begin to elevate the nuclear family and its attendant expectations of loyalty, obligation, and personal satisfaction. Even in this period, a significant percentage of the population did not experience this family form, and even those that did experienced it as a mother-child alliance and a formal husband-wife connection (Coontz, 1992). Far fewer contemporary American families reflect full blood and legal ties compared to families in the middle of the 20th century. This shift to valuing the nuclear family form, reflected in many Western nations, is not necessarily generalizable to non-Western nations.

The early 20th century bore witness to the Great Depression and two World Wars, each of which deeply affected American family life. World War II provided women with a taste of life in the labor force, a circumstance that created new workplace options for women. A post-war nation idealized marriage and family; suburbs developed, and life in single-family homes filled with children became the norm and/or dream for countless young couples who married during the late 1940s into the early 1960s. Because marriage was viewed as a "forever" commitment, parents attempted to ensure their offspring met the "right" potential mates

(Blumstein & Schwartz, 1983). Adoption agencies carefully matched adoptive parents and a child, in order to suggest a biological tie and save parents from the stigma of infertility (Riley & Van Vleet, 2012). This period became known as the "golden era of the American family" (Kendall-Tackett, 2001, p. 84). Other family variations received scant scholarly or journalistic attention.

Radical changes to the image and enactment of family life occurred during the late 1960s and 1970s; this period witnessed strong challenges to established familial relational patterns and assumptions. Family members' conflicts over the Vietnam War contributed to generational schisms. The Women's Movement persuaded many wives and mothers to leave the house in order to enter the workplace, while the "pill" provided women, married or single, with control over their fertility. Increasing numbers of women enrolled in college, meeting and marrying men from different classes, races, and religions. Divorce rates soared as women became more educated and financially independent, and as states passed no-fault divorce laws beginning with California in 1969. Political upheavals and personal opportunities forever altered the "Leave It to Beaver" image of "*The* American Family."

Academic writings on the family proliferated, much of it focused on marriage and children in the later decades of the 20th century. In 1973 sociologist Jessie Bernard published her landmark book *The Future of Marriage*, arguing that partners live within two marriages—his marriage and her marriage—and that his marriage involves greater control, power, and freedom. Such messages reinforced women's desire for greater gender equality. Yet, a decade later, Blumstein and Schwartz published *American Couples* (1983), a landmark study of four couple types—heterosexual married, heterosexual cohabiting, lesbian, and gay male—concluding that "The American family has changed more in the last thirty years than in the previous two hundred and fifty" (p. 25). They also acknowledged how little was known about the everyday lives of three of their couple types. Their book received extensive press, shocking academics and everyday adults alike.

Amidst growing change and upheaval, the nuclear family maintained its dominant and desirable image, privileging the qualities of heterosexuality, parenthood, biological children, marriage and legality, well into the last quarter of the 20th century. Legal recognition of other family forms remained difficult because, "The idealization of a natural nuclear family is preserved through constant reiteration and recitation of family ideology in political and social rituals—these images are reflected in law" (Fineman, 1993, p. 392). Although variations in family forms continued to be viewed as less desirable, the age of first marriage continued to rise as did divorce rates (U.S. Bureau of the Census, 1992). During this period transracial and transnational partnerships and adoption gained greater acceptance, creating multiple families formed through "visible difference."

The rise in transnational and transracial adoption also reflected the high number of single White pregnant women choosing to raise their children as single parents (Pertman, 2011).

By the close of the 20th century the nature of "The American Family" appeared more complicated and contentious. In 1992 Coontz argued that "Compared to the first sixty years of the twentieth century, then, there is now an increasing diversity of family types in America" (p. 183). For example, according to Footlick (1990), "In unprecedented numbers, our families are unalike" (p. 9). A 1990 *Newsweek* poll revealed that, by a ratio of three to one, respondents defined the family as a group of people who love and care for each other" rather than relying on a legalistic definition of a group of people related by blood, marriage, or adoption (Stacey, 1996, p. 9). Extending the conversation to a logical conclusion, the renowned sociologist Anthony Giddens (1993), theorized that the economic and social conditions of late modernity enabled a liberated practice of intimacy that he labeled "pure relationship" (p. 2). He went on to assert that, because it was now possible to separate sexuality from childbearing, individuals could pursue intimacy for its own sake and such intimate relationships would endure only as long as each partner experienced enough satisfaction to remain in it. The ongoing increases in sequential partnerships, voluntary childless marriage (Durham & Braithwaite, 2009), and same-sex partnerships (Lewin, 2009) serve to support his position. Arguments on the future of the family raged into the 21st century as various factions advanced various criteria for being a "real" family; in some circles they continue to rage.

## The Status of Marriage

Historically, marriage was viewed by many as the gold standard of adult relational life, a pact sanctioned by law and frequently by God—a commitment severed only by death. Yet, the history of American marriage reveals an "elusive traditional family" (Coontz, 1992, p. 10). Although images of the "until death do us part" ideal marriage remain to this day, everyday life belied such stereotypical images. Increasingly adults lived alternative partnered lives, yet little was known about their relationships, such as heterosexual cohabiting pairs and same-sex partnerships. Legal scholar Fineman (1993) depicted marriage as the venerated family form protected by legal and cultural institutions, warning that living in alternative intimate arrangements left individuals outside the protection of legal and cultural institutions. His warning went unheeded.

Today marriage remains an idealized partnership form, even though trends reveal that barely half of adults are currently married (Cohn, Passel, Wang & Livingston, 2011). First marriages take place later, usually after a period of cohabitation

(Wilcox, 2009). Yet, individuals increasingly opt for nontraditional partnerships. Within the past fifty years the lockstep pattern of long marriages with multiple children devolved to various lifestyle alternatives; many first marriages occur after the bride has borne one or more children, a significant reversal of the traditional U.S. marriage pattern but a replication of the Western European shift to marriage after children, if at all (Eurostat, 2012). Cherlin (2009a) characterizes contemporary U.S. marriages as more fragile than those in many other countries, attributing this fragility to the cultural assumption that marriage should fulfill each partner's personal needs and desires. Expectations of companionship, intimacy and security place strong demands on each partner; such expectations do not necessarily exist in many other cultures, especially in Eastern cultures.

Yet, although individuals and partnerships can thrive outside of marriage, it continues to be the most desired and most prestigious way to have a family—"the ultimate merit badge" (Cherlin, 2009a, p. 142). Given the economic pressures, marriage remains outside the reach of many lower income individuals while appearing personally or politically undesirable to others. Yet, given the opportunity, increasing numbers of members of same-sex partnerships choose to make a legal marital commitment to maintain a partnership "until death do us part." For many, marriage still remains an elusive dream.

## U.S. Population Trends

Recent U.S. Census data confirm major ongoing changes in family life, variations that eventually impact the family identity discourse that members engage in with outsiders and other members of their families. Therefore, a very brief overview of family life seems to be in order.

Americans are marrying at older ages. Between 2006 and 2010 the median age at marriage was 25.8 for women and 28.3 for men (Copen, Daniels, Vespa & Mosher, 2012). A 2009 Census Report indicates that later marriage contributes to the later age of divorce, and those who recently married had higher levels of education than the general population (Elliott & Simmons, 2011).

Marriage duration continues to decline. In the 2006–2010 period, the probability of a first marriage lasting at least 10 years was 68% for women and 70% for men and lasting at least 20 years was 52% for women and 56% for men. Those who married before age 20 had a lower probability of reaching the 20-year mark (Copen et al., 2012).

Birth patterns continue to change. Overall, the U.S. birthrate has fallen to a record low with the greatest drop occurring among immigrants (Livingston & Cohn, 2012). The trend in number of births dropped from 2007 (4,316,233) to 2012 (3,958,000) (Hamilton & Sutton, 2013). The mean age of first-time mothers increased by 3.6 years from 1970 to 2006, from 21.4 to 25.0 years old (Mathews & Hamilton, 2009). Among women, a higher percentage of first births occurred within a cohabiting union, although many such unions do not survive two years after the birth. Race and ethnicity also plays a role. Approximately 80% of first births to black women and 73% to black men were premarital, whereas 53% of first births to Hispanic women were and 56% of Hispanic men were premarital (Martinez, Daniels & Chandra, 2012).

Other family features and forms continue to alter the face of the family. One in seven, or 14% of 2008 marriages, were interracial or interethnic (Passel, Wang, & Taylor, 2010). According to a 2012 Gallup Poll, 3.4% of U.S. adults identify as LGBT (Gates & Newport, 2012). Over 8.5 million adoptees reside in the U.S. Every year about 140,000 children find adoptive homes (Riley & Van Vleet, 2012); approximately 400,000 children live within the foster care system, at any given time (Adoption and Foster Care Analysis and Reporting System [AFCARS], 2011).

The American family continues to change rapidly with no end in sight to the variations that will result from this evolutionary process, although, according to Stacey (2011), "the word *family* continues to conjure up an image of a married, monogamous, heterosexual pair and their progeny" (p. 4). Yet the reality demonstrates that as individuals live longer and the decrease in legal adult ties makes it easier for individuals to move on when dissatisfied with a current partnership, familial ties will become even more fluid. Therefore, family members will, of necessity, rely more heavily on discourse to establish the nature of their familial ties.

## International and Intercultural Differences

Much scholarly writing on family interaction overlooks cultural differences from a global perspective. In many Asian countries, for example, geographic migrations impact the traditional beliefs about filial piety and the significant role of family elders; the latter has undergone great change as young adults move to cities or countries far from home, making elder caretaking impossible. Many Chinese young adults from rural areas move to large cities for a university education or secure valued employment, leaving elderly family members with very limited contact and support from their adult children. Recently, in response to the outcry of older parents, the Chinese government passed a law requiring adult children to visit their parents regularly, or at least talk with them on the phone (Einhorn, 2013). Other recent major changes in Chinese families include the diminishment of the parent-child dyad, an increase in husband-wife decision making, a decline in favoring sons, and an increase in marriages based on romantic love (Lee & Mock, 2005).

International immigration practices also impact family interaction patterns. For example, Afghan Hindu refugee families who immigrate to Germany experience generational struggles due to generational differences in lifestyle expectations (see Chapter Fourteen, this volume). Currently many Filipino women struggle with mothering from a distance as they financially support their families through employment as childcare workers in other nations (Parrenas, 2001). Although most of these internationally separated families were established through traditional blood and/or legal ties, it is the lack of traditional family face-to-face interactions that challenges family identity in many cases.

In Western Europe differences in the ways couples manage work-life balance across countries create differential familial conflict issues. In their study of efforts to support parental work-life balance within the European Union, Crompton and Lyonette (2006) revealed mixed results for couples across countries. Survey results in Finland and Norway revealed significantly lower levels of family work-life conflict as a result of government childcare support than in other European countries. At the other extreme, support for childcare in France exacerbated family work-life conflict by challenging the traditional gendered domestic division of labor.

Finally, a comparison of American and European families reveals that, "Whether in marriage or cohabitation, Americans appear to have far more transitions in their live-in relationships (Cherlin, 2005, p. 46). This finding, coupled with the growing number of American families formed through cohabitation, reinforces the increasing reliance on discourse strategies to account for increasingly complex familial ties. The pace of relational change impacts families across the globe, necessitating ongoing negotiations about discourse strategies among current and former family members; American families exhibit the greatest need for a range of discourse strategies designed to convey the nature of complex family ties.

Over the years since Judith Stacey advanced the term *postmodern family*, or discussed "the contested, ambivalent, and undecided character of contemporary gender and kinship arrangements" (1996, p. 7), family life has become even more complex for U.S. families as well as for families across the globe. The following section examines family members' increasing reliance on discourse to construct, maintain, reconfigure, and deconstruct familial identity.

## Discursive Construction of Family Identity

The role of discourse in family formation and identity management assumed greater significance as new family forms evolved. Currently discourse plays a powerful role in the development of family identity. All families develop their identities, to some extent, through discourse. This occurs in two ways: first, all members establish their familial identity through the development of shared discourse patterns, as they implicitly create and reinforce a sense of collective identity. Second, increasing numbers of individuals rely on strategic discourse to address the nature of their family forms, and their personal place in their family; their communication repertoire contains a set of explicit, strategic messages regarding the nature of their familial membership. Such messages serve to instantiate the nature of members' familial ties for outsiders as well as for each other.

The more complex the family form, the greater the role of discourse in constructing and maintaining a family's identity. Therefore, as increasing numbers of individuals live within a wider range of partnered and parenting forms, often experiencing multiple family forms within a lifetime, such individuals rely increasingly on discourse to construct and convey their family-ness to those within, as well as outside, "the family." These complicated family forms include, but are not limited to, those created through same-sex partnering and parenting, transracial/international adoption, single-parent adoption, and the growing reliance on donor eggs and/or sperm to achieve pregnancy. The following sections address the role of discourse in establishing and managing identity in families formed, in whole or in part, outside blood and legal ties.

## The Role of Implicit Discursive Construction of Family Identity

Scholarly writing near the end of the 20th century addressed the role and significance of discourse in establishing family identity, reflecting the experiences of countless individuals living outside the traditional family forms. In other words, these individuals lived in incompletely institutionalized relationships (Cherlin, 1978). Gender, family studies, linguistics, and sociology scholars, among others, who viewed family as a socially constructed concept, turned their attention to the role everyday talk plays in constructing family identity.

The concept of *doing family* arose from the work of gender scholars writing near the end of the 20th century. The concept of *doing gender* emerged from the growing belief that gender is constituted through interaction involving a "complex of socially guided, perceptual, interactional, and micropolitical activities that cast particular pursuits as expressions of masculine and feminine 'natures'" (West & Zimmerman, 1987, p. 126). Multiple gender scholars have interrogated the family lives of gay males and lesbians through this lens.

An extension of *doing gender*, the term *doing family* provides grounding for understanding how communicative practices construct families. The *doing family* perspective implies "engaging in interactional work around the notion of family and we enact and react to both internally felt and externally applied notions of who makes a family" (Jacobson, 2009, p. 75). In his sociological study of gay and lesbian relationships and family life, Carrington (1999) asserted that every family is "a social construction or a set of relationships, recognized, edified, and sustained through human initiative. People 'do' family" (pp. 5–6). From this perspective, doing family emerges from, and reflects, members' everyday discourse as well as their personal everyday experiences. Building on this concept, Nelson's (2006) study of how single mothers "do family" led her to the assertion that creating family involves making decisions about who counts as family as well as assigning appropriate behaviors, tasks and obligations to persons so identified as family. From this perspective, *enactment* becomes the operative term, suggesting that "Family must be achieved and constructed on a daily basis" (Naples, 2001, p. 33). In other words, family is created and recreated over time through discourse and everyday life experiences.

The specific focus on discourse gained momentum through the writings of Gubrium and Holstein (1993), who assserted that "The central principle of the family discourse perspective is that the social world and its forms are made concrete and meaningful through everyday talk and interaction" (p. 66). Claiming that family is not objectively meaningful, these authors also proposed that this concept always remains under construction because they view "family discourse as a social process by which 'family' as a social form is brought into being as a matter of practice" (Holstein & Gubrium, 1999, p. 4). These scholars and likeminded others depicted a range of familial patterned practices, including discourse, that convey a sense of family to insiders and outsiders.

Given the radical changes in family life over recent decades, numerous scholars took the position that family is socially constructed and grounded in language use, recognizing that "Ties 'beyond biology' abound in a world where almost half of marriages end in divorce, one third of children are born outside marriage, and repartnering is commonplace" (Bernardes, 1999, p. 812). Relying solely on blood or legal ties to determine family-ness no longer seemed sufficient.

Yet, family identity research does not explicitly address strategic interactional patterns as serving to construct family ties. Instead, researchers tend to focus on the processes of assigning rights, privileges and responsibilities that serve to constitute membership. Such practices serve as implicit messages of belonging. For example, no scholarly response to Nelson's (2006) provocative article on doing family focused directly on enacted discourse. In her response to Nelson, Hertz (2006) claimed that doing family involves a dynamic of creating social ties while maintaining boundaries, whereas Sarkisian (2006) interpreted doing family as focusing on activities which create and sustain family ties while defining family boundaries. Similar writings do not evidence explicit or systematic attention to the role of strategic verbal or nonverbal messages in creating, managing, reforming, or dismantling familial boundaries.

The significant work of linguistics scholars, spearheaded by Deborah Tannen (2001, 2007), locates discourse as central to constructing family identity based on her studies of "the language of everyday conversation, and how it works—or fails to work—to create, reinforce, complicate, and improve relationships in the family" (2001, p. xvi). Her research team (Tannen, Kendall & Gordon, 2007) analyzed the role of discourse and identity in the everyday lives of four families, determining that "Families are created in part through talk: the daily management of a household, the intimate conversations that forge and maintain relationships, the site for the negotiation of values and beliefs" (Kendall, 2007, p. 3). More recently, Gordon (2009) described the role of intertextuality, or circumstances when "words are repeated across (rather than within) conversations" (p. 17), demonstrating how everyday language use actually constructs families by creating shared meanings and a group culture. Essentially, members "use language in making meanings, in creating themselves as a social group, and in extending their 'familyness'— including their family language ... to other people in their lives" (p. 7). Relying on linguistic repetition and intertextuality, Gordon's research reveals how family members create recognizable patterns of talk that serve to bind members together while demonstrating their connections to outsiders. Her work advances a constructionist view of family language as a "primary means of creating not only family meanings but family itself" (p. 28). The scholarship of numerous family communication scholars represents this position.

## Family Communication Contributions

Family communication scholars entered this conversation on the constitutive role of discourse over two decades ago. Many family communication-oriented scholars relied on transactional process definitions of family, reflecting a constitutive approach that "...asks how communication defines, or constructs, the social world, including ourselves and our personal relationships" (Baxter, 2004, p. 3). In the 1990s a small group of family communication scholars advanced the position that families, and images for families, are constituted through social interaction. They defined family as "a group of intimates who generate a sense of home, and group identity, complete with strong ties of loyalty, emotion, and experience" (Fitzpatrick & Vangelisti, 1995, p. 254). Increasingly these scholars employed what Fitzpatrick (1998) referred to as "definitions of the family that depend on how families define themselves" (p. 45). This definitional choice led to a claim that, in the future, communicative definitions would be privileged over structural ones (Whitchurch &

Dickson, 1999). More recently Edwards and Graham (2009) argued that definitions of family emerge implicitly from social interaction and symbolic experience, specifically highlighting how families become codified through storytelling. Over the past two decades family communication scholars have addressed the implicit role of discourse in establishing a sense of family-ness. Yet these efforts stopped short of addressing the actual enactment of discourse strategies designed to construct, maintain, reconfigure, or deconstruct familial identity.

## The Role of Strategic Discourse in Family Identity Construction

The discursive turn in communication scholarship emerged from the identity struggles of individuals living outside the family norms of biological and legal ties who enacted multiple family configurations without conventionally recognizable familial identities. Such individuals relied on discourse strategies to accomplish their identity work—"the process through which talk makes available to participants and observers who the people doing the talking must be" (Tracey, 2002, p. 7). Forecasting the role of discourse in constructing family identity explicitly, Holstein and Gubrium (1999) asked, "Where and when does family terminology—with its related social forms such as mother, father, child, and grandparent—and its classically connected sentiments—…get talked about?" (p. 14). Today family communication research extends previous scholarship by addressing the explicit discursive practices by which family members strategically manage their complex family identity.

As noted earlier, all families are constructed, at least in part, by discourse, but the more complex the family's form, the more members must develop communicative strategies to address their membership within the familial group or to respond to another's comments or questions. For example, an acquaintance might question a teenager about the source of her red hair because no other redhead exists in her immediate biological family. She could answer quickly and easily by saying, "My grandmother." The same question may confront a redheaded adopted or foster child with a dilemma about whether and to what extent she should reveal information about her familial status to a stranger or acquaintance. In most cases, the nature of the question, comment, or challenge, and the identity of the speaker, will influence the nature of the response and the respondent.

Although all families construct their identities through communication to some degree, increasingly more contemporary family members consciously enact identity-oriented discourse strategies in order to construct, maintain, reconfigure, and deconstruct their familial identities (Galvin, 2006). Constructing families formed partly or totally outside the bounds of biology and/or law requires that members engage in conscious, explicit and strategic communication designed to address and manage their family membership. In other words, "families formed wholly or partly without biological and/or legal ties depend heavily on discourse processes to create their 'stickiness'" (Galvin, 2006, p. 9). These families include those formed through transracial adoption, same-sex parenting, unrelated donor insemination, or multiple marriages, among other options. In such cases, members' discourse serves to: (1) provide outsiders with an understanding of their family identity and (2) establish and reinforce insiders' sense of family identity. Families in which members enact such ongoing, explicit, strategic discourse to establish their identities are considered to be highly discourse dependent. These family members bear a communicative burden that members of families formed fully through blood and/or legal ties do not carry.

The following framework of discourse-dependent families' use of discourse strategies depicts how family members consciously, explicitly, and strategically manage their external and their internal boundaries as they engage in identity work (Galvin, 2004). External boundary management involves using discourse strategies to reinforce family identity when outsiders challenge that identity or the validity of a specific family relationship is misunderstood. The following strategies, in order of imperative, include: (a) *Labeling*—creating titles or positions to indicate the nature of a familial connection (e.g., calling a stepfather "Dad" in front of other people or introducing a someone to your two mothers saying, "This is Momma Sally and Momma Ruth"), (b) *Explaining*—rendering the relationship understandable to others (giving reasons for using family terminology (e.g., "Ella is my stepfather's daughter but we view her as our sister"), (c) *Legitimizing*—invoking law or custom to justify a tie as genuine (e.g., "My parents adopted my deceased aunt's daughter, so Casey is my sister"), and (d) *Defending*—actively justifying a relationship against attack (e.g., responding to "Couldn't you adopt a White child?" by saying, "Love trumps color, something you would not understand").

Internal boundary management involves using communication strategies to maintain members' sense of family identity and members' ties. These strategies include: (a) *Naming*—choosing names/titles for persons considered as family but without blood or legal ties (e.g., calling a grandmother's second husband "Grandpa-B [B for bonus]"), (b) *Discussing*—talking about the nature of special ties that bind certain persons to a family (e.g., conversations explaining the concept of known versus unknown sperm donors to a child born through donor insemination), (c) *Narrating*—telling stories that (re)present the family's self-identity (e.g., repeating the complicated adoption saga that accompanied an international or foster adoption), and (d) *Ritualizing*—involving members in enactments of familial identity, ranging from holiday celebrations (e.g., sewing members' names on Christmas stockings) or ordinary events (e.g., attending Sabbath services together). Many family communication scholars have addressed specific identity management strategies enacted in families formed in various ways, including adoption (see Chapter Nine, in this volume) and sperm donor use (e.g., Harrigan, Dieter, Leinwohl, & Martin, 2012).

Conversely, discourse can also serve to deconstruct family ties (Galvin, 2009). Although relational distancing remains an understudied area (Hess, 2003), many individuals live within multiple family forms before reaching adulthood. Such experiences often involve loss and estrangement. When one or more family members act in ways contrary to the beliefs or values of other members, or are viewed as unwelcome for myriad reasons, offended family members might enact communicative deconstruction strategies, assertively or reluctantly, in an attempt to remove such persons from family membership. Also, occasionally individual members reject their close relatives' beliefs, values, or behaviors and, in doing so, explicitly or implicitly renounce their family membership. Such circumstances occur infrequently given that many families accept, even if unwillingly, a wide range of individual differences rather than disown a member. In many cases, for denial of membership to occur, there must be highly problematic circumstances reflecting deliberate, recurring behavior, viewed as extremely negative by other members. Numerous families experience difficult periods during which a member is disowned verbally, but within a reasonable time period, these tensions are forgiven or forgotten. To be considered as examples of deconstruction strategies, the interaction must involve deliberate, patterned behaviors evidencing a clear intent to dismantle the relationship.

Deconstruction also involves a range of verbal and/or nonverbal discourse strategies designed to convey a desire to dissolve familial ties. Members might disown an offending member through direct rejection messages; these involve statements such as, "You are dead to me" or "You are no longer part of this family." Usually recipients of such verbal messages are excluded from future familial social occasions. Examples of such precipitating circumstances include a member's decision to marry or partner outside the family's religion or race or become involved in a same-sex partnership; other examples include the discovery of a member's affair or a member's violent or criminal behavior. In such cases, affection, loyalty, and/or appropriate behavior is privileged as the "real" arbiter of who counts as family. Occasionally individuals choose to remove themselves from membership through distancing or overt rejection. Instances such as the rejection of a member's partner or one's commitment to religion unacceptable to other family members might trigger such messages. Outside of the divorce literature, involving legal termination, few academic studies have addressed the communicative processes involved in deconstructing families communicatively.

The previous discussion of managing internal and external family identity addressed singular issues, although many families reflect multiple complexities leaving them facing multiple areas of identity challenge (Hertz, 2009). For example, after struggling with infertility a heterosexual couple might adopt a transracial baby only to discover the woman is four months pregnant; a married father might come out as gay to his wife and children and then partner with someone similar in age to his children; a surrogate might present a single adoptive father with triplets. As families become more complex with each passing decade, discourse stands to assume an increasingly significant role in family identity construction.

## Conclusion

Given the changing nature of family formation experiences, the increasing numbers of exceptions or variations to the previous norms of blood and legal ties challenge any sweeping claims about family-ness. Researchers must continue to study why, and at what point(s) in a relationship, might individuals refer to certain others as "family" (Bernardes, 1999; Nelson, 2013). For example, groups of people whose life-course experiences and/or legal ties coincided for a lengthy time period might refer to themselves as "a family," but additional time and emerging differences could render certain individuals unacceptable or non-existent to other group members. Former in-laws or sorority sisters/fraternity brothers frequently fall into this category. Conversely, some familial ties might be viewed as sacrosanct, at least in most families. To make this point Bianchi (2006) critiqued the aforementioned Nelson (2006) article on single mothers, arguing that certain intergenerational bonds such as "those between a mother, her daughter, and her daughter's children—seem rather impervious to 'deconstruction'" (p. 812). Few studies, outside the divorce literature, address relational deconstruction; even fewer studies address communicative indicators and outcomes of such familial changes.

Evolving, complex family forms, sometimes referred to as *evotypical families* (Ferguson & Leoutsakas, 2013), continue to appear on the horizon. Evotypical families "emerge at the point when imagination, commitment or need overrides norms and traditions" (Galvin, 2013, p. 4). Initially such emergent families function without descriptive labels recognizable to the larger community because, "When family identity is involved, language follows lived experience" (Galvin, 2006. p. 15). In other words, by the time newer family variations appear on the horizon, those previously considered as evotypical family forms have been named and, in some cases, become more or less normative. Examples of current evotypical families include a family headed by a woman and her transgender (now female) partner (Boylan, 2013), a family in which a beloved pet assumes the role of a full-fledged member of the family (Walsh, 2009), or families formed through ties of half-siblings and a sperm donor (Hertz, 2009).

Acceptance of family identity variations comes slowly. Even as the *U.S. News & World Report* article, quoted in the epigram at the opening of this chapter, predicted future changes in the family tree, these new branches were depicted as "odd"—one more subtle indication of the difficulties inherent in society's acceptance of family change.

For over three decades family communication scholars have studied "the use of language to define our boundaries within these family forms that find themselves outside the traditional definitional mechanisms associated with families" (Le Poire, 2006, p. 192). Given the significant growth of research in this area, it is safe to predict that these scholars will continue to contribute to family identity scholarship by addressing emerging family forms and the strategic and intentional communicative practices enacted to affirm and manage such a family identity. By the year 2033 domestic and international family trees will sprout many new branches, many unforeseen by contemporary family scholars. As noted earlier, the more complex the family form, the greater the role of discourse in constructing and maintaining the family's identity. Therefore members of families on those branches in 2033 will, of necessity, continue the challenge of communicatively constructing their families' identities.

# CHAPTER THREE

# Theorizing the Communicative Construction of "Family"

## The Three R's

LESLIE A. BAXTER

Each chapter in this volume describes a particular form of "nontraditional family," and such localized understanding of specific family types holds inherent value. In addition to studying these family types discretely, however, it is important to ask what they share in common and to theorize those commonalities. As is evident in reading the chapters in this volume, much of existing research can be described as a-theoretical: research findings that have amassed without benefit of theoretical sensemaking. Future research can benefit from more theoretically informed work, and the purpose of this chapter is to discuss selected theories and theoretical issues that can be productive in framing our understanding of communication in post-nuclear families. The chapter is organized around the "Three R's" that are especially important: *Remaking, Resistance,* and *Resilience*.

Before turning to each of these R's, however, it is important, especially in an eclectic volume such as this one, to reflect on theory more generally. Lewin's (1951) oft-quoted claim that "there is nothing so practical as a good theory" (p. 169) underscores the usefulness of theory. Raw data (whether qualitative or quantitative) never speak for themselves; instead, they need to be rendered understandable, and that is what a good theory does. A good theory helps a researcher determine what to pay attention to in the overwhelming sea of phenomena available for study; it helps us sort out what patterns in data are more and less important to pay attention to. Post-positivistic theories draw researcher attention to patterns of co-occurrence between variables; interpretive theories draw attention to patterns of meaning-making—how meaning kernels combine to form themes or construct the meanings of phenomena of interest; and critical theories provoke researchers to examine patterns in the power relations between discourses or structural groups. Finally, a good theory helps us to understand the patterns that are identified. Post-positivistic theories value theories of causal explanation: a given pattern between two variables, A and B, is made understandable by identifying one as the cause of the other, both the result of a third causal variable, C, or one as a cause of the other mediated through a variable, D. Interpretive theories value a different kind of understanding than causal explanation; instead, such theories attend to the subjective meaning-making process guided by participant reasons and cultural rules. Critical theories achieve a third kind of understanding, one that seeks to unmask what is taken-for-granted or accepted as natural in society (e.g., the accepted superiority of one group over another or accepted practices regarded as inherent or natural) in order to unravel the power relations that often lurk below the surface.

A good theory can take several forms. Turner (1986) distinguished analytical schemes, modeling schemes, and propositional schemes. Analytical schemes are typologies or classification schemes intended to describe the properties of the phenomena under study. Chapter Two in this volume discussed an example of this kind of theorizing in Galvin's (2006) typology of discourse-dependent strategies used by family members in presenting their family identity both internally and externally. According to Turner, understanding through analytical schemes comes by producing an exhaustive set of mutually exclusive categories that create order for the social world of interest. A given datum is explained by finding its place in the classificatory scheme. As Turner stated, "Analytical schemes explain empirical events by finding their niche in a typology" (p. 11). Analytical schemes provide understanding of *what* a given phenomenon is. Turner asserted that analytical schemes are a necessary prerequisite for developing other forms of theory. Because of this, many scholars regard analytical schemes as pre-theoretical. Because such a view too easily creates unnecessary hierarchies in what is regarded as a "real theory," it is more useful to argue that analytical schemes are one fruitful kind of theorizing available to communication researchers.

A modeling scheme, the second type of theory discussed by Turner (1986), refers to "a diagrammatic representation of social events" (p. 18). Models are often oriented toward distal and proximal causal explanations of processes. They focus on *how* a given phenomenon happens, examining antecedent variables which function through mediating variables to produce predicted outcomes. Such models present a set of key concepts and a set of symbols (e.g., lines, arrows, etc.) by which those concepts are connected. An example of a modeling scheme relevant to this volume is Meisenbach's (2010) model of stigma management communication.

The model begins with positing the role of communication in marking a person's stigma, which is mediated through the individual's attitudes toward the stigma and strategic communication practices, to result in a variety of possible outcomes or consequences. Some researchers regard models as pre-theories, which creates a hierarchy of inferiority discussed above; it is more productive to view a model as a kind of theory that ought to be accepted on its own terms and as equally valuable to other approaches to theorizing.

A propositional scheme, according to Turner (1986), specifies the connection between two or more concepts. These schemes vary in their level of abstraction and the logical tightness of their organization and take one of two general forms: the axiomatic theory and the formal theory. Propositional schemes focus on addressing *why* a phenomenon occurs. Axiomatic theories rely on a hierarchical presentation of basic axioms, highly abstract statements, from which theorems are logically deduced and subsequently tested. Such theories are relatively rare in interpersonal/family communication. The most commonly found propositional theory in interpersonal/family communication is what Turner referred to as a formal theory. Formal theories consist of a set of abstract principles that are then deployed in "rather loose deductions to explain empirical events" (Turner, p. 15). Core concepts and principles are deployed as sensitizing devices to direct researcher attention to some phenomena and processes instead of others and to pose analytical questions with which to interrogate the data. Explanations in formal theory can focus either on causality, as in post-positivistic theories, or intelligibility, as in many interpretive/critical theories. Many of the theories represented in this volume could be described as formal theories. Two dialectical theories frequently cited in the volume illustrate differences in these types of formal theories. Petronio's (2002) communication privacy management theory (CPM) provides a set of basic principles and a set of factors (e.g., culture, context, gender, motivation, benefits/costs) that affect whether private information will be shared with others. Research using the theory has been used largely with a goal of making predictive, causal claims about the variables that influence the negotiation of disclosure or privacy between owner and receiver of private information. By contrast, relational dialectics theory (RDT; Baxter, 2011; Baxter & Montgomery, 1996) provides an example of an intelligibility-focused theory. It posits some basic principles (e.g., meaning-making is a struggle between competing discourses), and some key concepts (e.g., the distinction between diachronic interplay of discourses and synchronic interplay of discourses) that a researcher can deploy in rendering intelligible the patterns of meaning-making in utterances.

Theories, then, come in many stripes. They all share a common goal of helping researchers to understand the phenomena of interest. Within the limits of this volume, we are interested in theories that can illuminate the communication construction/remaking of "family." Theories useful to this goal will attend to three basic elements, the Three R's of Remaking, Resistance, and Resilience. These elements will be discussed sequentially, but this organization belies their inherent interdependence. For example, resistance and resilience are enacted communicatively, and resistance is futile unless it is enacted with optimism and perseverance, two of the qualities identified in resilient families.

## The Three R's of Theorizing the Communicative Construction of "Family"

### The First R: Remaking

The first R, Remaking, emphasizes the action of construction: the doing of family through a variety of social activities. Although a communication scholar is quick to argue that all social action, by the nature of its sociality, implicates communication, researchers in other disciplines often take communication for granted as either the outward representation of internal individual states and traits (cognitions and motivations, for example) or as a more or less neutral vessel through which social forces (such as roles or structural positions) are manifested (Sigman, 1995). In Chapter Two, Galvin productively addressed this point and presented her discourse dependence typology, which focuses on intentional, strategic communication practices, in order to draw explicit researcher attention to the role of communication in constructing a family identity. Galvin positioned communication as central to the project, rather than positioning it as a theoretical handmaiden that merely reflects or transmits other psychological or sociological factors. Galvin's goal of centering communication is important in a volume focusing on communication, but scholars do not need to limit communication to intentional, strategic activity in order to accomplish this goal. Unintended communicative practices are just as powerful as strategic efforts. Furthermore, an ecumenical view of the role of communication in constructing family should embrace both constitutive and effectual conceptualizations of construction.

The role of communication in constructing family takes one of two basic approaches: the *constitutive approach* and the *effectual approach*. Communication scholars who have been especially vocal in eschewing so-called representational or transmission views of communication have argued instead for a constitutive view of communication and have understandably aligned themselves with the interdisciplinary intellectual project known as *social constructionism*. "Constitutive" in this context means that the social world does not pre-exist communication but rather is constructed in and through communicative enactments. Burr (2003) has succinctly captured the essential assumptions upon which social constructionists agree: (1) a rejection of the post-positivistic assumptions of an objective reality; (2) a belief in the historical and cultural specificity of knowledge claims; (3) anti-essentialism; (4) language as a pre-condition for thought; and (5) a belief in knowledge created through social practices. Most importantly from the perspective of communication scholars, "social practices" often has been conceived as a catch-all that references all kinds of social behavior and need not focus on communication per se. For example, one can focus on the social practices of feeding the family (menu planning, shopping, cooking, serving, eating, and cleaning up) without ever focusing explicitly on the verbal and nonverbal communication that occurs in enacting these various aspects of family feeding. Communication can too easily be positioned as the taken-for-granted vehicle through which these various aspects are enacted without ever receiving explicit attention in its own right. At the end of the day, it is probably fair to say that communication scholars who reject a post-positivistic paradigm, and its attendant assumption of an objective reality that can be causally predicted and explained, hold family membership in the social constructionism project. But one can be a social constructionist without being a communication scholar. Thus, communication scholars who espouse a constitutive view of communication are a subset within the broader, interdisciplinary social constructionism project.

Furthermore, one can be a communication scholar committed to the significance of communication in constructing the social world but without holding membership in the social constructionist project. That is, one can reject a representational or transmission view of communication and not be a social constructionist at all, and in this sense, communication scholars do themselves a disservice by granting social constructionism monopoly rights in rejecting handmaid status to communication. Communication can construct the social world through the consequential effects it has in shaping outcomes of a variety of kinds, an alternative view to the constitutive view advanced by communication researchers who align with social constructionism. This effectual approach emphasizes the effects of communication in shaping the world as we know it, and this approach has a long disciplinary tradition that can be traced to Aristotle's classic work on persuasion. A focus on the effects of communication is precisely what post-positivistic communication scholars emphasize in examining how various aspects of communication function as independent variables in causally impacting various outcomes such as holding an identity as a (successful) family or being seen as a (successful) family by others.

It is useful to differentiate constitutive from effectual approaches to constructing family, because of two frequent abuses of the term "constitutive" among communication scholars (who shall remain unnamed). The first abuse is one in which the constitutive approach (with its intellectual roots in social constructionism) is used interchangeably with construction, functionally ignoring the merits of the effectual approach. The second abuse is one in which the term "constitutive" is used in reference to the effectual approach, thereby ignoring the social constructionist assumptions in which that term has been historically embedded. In short, I am suggesting that communication is a powerful player in constructing family through either the social constructionist focus on how specific communicative practices (of intentional or unintentional kinds) constitute the family or the post-positivistic focus on the effects of communication in shaping family. But these two approaches make different assumptions about the social world and come from different intellectual traditions. The authors in this volume all center communication in constructing the post-nuclear family, but some emphasize communication as constitutive whereas others emphasize communication as effectual. There is room at the theoretical table for both approaches.

Communicative construction/remaking builds on both psychosocial (functional) and transactional (identity-based and affection-based) conceptualizations of the family discussed in Chapter One. Both functional and transactional approaches emphasize communication, the former for its task capacities and the latter for its socioemotional capacities. Both of these approaches can draw strength from either the constitutive or effectual perspectives. Importantly, both approaches stand in sharp contrast to structural approaches which define a family along institutional and role lines, definitions that currently favor the nuclear family.

Galvin, in Chapter Two, has provided us with a useful list of communication strategies used by discourse-dependent families as they constitute "family." Most helpful conceptually, however, is her distinction between internal boundary management and external boundary management. Family communication scholars have for a long time privileged family interiors—what family members say to and do with one another—and this work needs to continue. As Foucault (1977/1995) observed, individuals socialized in a society police themselves, disciplining directed toward conformity to the dominant ideologies of their cultural memberships. Family members who occupy post-nuclear family forms thus need to convince themselves first that they are legitimate. As important, however, and for too long overlooked by family communication scholars, is an outward gaze to consider what family members do in presenting their family to others. Although we like to think of the family as the ultimate private world, it is constantly under surveillance, and thus judgment, by outsiders (Nelson & Garey, 2009). It is subject to public disciplining in any number of ways, including eligibility for marital status, access to income tax deductions, the protection of children through child welfare, school conferences, and so forth. Family communication, in short, is as much public as it is private, and it merits research that is focused both outward and inward.

Illustrative of the private-and-public nature of doing family is the process of deconstructing the family (Galvin, Chapter Two). Although we understand this deconstruction process through the lens of divorce, what has gone under-investigated is estrangement, which at its extreme is the severing of all types of interdependence among family members—emotional, instrumental, physical, and legal. In an initial investigation of the role of communication in parent-child estrangement, Scharp (2014) has found that the communicative work of maintaining a state of estrangement is as labor-intensive, if not more so, than the work of accomplishing the initial estrangement. Family members and outsiders alike refuse to recognize that the familial tie between parent and child can ever be severed. This communicative labor is testimony to the enduring belief that family is a nonvoluntary relationship in which blood ties are forever. However, the fact that so many are thought to have accomplished estrangement speaks to the agentic capacity of family members to transform even this presumably nonvoluntary relational bond to voluntary status.

Of the many communicative practices worthy of study, I draw special attention to four of the entries in Galvin's (2006) typology: narrating, ritualizing, naming, and labeling. Although Galvin locates both narrating and ritualizing internally among family members, they can function both internally and externally. Naming and labeling are conceptually similar and differ only in their internal vs. external location and will be combined for discussion purposes here.

As a genre of communication, a narrative is an "account of what happened to particular people—and of what it was like for them to experience what happened—in particular circumstances and with specific consequences" (Herman, 2009, p. 2). Narrative "is a basic human strategy for coming to terms with time, process, and change" (Herman, 2009, p. 2). It can be studied from both constitutive and effectual approaches, and it can be enacted either inside or outside a family's boundary. As Becker (1997) has astutely observed, a narrative is predicated on rupture of some sort; some crisis or anomaly happens to characters and we understand the implications of this as time unfolds. The mere existence of post-nuclear family forms is a rupture of the dominant cultural ideology, and narrative is ideally positioned as a central portal communicative practice in understanding how the stories family members tell (to themselves as well as to outsiders) construct the meaning and functionality of "family." All too often, scholars use narrative as a mere methodological tool in collecting reported stories whose content is then thematically analyzed. Instead, researchers need to draw upon the wealth of emerging narrative theories, including narrative performance theory (Langellier & Peterson, 2004),

RDT (Baxter, 2011), narrative completeness/coherence theory (e.g., Baxter, Norwood, Asbury, Jannusch, & Scharp, 2012; Koenig Kellas & Manusov, 2003), and narrative redemption (e.g., McAdams, 1997) and other narrative therapy theories. As these theories demonstrate, narratives are not merely a neutral method of transmitting a storyteller's memories of a prior experience. Instead, the act of telling a story, and a story of a particular type, constructs social reality rather than merely representing it.

Although some communication scholars argue that all communication is ritual (e.g., Carey, 1988), the concept is used by Galvin (2006) to refer to a particular genre of communication. As a genre, ritualizing refers to the enactment of "a voluntary, recurring, patterned communication event" that "pays homage to what [family members] regard as sacred" (Baxter & Braithwaite, 2006a, pp. 262–263). It is a powerful communicative practice that promotes family identity, negotiates both continuity and discontinuity with the past, enacts membership in larger cultural systems, and facilitates stress management (for a review, see Baxter & Braithwaite, 2006a). Rituals can be either internal or external to the family boundary, or both simultaneously. A wedding, commitment ceremony, or vow renewal ceremony, for example, is at once a private event for close family and friends and a public, cultural event that reinscribes the society's values (Baxter & Braithwaite, 2002). Ritual studies is an interdisciplinary enterprise that draws upon anthropology, religious studies, family studies, and communication. A variety of theoretical frameworks have been articulated to provide an understanding of why and how rituals are so meaningful: functional, semiotic/cultural, and performance (for reviews, see Baxter & Braithwaite, 2006a; Bell, 1997). Functional theories are guided by the general question of what functions are performed for individuals and social groups, such as families, by the enactment of rituals, and this tradition can be traced back to Durkheim's (1965) work on religious rites. In general, functional theories argue that rituals construct and maintain social cohesion. Semiotic/cultural theories examine the symbols invoked in rituals with a goal of understanding their cultural meanings. Turner (1969, 1974), for example, has argued that rituals are dense with multivocal symbolic meanings which assist in managing contradictory belief systems. Performance approaches move beyond the representational view that symbols reflect cultural beliefs and values to advance a constitutive position that rituals construct the social world. As Bell (1997) has stated, "Ritual does not mold people; people fashion rituals that mold their world" (p. 266). Performance theories emphasize the physical and sensory enactment itself rather than attending to its symbolic content.

At some level, distinctions among these three theoretical strands are quite arbitrary and are often folded together in the study of family rituals. For example,

Wolin and Bennett's (1984) family rituals theory combines functional, semiotic, and performative elements. Wolin and Bennett distinguished three forms of family rituals—celebrations (tied to broader cultural systems of meaning), traditions (tied to particular family history), and patterned interactions (which constitute family identity and honor it through everyday patterns of interaction). Family rituals, argued Wolin and Bennett, build and sustain family cohesion and identity, evoke a strong affective response among family members through their performance, tie a family to its past, buttress a family through challenges, and negotiate change.

The third and fourth of Galvin's (2006) strategies, naming and labeling, are particularly important in creating legitimated identities from a critical theoretical perspective. Wood (in press) has made the same observation in the context of her review of critical feminist theories: the acts of naming and labeling provide a vocabulary that enables recognition and legitimation of phenomena otherwise overlooked because they cannot be given voice. From a critical theory perspective, naming and labeling are key to knowledge/power. That which cannot be given voice is repressed because it cannot be heard (Foucault, 1978). Attention to naming and labeling is underscored by the discussion in Chapter One with respect to how the U.S. Census Bureau defines a "family" and who is left out by that definition.

In this regard, the work of Pahl and Spencer (2010; Spencer & Pahl, 2006) is illuminating. These scholars suggest that the dominant discourse of relating takes for granted a tidy binary, categorical division between "friends" and "family." The dominant discourse sorts relationships through these labels into these two relational bins—one that emerges through choice (friendship) and one that is given (family). Instead, they urge a shift in thinking to a different level, urging scholars to attend to individuals' personal communities, which consist of a set of important personal ties in one's life that blur boundaries between friends and family in a process they call *fusion*. Although the approach articulated by Pahl and Spencer is too cognitive to serve the scholarly interests of communication researchers, their concept of fusion begs for scholarly attention to the communication practices by which societal members discursively legitimize certain relational functions and assign them to one type of social relationship as opposed to another type through labeling/naming practices. As Allan (2008) has noted, "The boundaries between family and friendship are becoming less clear-cut in people's construction of their micro social worlds" (p. 6). Scholars with a critical theory orientation could productively examine the communicative practices of labeling/naming in order to examine ruptures in the tidy friend-family binary. In doing so, many kinds of social relations that currently fall through the cracks might gain legitimation, such as voluntary kin (see Chapter Eleven in this volume).

Ironically, one of the long-term consequences of attention to fusion might be a self-reflexive re-thinking of the too tidy intellectual distinction that communication scholars currently make between so-called "interpersonal communication" and "family communication." Change can be liberating.

## The Second R: Resistance

Resistance recognizes that post-nuclear families are somehow less legitimated—in public policy and in hearts and minds—than is the idealized nuclear family. In other words, these postmodern families are, to some extent, stigmatized (e.g., Goffman, 1963) or marginalized (e.g., Lehmiller & Agnew, 2006). Chapter One discussed at length the cultural idealization of the nuclear family, which positions post-nuclear families to be seen as inferior, second-best, incomplete, and nonnormative.

Although scholars of the postmodern family usually start the conversation with the stigma/marginalization concepts, it is not forcefully deployed theoretically. Beginning with early articulations of Erving Goffman in his classic 1963 book on *Stigma*, and continuing through more recent theorizing in our own discipline by Smith (2007) and Meisenbach (2010) on stigma communication, we have a rich theoretical toolkit that merits more than a token nod by scholars of the post-nuclear family.

The post-nuclear families represented in this volume vary with respect to which of the three legs of the nuclear-family ideological stool are challenged: co-residence, heterosexual marriage, and shared genes (through biological reproduction). Reasonably, stigma/marginalization should vary depending on how many of these elements are absent. But the extent of stigmatization/marginalization is more complicated than simply counting up the number of ideological missing pieces. Smith (2007) has cogently argued that stigmatization varies by the extent to which the stigmatized identity is publically "marked" (p. 463), or known, whether the stigmatized person is perceived as responsible through choices made, and the extent of social peril posed to the social order by the stigma. Some post-nuclear family members might experience less stigmatization/marginalization because they can keep their identity secret from others (e.g., pretending that an adopted child is a biological offspring). In such circumstances, Petronio's (2002) communication privacy management theory could be helpful in illuminating the communication process through which stigmatized family identities are revealed to or concealed from others (e.g., Smith & Hipper, 2010). Stigmatization can be mitigated to the extent that family members are not held responsible for their family choice (e.g., an involuntary childless couple). The perception of social peril might vary as well; currently, in some U.S. states, marriage between same-sex partners is doubtless regarded as a greater peril than in states which have legalized such marriages.

Experienced stigmatization/marginalization likely varies by how it is managed. Meisenbach (2010) has offered a model of how stigma is communicatively managed that can productively be compared to the typology advanced by Galvin (2006), particularly the external boundary management portion, although the two approaches are theoretically quite distinct from one another. For example, Galvin's strategies of explaining and defending bear close resemblance, on their face, to Meisenbach's strategy of challenging public understanding of the stigma. Galvin's strategy of legitimizing shows some correspondence with Meisenbach's strategies of reducing the offensiveness of the stigma or challenging public opinion.

Although post-positivistic (e.g., Meisenbach, 2010) and interpretive (e.g., Galvin, 2006) scholars can usefully investigate how stigmatized/marginalized persons communicatively manage their status, stigma/marginalization beckons family scholars to embrace critical perspectives to understanding communication. As McKerrow (1989) has observed, our communicative actions are either in the business of reproducing the status quo or of resisting and changing those circumstances. The critical project is about understanding resistance and change. Family communication scholars currently have but two explicitly critical interpersonal communication theories available to us in the theory toolkit. The first, Langellier and Peterson's (2004) narrative performance theory, builds on Foucault's (1972) work on knowledge regimes, and asks us to query how storytelling (re)orders social life: how the stories we tell and how we tell them functions to make some identities legitimate while rendering others illegitimate, how some are allowed to tell their stories while others are silenced, and how some are allowed to listen while others are not. Relational dialectics theory (RDT; Baxter, 2011) asks how our communicative acts are animated by dominant and marginalized discourses or systems of meaning and how interactants' words navigate the discursive fault lines of competing discourses in which they are enmeshed. As a field, family communication, like interpersonal communication, is dominated by those attracted to the post-positivistic paradigm, but postmodern families beg for a critical scholarly lens and agenda. How is it, from a critical perspective, that family forms that collectively comprise the majority are still marginalized as somehow inferior and nonnormative to the now minority nuclear family?

In addition to developing more home-grown critical theories of family communication, family communication scholars could productively draw upon a range of critical theorists that could illuminate important issues and processes involved in privileging some family forms as superior to others. Baxter and Asbury (in press) have discussed two broad intellectual traditions in the critical project: the modern and the postmodern. Space does not allow an elaboration of their discussion, but the essence of the difference in the two approaches is whether power is considered as a top-down dynamic in which social structures drive inequalities (the modernist approach), or power is considered as a bottom-up-and-out dynamic in which power and resistance are integrally wedded in localized, everyday practices (the postmodern approach). A modern critical project would focus on the power that resides in institutions and social structures such as the state and its effects on different groups organized by race, gender, and class. For example, as discussed in Chapter One, family forms in the U.S. are not equally distributed across racial/ethnic groups. Households headed by single women, with no spouse, are three times more common among Blacks or African Americans than among either Whites or Asian Americans. Because single-parent families are often viewed as inferior when compared to two-parent families, Blacks/African Americans are positioned to bear a larger stigmatization burden than others if their family form is single-parent. Because single-parent households often suffer economically in comparison to households with two adult income earners, this racial/ethnic divide becomes an income, and thus social class, divide, as well.

By contrast, a postmodern critical project would focus on how circulating discourses function to enable and constrain social action. For example, the heteronormative discourse of marriage makes it difficult for gays and lesbians to enact intelligible commitment ceremonies outside of the framework of the traditional wedding between a man and a woman (Goltz & Zingsheim, 2010).

Critical scholars informed by the postmodern critical approach could also interrogate the dominant circulating discourses that we often take for granted as the appropriate and necessary functional and affective elements of family. For example, if the discourse of the family views child rearing as a crucial function of family, then social connections that are without children cannot be legitimized as family. Similarly, distancing emotions are often regarded as illegitimate in idealizations of family (e.g., Hess, 2003; Scharp, 2014). Thus, critical scholars would interrogate the taken-for-granted psychosocial and transactional definitions by which cultural members legitimate some relationships as familial, based on the presence of accepted functions and affections, and deny this "family" label to others.

Critical scholars of the postmodern bent would doubtless take issue with Galvin's (2006) view that blood and law are located conceptually outside of discourse. Instead, premised on the theoretical assumption that the social world is constituted entirely through discourses, "blood" and "law" would be regarded as discourses that hold hegemonic status in mainstream U.S. culture. Critical scholars would argue that there is nothing "natural" or inherent in either blood or law; both are social constructions that are given meaning and value through communicative practices.

## The Third R: Resilience

The Third R places a premium on understanding risk and resilience for family systems. In general terms, the concept of resilience refers to "the ability to withstand and rebound from crisis and adversity" (Walsh, 1996, p. 1). Most commonly, resilience is studied as an individual phenomenon and refers to the personal qualities and skills of an individual that enable him or her to enact healthy and successful functioning or adaptation in the face of disruption (Lee, Nam, Kim, Kim, Lee, & Lee, 2013). From an individual perspective, the family is positioned as an environmental or contextual factor that functions as a source of risk for the individual (e.g., a child in an alcoholic family) or as a source of protection (e.g., a child who is raised in a supportive family environment). Walsh (1996), however, shifted resilience from the individual level to the family-system level, calling for research that examines risk and protective factors that affect the resilience of the family as a unit. Both approaches are valuable, but this discussion will focus on the family system as the focus of attention.

Family resilience research builds upon classic work in family stress and coping, for example, Hill's (1949) ABCX Model and McCubbin and Patterson's (1982) revision, the Double ABCX Model. However, unlike earlier work on family stress and coping which tended to emphasize variables that deterred family well-being, resilience research and theorizing tends to focus on factors that promote well-being in the face of stressors/risks (Afifi & Nussbaum, 2006; Walsh, 1996). This shift in focus is an important one, especially for post-nuclear families which can too easily be seen exclusively as deficit families because of their stigmatized and marginalized status. A risk and resilience focus urges scholars to look beyond challenges to identify those factors that enable these families to thrive. As Walsh (1996) eloquently noted, "Resilience is forged *through* adversity, not *despite* it" (p. 7). Challenges, in other words, are reframed as opportunities for strength.

Risk and resilience research and theorizing also tends to be more amenable to the study of developmental processes than was the case with earlier stress and coping work (Walsh, 1996). Although resilience research is a booming interdisciplinary project, a focus on process makes communication a central focus of scholarly attention. Family resilience scholars have identified a number of factors that predict resilience, including an attitude of optimism, spirituality, positive affection among family members, flexibility, financial management, spending time together as a family, shared recreation, the enactment of rituals, supportive networks, family problem-solving, communication openness, a proactive willingness to confront stressors, and family resolve or perseverance (Afifi & Nussbaum, 2006; Black & Lobo, 2008; Golish, 2003). In the context of post-nuclear families, the seminal work arguably is Afifi's (Golish, 2003) research on stepfamily resilience. These factors suggest both instrumental and affectional elements of resilience, informing psychosocial/ functional and transactional/affection approaches to family definition. Factors that are not explicitly communicative on their face (e.g., spirituality or optimism) should be studied to understand how they are enacted through communication practices. For example, the factor of financial management presumably involves communicative activity among family members, probably implicating family problem-solving, and the communicative details merit attention rather than being taken for granted.

Existing work on risk and resilience is informed largely by a post-positivist intellectual tradition with a conception of communication as effectual. However, resilience could productively be informed by scholars who bring interpretive/ critical perspectives in a focus on communication as constitutive. As even the early stress and coping models noted, the meaning that is attributed to stressors affects the stress level and the coping responses of family members, beckoning attention from interpretive scholars. The factors linked to family resilience from the functional, post-positivist perspective could usefully be studied through Galvin's (2006) typology, discussed in Chapter Two. For example, family narratives told both within and external to the family could emphasize a family identity of optimism or perseverance (e.g., "We Jones never give up!"). Similarly, family rituals could honor qualities that are linked to resilience. For example, regular family attendance at a church or synagogue could honor the family's spirituality.

Additionally, modern critical scholars should examine how different social groups organized by race/ethnicity, gender, and social class function with respect to risk and resilience, in part to adopt a stance of suspicion toward efforts to generalize findings identified among samples of largely White, heterosexual, middle-class families (Walsh, 1996). Postmodern critical scholars could usefully ask about the discursive formations that define resilience in taken-for-granted ways. For example, resilience might be defined differently depending on the cultural membership of a given family.

Communication theories of family risk and resilience are still needed to organize and explain what, how, and why communication processes produce family resilience. In the end, theorizing will need to identify factors that are common across family types and factors that are unique to the challenges of a given post-nuclear family type.

## Conclusion

This chapter adopts an ecumenical approach that welcomes a variety of intellectual traditions (post-positivist, interpretive, and critical), types of theories (typologies, models, and formal theories), and conceptions of communication (constitutive and effectual). The greater the number and diversity of theoretical voices at the table, the richer our understanding of communication in post-nuclear families. Most importantly, the study of the communicative remaking of "family" needs more concerted theory development. As subsequent chapters make clear, much of our understanding of communication in constructing post-nuclear families sits at the empirical level but without benefit of theories to help us understand and explain reported patterns in data. The relative paucity of theories demonstrates that communication research on post-nuclear families is in its intellectual infancy. The time is long overdue for family communication scholars to give these alternative family forms their theoretical, as well as empirical, attention.

# PART TWO

# Remaking "Family" beyond Traditional Marriage

# CHAPTER FOUR

# Families Centered upon a Same-Sex Relationship

## Identity Construction and Maintenance in the Context of Legally Recognized Same-Sex Marriage

PAMELA J. LANNUTTI

Galvin (2006) argued that while all families engage in some level of family identity building via discourse, families that are less traditionally formed are more dependent on discourse to manage and maintain their identity as a legitimate family. Families centered upon a same-sex relationship[1] are one type of "discourse dependent" family that Galvin described. Families centered upon a same-sex relationship fall outside of the "traditional" family model, because there is no heterosexual married couple as the family centerpiece. As a result, families centered upon a same-sex relationship often face discrimination and stigmatization that challenges their identity as a "legitimate" family. Yet, recent years have been a time of dynamic change in the legal and social status of families centered upon a same-sex relationship. In many locations across the globe and in the United States, marriages between same-sex couples are being legally recognized for the first time. Legally recognized same-sex marriage (SSM) provides families centered upon a same-sex couple with new opportunities to manage and maintain their family identity within the civil law system. However, SSM is also a source of challenge for families centered upon a same-sex relationship, and in some instances, the introduction of the opportunity for SSM has also introduced new experiences of delegitimizing communication for the families. This chapter discusses the ways that families centered upon a same-sex relationship discursively negotiate their identity as a legitimate family within the context of SSM.

## Same-Sex Marriage as a New Context

A large body of literature has focused on examining the qualities of same-sex romantic relationships, often in contrast to those of different-sex romantic relationships (e.g., Haas & Stafford, 2005; Julien, Chartrand, Simard, Bothillier, & Begin, 2003; Kurdek, 2004). Although some significant differences between different-sex and same-sex relationships for various relationship qualities have been found, the overarching finding from this literature is that same-sex and different-sex couples tend to be more similar than different (Kurdek, 2005). Despite their similarities, different-sex and same-sex couples do have a vastly different set of opportunities and challenges when it comes to social and civil recognition for their romantic and family relationships. Civil recognition and legal protection for families centered upon a same-sex relationship has been limited.

In addition to civil discrimination, these families often experience social stigmatization. Because same-sex couples are often stigmatized, members of these families might be more likely to receive support and acceptance from a fictive "chosen family" of friends rather than their families-of-origin, and might be fully recognized only as a family within that fictive kin group (Dewaele, Cox, Van den Berghe, & Vincke, 2011; Gabrielson, 2011; Oswald, 2002; Smart, 2007; Weston, 1991). Discrimination in the workplace, educational setting, and other arenas against families centered upon a same-sex relationship might lead to their identity as a family being completely or partially closeted. Regulating private information to remain fully or partially closeted might become a relational maintenance behavior (Patterson & Schwartz, 1994). Yet, recent trends toward expanding civil recognition for same-sex relationships, including SSM, are giving some families centered upon a same-sex relationship the opportunity to institutionalize their relationship and construct and maintain their family identity through a new mechanism.

The debates and legal maneuvering for and against legal recognition and protection for same-sex relationships have been ongoing globally for nearly two decades. The Netherlands legalized same-sex marriage in 2001, and was followed by other European nations (including Spain, Norway, and Sweden) and countries on other continents including Canada and South Africa (see "To Have and to Hold," 2012). Yet, other nations, including many in Africa and the Middle East, still prohibit homosexuality (see "To Have and to Hold," 2012). In some nations, civil relationship recognition for same-sex couples differs by state or province (see "To Have and to Hold," 2012). Such is the case in the United States where the debate over SSM has been a trend of American politics since the legal recognition of same-sex marriage in Massachusetts in 2004. At the time this chapter was written, 16 U.S. States and the District of Columbia were issuing marriage licenses to same-sex couples, while 33 states had either amended their State constitutions or passed laws to prohibit SSM (see Human Rights Campaign, n.d.). Because American families centered upon a same-sex relationship are currently experiencing a hotly contested and extremely dynamic SSM landscape, the experiences of these families provide important insight into how families discursively manage and maintain their family identity in a shifting and complex social and civil context. Thus, this chapter will focus on research examining American families' SSM experiences.

Before discussing how families centered upon a same-sex relationship experience SSM in relation to constructing and maintaining their family identity, it is important to recognize how SSM creates a new context for these family members and their relationships. When and where legally recognized same-sex marriage (SSM) is not available, many same-sex couples establish patterns of relational commitment and maintenance other than the traditional norms for romantic couples such as engagement and marriage (Reczek, Elliott, & Umberson, 2009). For example, couples often use joint home ownership or specific legal documents to establish and protect their relationship and to signal their commitment (Porche & Purvin, 2008; Riggle, Rostosky, & Prather, 2006). Outside of SSM, many same-sex couples have commitment ceremonies. These commitment ceremonies lack civil recognition, but serve as a means of expressing commitment and identity as a family. Yet, research has shown that commitment ceremonies might not be perceived to have the same psychological weight and social significance associated with traditional heterosexual marriage (Stiers, 1999). Civil unions or domestic partnerships offer families centered upon a same-sex relationship a form of civil recognition and definition for their family; yet, these legal mechanisms often lack the full legal and social benefits and impacts of marriage (Rothblum, Balsam, & Solomon, 2011). For example, an employer might not be required to recognize an employee's civil union or domestic-partnership partner when extending spousal health insurance benefits as the employer would for an employee married to a different-sex partner. Thus, these alternate forms of commitment expression and relationship definition for families are significant, but they are each different from legally recognized marriage.

SSM is the only opportunity for same-sex couples to institutionalize their commitment and to express family identity using the *exact same mechanism* as their different-sex couple counterparts. However, it is not just the opportunity to legally marry that is part of the SSM experience. Families centered upon a same-sex relationship must also contend with the civil and social debates and legal maneuvering that has surrounded the introduction or prohibition of SSM in their region. As such, I argue that SSM is a new context in which families centered upon a same-sex relationship live their relational lives. Indeed, research examining perceptions of SSM has indicated that lesbian, gay, bisexual, transgender, and queer (LGBTQ) individuals and same-sex couples recognize the opportunity to legally marry to be a significant change in the context for their relational lives and perceive shifts in their understanding of their current romantic relationships, future romantic relationships, and family relationships as a result of the opportunity for SSM (Lannutti, 2005; Lannutti, 2007a; Lannutti, 2013; Porche, Purvin, & Waddell, 2005; Schulman, Gotta, & Green, 2012). Other studies have shown that LGBTQ people and their families experience stress and negative relational consequences as a result of exposure to campaigns to ban same-sex marriage and other forms of same-sex relationship recognition (Arm, Horne, & Levitt, 2009; Horne, Rostosky, & Riggle, 2011; Maisel & Fingerhut, 2011; Rostosky, Riggle, Horne, Denton, & Huellemeier, 2010). Given the unprecedented and unique context that the introduction of SSM creates for families centered upon a same-sex relationship, it is important to better understand the opportunities and challenges SSM provides as these families construct and maintain their identity as a legitimate family.

To fully understand the impact of the new context of SSM on families centered upon a same-sex relationship and the ways they discursively construct and maintain their identity as a legitimate family, it is necessary to consider two interdependent aspects of families' experiences with SSM. Family communication scholars recognize that families manage various boundaries through their communication (see Petronio, 2002). As Galvin (2006) pointed out, less traditionally formed families have been found to engage in a variety of discursive practices that construct and maintain family identity within internal boundaries within the family and across external boundaries between those within the family and outsiders. Thus, in order to better understand the SSM experiences of families centered upon a same-sex relationship, it is important to understand the opportunities and challenges that SSM presents to constructing and maintaining family identity within the internal family boundaries. It is also important to examine the ways that families discursively manage the opportunities and challenges that SSM presents to constructing and maintaining family identity across the external border between family members and outsiders.

## Getting Married (or Not) and Communication about Family Legitimacy

A good starting point for examining the ways that legally recognized same-sex marriage (SSM) presents opportunities and challenges for constructing and maintaining an identity as a legitimate family is to look to the deliberations of same-sex couples as they decide whether or not to marry. For most same-sex couples, SSM is introduced into their region after they might already have been engaged in a long-term relationship with its already established ways of communicating commitment, engaging in relational maintenance, and understanding of their identity as a family (Porche & Purvin, 2008; Schecter, Tracy, Page, & Luong, 2008). In this way, most same-sex couples who get married do not have the same experience as different-sex couples who begin their courtship with the knowledge that legal marriage is possible. Instead, most same-sex couples considering SSM do so knowing that SSM is new, regionally limited, and uncertain because its foreseeable future depends on changeable political and legal decisions.

Lannutti (2008) asked LGBTQ individuals who were either married or engaged to describe their marriage decision making process. LGBTQ people discussed both attractions to marriage and obstacles to getting married. Among the attractions to marriage were the opportunity to use marriage to communicate their feelings for their partner and their identity as a family. Further research has suggested that marriage does have a changing effect on the experiences of self and relational conceptions of same-sex couples. Married same-sex couples have reported feeling greater relational satisfaction, more security in their relationship, and greater commitment to their partner as a result of getting married (Lannutti, 2011b; MacIntosh, Reissing, & Andruff, 2010; Ramos, Goldberg, & Badgett, 2009; Schecter et al., 2008). Married same-sex couples also have referred to changes in their sense of identity as individuals and as a couple as a result of getting married (Lannutti, 2007b; Lannutti, 2011b; Schecter et al.). For example, participants reported how using the terms "husband" and "wife" to describe their partners shifted and solidified their own understandings of their identity (Lannutti, 2007b; Lannutti, 2011b; MacIntosh et al.). Two participants in Lannutti's (2011b) study of the same-sex marriage experiences of older couples illustrate the effect of spousal terms on the married couples' identity construction:

Carlo:    There is something really nice about saying "my husband" without irony to it.

Walt:    We never really used that term….you know, before marriage was legal. But there is something really solid to it. Comforting.

Carlo:    "Husband" just seems like a better word. Stronger. More permanent. (p. 71)

Yet, some married same-sex couples struggle to maintain their self and couple identity in opposition to spousal terms (Lannutti, 2007b; MacIntosh et al.; Schecter et al.). Lannutti (2007a) reported on the ways that lesbian-bisexual married couples often "dealt with misgivings about heteronormative marriage by defining or redefining marriage-related terms in a way that fit better with their self-concepts" (p. 248). MacIntosh and colleagues discussed the ways that Canadian lesbian couples who wed attempted to reconcile patriarchal associations with the word "wife" while now using the term to describe each other. They described how married lesbian couples qualified the word "wife" with humorous uses of the term and redefined the word through feminist reclaiming much like the words "queer" and "dyke" have been reclaimed by LGBTQ people.

Married and engaged LGBTQ participants in Lannutti's study (2008) also identified attractions to SSM relating to discursive practice across the external boundary between the family centered upon a same-sex relationship and larger society. Among these attractions to SSM were conceptualizations of SSM as a means of gaining legal protections for family, the chance to make a public statement of commitment, and the chance to be a part of the marriage equality political movement (Lannutti, 2008). Although many families centered upon a same-sex relationship had engaged in various legal moves to protect their families outside of SSM (Porsche & Purvin, 2008; Reczek et al., 2009; Riggle et al., 2006), research has shown that married same-sex couples believe that their SSM provides a straightforward and secure level of legal protection for their family (Lannutti, 2011b; Ramos et al., 2009). In this sense, SSM is a means to communicate a family's legitimacy to the larger civil society and be bound by the same legal rights and responsibilities as married different-sex couples and their families. Galvin (2006) pointed out how families who are not defined by the law are dependent upon discourse to construct and maintain their identity as a legitimate family. By providing families centered upon a same-sex relationship an opportunity to define their family through the law, SSM is an opportunity to ease some of the discursive burden upon families centered upon a same-sex relationship.

Research has indicated, however, that SSM might not always relieve the discursive burden faced by families centered upon a same-sex relationship. Instead, there are some instances in which SSM might actually increase the delegitimizing challenges faced by these families. Although some participants in Lannutti (2008) were attracted to SSM because it provided a means to make a public statement about the couples' commitment, research has indicated that LGBTQ people see the public nature of SSM as an opportunity and a challenge. The power of marriage to help publically define a family as "legitimate" is seen as a benefit for many LGBTQ people and married same-sex couples (Alderson, 2004; Lannutti, 2005; Lannutti, 2007a; Lannutti, 2007b; Lannutti, 2011b; Schecter et al., 2008). As examples, a participant in Alderson's (2004) study of SSM in the United States and Canada stated, "People understand the word 'marriage.'... 'This is my wife' and they know what you mean" (p. 119), and a participant in Schecter et al.'s (2008) study of SSM in Massachusetts stated, "When I speak of him, out in the world, I speak of my husband..." (p. 415). Yet, participants in studies of SSM experiences have also discussed feeling uncomfortable with the increased visibility for their family brought about by SSM. As with other forms of civil relationship recognition for same-sex couples (Solomon, Rothblum, & Balsam, 2004), having an SSM has been found to increase the level of "outness" for families centered upon a same-sex relationship (MacIntosh et al., 2010). Some same-sex couples have expressed concerns about personal safety as a result of the increased "outness" and visibility associated with SSM (Lannutti, 2011b).

Another attraction to marriage discussed by married or engaged LGBTQ people in Lannutti's (2008) study is the chance to be a part of the marriage equality political movement as a result of getting married. The politics of SSM play a central role in the experiences of families centered upon a same-sex relationship as they consider SSM as a means of constructing and maintaining their identity as a family. Families considering SSM do so within the context of a dynamic and contested movement for marriage equality. As such, in getting married, a same-sex couple might be seen as motivated by a desire to not only express their identity as legitimate family, but might also be perceived to be expressing support for marriage equality itself. Research has suggested that while the former might be an accurate understanding of the motives of same-sex couples who marry, the accuracy of the latter might be less certain. Married and engaged LGBTQ people have cited the importance of "being counted" as participating in the movement for marriage equality through the symbolic act of getting married (Alderson, 2004; Lannutti, 2007b; Lannutti, 2011b; MacIntosh et al., 2010). Alderson (2004) discussed how some same-sex couples were motivated to marry in order to help preserve and extend marriage equality for future generations. One of Alderson's participants expressed this motivation in stating, "There is [sic] going to be whole generations of queer children growing up, not knowing – not believing that they couldn't get married" (p. 113). Yet, the literature has shown that married and engaged LGBTQ people also have concerns and criticism of the marriage equality movement even as they choose to get married (Badgett, 2009; Lannutti, 2007b; Lannutti, 2011b; Schecter et al., 2008). Most commonly, LGBTQ people express concern that SSM will serve as a means of "mainstreaming" or "straightening" LGBTQ people, same-sex relationships, and the LGBTQ community (Alderson, 2004; Lannutti, 2005; Lannutti, 2007a; Lannutti, 2007b; Lannutti, 2011b; Rolfe & Peel, 2011). LGBTQ people concerned about the potential "mainstreaming" effect of SSM but who choose to marry anyway often find ways to redefine or co-opt aspects of traditional weddings and marriage in order to construct and maintain a family identity they feel best suits them (Goltz & Zingsheim, 2010). As a participant in Lannutti (2008) explained, "We wanted to make sure our wedding wasn't like a straight wedding, because our relationship certainly isn't like a straight relationship" (p. 256).

The decision to get married creates opportunities and challenges for families centered upon a same-sex relationship as they discursively negotiated their identity as legitimate family, but what are the experiences of families in which the same-sex couple decides not to marry? Same-sex couples who live in regions where SSM is possible, but choose not to marry, must still address SSM as they construct and maintain their family identities. For those who choose not to marry, their unmarried status now takes on meaning that it would not have had if SSM were not available in their region. Being able to be married, but opting not to marry, places these couples in a position to have to explain their unmarried status while still justifying their identity as a legitimate family. Thus, for those who choose not to marry, the existence of SSM might add an additional type of challenge to their family identity.

Only a few studies have examined the reasons why same-sex couples choose not to marry and can provide insight into how these families construct and maintain their identity as a legitimate family in the context of SSM. Lannutti (2012) interviewed Massachusetts same-sex couples (average relationship length = 8.14 years) about their choice to remain unmarried even though Massachusetts has recognized marriage for same-sex couples since 2004. Two groups of unmarried couples emerged: couples who said they will never marry and couples who said they had chosen not to marry "for now." Members of both groups cited resistance from family-of-origin members, political criticism of marriage, concerns about further "outness," the uncertainty and limitedness of SSM, and a lack of a need for the legal protections of SSM as reasons for their decisions not to marry. Additionally, couples who said they had chosen not to marry "for now" discussed their uncertainty about whether or not they were ready for marriage, uncertainty about the need for legal protection for their relationship, and uncertainty about the need for protections for parenting as reasons to remain unmarried. Supporting the idea that SSM impacts the relational lives and communication of family identity of all same-sex couples in regions where it is available, all of the couples had partner discussions whether or not to marry and had discussed their decision not to marry with at least some friends and/or family members. This suggests that unmarried couples needed to reaffirm their legitimacy as family in conversation with others in light of their decision not to marry.

Some of the reasons not to marry expressed by participants in Lannutti (2012) are echoed in other studies examining the experiences of same-sex couples who could, but choose not to, have an SSM or other form of civil relationship recognition.

Unmarried Massachusetts same-sex couples who participated in a study by Porche and colleagues (2005) expressed concerns that even though SSM is regionally limited and not federally recognized, SSM would become the only recognized form of establishing their identity as family, and would therefore make mute other legal protections they had in place for their family. Unmarried older same-sex couples interviewed by Lannutti (2011b) also saw previous legal protections that they had established for their family as preferable to the limited protections provided by SSM. As such, SSM is seen by some unmarried same-sex couples as a challenge to the legal means they have already employed to construct and maintain their identity as a legitimate family.

Concerns with the increased level of "outness" that comes along with SSM or other forms of civil relationship recognition expressed by participants in Lannutti's (2012) study were also expressed by same-sex couples who had chosen not to have a civil partnership in the United Kingdom (Rolfe & Peel, 2011). Older unmarried same-sex couples identified SSM as "dangerous" because of the increased visibility it would bring to married same-sex couples (Lannutti, 2011b). As discussed by Rolfe and Peel, civil relationship recognition is not a panacea for the social oppression and victimization of LGBTQ people, and thus, many LGBTQ people feel their families are safer without the increased visibility brought on by civil relationship recognition. Finally, the concerns that SSM would lead to a devaluing "mainstreaming" of LGBTQ people, their relationships, their families, and their communities expressed by participants in Lannutti's (2012) study were also expressed by unmarried same-sex couples interviewed by Lannutti (2011b) and by Porche et al. (2005). Those concerned about "mainstreaming" wish to highlight and preserve the uniqueness of their self, relational, and family identities by rejecting the institution of marriage that they associate with heteronormative culture.

## Same-Sex Marriage and Communication about Family Legitimacy with Families-of-Origin

Much of the discursive negotiation of their identity as a legitimate family performed by families centered upon a same-sex relationship occurs in interactions with family-of-origin members. An attraction to marriage described by married or engaged LGBTQ people is the ability to use marriage as a means to gain acknowledgment from family-of-origin members for the legitimacy of the family centered upon a same-sex relationship (Lannutti, 2008). An example of seeking family-of-origin acknowledgment of the legitimacy of a family centered upon a same-sex relationship is provided by a participant in Lannutti's (2008) study:

"My folks like my partner, but would call her my 'friend.' We wanted them to see her as my wife, just like they see my brother's wife" (p. 254). Thus, same-sex couples used getting married as a means to communicate their identity as a legitimate family to their family-of-origin members. This discursive strategy highlights the lack of family-of-origin support faced by many families centered upon a same-sex relationship.

A finding echoed throughout much of the LGBTQ literature is that families centered upon a same-sex relationship experience a lack of approval and stigmatization within their families-of-origin (see Connolly, 2006; Peplau & Fingerhut, 2007). How does SSM impact the ways that families centered upon a same-sex relationship communicate their identity as a legitimate family to family-of-origin members and the reactions of those family members? Schecter and colleagues (2008) found that married same-sex couples report that marriage "brought them closer to their families...created extended families, and that family members 'mellowed' and 'transformed' in their acceptance of the couple" (p. 414). These findings suggest that the legal status of SSM eases some of the discursive burden placed on families centered upon a same-sex relationship when interacting with family-of-origin members. However, other studies have indicated diverse reactions to SSM from family-of-origin members including acceptance, ambivalence, and rejection (Lannutti, 2007b; Lannutti, 2013; Smart, 2007). In fact, research has suggested that for many families centered upon a same-sex relationship, the opportunity for SSM introduces and highlights delegitimizing messages from family-of-origin members. In a study of attractions and obstacles to SSM for same-sex couples, the most commonly mentioned obstacle to SSM was a lack of approval for the marriage from family-of-origin members, with 41% of the participating couples indicating that this obstacle was of concern to them (Lannutti, 2008). One of Lannutti's (2008) participants described how family disapproval challenged the couple's desire to use SSM as a means of communicating their family identity, "Marriages are supposed to be about joining families. ... But, her family is so against our relationship, we couldn't have that" (p. 256).

A study by Lannutti (2013) sheds more light on how families communicate about SSM and why so much friction exists in the communication between same-sex couples and their family-of-origin members about SSM. Using Petronio's (2002) communication privacy management theory as a guide, Lannutti described how a same-sex couple getting married triggered a shift, and often turbulence, in the privacy regulation practices of families. For some families centered upon a same-sex relationship, SSM affected privacy boundaries and identity with their families-of-origin such that same-sex couples were more integrated into the internal family communication than before their marriages. For example, because they were now married, same-sex couples were included more often in discussions of family history and family updates. In this way, SSM helped families centered upon a same-sex relationship to communicate their identity as a legitimate family to their family-of-origin members. SSM also affected communication and identity presentation across the boundary between family members and outsiders. Same-sex couples described how they negotiated with their parents about how to share the news of their engagements and marriages with those outside of the family. In this way, SSM helped the family-of-origin members to communicate the legitimacy of the same-sex couple as part of the family. Thus, SSM was not only a location for identity negotiation for the same-sex couple, but for members of their families, as well. However, for many families, SSM triggered a privacy dilemma for family members who had to decide how and when to "come out" as a family member of an LGBTQ person. As one participant explained (Lannutti, 2013), "I thought my brother was supportive of Mike and I [sic]....he was until we were getting married and he couldn't explain [Mike] as my 'friend' anymore" (p. 20). This "coming out" dilemma for family members of married LGBTQ people as a result of the family member's SSM is also described in Badgett's (2009) studies of the impact of SSM in the Netherlands. The "coming out" dilemma for family-of-origin members resulting from the introduction of SSM highlights another way that SSM creates challenges to identity and the communication of identity. Here, SSM presents a challenge to family-of-origin members as well as members of the family centered upon a same-sex relationship.

## Same-Sex Marriage and the Communication of Family Legitimacy for Families with Children

The idea that SSM can be understood as an opportunity and challenge to the construction and maintenance of the family's identity for all members, not just the same-sex couple members, is also central to understanding the interplay between SSM and families centered upon a same-sex relationship with children. Research has indicated that same-sex couples co-parenting children are more likely to be recognized by others as a "family" than are same-sex couples who are not parents (Baxter et al., 2009) and that the presence of children might offset objections and challenges to same-sex couples' identity and practice as a family (Koenig Kellas & Suter, 2012). As with interactions with families-of-origin discussed above, SSM serves to remove some of the discursive burden to show that they are a legitimate family experienced by families centered upon a same-sex relationship. Same-sex couples have cited increased legal protection and social acceptance for having children or wanting to have children as attractions to SSM (Lannutti, 2008) and as benefits of being legally married (Badgett, 2009; Hall, 2005; Ramos et al., 2009). Ramos and colleagues (2009) reported that 93% of married same-sex couples with children in their study believed that their children were happier and better off as a result of their marriage. Married same-sex couples with children also reported that their children felt more secure, have a greater sense of stability, and "saw their families as validated by society" because of their parents' SSM (Ramos et al., p. 1).

Research shows that same-sex couples believe that SSM is a tool to use to communicate the legitimacy of their family, but how do the children of same-sex couples describe their perceptions of SSM and SSM's role in their families' communication of their identity as a legitimate family? Research on the perceptions of same-sex marriage held by children of married same-sex couples is scarce. Hall (2005) reported on interviews with children of same-sex parents married in Massachusetts. According to Hall, the children of same-sex couples felt that marriage equality for their parents and other same-sex couples was important and "right," but that the children viewed their parents' wedding ceremonies and parents' marriages themselves as more meaningful to their parents than to them. Goldberg and Kuvalanka (2012) interviewed adult children of LGBTQ individuals about their perspectives on SSM. Their participants unequivocally supported SSM as a means for families centered upon a same-sex relationship to gain important legal rights, such as adoption rights and health care coverage. The children of LGBTQ people also cited symbolic benefits of SSM, including making the family centered upon a same-sex relationship seem more "intelligible and real" (Goldberg & Kuvalanka, p. 45). Yet, one quarter of Goldberg and Kuvalanka's participants also mentioned some criticism of SSM or the fight for marriage equality while acknowledging the legal and symbolic benefits. Among the concerns about SSM and the fight for marriage equality mentioned by their participants were suggestions that relationship termination might be more complicated after SSM and doubts about the high amount of energy and resources the LGBTQ community has focused on marriage equality. Although limited, the research on the understanding of SSM held by children of same-sex couples suggests that they recognize SSM as a mechanism for helping to communicate a family's identity as a legitimate family, but that they also have some concerns about SSM as a political focus and legal contract.

## Same-Sex Marriage and Communication about Family Legitimacy with Friends

Research has identified the role of friends in the lives of LGBTQ people as fictive "families of choice" (Dewaele et al., 2011; Gabrielson, 2011; Oswald, 2002; Smart,

2007; Weston, 1991). Thus, it is important to understand how SSM impacts the ways that families centered upon a same-sex relationship communicate their identity as a legitimate family with friends. Married or engaged LGBTQ participants in Lannutti's (2008) study of decision making about SSM indicated a desire to marry because marriage would be a means to gain acknowledgment for identity as a legitimate family from friends. Married same-sex couples have reported that being married has influenced heterosexual friends' perceptions of family such that they were now seen as more "legitimate" (Badgett, 2009; Lannutti, 2011b). Smart (2007) argued that SSM further blurs the boundaries between "(given) families and (chosen) friends" (p. 671) because of the ways that same-sex couples integrate both kin and friends into wedding ceremonies and celebrations. Thus, wedding ceremonies are discursive practices that not only communicate the legitimacy of the family centered upon a same-sex relationship but also serve to integrate friends into that family form.

Other studies have indicated both support and resistance from LGBTQ friends to the same-sex couples' attempt to construct and maintain family identity through SSM (Lannutti, 2007b; Smart, 2007). Participants in Smart's (2007) study indicated that same-sex couple friends who opted to not marry were sometimes "awkward" about the participants' wedding ceremonies. Some lesbian-bisexual couples who participated in Lannutti's (2007b) study described the ways that lesbian friends would voice challenges to the legitimacy of a bisexual woman's identity as bisexual given that she was marrying a woman. Thus, research on interactions with friends again shows that for families centered upon a same-sex relationship, the introduction of SSM was associated with opportunities to communicate the family legitimacy and challenges to their use of SSM in the construction and maintenance of their family legitimacy.

## Same-Sex Marriage Restrictions and Communication about Family Legitimacy

To this point, I have discussed how SSM itself is interwoven with discursive construction and maintenance of an identity as a "legitimate" family by families centered upon a same-sex relationship. However, SSM itself is only part of the context in which these families now find themselves since the battles for and against SSM have taken place and continue to take place. Many families centered upon a same-sex relationship live in regions where campaigns against marriage and relationship recognition for same-sex couples have been waged and won. How, then, do families centered upon a same-sex relationship discursively construct and maintain their identity as a legitimate family in light of experiences with anti-marriage and anti-relationship recognition campaigns and legislation?

Researchers have identified psychological consequences for LGBTQ people as a result of marriage and relationship recognition restrictions and their surrounding campaigns (Horne et al., 2011; Maisel & Fingerhut, 2011; Riggle, Rostosky, & Horne, 2009; Rostosky et al., 2010; Rostosky, Riggle, Horne, & Miller, 2009). Rostosky and colleagues (2009) examined the effects of anti-SSM state constitutional amendments through a national study comparing LGBTQ people who lived in an anti-marriage amendment state to those who did not. They found that LGBTQ people who lived in a state with a newly passed marriage restriction amendment were exposed to more negative messages about themselves and their relationships and experienced higher levels of negative psychological effects, such as stress and depressive symptoms, than did LGBTQ people who lived in other states. Rostosky et al.'s (2009) results echo those found by Russell (2000) in her study of the psychological consequences of the passage of Colorado's anti-gay amendment in 1992. Horne and colleagues (2011) found further evidence of negative message exposure and negative affect for LGBTQ people in states that passed a marriage-restricting amendment. Maisel and Fingerhut (2011) found that LGBTQ people in California experienced an increased sense of prejudice from society as a result of the campaign for the passage of Proposition 8, which would prohibit same-sex marriage within the state.

While there have been many negative consequences for LGBTQ people as a result of marriage and relationship recognition restrictions and their surrounding campaigns, research has also identified positive consequences for LGBTQ people in these situations. LGBTQ individuals have reported experiencing increased social support from friends, family, and other community members, increases in their political activity, and increases in feelings of pride as a result of experiencing marriage restricting campaigns (Lannutti, 2011a; Maisel & Fingerhut, 2011; Rostosky et al., 2009; Rostosky et al., 2010). Thus, the psychological and social consequences of marriage amendments and other legal restrictions on LGBTQ individuals are complex. Families centered upon a same-sex relationship who live in a state with an anti-marriage restriction will surely experience an increase in delegitimizing messages about their family and will have to discursively address these additional challenges borne of the campaigns against SSM and resulting legislation. At the same time, anti-SSM campaigns might also serve as a stimulus for newfound support for families centered upon a same-sex relationship from social network members and could inspire these families to express their legitimacy through new avenues such as increased political involvement.

Researchers have further examined the effects of marriage and same-sex relationship recognition restrictions on families centered upon a same-sex relationship. Even in regions where same-sex marriage is legally recognized, research has identified negative consequences for families centered upon a same-sex relationship as a result of campaigns to reverse the recognition of same-sex marriage (Lannutti, 2005; Lannutti, 2011b). Couples might choose not to marry because SSM is seen as unsteady, unpredictable, or even dangerous in the face of anti-marriage campaigns and legal maneuvers (Lannutti, 2007b; Lannutti, 2011b; Lannutti, 2012). For example, an older same-sex couple who participated in Lannutti (2011b) explained why they decided to avoid the "public statement" of marriage:

> You see those nuts with the 'God hates fags' signs down at the State House. We'd just as soon keep our life private and just between those we are close to. Not to be bothered by those stupid folks who are just ignorant. (p. 75)

Same-sex couples have reported feeling fearful about their ability to define and protect their family as a result of anti-marriage campaigns and legal maneuvers (Maisel & Fingerhut, 2011; Rostosky et al., 2010). Faced with anti-marriage legislation, many same-sex couples have described the great lengths they went through to be legally defined as a family and to attempt to gain protections for their family (Maisel & Fingerhut, 2011; Rostosky et al., 2010). An example is provided by one of Rostosky and colleagues' (2010) participants: "My partner and I had to fly from Texas to Massachusetts to have our child in order for both of us to be on the birth certificate. This was risky and shameful that we would have to do this in order to protect our family" (p. 306). The changing status of same-sex marriage across U.S. locations and across time has forced some same-sex couples to marry multiple times and in multiple locations in order to try to define and protect their family. An example of this is provided by a participant in Maisel and Fingerhut's (2011) study, "I have married the same woman four times. I also have a small child with her. Hopefully, this [California] marriage will not be able to be reversed, or retracted, as our marriage in Portland, OR was" (p. 253).

Same-sex marriage and relationship recognition restrictions and their surrounding campaigns have also been found to have consequences for families beyond same-sex couples and their children. Horne et al. (2011) found that family members of LGBTQ individuals who lived in a U.S. state that passed an anti-same-sex marriage amendment experienced greater amounts of emotional distress than did family members of LGBTQ individuals who lived in a state that did not have such an amendment on the ballot. Many family members of LGBTQ people in Horne and colleagues' study expressed concern for the well-being of their LGBTQ family member as a result of the anti-marriage amendments. The personal distress over anti-marriage amendments and concerns about LGBTQ family members as a result of anti-marriage amendments were also reported by participants in Arm et al.'s (2009) study. Family members of LGBTQ people interviewed by Arm and colleagues also indicated that their understanding of their own identities and relationships were affected by the anti-marriage policies and surrounding campaigns. For example, family members of LGBTQ people reported feeling an "identity quandary" as they reflected on their own religious beliefs, personalities and connection to the LGBTQ community in the face of the challenges to same-sex marriage. Family members of LGBTQ people also described how experiencing the challenges to same-sex marriage allowed them to recognize support for them and their LGBTQ family member from other friends and family members and to learn how to better articulate and understand their concern for their LGBTQ family member in the face of discrimination. Family members of LGBTQ people have often reacted to movements against same-sex marriage by increasing their own political activism in support of LGBTQ rights (Arm et al.; Horne et al.). As such, the challenges to SSM can be understood to have impacted the way that family members of LGBTQ people conceptualized and communicated their family connection and identity. However, research has also shown that family members of LGBTQ people have reported that challenges to SSM resulted in conflict, tension, and relational deterioration between them and their LGBTQ family member (Horne et al.). Thus, challenges to the marriage rights of same-sex couples appear to have negative emotional and psychological impact on family members of LGBTQ people and family relationships but also appear to be an opportunity for self-reflection, relationship re-evaluation, and renewed connections.

Same-sex marriage restrictions and their surrounding campaigns have also been shown to have an effect on the communication and relationships across the external boundary between families centered upon a same-sex relationship and non-family members (Arm et al., 2009; Lannutti, 2011a; Maisel & Fingerhut, 2011; Rostosky et al., 2010). LGBTQ people have reported feeling alienated from society (Rostosky et al., 2010), and they have perceived a lack of support from the "heterosexual community" (Maisel & Fingerhut) after experiencing a challenge to SSM. More detailed examples of the ways that same-sex marriage restrictions and their surrounding campaigns can affect the communication between families centered upon a same-sex relationship and larger society can be found in Lannutti's (2011a) study of communication about marriage amendments between same-sex couples and their extended social networks (e.g., neighbors, acquaintances, colleagues). Blau and Fingerman (2009) argued that extended social network members, with whom we might have both direct contact (one to one interaction) and distant contact (contact through a mutual third party), are essential and influential parts of our social lives because these people form the basis for our understanding of "society" and they create a web of social connections that can be relied upon for material and social support at key points in our lives without the daily relational maintenance behavior typically associated with close personal relationships.

Lannutti (2011a) found that families centered upon a same-sex relationship living in states that passed an anti-same-sex marriage amendment discursively constructed and maintained their identity as a legitimate family in interactions with extended social network members in three ways. First, same-sex couple members "came out" during discussions with extended social network members about the marriage amendment in order to communicate their identity as an LGBTQ person. Second, members of families centered upon a same-sex relationship engaged in socially supportive interactions with extended social network members in which they discussed their feelings related to the marriage amendment, were listened to, and experienced solidarity with the extended social network member. In these supportive interactions, the legitimacy of the family centered upon a same-sex relationship was confirmed by the extended social network member. Third, families centered upon a same-sex relationship experienced disconfirmation from extended social network members when discussing the marriage amendments. These disconfirming interactions were characterized by condemnation and avoidance of the families' discursive construction of legitimacy by the extended social network member.

## Conclusion

Recent battles for and against legally recognized same-sex marriage (SSM) have created a new context for families centered upon a same-sex relationship. This context is characterized by private family deliberation, intense public debates, and dynamic and uncertain changes in legal status for these families. SSM has provided many families centered upon a same-sex relationship an opportunity to define their family via the law and has served to relieve some of the discursive burden faced by these "nontraditional" families as they construct and maintain their identity as a legitimate family. Yet, for some families centered upon a same-sex relationship, SSM has also served as a stimulus for additional challenges to the families' discursive construction of their family legitimacy. Thus, families' experiences with SSM provide an interesting counterpoint to Galvin's (2006) argument that legal ties between adults in the family serve to make families less "discourse dependent."

Further research is needed to more fully understand the SSM experiences of families centered upon a same-sex relationship. The current research is limited in that it mostly focuses on Caucasian families and does not fully address the influence of cultural elements such as ethnicity, religion, and social class on families'

SSM experiences. Because SSM is regionally limited, the extant research tends to focus on certain countries, such as the Netherlands and the United States, and certain areas within countries, such as Massachusetts. Locations for research on SSM should expand as the battle for and against SSM expands to additional regions. As SSM unfolds, longitudinal studies examining the ways that families centered upon a same-sex relationship construct and maintain their identities as legitimate families over time will be needed. Thus, the research discussed in this chapter provides us with only a starting point for understanding the experiences and identity construction and maintenance of families centered upon a same-sex relationship within the context created by SSM.

## Note

1. The definition of a "family" as perceived by both scholars and lay people is complicated and contentious (Baxter et al., 2009). As discussed by Stacey (1999), labeling families led by a female-female or male-male couple is complex. I am using the term "families centered upon a same-sex relationship" to describe the families rather than the term "gay and lesbian families" as to avoid the assumption of gay or lesbian identity for individuals who might self-identify in another way, such as bisexual.

# CHAPTER FIVE

# Single-Parent Families

## Creating a Sense of Family from Within

TAMARA D. AFIFI, SHARDÉ DAVIS, AND ANNE MERRILL

The number of children living with a single parent has increased dramatically in the United States. Twenty-eight percent of children lived with a single parent in 2010, which is in sharp contrast to earlier decades (e.g., 9% in the 1950s; U.S. Census Bureau, 2010b). In addition, roughly 85% of these single parents were mothers (U.S. Census Bureau, 2010b). Single parenthood also tends to be heavily divided according to race, socioeconomic status, and education. For instance, Black women have historically been more likely to be single parents than women of other races. According to a 2011 United States Census American Community Survey (ACS), a random survey of women ages 15–50 who gave birth within the past year in the United States, 68% of the Black women surveyed were unmarried, compared to 43% of Hispanic women, 26% of White women (non-Hispanic), and 11% of Asian women (Shattuck & Kreider, 2013). Most (69%) of the mothers in this survey were also raised in families living in poverty.

These single-parent families are also formed in different ways. First, single-parent families can result from a divorce or the dissolution of the parents' relationship. Some of the parents could have cohabitated and never married or never had the opportunity to marry (e.g., gay and lesbian parents being denied the opportunity to marry and then dissolving the relationship). Second, many single-parent families are formed through out-of-wedlock births or the parent not being married at the time of the birth of the child. As the U.S. Census data from the ACS indicate (Shattuck & Kreider, 2013), the rate of out-of-wedlock single motherhood has become increasingly common in recent years. Finally, single-parent families can be formed through adoption. Each of these single parent forms is unique and requires its own discussion. In the current chapter, however, we examine the communication patterns that cross these different types of single-parent families.

In many ways, single-parent families face an uphill battle to validate their family to others. They are confronted with societal stigma against single parenthood and statistics about the negative impact of single parenthood on children. Even though single-parent families face numerous challenges, it is how family members communicate with one another and define a sense of family amidst these challenges that is important. When one looks deeper, the same communication processes create a sense of family and build strong family bonds across all families—regardless of family structure.

Researchers tend to examine the differences between single-parent families and traditional two-parent families, emphasizing the increased risks and problems for single-parent families. The bulk of this research suggests that single-parent families face unique challenges, including a greater propensity for role overload for the single parent, economic hardship, social isolation and stigma, and deficits in social support (see Amato, 2000). Despite these added challenges, however, many children from single-parent families grow up without significant problems (Parke, 2003), and many single-parent families report equally high amounts of cohesion and resiliency as two-parent families (Ford-Gilboe, 2000). Consistently approaching single-parent families as a problem, or analyzing them from a "deficit approach" when compared to two parent families (see Golish, 2003), impedes people's understanding of the communication patterns that create strength within single-parent families and how these communication patterns transcend family structure. Although it is true that certain stressors can threaten single-parent families, many single-parent families emerge strengthened, resourceful, and resilient despite such stressors (e.g., Brodsky & De Vet, 2000; Seccombe, 2002). The more crucial question is how single-parent families create, maintain, and articulate a sense of family despite these challenges and become resilient in the process.

Of particular importance in this chapter is why some children and parents who experience single parenthood are resilient to its accompanying stress, or adapt effectively when faced with the adversity of single parenthood and potentially grow from the experience, whereas others do not. We first examine the challenges or stressors of single-parent families—both from a research perspective and a societal perspective—that can be obstacles to legitimizing their families to others. We then discuss some of the ways single-parent families create positive definitions of family in spite of these challenges. Communication is the means through which single-parent families co-construct their family identity. In this chapter, we examine how single-parent families co-construct a strong sense of family by adopting a functional perspective in our focus on the attitudes and communication processes within single-parent families that foster resilience and strength when faced with the challenges of single parenthood.

## Obstacles of Single-Parent Families

### Research on Single Parenthood

The majority of the research has painted a rather bleak picture of the impact of single parenthood on children. Even though much of the literature focuses on single-parent families that are the result of divorce, other research has examined the impact of single parenthood on children regardless of divorce. Most of the research on single-parent families, whether single parenthood as the result of divorce or other circumstances, has compared single-parent families to two-parent families. In general, this research has shown that children of single-parent families, on average, tend to experience more behavioral, psychological, cognitive, and economic difficulties compared to children who grow up in two-parent families (see O'Connor, Dunn, Jenkins, Pickering, & Rasbash, 2001; Riala, Isohanni, Jokelainen, Jones, & Isohanni, 2003).

When one examines the specific stressors experienced by children in single-parent families, education and economic attainment surface repeatedly. Researchers have shown that children who grow up in single-parent families tend to be educationally disadvantaged. Research has found that, on average, children of single parents are less likely to attend the best schools, less likely to have access to educational resources, less likely to complete high school and attend college, and less likely to have high earning potential compared to children who are raised in two-parent households (e.g., Astone & MacLanahan, 1991; Barton, 2006). Single parents are often less able to support and monitor their children's academic progress and homework, resulting in lower academic attainment, higher dropout rates, and fewer career aspirations (Jeynes, 2002). Research also has shown that children who are raised in single-parent families are more likely to report a variety of externalizing issues compared to children in two-parent families. For example, children raised by single parents are more likely to engage in risky behaviors, such as increased drug and alcohol use and earlier sexual activity than children from two-parent families (Barrett & Turner, 2005; Griffin, Botvin, Scheier, Diaz, &

Miller, 2000; Wagner et al., 2010). When children are not monitored by their parents, they are more susceptible to outside peer influences and delinquency (Carlson & Corcoran, 2001).

Researchers have identified three primary reasons why children of single parents tend to be more disadvantaged than children from two-parent families: (1) economic hardship, (2) stress overload and the lack of another parent to buffer the stress, and (3) diminished parenting. One of the main reasons why children from single parents are often disadvantaged is because single parents, particularly single mothers, tend to have less disposable income than two-parent households. This can create economic hardship for children. For example, the poverty rate in the United States nearly doubles to 24.6% when considering custodial single parents compared to two-parent households, with 12.9% of custodial fathers and 27% of custodial mothers falling below the poverty line (Grall, 2009). When children grow up in poverty with a single parent, they are more likely to live in poverty and be single parents themselves later in life compared to children who grow up with two parents (Amato, 2005; McLanahan & Booth, 1989). When people are stressed financially, it increases the propensity for conflict and strain in the family, which can result in diminished parenting. This diminished parenting, in turn, can negatively affect children's well-being (Amato, 2000; Solantaus, Leinonen, & Punamaki, 2004). When parents experience economic hardship, they might have to work multiple jobs to pay the bills and, consequently, might not be as available to monitor their children's activities. Nevertheless, much of this research has assumed that economic strain is perceived as stressful. As Amato (2000) has noted, finances only become stressful if parents perceive them as stressful. Many single parents might not perceive their finances as stressful because they have learned to budget their money effectively or find resources within their family and community.

A related reason why single-parent families can be stressful is because of a lack of another parent to buffer the stress. Single parents often experience role burden or role overload because they are juggling multiple roles simultaneously without the assistance of another parental figure. They are more likely than married parents to suffer depressive symptoms and to feel socially isolated, largely as a function of taking on the stressors of single parenthood alone with diminished social networks after a divorce (see Anderson, 2008; Usdansky & Wolf, 2008). Even one stressor, if managed alone on a daily basis, can be extremely stressful. When a child misbehaves there might not be anyone available to offer support. If this happens on an ongoing basis, it can be overwhelming. For instance, when a child throws a tantrum in a two-parent home, one parent can ask the other to take over the parenting responsibilities to reduce the stress. Single parents might not have the luxury of having another adult who can buffer the stress. In this sense, the structure of single-parent families can be important because of the lack of another parental figure to help manage the stress. Many single parents, however, learn to rely on extended family and friends as sources of social support (see Ciabattari, 2007, for information on social capital and single parents).

The stress of single parenting can also affect one's parenting because of diminished executive functioning. The single parent might be experiencing ego depletion or the process by which individuals cognitively become overwhelmed with information, making it difficult to process new information (Baumeister, 2002). Single parents are probably more likely than other parents to become ego depleted because they are juggling responsibilities that would normally be distributed between two parents. When parents become overwhelmed, they are more stressed and their ability to parent their children effectively suffers. As Baumeister (2002) has contended, self-control is like a scarce resource or energy reserve that can become depleted through repeated use. Many of the changes and stressors associated with single parenting (e.g., divorce or death, moving, multiple jobs, less income) can slowly erode parents' emotional resources. Parents who are in high stress situations might begin to lose self-control, and consequently emotional control, because external demands have depleted their emotional resources. Over time, their emotional energy is drained and they may simply resort to "numbness" or baseline levels of coping, which can result in a lack of empathy or ability to read others' emotions (see Baumeister, Brewer, Tice, & Twenge, 2007; DeWall & Baumeister, 2006). This intrapersonal withdrawal could predict a greater inability to encode their adolescents' emotions and coping abilities.

As suggested above, growing up in a single-parent family can also affect children through diminished parenting. For example, research has shown that many single parents tend to be both permissive (too lenient) and authoritarian (dogmatic) in their parenting (Amato, 2000; Bulcroft, Carmody, & Bulcroft, 1998). Single parents become more permissive or lenient with their children because they are tired from assuming too many roles or managing multiple stressors alone. At the same time, they are equally likely to use corporal punishment when their children misbehave because they are overwhelmed and stressed. Because of the stressful nature of single parenthood, children are less likely to be supervised, but research shows that when the parental monitoring increases, risky behaviors and delinquency problems in adolescence are reduced (Griffin et al., 2000; Wagner et al., 2010). Research also has shown that parental warmth, affection, support, and parental monitoring can buffer the impact of stress on children's internalizing and externalizing problems in single-parent families and other family types (e.g., Evans, Kim, Ting, Tesher, & Shannis, 2007; Lanza, Rhoades, Nix, & Greenberg, 2010). In fact, researchers have found that children who grow up in rather extreme conditions (e.g., violence, poverty, discrimination) can be protected from these conditions if their parents are supportive, loving, and involved in their lives (Evans et al., 2007). Researchers have also reported averages across families. Many single-parent families function better than two-parent families, primarily because the quality of the parenting and other communication patterns within the family are more important than family structure in determining family functioning (see Amato, 2005).

## Research on Societal Attitudes about Single Parenthood

In addition to various economic, educational, and parenting stressors, single parents face social stigma regarding their family. Single-parent families often face challenges in communicating their family's legitimacy and completeness to others. Single-parent families are problematized by outsiders for not conforming to the traditional nuclear family ideal (Ford-Gilboe, 2000). Single parents and their children can encounter greater stigma in their daily life than two-parent families simply due to the societal perception of their "incompleteness."

Much less empirical research exists about how the lay public perceives single parenthood compared to what researchers have found regarding the impact of single parenthood on children. However, the literature that is available on the public's perception of single parenthood suggests that single parenthood is viewed negatively in the public sector. To investigate people's attitudes about single parenthood, Usdansky (2009) conducted a content analysis of attitudes toward divorce (without reference to single parenthood) and single parenthood (regardless of how it is formed) written in popular magazines ($N = 474$) and scholarly research articles ($N = 202$) published between 1900 and 1998. She found that negative attitudes regarding divorce in magazines and scholarly journals decreased significantly during the century. Part of this trend could be due to the fact that children vary considerably in how they respond to divorce (Hetherington, 1999). Some children function better if they are removed from a turbulent family environment, some children show significant difficulties as a result of their parents' divorce, and others do not seem affected at all (Amato & Keith, 1991; Amato, 2001). Consequently, people could have varied feelings about divorce. As Usdansky (2009) also postulated, people could have varying feelings about divorce because they differ in their beliefs about the conditions that are acceptable for divorce to occur—with more and more people later in the century believing that personal happiness is a valid reason for divorce (rather than more extreme circumstances like infidelity or adultery). Unlike the findings for divorce, however, the perceptions of non-marital childrearing in magazines and scholarly articles were critical and stable throughout the century (Usdansky, 2009).

Why might people have a harsher attitude toward non-marital childrearing than divorce? The marital trends in the United States might suggest that even if Americans have varied feelings about divorce, they still ultimately value marriage (Cherlin, 2009b). American families have undergone enormous change in the past few decades, but Americans still ultimately value marriage. The "ideal" of marriage that most people strive for in the United States is in sharp contrast to non-marital childrearing (Cherlin, 2009b). Having children out of wedlock continues to be something that is condemned by society (Thornton, 2009). What the literature has suggested, then, is that the American public still tends to privilege the definition of "family" as a marriage between a man and a woman who have children together.

Nevertheless, the perception of out-of-wedlock births and the acceptance of the single-parent family form varies significantly across cultures within the United States, which could affect the identity of single-parent families. Single parents across sub-cultures negotiate a healthy single-parent identity with the support of their extended kin in spite of the stigma from their own cultural group and country. Many single parents are outcasts in their respective social spheres but are accepted in close family sectors.

Perhaps the most obvious example of differing perceptions of single parenthood resides in Black families within the United States. Even though single parenthood is stigmatized within the larger U.S. culture, single parenthood is typically deemed a common and acceptable family form within the Black community (Murry & Brody, 2002). Black families have led in the trend toward single-parent family compositions, with nearly 50% of Black American children having lived with a single parent (U.S. Census Bureau, 2010b). An ethnic group's experience with single parenthood allows them to develop particular coping strategies that help them resist negative stereotypes about single parenthood. Additionally, the prevalence of single parenthood over a long period of time for Black Americans could lessen the stigmatization for this group, and possibly even afford parents the opportunity to socialize their children so that they are less susceptible to stressors of single parenthood. For instance, single mothers within the Black community send positive messages of self-worth and pride to their children as a means of socializing them to survive in a society that frequently devalues them (Murry & Brody, 2002; Suizzo, Robinson, & Pahlke, 2008; Thomas & King, 2007). In doing so, children are prepared to resist negative beliefs about Black people and the single-parent family structure, which translates into less internalization of negative attitudes and practices (Murry & Brody, 2002).

The different cultural norms within each sub-culture create subtle, and often juxtaposing, positions on single parenthood. For example, the family values embedded in the Latino culture help single-parent families forge strong relational ties with extended kin and create strong and healthy attitudes about their unconventional family type. Latino cultures, like Asian cultures, promote collectivist norms (Gomel,

Tinsley, Parke, & Clark, 1998), and similar to Black Americans, emphasize kin support (see Carlo, Koller, Raffaelli, & Guzman, 2007). Yet, young Latino children, particularly girls, are socialized at a young age to respect the sanctity of marriage, family, and motherhood. Latinos' strong support of familialism, or the importance of family, and close relationships with kin discourages divorce and reinforces positive views of marriage, with Latinas getting married at younger ages compared to White women (Bulanda & Brown, 2007; Carlo et al., 2007). Even though the divorce rates for Latinos are lower compared to Blacks and Whites, Latinas are not excluded from the growing trend toward single parenthood. Even though single parenthood is not as legitimated as marriage in the Latino culture, single Latino parents have ample resources from extended kin to meet the emotional, financial, and practical needs that a co-parent typically provides in a dual-headed home. As this brief explanation suggests, the introduction of culture into the investigation of single-parent identity negotiation is critical. Sometimes families can face social stigma against single parenthood within the larger culture and within their family network and other times they find extraordinary amounts of social support within their family and sub-culture that can build resilience against the societal stigmas of singlehood. The larger question to be considered is how single parents and their children create a strong sense of family when faced with such social stigma.

## Creating and Communicating a Sense of Family in the Face of Stigma

### Emphasizing the Quality of Parenting Rather Than Family Structure

Although research typically has pointed to the hardships of single-parent families compared to two-parent families, attributing these patterns merely to family structure misses important similarities across families that explain why some families function better than others under stress. An alternative approach is to focus on the communication patterns that characterize families and determine their functioning rather than the composition of the families (e.g., Ford-Gilboe, 2000; Lansford, Ceballo, Abbey, & Stewart, 2001; Simons, Chen, Simons, Brody & Cutrona, 2006). Single parents and their children co-construct their family identity, or who they think they are as a family, through the way they communicate with each other. This identity work can foster resilience when faced with the hardships of single parenthood, largely because the co-construction of the family identity comes from within the family itself. Single-parent families that have a strong sense of family are most likely better able to adapt to the stress of single parenthood than families that have a weaker sense of family. Certain communication patterns within families, regardless of structure, also serve a functional approach in that they create family strength and resilience. In the paragraphs that follow, we identify some of the communication patterns in single-parent families that promote resilience. Identifying specific communicative strengths that foster resiliency across families can contribute to the understanding that family strength is more than family structure.

Communication determines how a family functions, which tends to transcend family structure. For example, one of the most powerful predictors of long-term child well-being is interparental conflict (Afifi & Schrodt, 2003; Amato & Afifi, 2006; Taylor, Way, & Seeman, 2011). Research has demonstrated that children from married families with high interparental conflict experience poorer psychological well-being and adjustment compared to children in low-conflict married families and divorced families (Amato, 2000). Divorce is important, but not as important as the degree of interparental conflict. The children that tend to fare the worst are those whose parents have an extremely turbulent relationship yet stay married because their children cannot escape the conflict (see Amato & Afifi, 2006). Intense and chronic interparental conflict interferes with parenting quality, creates high amounts of stress for children, and teaches children poor communication skills, which can be transferred to adult children's own marriages (Amato, 2000). Therefore, scholars have argued that marriage is beneficial for children if the marriage itself is healthy and stable; marriage is more of a proxy for the beneficial interaction patterns and stability that are associated with positive child outcomes (Parke, 2003). If divorce or single parenthood results in a decrease in children's exposure to destructive conflict, the research suggests that these children's well-being can improve over time. Family conflict is an important distinguishing factor of risk and resilience across families.

In addition to the quality of the parents' marriage and the degree of conflict, the quality of the parenting is equally important to family functioning. As Amato (2005) has stated, "regardless of family structure, the quality of parenting is one of the best predictors of children's emotional and social well-being" (p. 83). The quality of caregiving from a parent is strongly linked to a child's coping and resiliency throughout the lifespan. Supervision, consistent discipline, active involvement, and open family communication patterns are some defining characteristics of high quality parenting (Armstrong, Birnie-Lefcovitch, & Ungar, 2005). In addition to these qualities, closeness between single parents and their children can be particularly important in child development and well-being. Kuntsche and Silbereisen (2004) found that although adolescents from single-parent families had higher levels of substance use compared to those from two-parent families, parental closeness in single-parent families decreased the likelihood that adolescents from both types of families used substances. Therefore, regardless of family type, adolescents can equally benefit from parental closeness because it can protect them from risky behaviors. These findings emphasize the importance of parenting quality as a predictor of family and child well-being, rather than only relying on structural explanations. The powerful effect of parenting, particularly as it pertains to parent-child closeness and parental involvement, has been shown to alleviate much of the impact of the stress of single parenthood on children (Davis & Friel, 2001; Kotchick, Dorsey, Miller, & Forehand, 1999; Kuntsche & Silbereisen, 2004).

## Valuing a Sense of Family and Building Resilience

Some single parents report that the stigma surrounding single parenthood helps motivate them to "show others that single-parent families can survive and thrive" (Ford-Gilboe, 2000, p. 51). The challenge of convincing others of the legitimacy and strength of one's single-parent family can serve as a motivation to be a strong family. Overall, the extent to which single-parent families are able to possess a sense of wholeness and pride in spite of these challenges is likely to contribute to their overall family well-being and hardiness.

Creating a strong family in the face of the challenges associated with single-parent family life is particularly important for minimizing vulnerability and increasing resilience to potential risks (Patterson, 2002). Single-parent families possess strengths that can assist them in recovering from adversity (McCubbin & McCubbin, 1996). Communicating these strengths is a hallmark for successful single-parent families because it helps them recognize and legitimize the family as a strong social unit. Numerous scholarly essays have been written about what constitutes family resilience (Anderson, 2003; Luther, Cicchetti, & Becker, 2000; Walsh, 2002, 2003). Family resilience can be thought of as factors that protect and help family members recover from stressors (Orthner, Jones-Sanpei, & Williamson, 2004). Research has identified several factors which promote resilience in families, such as the quality of intra-family relationships, open family communication, external social support, spirituality, flexibility, and a general positive outlook or optimism (Black & Lobo, 2008; Greeff & Ritman, 2005; Greeff & Van Der Merwe, 2004). Researchers also have argued that the ability to enact such resilience-promoting qualities is not limited by family structure. Family structure does not impede a family's ability to engage in adaptive processes nor does it determine its overall well-being. Creating and communicating a sense of family resilience is one way that single-parent families can co-construct their family identity.

Single parent families can co-construct a family identity by communicating a strong sense of purpose and a positive outlook when faced with stressful situations.

Communicating a positive outlook helps family members rise above adversity by reframing hardship as an opportunity for growth. Optimism repeatedly has surfaced in the literature as an ideal strategy adopted by high functioning families (Walsh, 2003). For instance, research shows that single mothers with an optimistic outlook can indirectly influence resiliency with their children because these mothers tend to use supportive and involved parenting practices (Jones, Forehand, Brody, & Armistead, 2002). Single-parent families identify optimism as a family strength, such that they are able to devise creative coping and problem-solving strategies to maneuver through life's stressors (Ford-Gilboe, 2000; Richards, 1989). As parents attempt actively to encourage their child's perseverance in the face of difficult times, they develop their child's sense of personal efficacy and resilience (Amatea, Smith-Adcock & Villares, 2006). Resilience does not arise solely from within the individual or in spite of detrimental family circumstances, but is built within the family unit. This resilience serves as an important buffer against life stressors.

Other ways have been identified by which single parents are able to communicate a strong family identity to their children and others outside the family. In a qualitative study, single mothers reframed the societal stigma and negative reactions to single parenthood, learning to view their single parenthood as empowering (Levine, 2009). The researcher argued that this reframing of stigma increases single mothers' resiliency by creating positive meanings in difficult times. Arguably, single parents who are able to reframe their identity from one that is stigmatized to one that is a source of pride are also more likely to communicate this pride to their children, social networks, and others outside their social networks, benefiting their family as a whole. This ability is likely to be most apparent in single-parent families if the single parents translate this message to their children; if children observe that their family is a strong source of pride, they will likely have a strong personal and family identity.

Similar to the notion of positively reframing stigma, single-parent families can rely on the strength within their family by emphasizing its cohesiveness. Relying on cohesiveness or solidarity can help single-parent families bolster their perception of family strength. Ford-Gilboe (2000) found that single parents reported cohesion or emotional closeness most frequently as a strong characteristic of their family. In this study, single parents indicated that cohesion and closeness were particular strengths that motivated them to cope with stress, and that having a sense of cohesion positively affected their physical and mental health. This source of strength might be particularly salient for divorced single parents because they often become closer to their children as a result of having experienced a divorce together (see Afifi, 2003). In other words, single-parent families might develop a strong sense of cohesion through shared stressors and experiences, which in turn, can bolster their resilience. Over time, these families can learn that their cohesion is a testament to their strength and legitimacy as a family—that they are able to weather stressors of life successfully as a collective entity.

The cohesion that single-parent families experience could be related to the greater parent-child equality in these families compared to two-parent families. In single-parent families, parents and children (particularly adolescent or young-adult children) often share power within the family and have less hierarchical distribution of power than in two-parent families. Single-parent family members are more likely to endorse living by the guideline of "power with" rather than "power over" other family members (Ford-Gilboe, 2000). In addition, single parents and their children report greater mutual intimacy and nurturance than do those from two-parent families (Walker & Hennig, 1997). For example, a spirit of togetherness can be fostered when single parents include their children in the decision-making process. Children can also learn independence when they are asked to assume more responsibility in the household. However, a more egalitarian family environment can also result in role reversals or parentification. Parentification occurs when children become their parents' emotional support system (i.e., emotional parentification) or help the parent with instrumental tasks (i.e., instrumental parentification) (Alexander, 2003; Jurkovic, Thirkeild, & Morrell, 2001). Although shared power can be a family strength for single-parent families, single-parents must also be wary of sharing too much personal information with their children because it can make them anxious and worried (see Afifi & McManus, 2010). If parents are able to maintain clear parent-child boundaries, however, cohesive relationships will only enhance one's definition of family.

Positive parent-child communication can also enhance children's academic performance, contributing indirectly to a sense of pride within the family. Research has suggested that children who engage in emotional interactions with other family members tend to feel comfortable with their ability to succeed in school and believe that the academic material is coherent (Wooley & Grogan-Kaylor, 2006). Having a cohesive family, parental involvement, an authoritative parenting style, and effective parental monitoring have also been identified as key factors to promoting school engagement for at-risk inner-city adolescents (e.g., Annunziata, Hogue, Faw, & Liddle, 2006). Incorporating these essential family factors into normal family routines can also prevent children's internalizing and externalizing problems. For example, family integration and support can predict avoidance of problem behaviors at school. Single mothers and fathers have the ability to avoid the deleterious effects of single-parent household composition that are commonly identified in the research by adopting some of these central family processes.

In addition to creating a safe, comfortable, and loving home environment, single parents should also instill core values of perseverance and determination with their children in order to promote success in school. Communicating messages of determination and perseverance is paramount for building resilience, not only within the family as a whole, but also within each individual child. For example, Amatea et al. (2006) found that high achieving students have a strong sense of purpose and resilience to tackle the challenges of school. Parents set goals and they expect their children to set goals for themselves and work hard to achieve these goals. These parents think optimistically about their life circumstances and teach their children to think optimistically, viewing adverse circumstances as an opportunity to learn. Verbal messages of determination and perseverance foster strength in children and help them function competently in the face of difficult circumstances (Crosnoe, Mistry, & Elder, 2002; Seccombe, 2002). These messages can foster strength in children regardless of family structure but might be more powerful in single-parent families, where there might be more challenges to overcome. As parents send messages that capitalize on family strengths and use the assistance of extended networks to promote positive communication patterns among family members, single-parent families' ability to face challenges becomes increasingly easier.

How families work through problems together can also contribute to a strong definition of family. Families who are hardy are more likely to be committed to working together to solve problems, are confident in their ability to do so, view life experiences as opportunities for growth, and think they have control over life events (Ford-Gilboe, 2000). Closely related to this conceptualization of family hardiness is communal coping, whereby family members perceive stressors as "our problem and our responsibility" or view a stressor as jointly owned and actively acting on it together as a social unit (Afifi, Hutchinson, & Krouse, 2006; Lyons, Mickelson, Sullivan & Coyne, 1998). The research on family hardiness and communal coping has found that engaging in collective problem-solving promotes feelings of agency and control over life stressors in ways that contribute to family resilience. In fact, Ford-Gilboe (2000) found a "strong connection between family strengths and their reported motivation to cope with difficult situations and/or health problems" in both single- and two-parent families (p. 51). Successful single-parent families also build a strong familial network through messages that enforce mutual support and collaboration to ease the strain of the stressors. Families can foster a spirit of togetherness by engaging in conversations about life strains (Conger & Conger, 2002), collaborative problem-solving, and open expressions of emotion (McCubbin & McCubbin, 1996). In sum, regardless of family structure, family members who are able to cope with problems as a collective (where appropriate) and who can rely on one another to face stressors together are likely to be more resilient to future difficulties.

Another way in which single-parent families construct a sense of family is by surrounding themselves with strong social support networks. Feelings of isolation can be problematic for single parents because they contribute to depressive symptoms, but they can also be detrimental for children if the children's needs are not being met (Carr & Springer, 2010). Creating and maintaining a social support network of family, friends, or community members might be particularly helpful for managing feelings of isolation and bolstering feelings of validation (Levine, 2009). For example, the role of grandparent involvement is more strongly associated with reduced adjustment difficulties for children in single-parent families than for those in two-parent families (Attar-Schwartz, Tan, Buchanan, Flouri, & Griggs, 2009). Similarly, adolescents living in multigenerational households (e.g., with a single mother and a grandparent) have similar, if not better, developmental outcomes than adolescents in married families (Deleire & Kalil, 2002). Both single parents and their children are likely to benefit from close ties with extended kin or friends, as these sources of support likely offer additional child care, social support and financial support for the parent, as well as greater attention and affection for the child. The construction of "wider families" for single parents is an important mechanism through which single parents and their children receive the benefits of social support and familial bonds with close others (Donati, 1995).

The additional instrumental assistance from outside network members also affords single parents the opportunity to accrue social capital, which is helpful for overcoming adversities related to single parenthood. Social capital refers to people's access to resources through involvement in social networks, such as connections with friends, relatives, businesses, community organizations (e.g., church), and government agencies (Portes, 1998). Networks that are dense, i.e., networks in which many of its members are highly interconnected, are particularly likely to provide its members with social capital (Ciabattari, 2007; Widmar, 2006). Social capital is especially important for single parents because social connections can increase their involvement in their children's school, enhance their career or job mobility, and provide other emotional and instrumental resources for the family (Ciabattari, 2007).

Culture plays an instrumental role in families' access to outside network members. Collectivist cultures value self-sacrifice for the well-being of the group (Hofstede, 1991). Black, Latino, Asian American, and other cultures embody this cultural orientation and put forth great effort to assist single-parent families when it is needed. Although families from non-collectivist cultures, such as White Americans, might also feel obliged to help provide these resources, research suggests that network support is more heavily emphasized in various collectivist cultural groups (e.g., Murry, Bynum, Brody, Willert & Stephens, 2001; Waites, 2009). Black American children also have the support of their extended kin to fortify them against negative mainstream American attitudes. For instance, intergenerational families and multigenerational kin serve as a critical component in the preservation of Black American families (Waites, 2009). Friend and kin networks, particularly females, engage in instrumental support patterns, such as help with childcare, transportation, and household work (Sarkisian & Gerstel, 2004). This social capital can help Black single parents build resilience against adversities associated with singlehood. Although some research investigating kin support for single-parent families suggests that kin networks can be a source of stress rather than support (Rowley, 2002), most of the research shows that Black American mothers are able to form a strong in-group among their blood-linked and fictive kin network in order to resist the stigma of being a Black single parent (e.g., Murry et al., 2001). Research on social capital also has suggested that although Whites have greater access to social capital in terms of job mobility and access to government agencies than minorities, minorities appear to have greater access to social capital in the form of extended kin (see Cheong, 2006). Notions of collectivism and social capital within larger social networks could explain why some families can function effectively in the midst of adversity whereas others cannot.

## Concluding Thoughts

As we illustrated in this chapter, single-parent families often face numerous societal and personal challenges that can make it difficult for them to legitimize their family to themselves and to others. They might feel the need to defend their family or justify its worth, particularly when research and societal perceptions tend to problematize single-parent families. These societal biases and stressors likely reveal themselves differently depending on the type of single-parent family. The challenges that were discussed in this chapter, such as financial strain, educational attainment, and lack of another parental figure to buffer stress, are often experienced by many single-parent families regardless of how they are formed. Many of these challenges are simply due to the structure of single-parent families; there is one less parent to earn an income, help parent the children, and offer support in times of stress. At the same time, single-parent families are not unitary. Different types of single-parent families face different types of challenges, which likely influence how they construct their family identity and communicate it to others. For instance, a gay male parent who recently experienced a divorce or breakup faces challenges that are very different than the heterosexual male parent who recently experienced a divorce. The gay parent might be "doubly" stigmatized because he not only has to manage the stigma of a divorce, but the stigma of being gay in a predominantly heterosexual society. Similarly, single parents who adopt children might have societal challenges and stigma that are different than the single parents whose children are their biological children. Within adoption, there are also vast differences in experiences (e.g., international adoptions, adoptions of children of a different race, older adults adopting children, a single male adopting a child, a gay parent adopting a child). These differences are important and shape how the family co-constructs its family identity and communicates it to others. We do not address these differences here, but they should be the focus of future research.

Additional attention also needs to be focused on how the social construction of family through Galvin's (2006) discourse-dependence strategies complements the functional perspective provided in this chapter. For example, creating resilience in the midst of struggle undoubtedly happens, in part, through family narratives. As Koenig Kellas (2005) demonstrated, family identity and emotional connections are solidified and communicated to others through jointly told stories. Families often tell stories of stressful times, and often find humor in those difficult moments, in an effort to reaffirm their resilience. An interesting avenue of future research would be to examine how the social construction of identity through jointly told stories is different and similar within different types of single-parent families (e.g., single-parent families formed through adoption, out of wedlock births, divorce, etc.).

Rather than focusing on differences between single-parent families and two-parent families using a deficit approach, an alternative orientation is to examine the strengths within single-parent families and the similarities in communication patterns that cross family types. After all, it is the communication patterns that determine how a family functions more than its structure. In order for any family to communicate a strong identity to others, it needs to first create a strong identity within itself.

# CHAPTER SIX

# "I'm the parent *and* the grandparent"

## Constructing the Grandfamily

MELISSA W. ALEMÁN

*Sarah was unusually quiet on that Thursday morning at the beginning of her first-period English class. Eyes turned downward toward her desk, her long bangs hid her watery eyes and unusually blank expression. Her friends, Tom and Alison, were busy flirting next to her, their conversations just a scrambled din in her mind, as were all the others busy caring only about themselves, laughing and shouting across the room. Sarah pulled out the form that was due today, a template for graduation announcements. "The daughter of _____ " it began.*

*Many of the others in her class filled the form out immediately, but Sarah's form sat on her desk. "If I put down my grandparents' names, then what does that say about my mom?" she frets. "What will other people think? What will my mom think? That is, if she comes to my graduation at all. But if I put my mom's name, it might really hurt my grandma." As if it was an unwelcome graded test, she crammed the blank form back into her backpack.*

*The next morning, Sarah's English teacher stopped at her desk, "Do you have your graduation announcement form? Today's the last day you know."*

*The form remained crumpled at the bottom of her backpack. She never brought it up with her grandparents. "No, I forgot it," Sarah lies. "It's OK, I don't need to have my information in the program."*

*Sarah's teacher looks at her curiously but doesn't push further. Instead she moves on to the next person.*

In their study of young adults' retrospective accounts of being raised by their grandparents, Dolbin-MacNab, Rodgers, and Traylor (2009) found that grandchildren felt considerable ambivalences and loyalty conflicts regarding their family life, yet simultaneously experienced grateful and loving affection toward their grandparent caregivers. One of their participants, whose account formed the basis of the opening story, reflected on the experience of preparing her graduation announcement, stating: "The daughter of? Where did [mother] fit in? We can't leave her out because she is my mother. I didn't want to offend my grandparents by insinuating that either one is less important than the other" (p. 170). "Sarah's story" and experiences of many grandchildren like her have demonstrated the multiple audiences and identities at work in answering the question: *Who are we as a family?* Like other family forms that lack institutional support and clear role definitions, grandparent-headed households have relied heavily upon communicative resources to answer that question.

Grandparents have long served as surrogate parents to their grandchildren throughout history, particularly in African American and Latino/a communities where such roles have sought to preserve families in the face of institutionalized oppression and during periods of migration, and to maintain cultural values of kinship and familism (see Cox, 2000). Yet, over the past several decades the number of grandparent-headed households in the United States has been on the rise. In 2000 there were 5.4 million children living in grandparent-headed households in the United States, a 20% increase since 2000 (U.S. Census Bureau, 2010a). Among multigenerational households between 2009–2011, 64.6% were headed by grandparents and included the child of the householder and the grandchild (U.S. Census Bureau, 2012, October 25), while 34% of these households received *no support* at all from the parents of the grandchildren—so-called "skipped generation" households (Fuller-Thomson, Minkler, & Driver, 1997, p. 406). Further, studies have shown trends demonstrating that grandparents are increasingly providing substantial daily care for their grandchildren whether or not they are providing sole custodial care (Casper & Bryson, 1998; Musil & Standing, 2005).

Grandparents have taken on the full-time care of their grandchildren for a variety of reasons, including parental death, teen pregnancy, parental incarceration, parental drug and alcohol addiction, neglect and abuse, and parental unemployment (Hayslip & Kaminski, 2005; Jendrick, 1994). Further, grandparents have often been relied upon for caregiving support when their grandchildren displayed behavioral problems (Hetherington, 1989). Although it is not clear as to the origins, grandchildren in grandparent-headed households more often have more significant psychological and behavioral problems than those raised in other family contexts (Shore & Hayslip, 1994; Smith, Palmieri, Hancock, & Richardson, 2008).

Likewise, grandparent caregivers have not been free from the stress of the situation; an abundance of research suggests that raising grandchildren has contributed to many physical, psychological, and material stressors that grandparent caregivers experience, including depression (e.g., Minkler, Fuller-Thomson, Miller, & Driver, 2000), poverty and financial strain (e.g., Smith, Beltran, Butts, & Kingson, 2000), and various physiological burdens (e.g., Marx & Solomon, 2000). Such circumstantial and structural conditions set the contexts for a variety of communicative challenges facing what scholars and practitioners call *grandfamilies* (Edwards, 2001, p. 199).

Despite the challenges facing grandfamilies, studies have reported that grandparents and their grandchildren describe this relationship and family structure as a blessing for which they are grateful (Erbert & Alemán, 2008; Dolbin-MacNab et al., 2009). Grandchildren have claimed that their grandparents "saved them" (Dolbin-MacNab et al, 2009), while grandparents reflected on the valued opportunity to be a stable force in the lives of their grandchildren (Waldrop & Weber, 2001). Indeed, Hayslip and Goodman (2007) argued that researchers need to move away from a problem-oriented approach to see the ways in which grandfamilies "are resilient in the face of complex situations which are often imposed upon them" (p. 119).

This chapter responds to Hayslip and Goodman's call for perspectives that offer insight into the agency and resilience of grandfamilies, forwarding that families themselves are constituted in their communication both within the family and to external audiences (Galvin, 2006). Specifically, I explore the manner in which grandfamilies use narrative resources to make sense of their own being, while also framing their composition and existence to others in ways that manage the complex challenges of their situation. In doing so, I recognize that grandfamilies are but one of many family forms that are unsupported by the discursive biases of structural and biogenetic-developmental assumptions about the ways in which family is organized (Galvin, 2003). Such an approach does not, however, ignore the discursive challenges of grandfamilies, nor does it create an idealized portrait of those families. Instead, I argue that a narrative lens enables an examination of the complex ways in which grandfamilies are faced with and respond to discursive challenges and constraining societal discourses. Further, narrative theorizing showcases how storytelling practices can serve to empower families and foster resilience in the face of such challenges.

## The Discourse Dependency of Grandfamilies

Indicated by the collected chapters in this volume, a growing body of research in the field of communication studies asserts that biogenetic and structural definitions limit our understanding of the lived experiences of members who are situated outside of the traditional institutional boundaries of family life. Still, few studies in the communication field have explored nonnormative contexts of grandparenting, such as surrogate parenting, leaving us with limited understanding of the discursive strategies used by grandfamilies to manage their identities. Of those grandparent caregivers, only a fraction have legal custody of their grandchildren, with many more serving as caregivers with only tacit agreements as a condition of the situation. Grandparents without legal custody of the grandchildren they are parenting have expressed frustration about the lack of legitimation and rights to support their needs (Backhouse & Graham, 2012). Yet, the choice to enter into the foster care system or to pursue legal custody of their grandchildren has come with familial consequences and constraints for both the grandparents and grandchildren. For example, Gladstone, Brown, and Fitzgerald (2009) found that one reason grandparents were hesitant to seek legal custody was because such permanency "ended their hope that their grandchildren might someday return to their parental home" (p. 69), while others feared that entering into an institutionalized arrangement of kinship foster care formalized and constrained their relationship with their grandchildren, leaving their families "subject to more demands and scrutiny" (p. 68). Grandparents in this study also reported worries that the pursuit of legal custody had the potential to alienate them from their adult children. Findings such as these suggest that institutional legitimization does not free members of grandfamilies from definitional challenges.

Whether members of grandfamilies are accounting for their relationship to institutionalized forces or to one another, they are called upon to make sense of their identities and roles within their family. Galvin (2006) argued for the need to examine the communicative resources that such discourse-dependent families rely upon to constitute their family identity to themselves (internal focus) and to others outside the family (external focus). Specifically, she asserted that such "families are formed and maintained through processes of *adhesion*, rather than *cohesion*" (p. 9, emphasis in original), meaning that discourse provides the glue that binds family members together and demonstrates to outsiders the boundaries of that family.

Grandfamilies, while often bound by biogenetic ties, still embody a nonnormative relational context and are situated outside the constraining (Western) assumptions of the biological parent-child family structure (i.e., the nuclear family) (Cox, 2000). Therefore, members of grandfamilies are faced with the need to account for their existence to a variety of external others (e.g., children's teachers, other parents, friends, social networks, and other family members) and to one another. Such calls to defend and define their family can be both frustrating and isolating for grandfamilies. For example, Ehrle (2001) found that grandparents often felt out of place or "viewed negatively by parents and teachers of the peers of grandchildren" (p. 220), leading to the experience of social isolation and the need to defend and legitimize their family. Such social isolation is exacerbated when grandparent caregivers face conflict and criticism from other family members, particularly from their other adult children. Ehrle further claimed that such jealousy and criticism within the larger family system from adult siblings led grandparent caregivers to defend their role, time and money as parent: "In these families, grandparents reported frustrating and tiring conflict that often led to alienation from one or more of their adult children as well as the grandchildren of those children" (p. 220). Grandfamilies navigate discursive challenges, such as those found in Ehrle's study, in a variety of ways. In the following sections, I show how narrative theorizing and research offers a valuable lens to explain both the discursive challenges facing grandfamilies and the resources they draw upon to foster resilience.

## "Doing Grandfamily": Narratives and Storytelling

Across cultures, grandparents have been viewed as family storytellers, key participants in promoting family legacies (Thompson et al., 2009), important kinkeepers (particularly grandmothers) whose stories reinforce ground rules for family life (Stone, 1988/2008), and significant figures in constellations of family identity and memory (Trujillo, 2004). Although the role of the grandparent as surrogate parent falls outside normative expectations, the cultural valuing of *grandparent as storyteller and kinkeeper* serves as an important narrative resource from which grandparents can draw in responding to the diverse challenges facing their families. Further, such cultural values provide grandfamilies with a locus for resilience as grandparents are looked upon to facilitate sensemaking processes and to assist in narrating a hopeful future for their grandchildren.

Both grandparents and their grandchildren inherit family histories that guide them in the construction of their new stories as a grandfamily. According to Goodall (2006), *narrative inheritance* is the body of stories told by our forebears that provides families with sensemaking tools from which they create their own narratives and craft their identities:

> The narratives we inherit from our forebears provide us with a framework for understanding our identity through theirs. It helps us see our working logic as an extension of, or a rebellion against the way we tell the story of how they lived and thought about things. It allows us to explain to others where we come from and how we were raised in the continuing context of what it all means. (p. 23)

One's narrative inheritance need not have coherence, be complete, or affirming of a positive family identity. Indeed, Goodall invited us to ask how family members create coherence out of a narrative inheritance that is incomplete, problematic, or ultimately disruptive.

As is the case for many grandfamilies, the experience of ambiguous loss (Boss, 1999) can characterize their inheritance, as both grandparents and grandchildren grieve a loss of not just the parent, but also what might have been or their vision of what was to become. Specifically, Boss (2010) defined two types of ambiguous loss: the loss experienced (1) when a loved one is physically absent, but psychologically present (e.g., a family member missing in wartime action); and (2) when a loved one is physically present, but psychologically absent (e.g., a partner who has dementia). For grandfamilies, this ambiguous loss has been characterized by the former condition in which the parent is physically absent, yet present psychologically through family narratives. Boss (2010) has described that such family members are "kept psychologically present because they might reappear" (p. 138).

Lever and Wilson (2005) highlighted how both grandparents and the grandchildren in their care experienced such losses and showcased how narrative provides a means for coping with grief. The grandmother in their study recounted:

> I feel guilty when I can't give Rachel what she wants. She already feels abandoned by her mother. I remember Rachel would sit by the front windows for hours waiting on her mom because her mom had promised to come see her. She would be so excited you know ... until she finally realized that her mom wasn't coming. That used to break my heart. (p. 170)

In this case study, the grandchild, Rachel, exhibited behavioral problems that required therapeutic treatment. The authors argued that as a result of role-playing and other interactional exercises in therapy, Rachel was able to re-story herself and her family, "then able to talk about and process the grief associated with her biological mom's abandonment" (p. 170).

Understanding how grandfamilies respond to a narrative inheritance of ambiguous loss, or one that is characterized by equivocations and family secrets, is key to exploring how families craft future narratives as a response. How do families respond, reframe, and sometimes reject their narrative inheritance as defining of *who they are* and *who they might come to be* as they build their stories moving forward? Ballard and Ballard (2011) extended Goodall's conceptualization of narrative inheritance through an examination of conversational and joint properties of storytelling, offering that our narrative inheritance is shaped through intergenerational dynamics. Such interactive storytelling builds what they called "narrative momentum" and thrusts the family stories into a distal future (p. 81). Specifically, they asserted that "storytelling is the site where we jointly, interactionally, collaboratively, and in a shared way make sense of the narrative we have inherited while simultaneously constituting who we are—our identity—as a family" (pp. 73–74).

Langellier and Peterson's narrative performance theory (2004; 2006a; 2006b) provides a useful lens for understanding how families are constituted and continually reconstituted through the practice of storytelling, and thus how narrative inheritance and momentum can be viewed as a defining activity of family. They have theorized family storytelling as "both performance, *something a family does*, and performative, *the doing of storytelling that constitutes and forms the family*" (Langellier & Peterson, 2004, p. 34, emphases added). Further, they asserted that a narrative perspective focuses on an understanding of family as a small group culture rather than a pre-determined structure or biogenetic formation, opening up the possibilities for how we understand family processes:

> Approaching family storytelling as small group culture resists the idealization or romanticization of a "natural" family to examine how communication practices produce family.... Family storytelling is survival strategy of small groups in which they articulate who they are to themselves, for themselves and for the next generations, engaging memory and anticipation as embodied and material practices of human communication. (Langellier & Peterson, 2004, p. 35)

Such a framework highlights an understanding of narrative as a way of "doing family" (Langellier & Peterson, 2006a, p. 109), but also recognizes that narrative performances enable families to confront and critique social norms and offer alternative ways of being (Langellier & Peterson, 2004).

As performances, the collaborative nature of storytelling is important toward understanding how grandfamilies narrate resilience in the face of challenging and sometimes traumatic circumstances. Researchers have shown, for example, that the joint storytelling of difficult experiences is important to family sensemaking processes (Koenig Kellas & Trees, 2006), offers therapeutic value for family members, and assists families in creating a shared frame for their past experiences and future (Kiser, Baumgardner, & Dorado, 2010). Such collaborative storytelling is particularly important for families who have experienced trauma or are navigating difficult relational conditions. Still, Kiser et al. (2010) asserted that trauma can "derail family storytelling," interrupt collaborative processes, and make it difficult for family members to coordinate their narratives (p. 245). Yet when families have been able to work collaboratively to craft a narrative that both affirms the experiences of the individual family members while building a hopeful, coherent narrative that is larger than the problems of their circumstances, they have become "witnesses of their own resilience" (p. 248).

In addition to the collaborative character of family storytelling, it is important to understand the cultural forces at work in the content of stories. Individual family stories are shaped by and simultaneously shape cultural codes about the nature and obligations of families (see Stone, 1988/2008). That said, considerable diversity exists in beliefs about kinship care across cultures, particularly with regard to beliefs and assumptions that normalize or pathologize extended family providing parental care for children. For example, cultural values toward *familism* found in many Central and South American cultures have fostered beliefs that "family members have a moral obligation to help extended family members" in need (Fuller-Thomson & Minkler, 2007, p. 6), a cultural code that normalizes more patterned grandparent caregiving and intergenerational households. Such codes might help to explain why Latino grandmothers have reported higher levels of well-being as co-parents, as opposed to African American and White co-parents[1] (Goodman & Silverstein, 2006). Still, when surrogate parenting by grandparents occurs in a stigmatized context, such as the parental neglect, abuse or incarceration of their adult children, norms of familism might not protect against feelings of blame and shame expressed by those grandparents.

An exploration of the common narrative challenges that grandfamilies face can help scholars begin to understand the discursive strategies of grandparents and their grandchildren who seek to define and defend their families. Further, exploring research on grandfamilies in the fields of social work, psychology, and gerontology through a communication lens points to the important contributions still yet to be made by communication scholars and offers several points of departure for future research.

## Narrative Challenges in Grandfamilies

*Marta quickly closes the front door trying to keep it from slamming shut and walks back toward the living room. Tina and Kean, 5 and 7 years old, come running in from the kitchen, "Mom's here!" they clamor in unison. Noticing the door is closed, their cheers turn quiet, they stop short at their grandmother's feet and look up at her, "Who was there?" Kean asks, eyebrows raised.*

*"Oh, no one." Marta says waiving her hands at them, gently putting her hand on Kean's shoulder and directing them back into the kitchen with a nudge. "Just somebody trying to sell me something worthless. Go on now. How about you go in the backyard and play for awhile?" Kean grabs his brother's hand and pulls him toward the kitchen door, looking back at his grandmother.*

*Marta, feeling defeated, falls back into her chair and looks up as her husband slowly shuffles into the room. "That was Tara, wasn't it," he claims more than asks.*

*"You know it. Right on time, a week late. The boys called out for her every time someone came to the door this week. She wasn't right though. She smelled bad and was strung out. I couldn't let the boys see her that way. I've just got to protect them. We've got to do better by them."*

In the above story, Marta chooses not to tell her two young grandchildren about her daughter's attempt to visit but instead accounts for her decision to her husband. Like Marta, members of grandfamilies confront numerous challenges in narrating themselves to one another and to others, with each performance of a story begging numerous questions. Who can participate in the storytelling performances and what are their roles? What are the conditions of their participation? What information is privileged and hidden? What family codes are expressed in such stories and how are identities managed in the telling? The stories told by grandfamilies seek to answer the question: *who are we as family and who are we to be to one another?* In the following section, I describe four narrative challenges that have emerged in the cross-disciplinary literature on grandfamilies: (1) definitional challenges; (2) developmental dissonance and disruptions; (3) societal stigmas regarding perceived parental failures; and (4) competing family loyalties and painful narrative inheritance.

## Definitional Challenges Facing Grandfamilies

First and foremost grandfamilies face the basic challenge of defining who they are to one another as they account for their changing roles. Grandfamilies' accounts of definitional activities have included the challenges of navigating role ambiguity and conflict, as well as negotiating naming practices. Indeed, these two activities are intricately connected as decisions about what to call one another have often been embedded in and challenged by cultural narratives about idealized relationships between grandparents and grandchildren. For grandparents and the grandchildren they are parenting, there has been considerable conflict and disagreement about role expectations for behavior that resulted in the need for extended discussion among family members. For example, many grandparents have reported frustration at wanting to embody traditional roles of the permissive and loving grandparent, only to be faced with perceptions of grandchildren that they are instead the "mean" disciplinarian as "parent" (Langosch, 2012).

Role ambiguity and conflicts have also been expressed through the discussion of the sensemaking involved in naming practices of grandparents and their grandchildren. Erbert and Alemán (2008) observed this negotiation throughout the accounts of 45 surrogate (grand)parents, as they described the naming processes that take place over time. In some cases, grandparents retained names such as "grandma or granddad," in others they adopted the name "mom or dad." One grandmother reflected on conversations she had with her grandchildren and her ambivalent position about her role expectations as parent and her avowed identity as grandparent, stating:

> Well, she wants to call me mom, but I don't let her, because I am her grandmother. And periodically her mom will call, you know, and ask could she see her. And I let her. Because after all that is her mother. You know, but–no, all of them have asked if they call me mom, and I'm their grandmother, so you know, it's not right for me to step in and be their mom, when I am their grandmother. But I primarily do everything for them. (p. 685)

Studies have thus highlighted the ways in which labeling practices corresponded with how grandparent caregivers viewed themselves and emerging understandings of their changing roles. One participant in Bailey, Letiecq, and Porterfield's (2009) study of grandparent caregivers expressed the following realization:

> It took us the first two years of this whole thing to realize and conversations with each other that – wait a minute – we've finally got to quit being grandparents. We can't be grandparents anymore. We're now parents … You have to physically say "hold it, I'm doing this wrong. I'm trying to be Grandpa." I can't be Grandpa and that is a hard thing for grandparents to give up. (p. 152)

For others in their study, the naming practices seemed to move back and forth depending on the situation and the needs of the children, "They call me 'Grandma,' they call me 'Mom,' they call me 'Mommy.' Depends what's going on … they can call me what they want to" (Bailey et al., 2009, p. 152).

Caregivers are placed in the complicated position of making sense of their identity expectations as a *grandparent*, as it conflicts with those identities associated with *parenting*. Indeed, these cultural discourses of grandparenting and parenting begin with the meanings family members associate with "grandparent." Although the role expectations of grandparenting are often vague (Troll, 1983), for many grandparents this is a role filled with expectations for delight and fun (Glass & Huneycutt, 2002). This set of conflicting expectations is highlighted in the following grandparent's feelings:

> I feel guilty for not feeling like a grandmother. The typical grandmother thoughts aren't what I have. I think I'm not being a good grandma. The kind that makes you feel good – like a big lap, smile, and bun on the back of your head. (Landry-Meyer & Newman, 2004, p. 1019)

Members of grandfamilies have recognized the nonnormative character of their family and the challenges that cultural discourses place on how family members view themselves and talk about themselves as a family. Another participant in Landrey-Meyer et al.'s (2004) study pointed to the ways in which grandchildren utilize fantasy narratives when contrasting their family to those around them:

> I live in [a neighborhood] with the most normal families I have ever run into. They
> have two sets of grandparents that come and visit, and they visit them. Each of the
> families have a father and a mother. Ozzie and Harriet [neighborhood] or something.
> It's nice that it's so solid and family-oriented, but it's hard on [my granddaughter]
> because she sees the daddy and the grandparents and she misses that. She says I want
> him to be my grandpa – she'll pick somebody. It's hard. (p. 1017)

Both children and their grandparents thus confront cultural expectations for family
roles and struggle with the conflicts between conforming to those expectations and
creating a unique family relationship.

## Developmental Dissonance and Disruptions of the Grandfamily

Such role ambiguity and conflicts are heightened by developmental expectations
of both the grandparents and social network members, calling upon grandparent
caregivers and their grandchildren to account for the generation gap and age-
related context of their parenting relationship. Langosch (2012) argued that this
shift to "parent again" creates a developmental dissonance for grandparent caregivers, as it "alters the usual course of middle and old age" (p. 163). This developmental dissonance is evidenced in grandparents' accounts that parenting again
sacrifices their expectations for retirement, financial stability, and need to focus on
their own health (Dolbin-MacNab, 2006). Concerns about the health and well-being of the grandparents and their ability to care for their grandchildren to maturity
have been featured in accounts of grandparents and grandchildren, characterized by
a fear that the children will end up in foster care or back with unfit parents (Erbert
& Alemán, 2008). This requires grandparents and their grandchildren to process
their fears and concerns, sometimes resulting in grandparents' narrative affirmation
that they will be there for their grandchildren and have a plan for their future.

Further, the lifespan expectations for older adults, both by the grandparents
and to a lesser extent by others, set into conflict expectations of appropriate
behavior, desires, and relationships. For example, a central theme in Bailey et al.'s
(2009) study of coping and adaptation among grandparents raising grandchildren
dealt with the shifts in role identities associated with the lifespan expectations of
the empty nest and retirement planning. As one participant reported, "We were
used to peace and quiet. [We] didn't have anybody here. [We were] coming and
going whenever we wanted. [We went from] quiet to chaos" (p. 149). For some
participants in this study, this shift required grandparents to return to work and
the breadwinning role that preceded retirement.

Caregivers' grandchildren have also highlighted the generation gap they have
experienced between themselves and their grandparents who are perceived to be

out of touch with their peer group norms and contemporary disciplinary practices. Some grandchildren have made sense of their grandparents' strict philosophy regarding discipline as being outdated or a result of their old age, and they reported their response to such strict environments as rebellion against their caregivers (Dolbin-MacNab et al., 2009). Indeed, grandparents have expressed awareness of the changing demands of contemporary parenting and voiced concerns about dealing with the new pressures facing their grandchildren, particularly in their teenage years, but many also felt that their parenting strategies left their grandchildren prepared to make good decisions (Musil, Warner, McNamara, Rokoff, & Turek, 2008).

In some instances, grandparents faced patronizing communication from outsiders who failed to acknowledge what they perceived as their hard-earned respect as knowledgeable parents, highlighting the developmental dissonances involved in second-time parenting. For example, in their qualitative study of grandparent caregiver roles, Landry-Meyer and Newman (2004) found that half of the participants voiced frustration with the challenges of the "recycling the parent role" (p. 1015), especially when non-family members failed to recognize that they are performing a role again. One grandparent highlighted this frustration in talking with professionals, "Respect [the grandparent's] position. They have been parents ... We don't need to be taught the basics, I guess. Respect their knowledge" (p. 1015). In this instance, the grandparent pointed to the struggle to define their relationship and role as skilled and knowledgeable parents.

## Navigating the Stigma of Perceived Parental Failure

Grandparents' struggles to narrate themselves as competent and knowledgeable second-time parents are situated within the discursive challenge created by societal beliefs (real and imagined) that parents are responsible for their children's failures (Hayslip & Glover, 2008–2009). Thus they often bear the heavy emotional and rhetorical challenge regarding *perceived* responsibility and shame for their own adult children's *parental* failures, particularly in circumstances in which their children were neglectful or abusive toward their grandchildren, incarcerated, or addicted to drugs (Fuller-Thomson & Minkler, 2000). For example, some grandparents perceived their children's failure to parent effectively as a direct reflection on their own failures as parents and thus experienced additional stressors related to this new role (Musil, Schrader, & Mutikani, 2000), creating a narrative inheritance characterized by the stigma and fears of inadequacy. Grandparents have responded to such inheritances by reframing the situation and crafting narratives of surrogate parenting as an obligation to preserve the family and a second chance to "do it right."

Given that the majority of situations in which grandparents are parenting grandchildren resulted from problems of their adult children, it is not entirely surprising that grandparent caregivers have expressed anger and resentment or responsibility for their adult children's mistakes (Ehrle, 2001). Musil et al. (2008), for example, found that grandmothers reported frustration with their adult children's "inability to 'get their lives together' to care for their children" (p. 107). However, "for some grandparents, the stresses of raising their grandchildren are mitigated by carrying on the legacy of their family" (Hayslip, Shore, Henderson, & Lambert, 1998, p. S165).

Grandparents have negotiated expressions of guilt and stigma in their accounts of their reasoning for taking in their grandchildren and the need to protect their grandchildren from their adult children, just as Marta did in the story that opened this section. Such accounts serve to reframe their stories away from stigma to obligation, family preservation, and the well-being of the grandchildren. In Erbert and Aleman's (2008) study of the experiences of grandparent caregivers, one 68-year-old grandmother reported the tensions she felt in her need to protect her grandchildren:

> I felt obligated, you know, because they were my grandchildren, and I didn't want them to be in the streets like her [the mother] ... Now to me, I was raised another way, than to see these things happening. I said, "Well, I guess God wants me to take care of these grandchildren until something comes up." And that's the way those kids were, with me all the time. (p. 680).... I'm gonna protect these kids. She's [my daughter] already a grown up. She can do whatever she wants, but these kids are going to be protected by me. And that's how we figure that we cannot just let these kids be in the streets with her. No way. (p. 681)

Numerous studies have mirrored narratives such as this one and have reported that grandparents take responsibility for raising their grandchildren in order to create a stable family life for them (e.g., McGowen & Ladd, 2006). Grandparents have contrasted this to the alternative of placing their grandchildren in foster care, creating a frame that the very existence of their grandfamily provided stability in the face of the changing and uncertain status of the grandchildren's parents' role in their lives.

Such accounts help to show how grandfamilies navigate the terrain of ambiguous loss and provide coping responses for the grandparents and grandchildren alike. For example, one participant in Williamson, Softas-Nall, and Miller's (2003) study of grandmothers raising grandchildren expressed the gratification in knowing that she created a stable environment for her granddaughter:

> I would never let my grandkids go to somebody else ... we wouldn't let Lisa go into a foster home. You don't know who that person is who is going to be raising that

child. …You bet it's rewarding, to see a healthy well-adjusted child that doesn't have to live in a foster home. (p. 29)

Still, grandparents in other studies reported greater ambivalence, recognizing that raising their grandchildren was not ideal, but it was the only option. A grandfather in Bullock's (2005) study narrated a more resigned position, yet still favored the stability of his grandchild over his own expectations for his life:

I don't feel I'm ready to take care of a small child this late in life, but we didn't have any choice. My wife said we [were] all the child had left. What in the world would have happen[ed] to the child if we didn't do [it]? (p. 48)

In addition to the frames of obligation and family preservation, many grandparent caregivers have instead framed the experience of parenting their grandchildren as a second chance, an opportunity to make up for the mistakes they made in the parenting of their own children (Ehrle & Day, 1994). Bailey et al.'s (2009) qualitative study of role transitions found that almost all grandfathers participating reported the new grandfamily context as a second chance opportunity to be a primary caregiver, as opposed to their primary role as breadwinner when parenting their own children. "Grandfathers lamented that when their own children were young they were working hard to provide and missed out on many of the joys of parenthood" (Bailey et al., 2009, p. 150). This alternative framing of custodial grandparenting as a "second chance" opened up a discourse that highlights the role shift as *opportunity*, rather than *obligation*. One grandfather in the study stated, "I missed things because I was working. I never did bond with those three kids. [I] had them in my heart, but nothing like with [our granddaughter.] [Having her] was just like having a child" (Bailey et al., 2009, p. 151). Indeed, Hayslip and colleagues (1998) similarly found that custodial grandfathers, more so than traditional grandfathers, scored higher on measures of positive grandparental meaning. They concluded that for custodial grandfathers "raising their grandchildren can indeed permit them to derive a greater sense of personal meaning from the role, despite its negative impact on well-being, relationship quality, and relationship satisfaction" (p. S170).

Although the few studies of custodial grandfathers have suggested that they relished the opportunity to parent (again) and had a heightened sense of purpose in their relationships with their grandchildren, the more numerous studies of grandmothers have cast a portrait of perceived parental wisdom that they did not have as first-time parents. For example, Dolbin-MacNab's (2006) study of custodial grandmothers found that nearly one-quarter of the grandmothers interviewed expressed that "they brought greater wisdom and experience to parenting their grandchildren" (p. 560). One grandmother specifically highlighted her confidence in parenting a second time around stating, "I know what to do now. I didn't know what to do then" (p. 569).

## Competing Family Loyalties and Painful Narrative Inheritance

Members of grandfamilies often experience intergenerational loyalty conflicts, or triangulations, that impact the well-being of family members (Goodman, 2003). Although loyalty conflicts exist in relationships with extended family networks, they are most salient in the triad comprised of the grandparent, their adult child, and the grandchild (Goodman & Silverstein, 2001). These triangulations, along with the experiences of role ambiguity, construct relational contexts of intergenerational ambivalence in grandfamilies (Dolbin-MacNab et al., 2009), a phenomenon characterized by relatively enduring contradictions experienced in cross-generational relationships, typically grandparents and their adult children (see Letiecq, Bailey, & Dahlen, 2008, for an extended theoretical discussion of ambivalence in grandfamilies).

For grandparents, loyalty conflicts have the potential to guide the kinds of stories they tell about themselves as parents, and in particular set the context for how they account to one another, their adult children, and their grandchildren about their parenting decisions. In particular, such triangulations form a powerful role in the characterization of family members that drives the narratives of grandfamilies, particularly with regard to rights and responsibilities. For example, grandparents have storied tensions regarding the rights of their adult children to "have a say" in the rearing of their grandchildren coupled with their simultaneous frustration that their children have given up that right (Erbert & Alemán, 2008).

For some grandchildren loyalty conflicts between their parents and their grandparents are a source of stress that leads them to characterize their parents as acting outside of their proper role in the relational triangle. Dolbin-MacNab and Keiley (2006) found that some grandchildren perceived their parents to assume roles that belonged instead to their grandparents, leading them to create distance from their parents. Such role tensions left grandchildren caught between their grandparents and parents. Dolbin-MacNab et al. (2009) found that their grandchild participants "disliked being caught in the middle of conflicts between their parents and kinship caregivers and described how this position resulted in confusion, distance, conflict and tension with their caregivers" (p. 170). Specifically, they found that children withheld criticisms or hurt feelings about their parents to avoid upsetting their grandparents who might feel defensive and protective of their adult children.

Not surprisingly, grandparents have expressed feeling protective of *both* their adult children *and* their grandchildren, influencing the ways that they talk with their grandchildren and narrate their grandfamily. Thus, grandparents have often made decisions to conceal the reason for the parent's absence as a means of protecting both their adult children and grandchildren, or frame the parent's absence as one of love, rather than neglect. The latter is showcased in the following narrative:

> "Yes, because I love you and you're my grandson, but your mom does thing[s] for you." He says, "No Grandma, she doesn't do nothing because she doesn't love me." You know I tell him, she does love you, she just can't be around you right now because she's getting herself to be a better mommy. Where's she's going to school so she can be a better mommy with you all. I say "It's not that she doesn't love you, but that she does love you that's why she's going to school." (Erbert & Alemán, 2008, p. 686)

This example illuminates the ways in which the framing practices of narratives help to create diffuse loyalty conflicts, as well as respond to the painful narrative inheritance that has been left.

For grandfamilies, narrative inheritance includes their origin stories, *how they came to be a grandfamily,* and is often characterized by trauma, separation, and loss. Depending on the contexts of the grandfamilies' formations and the ages of the children involved, grandparent caregivers must make decisions about how to characterize their family members, including their adult children, in the stories they tell. That is, their stories of their grandchildren's parents have been characterized by a simultaneous move to protect their grandchildren through keeping information about their parents a secret, while being open with them to maintain a trusting relationship (Erbert & Alemán, 2008). Although grandparents express this tension in a variety of ways, some studies have suggested that grandparents' inability to talk effectively with their grandchildren about their parents "could create difficulties for the grandchildren" (Kluger & Aprea, 1999, p. 16). That is, the character of the stories about their family origins told between grandparents and their grandchildren is important to understanding challenges to grandfamilies moving forward and to the individual family members' well-being.

## Communicating Resilience in Grandfamilies

In the face of the confluence of narrative challenges described above, one might expect grandfamilies to craft a problem-centered future orientation. Yet, research shows that grandfamilies communicate considerable resilience in crafting their new, sometimes temporary, families. From a communication perspective, Lucas and Buzzanell (2012) have defined resilience as "the process of meaning making through everyday messages and stories that enable reintegration from life's disruptions" (p. 190). Considerable research in social work and family therapy has demonstrated the resilience of grandfamilies and the optimism they convey in the face of their challenges. Bailey and colleagues (2009) found, for example, that many grandparents in their study "were able to reframe perceptions and look to the future with hope rather than ruminating in the past" (p. 156). Still, Brown-Standridge and Floyd (2000) argued that it is unwise for grandparents to either wholly embrace the dark relational contexts in which grandfamilies often emerge, or to ignore troubling dynamics and family histories as they craft new narratives that define their family. Specifically, they asserted that grandparents' opportunities to purposefully craft family legacies could be a source of empowerment for grandfamilies.

Indeed, Lucas and Buzzanell (2012) have claimed "rather than dwelling on what might have been, resilient individuals and families seek to normalize that which is reassuring about the present" (p. 192). Reassuring stories characterized by experiences of stability, love, support, and family preservation are themes that run through grandfamily accounts. Relational themes found in the narrative accounts of grandchildren, such as closeness, trust, gratitude, and support, offer insights into the manner in which grandchildren story their resilience through close bonds with their grandparents (Dolbin-MacNab & Keiley, 2009). Explorations of the manner in which narratives are used in support, family resource materials, and interventions can offer insight into the generative narrative momentum constructed from the complex narrative inheritance outlined in the sections above.

Support programs based in narrative have shown considerable success. For example, the "Relatives as Parents Program" in Orange County, New York, describes their "Kinship Family Portraits Project" as exceeding their expectations for success (Reynolds & Variano, 2009). This program sought to enable youth and their families to craft their family histories and stories through a variety of artistic media, including writing, photography, and art. The program, "born out of the firm conviction that there are many different types of healthy families and each deserves to be recognized and noted for its individuality" (Reynolds & Variano, 2009, p. 328), demonstrated the possibility of narrative momentum that projects family histories into the future. One youth described the project by claiming, "This is the best thing I have ever done. It makes me think that my family is right in front of me ... in my life" (Reynolds & Variano, 2009, p. 331).

Family communication scholars have an important role to play in contributing to the theoretical and applied understandings of the relational dynamics of grandfamilies. Although there is a robust literature in the fields of social work, gerontology, family therapy, and sociology that implicates communication processes, there is a dearth of literature that offers direct examination of communication in grandfamilies. As this exploration of the literature and the rich accounts of members of grandfamilies suggest, communication plays an important constitutive function, provides family members with resources for navigating complex discursive challenges, and equips families and practitioners with tools for crafting hopeful narratives for their family that showcase their resilience.

## Note

1. Co-parenting is when the parent is present in the grandparent-headed household, thus parenting is shared. Such cultural differences do not hold when the grandparents are serving as custodial parents.

# CHAPTER SEVEN

# Remaking Hindu Arranged Marriages in the Narrative Performances of Urban Indian Women

DEVIKA CHAWLA

Even as arranged marriages continue to receive attention in popular media both in India and the West, they remain a neglected subject of academic discussion and social analysis, particularly within the field of communication studies (Chawla, 2004; Rodriguez & Chawla, 2010). Such marriage forms are a cultural, religious, and social norm in many Asian cultures including, but not limited to, China, Japan, Korea, Pakistan, Afghanistan, and Bangladesh. In this chapter, I focus on Hindu arranged marriages among young urban women in North India to explore how women continue to choose this arrangement, yet discursively reframe its traditional understanding. In doing so they are able to alter their own status within the marriage form and transform what such marriages can mean in a largely urban Indian environment. My overarching goal is to illustrate the discourse dependence (Galvin, 2006) that is evident in how urban Indian women narratively perform their marriages. This chapter is an amalgamation of my ongoing work on women's experiences in Hindu arranged marriages that started in 2003, and I rely on my previously published research and essays dealing with resistance, conflict, and narration for the discussions here (see Chawla 2004, 2007, 2008; Rodriguez & Chawla, 2010).

My analysis and discussion of narrative performances is significant in the "remaking" of family communication studies in a few critical ways. It provides discussions about an under-studied context in marriage and family life, the

Hindu arranged marriage, and answers recent calls by family communication scholars who urge an expansion of the contexts in the study of family life (Baxter et al. 2009; Segrin & Flora, 2011; Turner, 2006; Turner & West, 2011). Further, the reframing strategies discussed here stretch the scope of Galvin's (2006) notion of external boundary management in discourse-dependent families.

## Traditional Hindu Marriage and Family

Contemporary arranged marriages—both rural and urban—continue to be organized by parents and elderly kin (Sur, 1973). In earlier times, intermediaries called *sambhalas* or traditional matchmakers were employed to keep the genealogical history of each family and to make sure that the bride and groom were not related for five to seven generations back—a prerequisite in Hindu marriages (Sur, 1973). In more recent times, these criteria have stretched to include other characteristics. Mullatti (1995) outlined seven criteria that are currently followed by matchmakers, kin, parents and relatives: caste, social structure, moral value compatibility, academic compatibility, occupational compatibility, the family's moral history, and horoscope compatibility (although not necessarily in this order). In the past two decades, parents have begun looking for marriage partners for their children through matrimonial columns in newspapers, magazines, and the internet, and some recent anecdotal evidence suggests that arranged marriages might be taking place even across caste lines (Chawla, 2007, 2008; Mullatti, 1995).

In its traditional understanding, the most "appropriate" and "righteous" type of Hindu marriage was a union arranged by parents and kin (Bowman & Dollahite, 2013) and is said to be derived from laws interpreted in the *Dharmashastras*, which in turn have their roots in the 3000 year old hymns called *Vedas* and *Smritis*, the oldest surviving documents of the Indian civilization recorded between 4000 B.C. and A.D. 1200 (Kapadia, 1958).[1] A general theme across these scriptures was that marriage was a duty and a religious sacrament required of all human beings for the well-being of the community. In fact, both marriage and procreation were/are one of the four necessary stages in a Hindu's life, with marriage constituting the second stage, *grahastha*, aimed at progeny and sexual activities. Historically, there were eight forms of Hindu marriage of which four, considered *dharma* or "righteous," were always arranged by kin. The other four, considered *adharma* or "non-righteous," were self-arranged by the bride and groom and involved either love, elopement, or abduction (Chawla, 2004, 2007; Kapur, 1970; Sastri, 1972, 1974). In their modern iteration, these "inappropriate" forms of marriages came to be referred to as "self-arranged" or "love marriages."

Little evidence in the scriptures suggests that any of the life stages were structured toward women (Mullatti, 1995). It is easy to conclude that while marriage was required of all Hindus, its advantages were primarily enjoyed by men, who benefited from both the spiritual and economic understandings of the Hindu marriage (Mukherjee, 1978). Spiritually, men benefited because they married in order to beget sons who would light their funeral pyre. This funeral rite ensured the male line a place in heaven, rebirth in the next life as a human being, as well as the liberation of future generations of the family from cycles of life and death (*moksha*). At the same time, the need for a male heir was an economic necessity; male heirs were desired because they alone could continue the family line and inherit ancestral property. Therefore, historically, the Hindu arranged marriage is referred to as "male-emphasized" (Mukherjee, 1978). Moreover, in some linguistic interpretations, the word "wife" is often used interchangeably with "household" (Mukherjee, 1978; Sastri, 1972, 1974; Shastri, 1969), casting the woman's role in her natal and marital home as both instrumental and objective.

Once married, a Hindu woman would invariably enter a joint family system. An ideal Hindu joint family (even in contemporary India) consists of a man and wife, their adult sons, their wives and children, and younger children of the parental couple (Gore, 1968; Sharma, 1997; Shastri, 1969). A joint family can often be looked upon as a multiplicity of genealogically related nuclear families living under the same roof and sharing in worship, food, and property.[2] Very often, a joint family has been described as a group of adult male coparceners and their dependents—wives and children. For instance, if a father has two sons and one daughter, under Hindu Law the sons would be considered joint heirs (coparencers), but a daughter would not inherit property (Gore, 1968).[3]

The very structure of the joint family contributed to an overall subordinate status of women. Formal authority was always given to the oldest male and thereby hierarchically bound by age. This hierarchy manifested itself at many levels. Women were married and brought into the family that consisted of men who were all related by blood. Women were thus not only biologically on the outside but also treated as symbolic outsiders until they birthed a son and in doing so became completely included in the family. If they did not beget a son, then a new wife could be brought into the joint family, although this changed with the Hindu Divorce Bill in 1952 (Kapadia, 1958). Once married, the conjugal relationship between partners was discouraged from becoming too romanticized because the emphasis was on the socioeconomic welfare of the family. This contributed to the degradation of women's status in the family, which in turn was supported by denial of property rights to women and by women's inability to achieve economic independence. Role and authority segregation of men and women were therefore essential to the economic well-being of a Hindu joint family. Even though women remained necessary to the family, they remained powerless, property-less, and dependent within the household that they, in principle, symbolized. Women were therefore largely seen as an instrument of procreation in the Hindu marriage system.

## Social Scientific Research on Arranged Marriages: A Brief Review

Hindu arranged marriages in India vary from region to region. Although they are varyingly understood, in general these marriages continue to be premised on the conception of the traditional Hindu marriage described above (Mullatti, 1995). Notwithstanding the forces of liberalization, globalization, and urbanization, the number of arranged marriages in India far outnumbers "love" or "self-arranged" marriages. Approximately 95% of all marriages in India continue to be arranged marriages (Bumiller, 1990; Chawla, 2004, 2008; Kapadia, 1958, Kapur, 1970; Mullatti, 1995). This statistic is strong evidence that such marriages are the norm rather than the exception.

Academic research on arranged marriages has been limited to historical and sociological analyses. The historical literature consistently focuses upon the structure of the family, interpretation of Hindu religious texts, discussions about caste, and Hindu norms and traditions. Moreover, for about five decades, social scientific research on this marital relationship has primarily emphasized comparisons between "arranged" and "love" marriages wherein the two forms are treated as static historical formations, the former belonging to the East and the latter to a more progressive West (Kapadia, 1958; Chawla, 2007; Kapur, 1970; Kumar & Dhyani, 1996; Netting, 2010; Rao & Rao, 1975; Ross, 1961; see also Sprecher & Chandak, 1992). In other research, sociologists and historians at Delhi University have approached arranged marriages from the standpoint of kinship, sexuality, same-sex relationships, marital laws, legal history, and the role of the nation state (Uberoi, 1993, 1996).

A few influential sociological studies examined urbanization and Hindu family life. For instance, Kapadia (1958) traced the history of the marriage form until the 1950s and concluded that while marital trends might have shifted owing to industrialization and urbanization, marriage among Hindus continued to be held up as a holy sacrament (not different from religiously defined marriage in other groups), and as an obligation and duty that transcended socioeconomic-cultural progress. Gore's (1968) study complements these findings in that Hindu traditions over-rode forces of urbanization in both rural and urban areas (see also Kapur, 1970; Ross, 1961).

Other social research on arranged marriages dealt with attitude changes among college students and further comparisons between arranged and love marriages. The results, based on urban samples, are contradictory. For instance, Rao and Rao (1975) found that 91% of their gender-balanced college student sample disapproved of the traditional form of "arranged" marriage, attributing the high disapproval to factors such as modernization, industrialization, education, and the breakdown of the joint family system. A related survey study by Sprecher and Chandak (1992), almost two decades later, found that over half of their sample approved of the traditional system, thereby pointing to a reversal in the modernization trend. However, with an unevenly distributed gender sample that had three times more women than men, the reliability of the procedures seems suspect in this latter study.

Studies on marital adjustment and satisfaction, on the other hand, show some consistent results. Kapur's (1970) socio-psychological survey investigated marital adjustment among Indian urban working women, finding that women in self-arranged marriages did not adjust better or worse than those in arranged marriages. Kapur's study continues to be the most descriptive document available on the arranged marriage relationship. She used a combination of qualitative and quantitative data in presenting her conclusions. However, her qualitative data were used merely to support her findings while the narratives of women in the study were left unanalyzed. Moreover, Kapur's study, although influential, is now over three decades old. A more recent study (still two decades old) by Kumar and Dhyani (1996) examined the relationship between type of marriage, marital duration, sexual satisfaction, and adjustment among urban women married for at least one year. They found that type of marriage and marital duration had no significant relationship with marital adjustment.

Although limited in scope and analysis, these survey studies are invaluable in that they address a marital form that is vastly understudied, and they shed some important light on Hindu family structure and family members' roles within that structure. More importantly, their limitations are an impetus to uncovering and understanding women's contextual experiences in arranged marriages.

The research that I present in this chapter focuses on a contextual understanding of urban Indian women's experiences in Hindu arranged marriages. I examine the narrative performances of young urban women from an ongoing ethnographic life-history study of 20 urban Indian women in Delhi, India.[4] In particular, I attend to four basic performative reframing strategies emerging from their storied performances that are critical to understanding how my participants were involved in the task of discursively dislocating a traditional marital structure and performing a reframed story of their marriages. First, I briefly explain my fieldwork practices for the study, then I present the performative strategies deployed by my participants.

## Theoretical Framing and Research Practices

Surprisingly, women's voices have been largely silenced or at best marginalized within the research literature, and their experiences of marital life continue to be largely unexplored. Aware of this silence, in 2003, I began an ethnographic life-history study to explore the experience of urban Hindu middle-class Indian women who had voluntarily chosen to be in arranged marriages. Such methodological approaches are crucial in understanding diversity since they are sensitive to context, dynamic processes, and subjective perspectives of both the researcher and the participant (Denzin & Lincoln, 2011; Reissman, 2008). In the study of women's lives, life histories are considered exceptional resources because they enable access to "women's lives at different points in their life cycles in specific cultural and historical settings" (Geiger, 1986, p. 338). Life histories, as personal narratives, "illuminate the course of a life over time and allow for its interpretation in historical and cultural context" (Personal Narratives Group, 1989, p. 4). Additionally, giving narrative form to a life, or to a portion of it, requires exploring the individual and social dynamics that are inevitably significant in shaping a life.

As such, the life histories in my field research can be better understood within the umbrella of a performance paradigm. "Performance," noted Langellier (1999), "is the term used to describe a certain type of particularly involved and dramatized oral narrative" (p. 127). Further, Langellier (1989) proposed that a "story implies storytelling" and "storytelling … is a way of speaking by a storyteller to an audience in a social situation—in a word, a performance" (p. 249). Within a performance frame, storytelling is a conduit between the experience and the story, what Langellier (1999) described as, "the pragmatic of putting narrative into practice, and the functions of narratives for participants" (p. 127).

Understanding narrative from a performance standpoint brings together two key characteristics of narratives—making and doing. Explicating this coupling in a landmark essay, Peterson and Langellier (2006) wrote:

> The understanding of narrative as *a making* is evident in investigations into the elements, aspects, and structures that make up narrative. Such efforts locate narrative as an object, work, or text that is imagined, fashioned, and formed. … The turn to performance [recognizes] that the creative potential or force of such "makings" is not limited to the aesthetic realm of literature, ritual ceremonies, dramatic productions, or festivals. … Performance makes what would otherwise be mundane into something more: it distinguishes or frames itself from what surrounds it, it marks itself off and thereby turns back to comment on its context. (p. 174)

Understood this way, narratives are not merely the recognition, representation, or recounting of past experience, but additionally emerge from the lived realities of bodily conduct (Peterson & Langellier, 2006). In other words, narratives are *performative* in that they re-produce their referent (Butler, 1990). Adding performativity to performance, according to Langellier (1999), highlights:

> the way speech acts have been extended and broadened to understand the constitutiveness of performance. That is, personal narrative performance constitutes identities and experience, producing and reproducing that to which it refers. ... In performativity, narrator and listener(s) are themselves constituted ("I will tell *you* a story"), as is experience ("a story about what happened to me"). Identity and experience are a symbiosis of a performed story and the social relations in which they are materially embedded: sex, class, race, ethnicity, sexuality, geography, religion, and so on. That is why personal narrative performance is especially crucial to those communities left out of the privileges of dominant culture, those bodies without voice in the political sense. (pp. 128–129)

Approached from the standpoint of performativity, the "*personal* in personal narrative performance is a struggle for agency," and shows a process of an emergent (through making and doing) rather than a stable self (Langellier, 1999, p. 129). In my study, I focused on the life histories as emergent performances of identity that, in the process of the telling, reframed the arranged marriage experiences of the women. I posit that in the narrative interview performances, the arranged marriage is re-articulated and reframed for both the performers (my participants) and for me (audience; participant-observer).

The participants for my study included 20 urban women who either worked outside the home or were home-makers. They ranged in age from 27–44, who had been married in the early 1980s, 1990s, and 2000s.[5] Their occupations included corporate executives, sexual rights activists, medical doctors, teachers, special education counselors, journalists, day care workers, and private entrepreneurs. I gained access to my participants through a snowball sampling strategy (Agar, 1996), and many of them were referred to me by families in the Delhi neighborhood where my own family lives (Delhi being my erstwhile home).

My life-history interview protocol was open-ended yet designed around three broad domains—girlhood, pre-marriage, marriage. Each life history was engaged as a personal narrative performance. My participants performed their stories in a combination of Hindi and English; these were audio-recorded prior to verbatim transcription (by me). I relied on a dialogic/performance analysis proposed by Reissman (2008) to engage the personal narrative performances. Reissman described dialogic/performance analysis as a broad, flexible, and varied interpretive approach to oral narrative that "interrogates how talk among speakers is interactively (dialogically) produced and performed as narrative" (p. 105). Instead of relying merely on what is and how something is spoken (i.e., narrative as making), this approach asks "'who' an utterance may be directed to, 'when,' and 'why' that is, for what purposes" (Reissman, 2008, p. 105). Since the life story performances were intertwined with my own presence and role in the field as an insider-outsider (insider as a consequence of belonging to a similar socioeconomic-geographic location, but outsider because I have not been involved in an arranged marriage), this approach to analysis was critical in engaging the narrative performances as both a making and a doing. Such an analysis focuses on broader questions such as how a story is "co-produced between teller and listener, speaker and setting, text and reader, and history and culture" (Reissman, 2008, p. 105).

In carrying out a dialogic/performance analysis, I discerned four performative reframing strategies used by my participants that show a perceptible shift in the way that arranged marriage was experienced and performed in those moments of interaction with me. For the purposes of this chapter, I have chosen to focus on the narrative performances of younger women who were in their 20s and their 30s.

# Performative Reframings

In this section, I discuss four performative reframing strategies which emerged in the process of the storytelling performances. I illustrate how these reframings reconstructed the traditional marriage from a structural to a non-structural arrangement. As noted in the discussion on the Hindu marriage, among traditional Hindus, marriage simply falls under two broad categories—arranged or love. I began fieldwork equipped with these binary categories. I was keen to know how my participants viewed their marriages in general but particularly so when they were choosing between these two forms in their pre-marital days. Quite early in my fieldwork, it became evident that my participants approached their marriages outside of these two conventionally prescribed categorical forms. Disregarding the categories of "love" or "arranged," their storytelling performatively reframed their marriages as *comfort, playing wife, romance,* and *egalitarian friendship.*

## Marriage as Comfort

Even a cursory look at definitions of arranged marriages shows that arranged marriages are seldom associated with the notion of comfort (Chawla, 2007; Kapadia, 1958; Nussbaum, 2000). To the contrary, for non-Indians and many urban Indians, the term *arranged marriage* inevitably evokes qualities of imposition, duty, obligation, and constraint.

The performance of marriage as comfort emerged during a point in their life histories when I would ask my participants to recall any criteria that they had envisioned for their future husbands. Unsurprisingly, a majority of my participants shared the view that material wealth, good jobs, and higher educational attainment were necessary prerequisites for a husband, qualities that would allow them to live in comfort. When I first encountered articulations of these qualities, I viewed them as materialistic, even manipulative. After all, many of my participants were working professionals who could attain economic independence, and comfort, on their own. I remember being disturbed by their desire for comfort and also by my own interpretation of these women as manipulative. But when the desire for comfort persisted in life history after life history, I began asking questions such as: What did comfort mean? A comfort with what? In keeping with a dialogic/performance analysis, I began probing, and my participants were quick to elaborate. Most of them clarified by telling me that they grew up having been told to learn how to cook, clean, and generally to become adept at housekeeping because this was something that would be expected in their marriages. They talked of watching their mothers and grandmothers living lives tied to the hearth and home, of spending most of their days working in the home. For many of them, this "chore-like" quality of marriage had deeply influenced the criterion of comfort that they put forth in the stories they told me. They insisted that they were determined to not re-perform/imitate this type of wifely identity. Theoretically, they were making a performative break from the gendered marital identity performances that they had been privy to as young girls and later as young women. By doing so, they were making an intervention by resisting the repetitiveness of acts that reproduces conventions (Butler, 1990; Madison & Hamera, 2007). In the examples below, I illustrate some of these interventions.

Jhumpa, a journalist, explained that she was insistent on marrying someone with a professional degree. She chose to marry a man who had a high paying job in the corporate world because his salary would allow her to continue to live in the manner to which she was accustomed in her natal home. His higher paying job would ensure that she could skip household work and work outside the home if she desired. Other women told similar stories:

> I wanted a comfortable house, a room of my own, you know? Work in the morning and cook in the evening, then back to office, back to cooking, back to cleaning – that was not something that I could have done. So, I expected all these things when I married. (Geeta)

Meena echoed this same focus on comfort:

> If someone used to ask me what kind of a boy I wanted, I would say, "Someone who had a nice kitchen, who had a good bathroom, who was smart and handsome." My husband's salary did matter to me. It had to be good, so that I could have a luxurious

and comfortable life. That is what I liked about my husband—he had studied in a very good institute and his salary was also very good at that time.

Jhumpa, Geeta, and Meena negotiated the conditions of the matchmaking bargain, and seemed to have achieved the negotiation of comfort, at least in the ways that they related it to me. Once they succeeded in these negotiations with their parents, they told me that their marriages seemed more "playful" because they did not have to worry about material comfort. I sensed, in how they performed their stories, that these women were keen on reframing marriage from "chore" to "comfort."

## Playing Wife

Engaging marriage as comfort and identifying comfort as a key criterion in the marriages they desired, these women were reframing their own understandings of marriage from a space of work and chores to one of play. In a sense, by telling about their bargaining for comfort, they were performatively maneuvering out of the structural constraints of the Hindu marriage. In my interpretation, bargaining for comfort as a condition to marriage "bought" them out of the prescribed traditional role of "householder," which is a structural reality in the Hindu marriage. In Sanskrit, the language of the Hindu scriptures, even the word "wife," in some translations, stands for household and ties women's identities to home and hearth (Chawla, 2004). Escape from the structural constraints of the wife role, these women were free to play at being a wife on their own terms, making choices based on their own desires rather than on the householder role obligations.

"Playing wife" was keenly evident in the manner in which Radhika reframed her marital story. A practicing anesthesiologist, Radhika quit professional work briefly upon her marriage in order to join her husband in another city, where he was finishing his medical education. Describing those times, Radhika said: "He had long hours of working, but I just loved being the housewife. Generally, you know? I picked up a lot of cooking and I used to try out my cooking on him." For Radhika, this cooking was not a chore, but was fun because she had made the choice to cook; it had not been imposed on her. This play was made possible by the comfort afforded her when she chose to marry a man of sufficient income. Jhumpa shared a similar anecdote: "I had a very good time in Chennai. I had a cookbook and all and I used to, (I was not working at the time), experiment in the kitchen and stuff like that. I used to play housewife."

For other participants, "playing wife" came in the form of decorating the home at leisure, taking small vacations with the spouse instead of spending holidays with the natal or in-law families, and even small things such as impulsively going for dinners in the middle of the week. These performances were "breaks" from what they had witnessed in the lives of their mothers and grandmothers. Play was closely linked with being able to perform a self outside of the wifely role imposed by traditional arranged marriages. In performing "comfort" and "playing wife," these women were presenting features of their arranged marriages that functioned to resist normative understandings, thereby constructing an alternative meaning of the arranged marriages.

## Romance

A third performative reframing that is both complementary yet separate from comfort and play was "romance." To a Western reader, to reframe a marriage by centering romance in the relationship might seem like an obvious notion. But as noted previously, arranged marriages (and even Hindu marriages broadly) are rarely associated with romantic emotions. The non-romantic nature of the arranged marriage is reinforced in contemporary writings, and even today, "love" is considered a frivolous idea entertained by teenagers, celebrities, and Bollywood (Bumiller, 1990; Rodriguez & Chawla, 2010). Nussbaum (2000) noted that in middle-class India, love is mostly considered a threat rather than a goal of marriage. Therefore, even as women in the contemporary West continue to be socialized to the idea that their life's meaning is to be found in a relationship of romantic love, such a goal is uncommon among (many) Indian women. In the Hindu marriage, wrote Nussbaum, "even though marriage is prized, its *raison d'etre* is not taken to be romance" (p. 259). In fact, closely aligned with historical understandings of Hindu marriage, middle-class Indians continue to understand love as commitment and devotion to family (Nussbaum, 2000).

Hence I was surprised that my participants consistently expressed a desire for and addressed romance in their storytelling performances with me. This longing was keenly elaborated in their descriptions of their "first meetings" with their husbands. A first meeting in the context of an arranged marriage generally involves a meeting between two sets of parents and the potential bride and groom in a public area such as a restaurant, a relative's or a common friend's home, or some other neutral area. It is not a "date" between prospective bride and groom and is, in fact, a first meeting of the two families together (Chawla, 2004, 2007). Given the significance of this meeting as a punctuated event in one's life-cycle, it was unsurprising that all my participants recollected and then performed it in intimate detail. Geeta, for example, re-enacted (for me) her first meeting with a romantic flourish, even though she met her husband in the company of a few members of their respective families:

I saw my husband and I was like completely floored. He's not very good-looking, but he has a very honest face. He's got big and beautiful eyes. So I think I was completely head over heels in love with him. I could see that. So, I tried not to show it.

Geeta's anecdote re-plotted a family-arranged event into a romantic event, by re-enacting the "first meeting story" into a "love at first sight story"—a sort of performative re-arrangement, yet another intervention against the social convention. Such shifts were expressed in a variety of ways in other participants' narratives. For instance, Reema's entire marital definition was centered on romance and what she desired in a husband:

See first time you see only physically. You want a loving, caring and smart boy. Mainly, he should be caring, he should listen to you, and he should be loving. He should understand you. It used to feel good that not only will I have so many clothes to wear and jewelry, but that we will go out and there will be someone to love me and care for me.

The focus of Reema's narrative was on her romantic courtship moment and subsequent "loving" moments with her husband. As their marriage progressed, this romance diminished because her husband was overtly loyal to his mother who lived with them in the joint family. Describing this tug and pull, Reema confided:

That was very bad. Then you see these actions (him siding with his mother) and you can't love the person. And the wife's thing is that she wants him to be hers alone and nobody should share your husband. That he should be listening to you alone.

This strain took a toll on Reema's marriage for some years, but she and her husband rebuilt their trust by taking one vacation every year as a couple:

We go out every year on our anniversary. We don't take our kids. We go out and that is a good change and we can discuss all our problems. You have all the time. It gives you a break from work and household tensions. You can discuss problems and say what things should not happen. Like I tell him, "You should not scold me, you should not say this in front of everybody."

Romance in Reema's performed story migrated from desire, to longing, to loss, and now, ultimately, a replenishment. Romance was central to the expectations, definition, and experience of her marriage.

Ultimately, in my interpretation, reframing their marriages from a contractual arrangement between families to a romance between heterosexual partners allowed my participants to performatively shift the traditional marital story that they were living. While comfort, playing wife, and romance were critical to the reframing of the structure of the arranged marriage, the notion of a "husband as friend" was an additional performance that further elucidates how my participants were shifting the frames of a normative tradition.

## Egalitarian Friendship

In addition to redefining their marriages in the ways I have explored, a linked yet separate discursive framing performed by my participants was the desire for a marital relationship that was exclusive of the family. "My husband is my (best) friend," or "I want my husband to be my best friend" was a sentence I heard repeatedly across a majority of the life histories. I came to view it as a resonating narrative performance that illustrated the aspiration for a "new" and "different" type of marital relationship in which the couple viewed themselves as a core unit that was more important than the larger extended family.

My participants spoke at length about their commitment to having a meaningful relationship with their husbands, one that was outside of the extended family; they constructed the nurturing of this equal-partnership relationship as central to how they had re-defined their marriages. There are two implications to this performative reframing. First, it implied that for these women in the stories they told in those moments with me, marriage was a distinct relational unit, a dyadic unit that consisted of husband and wife, instead of the entire family. These women had entered their arranged marriages prioritizing the marriage and the relationship with their husbands as more significant than their role or inclusion in the in-law family. Second, this unit was egalitarian, democratic, and consisted of two individuals who gave to it equally, as best friends.

The privileging of the marital relationship over the well-being of the extended family was illustrated in the manner by which my participants described their marriages and their husbands. Meena noted how she and her husband understood each other:

Meena:     We shouldn't give much importance to other people.

Devika:    Other people?

Meena:     The other family members. It should be just between husband and wife, about our relationship. We should understand each other and not ruin our relationship because of our parents. Maybe my husband doesn't like [a] few things about my parents and even I don't like things about his. So, I think now I've understood this, you can't fight over these things. I mean we have to live together. They are just *sidey* [bystander] people who, once in a while, you have to meet. So you can compromise on all this.

The women emphasized that their relationships with their husbands were like close friendships: fun-filled and egalitarian relationships in which they could be both carefree and honest. In talking about her relationship with her husband Radhika cheerfully recalled the fun and excitement of her honeymoon:

Radhika:     He's a nice man. He's a very exciting man also. You know how we spent our honeymoon (laughs)?
Devika:      How?
Radhika:     Trying to kill each other, I think (laughs louder). We went paragliding; we went river rafting; we went skiing—everything. It was a sponsored package, my brother had given it to us. Like this guy, the tour guide, was supposed to help us with our tours and everything, and he said, "What were they trying to do on their honeymoon? That's not the way you are supposed to spend your honeymoon" (laughs). But we were having a lot of fun together.

Geeta emphasized that she could be herself with her husband:

Geeta:       So, I realized that he is the best friend that I have. I have to be at the best of my behaviors or even better behavior with each and every person that I have around me—could be you, could be my colleagues, could be my in-laws, my own brothers—but, I don't have to be the best of me with him. I can misbehave; I can abuse; I can slap him if I want to (laughs), and he would still be the best friend.
Devika:      How did he indicate that to you that you could do what you wanted?
Geeta:       I just gradually got to know. I mean once you do it the first time and the second time he tells you that, "Okay you are in a bad mood again, sit and speak to me. Relax, if you want to abuse me then sit here and do that, and it doesn't matter I am going to listen to each and everything that you have to say." So that came gradually, it took us about a year, I would say, to come to that kind of understanding.

In my view, these four reframings, when approached from the perspective of discourse dependence, are powerful tools that rewrite the deeply traditional marital scripts that are a part and parcel of arranged marriages in their traditional iterations.

## Conclusion

Galvin's (2006) approach to discourse dependence takes a Westernized view in its consideration of diverse family forms that sit as alternatives to the U.S. heteronormative norm. However, I want to suggest that transformations of traditional family forms in other cultures can also be viewed as instances of discourse dependence. The concepts of family and marriage and what they mean is in flux, not only in the United States, but also in other parts of the world (Coontz, 2005). I have argued that discourse dependence—the idea that contemporary families increasingly use communication to define themselves—can be stretched to understand diverse forms of communicative construction outside of the U.S. In particular, the construct of discourse dependence can be used to understand how women in contemporary Hindu arranged marriages are changing the definition of the normative traditional arrangement by using performative strategies to reframe the marriage and consequently reconstruct and re-envision their relationship with their husbands. In performing their stories, my sample of urban Hindu women shifted the way that they viewed and engaged their marital relationships. This reframing shifted the arranged marriage from a structurally fixed idea that relies on gendered notions of duty, sacrament, and obligation to one that is self-defined and experienced, in criteria and expectations, via comfort, play, romance, and egalitarian friendship. This reframing can also be approached as resistance to a male-centered marital structure and as an assertion of agency on the part of women (Chawla, 2007). As Peterson and Langellier (2006) argued, "performing narrative makes it possible to resist, thwart, and alter" existing structures and power relations (p. 178).

Historically, this reframing may also be understood as a universal development that, according to Coontz (2003), shapes our modern values about what and how to communicate in marriages. She noted a "long-term trend that to a greater and lesser degree affects people of almost every race, ethnicity, and region in the modern economy. That is the erosion of the traditional ways of organizing and sustaining personal intimacy" (p. 189). This growing role of "personal attraction and compatibility" in the context of marriage and the "eclipse of kinship" is also an outcome of socioeconomic changes with women entering the workforce, gaining economic independence from family units, changes in inheritance laws, industrialization, and so on (Coontz, 2003). As a consequence, the impact and influence of communication within the family will continue to grow and so, noted Coontz (2003), "in an increasingly diverse society, the search for identity and connection through the exploration of individual feelings—as opposed to the confirmation of social conventions—will undoubtedly continue" (p. 190).

We cannot ascertain that the arranged marriage in urban India is in a "definitional crisis" since the number of persons involved in such marriages remain relatively steady. However, emerging trends from this particular life-history fieldwork seem to suggest that its definition is being remade performatively by the discursive terrains and subsequent lived strategies of the women who choose this traditional form of marriage.

# Notes

1. These scriptures were written by male Aryan sages who inhabited the areas across the Indus river, long before the word "Hindu" came to be associated with religion. "Hindu" is simply an evolved Persian word for the people that lived across the river "Indus" or "Indu." An influential interpreter of the scriptures, the sage Manu is said to have been responsible for laying out marital laws in his work *Manu Smriti* that are still in use (Shattuck, 1999).
2. In my research I use "joint" and "semi-joint" to refer to family structure and co-habitation patterns. A semi-joint family could be one in which one son and his family live together with his parents, while the other siblings live elsewhere.
3. This legal history underwent transformation with the passing of the Hindu Marriage Act by the Government of India in 1955 allowing for the dissolution of marriage via divorce or annulment, and property for women, daughter, wives, widows, and daughter-in-laws. In her 2005 work, *Marriage, A History: From Obedience to Intimacy Or How Love Conquered Marriage*, family sociologist Stephanie Coontz argues that even in the Western world, marriage was a deeply economic institution and was separated from love and intimacy; individuals were expected to find the latter and former outside of the marriage.
4. This study received human subjects clearance by the Institutional Review Board of Purdue University. All participant names and any identifiable information have been changed to maintain confidentiality and protect the identity of the participants.
5. The women in the original study were interviewed in cohorts, as women who were married in the 1980s, 1990s, and 2000s in the age range of 27–44. While there were many differences in the ways that participants articulated their marital lives based on life-course and life-cycle, there were also several domains of similarities. The discussions in this chapter are based on those domains of similarity.

# PART THREE

# Remaking "Family" beyond Biological Ties

# CHAPTER EIGHT

# Life without Kids

## In(Voluntarily) Childless Families

KELI RYAN STEUBER

In our pronatalist society, the assumption is that individuals will become parents one day, regardless of reproductive ability. Parenthood is often viewed as a rite of passage and a critical stage in development and maturity (Scott, 2009). However, an increasing number of families find themselves childless either by choice or chance. Whereas many of the families being discussed in other chapters of this book must work to legitimate the *presence* of a non-biological or non-legal relative as part of their family unit, these families are burdened with legitimating their identity as a family with the *absence* of an expected member of a nuclear family unit: a child.

## Composition of Childless Families

The childless population is comprised of individuals who are purposively childless, those who are biologically unable to have children, and those who are temporarily childless (Park, 2005). There is an increase in the number of couples who are purposively choosing to remain childfree (Durham, 2008). Although it is difficult to ascertain specific and current numbers, especially for men, researchers have found that the number of women of childbearing years (15–44 years) who have selected a voluntarily childfree lifestyle has increased over the past 20 years (Paul, 2001).

Despite the increase in this trend, voluntarily childless families are still uncommon (see Durham & Braithwaite, 2009). Compared to individuals with children, the voluntarily childless are more educated and more likely to secure professional occupations, less religious, and less conventional and traditional (see Durham, 2008). Statistics about family planning are virtually nonexistent for single, gay, lesbian, and transgender couples; however, with advances in assisted reproductive technology and adoption, these couples have a variety of family-planning options to consider.

Another major reason that families are childless is because couples are biologically unable to reproduce. The inability to reproduce can encompass heterosexual infertile couples, as well as individuals or couples who need to rely on assisted reproductive technology or adoption to have a child. In terms of infertility, an estimated 15% of couples, or 4.3 of the 28 million marriages in the United States, face conception difficulties at some point in their reproductive lifespan (Chandra, Martinez, Mosher, Abma, & Jones, 2005). People coping with infertility are often desperate for the experience of parenthood, and psychologically cope with increased risks of depression (Peterson, Newton, & Feingold, 2007), and with issues of blame, treatment stress, and relationship uncertainty (Steuber & Solomon, 2008) related to their inability to give birth. Gay, lesbian, and transgender individuals might also cope with infertility as a medical condition; however, if they are going to have biological children, they must rely on reproductive technologies, surrogacy, and sperm or egg donors. Accordingly, a variety of circumstances can find an individual categorized as biologically unable to reproduce.

People also can be childless temporarily. A variety of circumstances can categorize individuals as temporarily childless (Park, 2002). Decision-making within a couple, health issues, or relationship status might position someone as childless for a given frame of time. For example, people can be temporarily childless because they have yet to make a decision about parenthood individually or within their relationship. Non-infertile, heterosexual couples might have divergent views about their transition to parenthood, thereby delaying an active decision about having children. For single individuals, perhaps there is a delay in parenting until finances are available, especially because adoption and the assisted reproductive technologies necessary for a single adult to become a parent are costly and time-consuming. Gay individuals might face stigma unique to their sexual orientation, perhaps complicating family planning decisions (see Biblarz & Savci, 2010, for a review). Once they decide to reproduce, they too must explore the adoption or assisted reproductive technology processes. Taken together, there are a variety of circumstances both unique to and spanning across the various compositions of childfree individuals that can categorize them as temporarily childless.

Despite these three differing circumstances, much of the research on childfree couples has focused on those who are infertile, although an increasing number of studies examine the stigma and decision-making processes of those who are voluntarily childfree (e.g., Durham, 2008; Durham & Braithwaite, 2009; Thornton & DeMarco-Young, 2001). No research exists in the communication or related disciplines that focuses on temporary childlessness directly, despite the fact that a large number of individuals and families can be categorized as such.

This chapter will focus on individuals who have permanently decided to remain childfree or who are experiencing unexpected challenges in their attempts to become pregnant (i.e., infertile couples). I will review literature that illuminates the identity struggles that childless families manage, as well as the communicative ways these individuals attempt to legitimate their family in its current state. Although there are varying reasons why individuals do not have children, most of them share outsiders' perceptions that they are in some way an incomplete family. This shared assessment is important; however, the experiences of each of these families are incredibly unique.

## Expectations for Parenthood

Individuals and couples must make decisions about their goals for parenthood. If single, individuals need to decide not only if they want to parent, but what steps they will take to meet their goal of becoming a mother or father. If choosing parenthood, decisions need to be made about adoption or donor insemination or surrogacy. Both of these options bring with them emotional, financial, and practical components. In the case of couples, individuals need to manage not just their own preferences for parenting, but they also must consider the partner's desires. In situations in which there are divergent goals for parenthood, couples must negotiate the best way to approach this pivotal issue. In the case of gay and lesbian adults, decisions must be made in general about their desires for children, as well as the logistical points about adoption, surrogacy, or donor insemination, and additional stigma that might surface from their decision to parent in a heterocentric society (see Chabot & Ames, 2004). The decision to have a child is a big one, and it often has long-term implications for families. In an eight-year longitudinal study of married couples, couples with children had a more rapid relationship deterioration than their non-parenting counterparts (Doss, Rhoades, Stanley, & Markman, 2009). Although there is a plethora of data showcasing the impact of a child during the transition to parenthood (see Kluwer, 2010), there is far less research examining the communicative strategies leading up to the decision to have a child. Put differently, we know much more about how couples communicate outwardly about their child-rearing decision than we do about how they make this decision internally between partners.

The family planning process, situated within the individual or a relationship, is often viewed as a collective process by outside family members (Steuber & Solomon, 2011a). Potential grandparents often make requests for when their children are expected to expand their family, friends and siblings might make lighthearted inquiries about when people are going to start "trying," and people in general often offer unsolicited advice in terms of when and how to make the family planning decisions. Complicating matters more for childless families is the fact that their family planning struggles or decisions are difficult to conceal (Steuber & Solomon, 2011a). The mere absence of a child is an indicator of an incomplete family (see Dorow & Swiffen, 2009), and outsiders often begin making sense of that observation with or without accurate information. For that reason, childless families must make the decision whether, and how, to communicate their situation to their social networks. Unfortunately, even if they choose to conceal information about their childless state, they will often be forced into interactions that require some form of a communicative response.

These interactions, often uncomfortable for childless families, force the childless person or couple to legitimate their family status. Unfortunately, interacting with social networks about their childlessness can be a contributing source to the stigma these families experience, as well as a site in which to legitimate, defend, and explain their situation. Galvin (2006) has argued that families that are considered nonnormative must work to legitimate their identities. In the following paragraphs, I will situate both childless by choice families and infertile families within the context of a pronatalist society. Simultaneously, I will illustrate through examples how childless couples communicate to validate their family form. Finally, I will discuss areas for future research within the childless context.

## Childless by Choice Families

Childless by choice (CBC) families are those individuals or couples who make a conscious decision not to have children. CBC families have various motivations for their decision, ranging from loving their life in its current state, to valuing freedom and independence, to being concerned with bringing a child into the world in its current form (see Scott, 2009, for more). Despite their positive assessment of life without children, these families have the job of legitimating their childfree family as "complete" in its current state. CBC individuals are often assumed to have character flaws, such as being selfish or too career driven (Scott, 2009). In addition, religions predominantly endorse procreation (Durham, 2008), and people consider parenthood as a pivotal point in the developmental process. With these social pressures in place it is not surprising that the choice to remain childfree is often met with negativity. Especially for women, non-mothers are deemed selfish, neurotic, childish, and immature (see Vinson, Mollen, & Smith, 2010, for a review). They are also viewed as more driven, and less warm, caring, and emotionally healthy than mothers (LeMastro, 2001; Mueller & Yoder, 1997).

These perceptions bring with them implications for these families. Consistently, researchers have found that CBC individuals experience stress or guilt because of their decision (Durham, 2008; Thornton & DeMarco-Young, 2001). These individuals often communicate frustration with having to legitimate their childfree choice (Scott, 2009) and, accordingly, make selective decisions about whom to reveal their life-choice and justifications outside of their marriage (Durham, 2008). The following paragraphs further discuss challenges faced by CBC families.

## "It's selfish"

One of the dominant assumptions linked to childfree living is the perception that adults who do not want to reproduce are selfish. They are perceived to prioritize their own successes, either in career or travel or monetarily, at the cost of giving the gift of life and reproducing. Park (2002) argued that the intentionally childless are often perceived to have excessive lifestyles and to value individualism over familial bonds. Callan (1985) reported that the fewer children people have the more negatively they were viewed, and that childless individuals were seen as individualistic, career-oriented, selfish, and materialistic. Taken together, many CBC families are judged to be self-focused and thus alienated because of their decision to actively avoid parenthood.

In light of the negative stereotypes, such as selfishness, that are associated with CBC decisions, individuals might allow outsiders to assume their family status is something other than voluntarily childless. Some individuals will engage in *identity substitution*, a form of labeling that is a primarily reactive response involving assuming another, less stigmatizing, identity (Park, 2002). In these situations, childfree couples label themselves as something different than they are to avoid the stigma or judgments associated with their nonnormative family status. For example, individuals can make vague statements about parenthood not being in their future, which might suggest the possibility of infertility to outsiders. The vague statement, then, helps them to pass as potentially having reproductive challenges. This ambiguity can serve as a shield for the childfree, as people might feel sympathy at the thought of the person not being able to have a child rather than outwardly express disapproval or use silence related to their voluntarily decision not to have one. According to Durham (2008), "people are likely to perceive voluntary childfree couples as suffering from character flaws, as opposed to pitying or sympathizing with infertile couples" (p. 133). It should be noted, however, that some couples do not report passing (Durham, 2008), perhaps in an attempt to legitimate their status through actively identifying as childless.

## "You'll regret it later"

Another main assumption from outsiders is that childfree families will grow to regret their decision (Gillespie, 2000). Many childfree individuals have been told that they will eventually realize the joy they missed out on due to bypassing parenthood, especially as everyone around them begins to have children and, eventually, grandchildren. Outsiders also believe that regret might surface with age, particularly during times when adult children assume the caregiving role for their parents (Gillespie, 2000). The assumption that individuals will grow to regret their childfree state might be one reason that many women face sterilization opposition from their medical care providers when they claim they want to be childfree. Individuals have experienced doctors refusing sterilization procedures to young women because the physicians believe the women will come to regret their decision and then find themselves physically unable to reverse the procedures (see Kelly, 2009; Scott, 2009).

When people perceive that CBC families will have future regret, they position CBC family status as temporary. For example, many childfree individuals (single, partnered, or married) in Scott's (2009) study reported being told that they were young and would eventually change their mind and desire parenthood. A salient assumption for women specifically is that they will grow into a desire for motherhood (Gillespie, 2000). Put differently, the thought that individuals might actually actively desire to remain childfree is often shocking for outsiders to process, resulting in assumptions that CBC individuals are unaware of themselves and their goals for parenthood. This predicament forces individuals to then justify their decisions to outsiders. CBC individuals often provide explanations for their deliberate decisions, offering accounts such as asserting that they do not perceive a baby to improve the quality of their relationship and, in fact, claiming that a child would be detrimental to their partnership (Scott, 2009). Research has supported the view that relationships decrease in quality after a child is born (Doss et al., 2009), and many CBC families argue that they do not want to risk that relationship decline. A second popular explanation is that the childfree families value freedom; some families choose to communicate that good parenting requires a lot of sacrifice, and they recognize that they are not willing to make those life changes at this point (Scott, 2009). Finally, many individuals simply state that they do not feel any parental instinct (Scott, 2009). This type of statement is especially poignant to outsiders inquiring about their childfree state, as it is hard to suggest that someone should have a baby when they claim to feel no natural tendencies towards caring for it. By identifying a feature of parenthood that is unwelcome to them, such as fear for changing their relationship and sacrificing freedom, CBC families are explaining to outsiders why it is the appropriate decision for them not to move forward with having a child. Feeling a void in terms of maternal or paternal instinct is another viable explanation—one that leaves little room for rebuttal because the well-being of a child might be challenged. Of course, these more convincing rationales are also the ones that feed the stereotype of CBC individuals as selfish or different.

## "You're incomplete"

One way that CBC families can defend their situation from being judged as nonnormative is to label their family as complete. Durham (2008) found that while individuals and their spouses held what they considered a more progressive perspective on "family," their relatives held a much more traditional view that prioritized the inclusion of children. This perspective often forces CBC individuals to legitimate their family form in the "absence" of a child, labeling themselves as "complete" or "whole" or "just the two of us." Although many couples report using these labels in their interactions with outsiders, others are emotionally taxed by this exercise (Park, 2002). Accordingly, in some situations, CBC families report that they control information by *passing*, introduced above as the act of suggesting their situation is something different. One way to pass is to suggest they were simply postponing the excitement of parenthood temporarily. Individuals reported that they avoided the negative reactions of their inquirers by simply adhering to the social norm, thereby labeling themselves as "postponers" or "late bloomers" (Park, 2002). A second form of passing is to allow outsiders to believe they are coping with conception difficulties, a strategy discussed above. In this way, childless families legitimate their situation by identifying as infertile, not childfree by choice. This behavior situates them more clearly within the norm and, in this case, the label of infertility offers an explanation for their childless state.

When relationships are being challenged as not genuine or unrecognized in its current form, CBC families often legitimate their status in an attempt to have others identify or recognize the family form as "real." Further, CBC families must legitimate their dyadic unit as *happily* complete without a child. The legitimation seems to stem not from whether they are a "real" family, but more that they are a happy family in their current state, without a child. Individuals might illustrate their happiness by discussing the enjoyment of traveling, the lack of resentment because of career sacrifices, and the ability to spontaneously join each other on business or leisure trips (Scott, 2009). In fact, when asked if he thought he would miss having a family down the road, one CBC husband in Scott's (2009) study stated, "I don't need to have a family to complete the bond. I've got my partner; that's all I need" (p. 147). Another woman from the same study stated, "It's more important to me to have a good relationship with Tom, and be the best person that I can be, than to have those two things suffer and try to be a parent" (p. 141). These quotations are representative of many of the feelings articulated by CBC families. These couples are happy in their childless state, and to them that happiness legitimates their decision to go against the normative expectations to have children.

In light of the pervasively negative attitude associated with childfree status, it is not surprising that families must work communicatively to legitimate their family planning decision. These examples illustrate some of the social and structural responses that people have towards childfree living: the belief that it is temporary, that people will "mature" and evolve into wanting to parent, that they will come to regret their decision for a childfree life, and that CBC families are incomplete. These cultural assumptions force families to communicatively defend their CBC status, which can be an emotionally taxing process.

## Infertile Couples

Infertility is medically defined as the inability to produce a live birth after twelve months of unprotected, regular sex for individuals under the age of thirty-five, and within six months for individuals over the age of thirty-five (Domar, 2002). As indicated by Greil, McQuillan, and Slauson-Blevins (2011), regardless of the healthcare definition of infertility, "couples do not define themselves as infertile or present themselves for treatment unless they embrace parenthood as a desired social role" (p. 737). This point draws the distinct line between childfree couples by choice and childless by infertility. As Letherby (2002) so aptly stated, infertile couples "are both within and outside" the dominant pronatalist discourse. These families are nonnormative in the sense that they are, at least temporarily, unable to have children; however, they desire to embrace the normative expectations of parenthood. This desire complicates the ways they legitimate their family form in comparison to CBC couples because these families do not perceive their current family status to be complete as is. In fact, they often see it is as more of a work in progress.

These couples are forced to legitimate their family status in two ways. First, they work to situate themselves within the normative while simultaneously defending their current family form. Second, these families often find themselves having to justify their responses to infertility. Although more diverse than the pro-natalist perspective, society has expectations about how families should respond to infertility. These expectations range from not treating at all to treating too aggressively, which puts infertile families in the position of having to answer to a plethora of contradictory assumptions. The following section will review some of the stereotypes infertile families face and then offer examples for how they work to communicatively legitimate their current status, as well as their decisions in how to respond to infertility.

## "You waited too long"

In her 2002 book, Hewlett declared that, for most successful women who found themselves childless at midlife, their childless status was a non-choice that snuck up on them. The message that women are "waiting too long" to have babies became pervasive in the media, with talk shows and magazine covers privileging the idea that midlife women without children were all experiencing regret that they prioritized their careers over motherhood. The action step from these outlets was clear: We need to start educating women that they need to plan ahead if they want to have it all, or else they will find themselves alone and married to their career. This societal perception easily permeates into discourse related to infertility. If childless women were in their thirties, the problem had to be their age. Interestingly, this stereotype dominates society's view of infertility when, in fact, reproductive challenges stem from female-only health issues only 35% of the time. According to the national infertility association, Resolve (n.d.), the causes of infertility are split evenly between male and female factor issues, each with a 35% chance of causing the reproductive challenge, and a 20% rate of both contrib-uting to the diagnosis, and a 10% unexplained rate. Is age a factor for infertility? Of course. But is it the predominant cause of infertility? Absolutely not. If families do decide to disclose their diagnosis of infertility, most are met with the assumption that they "dug their own grave," or created the problem themselves and are now dealing with the consequences. For those cases of infertility that are age-related, how are women supposed to follow Hewlett's (2002) advice to be "strategic" when, as Bute, Harater, Kirby, and Thompson (2010) pointed out, "their choices are limited by lack of access to paid time off, inadequate child care, or fear of losing their jobs?" (p. 63). The message is clear: Women deserve to have it all, but if they do not, they must not have planned well enough. The stereotype remains, then, that if it is age related, it is their fault for waiting too long. If it is not age related, the assumption that it is still remains.

One strategy that varies greatly from CBC couples' behaviors is that some infertile families want to label themselves clearly as infertile in an attempt to explain their nonnormative family form. Many infertile couples who work to label themselves do so in part because they believe that the alternative identity, of not wanting to have children, is worse than the identification of being infertile. In one interview we conducted as part of a larger study (Steuber & Solomon, 2011b), a mother of two children was struggling to conceive a third child. She said:

> Children are a gift from God and they're a blessing. And that's really hard, [be]cause a lot of women I know are limiting their family size, they're not having more than two kids. They're having one and two, and I know I'm young and I think I even look younger than I am, you know? So there's this, yeah, maybe a little bit of a question about is she this gung-ho career, power woman? As opposed to this nurturing mother who wants to care for her children and have a larger family. (Interview 7)

This quotation is representative of the pronatalist pressures career women experience. One element is the suggestion that people might think the family delayed parenthood in favor of a career, thereby adhering to the thought that career women who are infertile contributed to their reproductive challenges by waiting too long to begin mothering. This quotation also nods to the stereotype that CBC families face—a perception that choosing a career over parenthood is selfish. In this case, this woman identified as a career woman and a mother. She responded to her concerns about people thinking she wanted to limit the number of children by wanting to clarify that it was not by choice. Indeed, studies have shown that infertile women feel that the stigma tied to being voluntarily childfree was worse than the judgments associated with infertility (Miall, 1985; Steuber & Solomon, 2011a). In fact, it seems that women are more likely to disclose details of their infertility if they believe they are being stigmatized because of it, perhaps to try to clarify that their childless state is not by choice (Steuber & Solomon, 2011a).

## "You're not trying hard enough"

One prominent issue that has emerged in my research with infertile women is the suggestions they receive from social network members indicating that they are not doing enough in terms of treating their infertility. Many times the unsolicited advice comes from individuals who know little about the condition of the infertile couple, thereby giving uninformed "encouragement." One woman we interviewed (Steuber & Solomon, 2011b) had sisters who kept intervening. When she took a break in her aggressive treatment plan, fueled by both emotional and financial stressors, at least one of her sisters would interject:

> And I'm tired of that and now that we're not doing anything I feel so much better. There might be a sister or two that's like, what are you doing? You're not getting any younger. And I'm like leave me alone, I'm fine. Just leave me be, so that can be annoying. (Interview 5)

In the same study, another woman commented that people always wanted to offer some advice, perhaps because they believed they were experts on reproduction if they had successfully birthed a child. She said, "Everybody wants to give you something. Just stick with it! Just keep going! Just try!" (Interview 14). Similarly, in a focus group study of social support for infertile women (Steuber, 2013) one woman stated, "I don't want somebody to, 'Oh, no, just keep going. It will happen. You're just not doing it long enough'" (Focus Group 4, Participant 4). For those couples who are pursuing aggressive treatment, people often make comments when they take a cycle off or try less expensive or less invasive procedures. As indicated on Resolve's (n.d.) website, individuals cannot pursue medical treatment forever, and they should not be encouraged to do so. In a society where the expectation is that every person should want to become a parent, there is often judgment when an infertile family handles their infertility medical care in different ways than their friends and family desire. Taken together, couples who have elected by choice or financial constraint not to pursue aggressive medical intervention (i.e., intra-uterine insemination, in vitro fertilization) are often critiqued for not fighting their infertility and, therefore, not adhering enough to the normative expectations for parenthood (Steuber & Solomon, 2011b).

## "You're trying too hard! Just relax!"

Infertile individuals frequently comment that one of the most frustrating and anger-inducing statements a person can make to them related to infertility is to "just relax!" One woman we interviewed (Steuber & Solomon, 2011b) voiced her anger at the unsolicited advice she often received, "'Don't think about it and it'll happen!' I'm like, yeah. You try being in my situation" (Interview 5). In this particular case, this woman had a health condition that drastically decreased her chance of reproduction without intervention. What many people do not realize is that infertility is not a sexual disorder; it is a medical condition. Although low stress is better for overall well-being, it alone cannot "treat" most of the medical diagnoses that contribute to infertility (Resolve, n.d.). In a focus group study I recently conducted (Steuber, 2013), one woman shared the frustration she felt about her friend suggesting she should calm down about treatment outcomes, "She one time said something about needing to relax, just not get so stressed about it. She said, 'I'm worried about how stressed you get.' That was her line" (Focus Group 5, Participant 1). This statement is often directed at women, and it implies that personality characteristics such as being high-strung or obsessive obstruct their ability to have a child. In the same focus group, one woman mentioned that her mother-in-law would suggest to her son that the level of treatment they were pursuing was not necessary, "And like I said, he had his mom in his ear kind of, 'It'll happen when it happens'" (Focus Group 5, Interview 3). Simultaneously, people will attach criticism to treatments if they think they are trying too hard, such as spending too much time or money on a certain procedure or allowing their schedules to be overridden with infertility attempts. One woman interviewed in a focus group (Steuber, 2013) commented:

> And so we've been doing everything out of pocket and people say to us, "Why are you spending all this money? Why don't you just adopt? It's a waste of money. Every time you do this, it's just a waste." And I say, "I'm putting a new sewer system in my house. If I'm going to spend it on that, I'm going to spend it on this for me. This could make a difference." (Focus Group 1, Interview 1)

The frustration at these unsolicited comments is clear, and oftentimes people coping with infertility must legitimate their treatment approaches and intensity to outsiders who know little about their situation.

## "You want kids, right?"

Similar to CBC families, infertile individuals must also manage the perception that their family form is incomplete in its current state. This belief often coincides with inquiries about existing children or when they are going to start having children (Steuber & Solomon, 2011b). Questions about whether or not they have children can be perceived as challenging the legitimacy of their current status, enticing people to respond by revealing that the reason they do not have children is because they are unable to do so. As one woman stated in a recent focus group, "Yeah. I just wanna wear a T-shirt that says, 'I can't conceive.' Here you go" (Steuber, 2013; Focus Group 3, Participant 2). This type of defensive response was indicative of the frustration infertile women felt towards inquiries and comments members of their social network made regarding their childless family form. Another example of defensiveness was offered in the focus groups:

> I'll be honest, I sometimes take a little sick pleasure in that. Because I hate the question, "Oh, do you have kids?" That's the most awful question on the planet. Or,

"Are you a mom?". … Those questions sucked going through infertility treatment, especially that first year after I lost the pregnancy, sort of quadruple sucked. So after I lost the pregnancy, I've started to say to people, "None that's survived," to shut them up real fast. I know it's an innocent question. I know they didn't mean it the way it felt. But it's like a knife to the gut. (Steuber, 2013; Focus Group 5, Participant 2)

As reported by Galvin (2006), defending often comes in straightforward and indignant statements and are often in response to threats to the legitimacy of the family form. In the case of infertile families, these defensive comments are in response to inaccurate assumptions or inappropriate inquiries about their family planning process.

These cultural beliefs associated with infertility are examples of just some of the many issues that infertile couples must defend themselves against. Although infertile couples align with the normative expectations of wanting to have children, they find themselves in an ambiguous state of desiring parenthood, but being unable to attain it.

## Implications and Future Directions

As more couples face infertility or forego having children, it becomes even more important to understand the experiences of childfree families. Much of the academic research highlights the struggles these nonnormative families face, making it critical to document positive outcomes, identities, and communication that are associated with these couples. As the number of childless families increases, more nuanced examinations of the perspectives of each member of these dyads are needed.

### Men and Childlessness

One obvious area of needed research is on men's perceptions and behaviors of childlessness. This book is about how families collectively legitimate their nonnormative family; however, this chapter was largely from the perspective of women. When it comes to reproductive health, men are notoriously less communicative in their relationships (Steuber & Solomon, 2008, 2011b). In my experiences recruiting infertile families specifically, it is difficult to get a response rate from men without recruiting the entire couple. In addition to men disclosing less about their reproductive-related behaviors and emotions, infertility has been medicalized to focus mostly on women. Many of the assumptions of infertility causes and focuses of treatment are related to women's bodies, making more of the research centered around the female perspective. Childfree women perceive more stigma for their lack of parenthood than their male counterparts (Steuber & Solomon, 2011a), which contributes to an understandable focus on women's perspectives. Although examination of women's perspectives is necessary and important research, it is limiting. Accordingly, future research needs to begin representing the male voice in childlessness topics.

## Singles and Childlessness

Much of the research on childlessness uses the individual as the unit of analysis; however, these individuals are often members of a couple. Alternately, it is becoming increasingly important to explore single individuals' perceptions of parenthood, along with the challenges or stigma they perceive that might contradict some of the ones couples experience. Put differently, do single people who want to become parents without a partner face scrutiny for their decision to bring a child into a one-parent home? What are their experiences both relationally and within the medical community? What factors contribute to their likelihood to pursue parenthood individually and what obstacles do they face? Research explores single parenthood, or unexpected pregnancy out of wedlock, but there is an increasing number of people who make the active decision to parent alone. Communication scholars need to spend time exploring the family planning process of prospective parents who are single.

## Loss of a Child

Families can vary in the reasons they are childless, but one important stage of childlessness more research needs to consider is when an expecting individual or family loses a child at some point in their pregnancy. Many times, as in cases of miscarriages, families are categorized as infertile; however, when they lose their baby after the pregnancy has been announced or they are visibly expecting, such as late-term miscarriage, stillborn births, or the loss of a child at any age, these individuals likely experience a unique childlessness experience. In addition to the communication and support experience likely being different from some of the experiences discussed in this chapter, these individuals also must cope with having been parents and now managing their identity as non-parents. Research in this area is especially important because this loss can shape their reasoning behind their parenthood choices (such as whether or not to attempt to have another child), and because it might inhibit them from celebrating the normal excitements of parenthood if they do try to have another child. Negotiating how to communicate their situation while protecting their right to grieve privately can be taxing on these individuals, and it might make the stigmas associated with CBC couples or infertility especially hurtful.

## Long-Term Outcomes

Many people believe that childless couples, either by choice or infertility, are less happy than their child-bearing counterparts. Findings challenge this perception, and there is no evidence of negative associations between childless status and well-being. Recent research is beginning to document trends that suggest childless-by-choice couples experience less relational decline than their married counterparts (Doss et al., 2009), and the experience of infertility can actually contribute to increased bonds in couples (Resolve, n.d.; Steuber & Solomon, 2008). Further, researchers have found that CBC couples are predominately happy (see McQuillan et al., 2012). Research should approach studying these families for the benefits they acquire because of their childless status, which will perhaps slowly challenge the nonnormative labeling they receive.

## Positive Interactions about Childlessness

Many of the first-hand accounts presented in this chapter underscore the negative perceptions related to childless families. There are plenty of examples, however, of positive support that these families receive. For example, Scott (2009) talked about how some CBC families reported that parents would approach them and reveal how much they love their children, but that they wish they had the foresight to consider how their life would have been different without them. These conversations also addressed the way many people slide into parenthood without considering if the normative expectations are best for their lives. Similarly, infertile families frequently comment that the positive support they receive often outweighs the negative, as well as an understanding for how difficult it must be for friends and family to know how to support them as they cope with reproductive challenges (Steuber & Solomon, 2011a). Although these two types of childless families are nonnormative, they still have positive social experiences. Future research should study how these families are communicatively supported by their friends and family with regard to their family status.

## Revelations about Surrogacy and Donors

In addition to the availability of in vitro fertilization and adoption, another choice available to individuals with biological limitations is surrogacy, the process in which one woman carries a pregnancy on behalf of another woman, man, or for a gay couple. This arrangement is agreed upon prior to the conception of the child (see MacCullum, Lycett, Murray, Jadva, & Golombok, 2003). Traditionally, surrogacy consisted of the surrogate mother and the commissioning father being the genetic parents of the child; however, more recent technology has allowed the commissioning of mother's eggs or donor eggs to be inseminated into the surrogate mother. This option creates the potential of both parents being biologically related to the child. Or, in situations when a single parent or a gay couple commission a surrogate, there are multiple genetic links possible.

These new advances bring with them important considerations. Couples need to coordinate their comfort levels with surrogacy and donor arrangements between themselves, and both single parents and couples alike must consider how to share this news with external family members and, in the future, with their children. Although research is beginning to explore privacy decisions related to these issues (e.g., Jadva, Blake, Casey, & Golombok, 2012), less research focuses on the long-term perspectives of the children and the surrogates or donors themselves. As this book illustrates, "family" can be defined in many ways. In light of the increasingly open histories of surrogacy and donors, how will people define their families in these situations? How will divergent preferences be managed among parents and children? How will rituals, traditions, and everyday familial communication be adjusted to account for the many ways families can be built and maintained? A recent study found that parents who use a genetic surrogate are more inclined to postpone revealing their child's birth information (Jadva et al., 2012). Exploring how disclosure decisions and timing impact children's narratives of their birth is an important avenue of study.

## Conclusion

Taken together, there are a variety of compositions of childless families to consider. Two major groups are the individuals who choose to be childfree and those who have biological constraints on their ability to have a child. Despite the vast differences in the reasons behind their childlessness and their desires for parenthood, people from both camps face the predominantly negative stigma of childlessness in a pronatalist culture. This chapter outlined the various ways individuals communicate to legitimate their family as it currently is or how they hope it to be in the future. Despite the substantial research available on this topic, much work is needed to expand our understanding of the diversity of families who are childless and the decisions they face and make in regard to parenthood.

# CHAPTER NINE

# The Adopted Family

ELIZABETH A. SUTER

Almost half of American lives have been personally touched by adoption. A recent survey found that 47% of Americans were adopted as a child, have adopted a child, or have an adopted family member or close friend (Dave Thomas Foundation, 2007). According to the most recent U.S. Census data, adopted sons and daughters comprise 2.1 million children or 2% of all U.S. children (Lofquist, Lugaila, O'Connell, & Feliz, 2012). Two types of adoption exist in the United States—domestic and international adoption. Domestic adoption refers to the adoption of U.S. born children and includes both foster-care adoption and private adoptions. Foster-care adoption involves adopting children out of public state care, while private adoptions are arranged via privately funded, licensed adoption agencies. International adoption, on the other hand, refers to the adoption of children born outside the U.S. Many international adoptions are not only transnational, but also transracial, meaning the child and adoptive parent are of different races.

Galvin's (2003) research agenda ignited communication research on adoptive families. Then, in 2006, Galvin articulated a typology of discourse-dependent families' internal and external boundary management practices. The aim of the current chapter is two-fold. First, this chapter aims to synthesize extant literature and stimulate future research. Second, this chapter proposes a revision to Galvin's (2006) initial typology. In addition to Galvin's two previously identified categories of internal and external boundary management processes, this chapter proposes that a third category, labeled narrative, exists. In this new category, the discursive practice of narrating, initially conceptualized by Galvin as solely an internal boundary management process, is reconceptualized to first include not only the discursive work that narratives do within families, but also the work that narratives do as families interact with outsiders. Second, narrating has been reconceptualized to also include the work narratives do across familial internal and external borders. This border-crossing function of narratives is conceptualized here as border work. As such, the narrative category is sub-organized in terms of internal boundary management processes, external boundary management processes, and border work processes. As a whole, this chapter is organized first in keeping with Galvin's original typology of internal and external boundary management processes. It then turns to the new category of narrative, which extends Galvin's initial conceptualizing. First, this chapter considers the internal boundary management processes of naming, discussing, and ritualizing.

## Internal Boundary Management

This first section addresses three of the four internal boundary management processes originally laid out in Galvin's (2006) typology—naming, discussing, and ritualizing—that discourse-dependent families use to manage internal identities. The internal work of the fourth, narrating, will be discussed later in the newly conceptualized Narrative section.

### Naming

In the context of adoption, naming, the ways in which members internally indicate familial status, is an understudied internal boundary management process. Suter's (2012) study of the naming practices of international adoptees is the only naming study to date explicitly framed within Galvin's construct of discourse dependency. Despite the fact that names are typically bestowed on international adoptees in an impersonal and often institutional manner (e.g., by an orphanage director), adoptees do not arrive in the U.S. unfettered, unnamed, or unclaimed. Rather, "regardless of the often tenuous and transitory nature of these claims, international adoptees do indeed arrive in the United States replete with birth culture names" (Suter, p. 3).

Thus, Suter's (2012) study asked what internationally adoptive parents do with these names and why they do what they do. Suter conducted focus groups with 32 U.S. White adoptive parents of an internationally adopted child. Her results present a catalog of four international adoptee naming forms: (a) Full Birth Culture Name as Middle Name (38%) (e.g., "Mary Wang Xiao Hong Smith); (b) Alteration of Birth Culture Name (42%) (e.g., "Mary Xiao Smith"); (c) Creation of a new Chinese or Vietnamese Name (9%) (e.g., Mary Mei Smith); (d) Exclusion of Birth Culture Name (11%) (e.g., Mary Sue Smith).

When justifying these naming forms, parents appealed to two primary motivations—identity and pragmatism. Depending on the naming form, parents sought to build three types of identity—ethnic, family, and individual (a child's sense of connection to his or her birth country, family, or understanding of the self, respectively). For instance, parents who retained their child's full birth culture name as middle name were primarily concerned with fostering ethnic identity, whereas parents who enacted exclusion of birth culture name were more concerned with building family identity by re-naming the child after a member of the adoptive family. On the other hand, for parents who altered or created a new name, concerns about ethnic, family, and individual identities were often tempered by pragmatic concerns. Adoptees' names were changed to accommodate U.S. English naming sounds and conventions.

Similar to Suter (2012), Anagnost's (2000) and Quiroz's (2012) studies of internet postings of internationally adoptive parents found parents negotiating difference and identity through a variety of naming practices. Unlike others, Anagnost found that some parents renamed themselves by adopting their child's surname as their own middle name, in effect reshaping their own identity and merging it with that of their child. Both Anagnost and Quiroz critiqued the practice of renaming (what Suter labels exclusion of birth culture name). For Anagnost, "the violence of renaming [equates to] the erasure of a difference that will eventually reassert itself with a vengeance when the child begins to raise the question of his or her origin" (p. 408). For Quiroz, renaming is fraught with White privilege (advantages bestowed on Whites because of their majority status) and fails to consider the adoptee's loss of ethnic identity. Indeed, Scherman (2006) found that parents who renamed scored significantly lower on cultural sensitivity.

To date, naming has only been explored from the perspective of the parent in the international adoptive context. Most notably, the domestic context and the perspectives of other members of the adoption triangle (i.e., the adoptee and the birthparents) have yet to be explored. Although the perspective of the birthparents is unlikely to be examined in the context of international adoption given that these adoptions are primarily mediated between the sending country and the U.S., the perspective of the international adoptee is ripe for investigation. Indeed, the topic of naming surfaces in adult adoptee informal narratives and song writing. As Vietnamese adult adoptee Jared Rehberg's (2009) song lyrics to "Waking Up American" denote, "Without me, without you. I'm living in America with a brand new name" (p. 132). Indeed, international adoptees come to their adoptive parents with their identities already marked by a name. Oftentimes these birth culture names include toponyms, or placenames, that bind them to their geographic cities and counties of origin and while often shared in part by their orphanage or foster mates, bind them to the children of their past. What meanings do international adoptees make of the naming form bestowed on them by their adoptive parents? Do some forms promote adoptive identities (ethnic, familial, and individual) more or less than others? Do naming forms that alter or exclude birth culture names engender loss and grief or do such forms promote a higher sense of family identity like adoptive parents hope? Does maintaining the full birth culture name actually foster adoptee ethnic identity or does this form leave adoptees feeling marked as different? These are just a few of the questions that might be pursued in future research on the adoptee perspective in the context of international adoption.

No research to date has been conducted on naming in the domestic adoptive context. Given that domestic adoptions are often mediated directly between birthparents and adoptive parents, the birthparent perspective, obscured in the international context, is open to investigation. Baseline research might begin by examining if there are any patterns to the ways domestic adoptees are named, similar to Suter (2012). Research might then go forward by investigating the discursive identity and meaning-making processes of these forms *across* members of the adoption triad.

Future investigations on naming within the domestic foster-care adoption context might be particularly warranted as foster-care adoptions often involve older children who come to their adoptive families with names (both first and last) binding them to their past. Future research might begin to examine the identity implications and meanings surrounding foster children's (re)naming. For instance, does retention of the foster child's legal name(s) promote the child's ethnic and individual identities? Or, does retention bind the child to a negative past, obstructing actualization of the self in their new familial context? Does changing the foster child's last name to the adoptive parent or adoptive family name promote the child's sense of family identity? What are the meanings members of the adoptive triad attribute to the processes of changing or not changing adoptee's name(s)?

## Discussing

In the context of adoption, Galvin's (2006) internal boundary management process of discussing has been widely studied. Much research to date demonstrates that internal family communication about adoption builds positive identities for both adoptees (Hawkins et al., 2007) and the adoptive family as a unit

(Jones & Hackett, 2007). For instance, discussing promotes adoptees' information seeking about his or her adoption or birth family (Skinner-Drawz, Wrobel, Grotevant, & Von Korff, 2011), reduces negativity about birth mothers and adoption (Le Mare & Audet, 2011), and mitigates uncertainty and loss (Powell & Afifi, 2005). Colaner and Kranstuber (2010) found discussing reduced uncertainty through two distinct discursive patterns—negotiating information with adoptees, and explaining the meaning of adoption.

Yet, these identity-building conversations are never easy (Jones & Hackett, 2007). Difficult topics (e.g., visible differences, birthparents, the circumstances of the child's relinquishment) pose challenges (Harrigan & Braithwaite, 2010). Fathers are less involved overall, and ambivalence about marriage decreases conversational involvement for both mothers and fathers (Freeark, Rosenblum, Hus, & Root, 2008). Children experience difficulties discussing adoption issues nearly twice as often as parents realize (Hawkins et al., 2007). White parents of transracial adoptees often fail to recognize the impact of race and ethnicity (Kim, Reichwald, & Lee, 2012), and their race lessons have been found to reaffirm existing racial hierarchies (Smith, Juarez, & Jacobson, 2011). For instance, although well-intentioned, parental race lessons, reflecting a liberal humanist approach to race, tend to reify the assumption of White racial innocence.

Despite the positives associated with early disclosures of adoptive status and ongoing discussions of adoption-related topics, some parents remain uncomfortable discussing adoption details. Such parents either withhold information or disclose in uncomfortable ways, often getting upset by the interaction. Such actions often lead children to avoid these interactions in order to protect their parents (Wydra, O'Brien, & Merson, 2012).

Harrigan (2009) examined dialectical tensions (Baxter, 2006, 2011) surrounding discussing and not discussing in the context of transracial domestic and international adoption. Harrigan identified three parental discursive patterns. In the first pattern, spiraling inversion, parental communication is closed until openness is triggered by external events or happenings (e.g., children's pointed questions), adoption-related rituals (e.g., anniversary of adoption day), or emergent situations that present opportunities for adoption-related conversations. In the second pattern, segmentation, parents discuss certain adoption-related topics, but remain closed on other topics (e.g., reservations about the adoption process, negative thoughts about the child's birth culture, circumstances of the child's abandonment). In the third theoretically distinct discursive pattern, balance, parents discuss adoption, but simultaneously limit the information shared.

Harrigan and Braithwaite (2010) illuminated two ways in which competing meanings of adoption were intertwined with one another, a discursive practice known as *dialectical unity* (Baxter, 2011): (a) pride and imperfection, and (b) love, constraint, and sacrifice. The discursive struggle of pride and imperfection was evident in parental talk about the child's birthplace. The interplay of these discourses rendered the birthplace as something worthy of pride, yet imperfect at the same time. The discursive struggle of love, constraint, and sacrifice was also evident in parental talk about the child's birthplace. The interplay of these discourses constructed birthparents as persons who loved the child (love) but who could not parent the child (constraint) and, as such, had to make an adoption plan aimed at ensuring the well-being of the child (sacrifice).

Docan-Morgan (2011) turned attention to adoptee topic avoidance, specifically interrogating topic avoidance about racial derogation (i.e., appearance, ethnicity, or physical attacks) in the context of international, transracial adoption. Docan-Morgan found that most adoptees avoided talking with their parents about these experiences due to parental unresponsiveness or self-protection (i.e., the desire to blend into their mainly White families and communities). As such, adoptees developed a privacy rule (Petronio, 2002) defining racial derogation as private information and remained closed on the topic. The permeability of adoptees' privacy boundary surrounding discussing racial derogation shifted developmentally with disclosure rates highest in the early years, lowest in the teen years, with an upswing again in early adulthood.

Research to date on the identity-building properties of internal family discussions about difference is mixed. Clearly adoptive family members struggle with these conversations, at times promoting positive identities, at other times yielding less than positive meanings, and in some cases, leading to topic avoidance.

In the case of transracial adoptions, whether domestic or international, as the findings of Kim et al. (2012), Smith et al. (2011), and Docan-Morgan (2011) underscore, the mainly White adoptive parents in these families are often underequipped to manage discussions about race in ways that promote positive adoptee identities. As such, it seems important that future research continue to identify not only the disparities in meaning between adoptees and their adoptive parents, but that research also begins to illuminate the interactional and discursive processes leading to these disparities. Study designs such as the one used by Kim et al. (2012), comparing the meaning-making of adoptees and adoptive parents of the same conversation, seem particularly promising. To move beyond identification of discrepant meanings between parent and child to focus on the underlying communicative processes might suggest a need for the collection of naturally occurring conversations analyzed through a conversational or discourse analytic lens. It remains possible that such communication research might not only advance scientific knowledge about adoptive families, but might also serve practical ends and produce results that could be translated into advice for helping adoptive family members discuss difference in ways that promote positive adoptive identities not only for parents but also for adoptees.

## Ritualizing

Research on ritualizing is limited. In examining the role of parental discourse in adoptee uncertainty management, Colaner and Kranstuber (2010) identified two common forms of ritualizing: celebrating the anniversary of the adoptee's adoption day and writing annual letters to birthparents. Adoptive parents' ritualizing efforts reduced adoptees' uncertainty by highlighting known aspects of the adoption and downplaying uncertain aspects, which in turn resulted in a more coherent overall adoptive identity for adoptees.

The bulk of research to date on ritualizing has been framed within Jacobson's (2008) construct of *culture keeping*. Culture keeping consists of a variety of ethnic socializing practices (e.g., attending culture or heritage camps; befriending other international-adoptive families; hosting adoption travel group playdates, monthly dinners, and reunions; celebrating birth culture holidays) aimed at promoting healthy ethnic identity development. The primary ritual means of culture keeping studied to date is heritage or culture camps. A post-adoption resource, heritage camps include cultural activities, food, and celebrations alongside adoption-related programming for adoptees and their adoptive parents.

However, the identity-building properties of heritage camps are subject to critique. A disjuncture between parental motivations and adoptees' actual experiences at heritage camps has been reported. Randolph and Holtzman (2010) found that parents were satisfied with heritage camps because they felt the camps positively promoted individual- and familial-level identities by simultaneously acknowledging difference and reaffirming their family form as normal. By contrast, adoptees did not feel heritage camps significantly impacted their individual or family-level identities. Adoptees constructed camp activities as relatively superficial and ineffective in addressing the racial differences and prejudices experienced in everyday interactions.

As the responses of the 234 adoptees suggest in a study by McGinnnis, Smith, Ryan, and Howard (2009), ritualizing needs to go "beyond culture camp" (the title of the study) to positively promote adoptive identities. The study reported a distinct need to move beyond the strategy of cultural *socialization*, as embodied in culture keeping rituals such as heritage camps, towards experiences that foster racial and cultural *identification*, such as traveling to the birth country, interacting in diverse settings, with both same-race role-models and other adopted individuals. Quiroz (2012) argued that Jacobson's construct of culture keeping is better characterized as cultural tourism. Quiroz's suggestions for more authentic experiences are similar to those proposed by the Beyond Culture Camp study; however, she added practices that require even more accommodation on the part of the adoptive parents. She suggested adoptees need to not only visit the birth country, but do so on a regular basis, speaking their native tongue, and having intimate relationships with members of their birth country.

As this review indicates, the bulk of research to date on ritualizing has been conducted within the context of internationally adoptive families on the ritual of attendance at heritage or culture camps. Given the popularity of these camps and the sheer numbers of internationally adoptive families that attend annually in locations across the country, research that identifies the ways the discursive practices at these ritual events might be altered to redress the critiques is particularly warranted. How might the culture camp ritual event better create experiences that foster more positive identities and meanings? Moreover, what are the existing discursive practices within this ritual that currently promote positive identities not only for parents but also for adoptees? How might these successful practices serve as models for change? Likewise, future researchers might study the talk within alternate ritual practices suggested by Quiroz (2012) and McGinnis et al. (2009) (e.g., regular visitation to the birth country) for additional models for change.

By comparison, ritualizing within the domestic context is far less studied. Colaner and Kranstuber's (2010) results provide some insight, as their sample was mainly domestic adoptees, but there is still far more that remains unstudied. For instance, how might the discursive practices within ritual events vary across closed versus open adoptions? Closed adoptions are confidential with no contact between the child and his or her birth family. Open adoptions, on the other hand, allow contact and the exchange of information, but these arrangements exist on a continuum of openness, ranging from minimal disclosure mediated through an attorney or adoption agency to full disclosure and ongoing face-to-face contact (Seigel, 2013). Within open adoption ritualizing, are there some rituals that pose particular challenges to adoptees' identity constructions? Open domestic adoptions often require adoptees to make sense of their dual positionality as a member of a birth family challenged by life circumstances that did not allow them to parent and as a member of an adoptive family alternately positioned with the social and economic capital necessary to parent, but lacking in a child. What are the discursive practices that adoptive and birthparents invoke that help or hinder adoptee identity understandings and meanings across and within particular ritual practices? Moreover, as Baxter (2011) wrote, ritual holds the potential to be an aesthetic moment. What might be the transcendent ritual moments that bring adoptee identities into a coherent whole? Most importantly, in what ways might adoptive triad members' discursive practices positively facilitate these identity integrations?

# External Boundary Management

As compared to internal boundary management, external boundary management is far less studied. This disparity likely reflects family scholars' longstanding interest in understanding internal family dynamics and affirms Baxter's (2011) call for relational researchers to become students of culture, deepening our understandings of the interrelationships among culture, society, and relationships.

Given this dearth of research, there is insufficient evidence to divide this section into Galvin's four external boundary management processes as was done above for the internal boundary management processes. Rather, this section provides an overall review of external boundary management, organized around three subsections: outsider remarks, parental responses, and adoptee perspective, using findings to date to articulate an agenda for future research.

## Outsider Remarks

To date, external boundary management has been studied only within the context of visibly different transracial, international adoptive families. Jacobson's (2009) construct of *interracial surveillance* (i.e., the monitoring of families by strangers in public settings) provides a useful framework for understanding these interactions. Drawing upon Foucault's (1977/1995) notion of the normalizing gaze, interracial surveillance captures how the visible difference between transracial, international adoptees and their primarily White adoptive parents draws public interest and scrutiny. Visible difference invites outsider remarks; interracial surveillance is characterized by near-constant remarks on family difference.

In spite of the increasing pluralization of the American family, the two-parent, biologically connected family form continues to be the most valued (Baxter et al., 2009). This conservative U.S. family ideology has been found to make its way into social interactions. Everyday encounters remind transracial internationally adoptive parents that they have transgressed the traditional view of family given the racial dissimilarity between family members; the construction of family via adoption; and the adoption of a child born outside the U.S. (Suter, Reyes, & Ballard, 2011a). In short, U.S. culture continues to narrate that adoption is "still not quite as good as having your own" (Fisher, 2003, p. 335).

Adoptive parents experience outsider remarks as invasive (Jacobson, 2008, 2009). The forty White adoptive mothers of Chinese children in Jacobson's (2008) study construed outsider remarks as invasive based on their bluntness, consistency, unidirectional nature, the right and entitlement others feel to ask and receive answers, as well as outsiders' lack of awareness of how their remarks are received.

While parental experiences with these encounters lead parents to invoke the term "attack" to characterize public encounters (Suter, Reyes, & Ballard, 2011b), interracial surveillance of transracial international families does not result in either structural discrimination or physical intimidation. But rather, Jacobson (2009) argued that interracial surveillance and the loss of biological privilege challenge the privacy and integrity of these families. As such, Jacobson situated this loss of privilege as a symbolic loss of normativity. However, she was careful to point out that this symbolic loss of normativity is not inconsequential, but rather can lead to negative material as well as social and psychological impacts. In fact, consistent with stress proliferation theory, which posits that stress experienced by one family member can negatively impact the well-being of other family members, Lee and the Minnesota International Adoption Project (2010) found a significant relationship between parental perceived discrimination as manifested in external remarks and problem behaviors for transracially internationally adopted children from Asia and Latin America.

Outsider remarks have been found not only invasive, but also troubling to identity. Explicitly framed within Jacobson's (2008, 2009) construct of interracial surveillance and Galvin's (2006) constructs of external boundary management and discourse-dependent families, Suter and colleagues (Suter, 2008; Suter & Ballard, 2009; Suter et al., 2011a, 2011b; Suter, Morr Serewicz, Hanna, & Strasser, 2013) have conducted a series of studies examining this discursive negotiation of family identity. Although previous research had suggested that social interactions might challenge the identities of families with adopted children from China, the extent of the challenge experienced and how families negotiate these interactions remained unknown. As such, the purpose of Suter (2008) was two-fold: (a) to investigate the degree to which remarks from others either support or challenge family identity and (b) to investigate the degree to which parental response strategies either support or challenge family identity. She found that the majority of outsider remarks were experienced as challenging to family identity. Analysis of open-ended narrative data revealed that parents felt particularly challenged by interactions that indexed the visible difference between family members (e.g., "Are they *really* sisters?"). Analysis of closed-ended data revealed that the most identity-challenging remarks by outsiders are: (a) negative remarks about China's history or culture ("You know in Asia, they *kill* their babies"); (b) stereotypes of Asians ("The problem with Asian children is someday they always want to go back"); and (c) remarks that characterize adoptive parents as "wonderful" for "saving" a "poor orphaned girl."

## Parental Responses

Parental responses have been found to redress these challenges and affirm identities. Suter (2008) went on to explore the degree to which parental responses either support or further challenge family identity. She found that parental responses to these identity-challenging interactions are supportive of family identity as they validate the family as a construct and the relations between members as genuinely familial. The three parental response strategies that most support family identity are: (a) answering directly; (b) educating; and (c) asking if the other is considering adopting from China.

Whereas Suter (2008) established that in the face of identity-challenging interactions, parental responses tend to affirm family identity, the decisions that lead to affirmation remained uninvestigated. As such, Suter and Ballard (2009) illuminated the decision-making criteria underlying parental identity-affirming responses and ascertaining how these criteria change over time. Overall, Suter and Ballard found that parents do not discursively affirm family identity by employing static, rehearsed responses, as had been previously suggested by popular/educational writings on adoption. Rather, they found that parental response decisions are relationally and interactionally contingent. Parents consider contextual factors (e.g., situation, presence or absence of child, age of child, relationship with questioner) when deciding whether and how to respond in the face of challenge. Additionally, Suter and Ballard found that external boundary management improves across time. With increased insight, self-assurance as an adoptive family, and sheer experience, parents develop increasingly competent responses that better manage their sense of privacy and integrity as a family.

Despite this knowledge, parental sense-making and identity-positioning during interracial surveillance remained unknown. As such, Suter et al. (2011b) examined the metaphorical discourse parents invoke when talking about managing interracial surveillance. Two disparate metaphors emerged—adoptive parent as protector and adoptive parent as educator. Protectors attempt to *guard* identity by enacting defensive, somewhat reactive discourse; meeting invasive remarks straight-on; and by using confrontational, strategic, and toughening discourse. By contrast, educators attempt to *build* identity. As such, their discourse is less reactive and more intentional than protectors. They aim to build identity through discourses of preparation, modeling, and debriefing.

Two recent studies have examined parental privacy management of intrusive outsider comments. Suter et al. (2013) categorized parents in terms of their privacy rule structures, ranging from parents who tend to reveal all adoption-related information to families who have a highly developed nuanced set of rules for who, how, and why they reveal or conceal information. Findings also illuminated the attributes of these parental rules, discriminating the topics (e.g., child's pre-adoption story), targets (e.g., extended family), motives (e.g., instrumental need) and contextual criteria (e.g., presence of child) most frequently motivating privacy rule development. In a related study, Harrigan (2009) found three patterns of parental (non)disclosures of adoption-related information to persons outside the family. In the first pattern, parental (non)disclosures ebbed and flowed across time. Although keeping adoption-related information private was the norm, parents would disclose information when doing so seemed like a way to build relationships, to show pride in the adoptive family, or to meet the demands of the situation (e.g., doctor visits, public celebrations of adoption day anniversaries). In the second pattern, parental (non)disclosures varied in accordance with context. Parents would reveal certain adoption-related topics to outsiders (e.g., basic facts about the adoption) while concealing other topics (e.g., child's birth family history). In the third pattern, although parents answered outsiders' questions, they often provided ambiguous answers allowing them to maintain a comfortable level of privacy.

## Adoptee Perspective

As evidenced by this review, research to date on external boundary management is decidedly focused on the adoptive parent. Docan-Morgan (2010) is the only study to date that has interrogated the adoptee perspective. Examining Korean adult adoptees' retrospective accounts of intrusive interactions, Docan-Morgan reported a typology of adoptee intrusive interactions. Further, Docan-Morgan reported on the external boundary management strategies Korean adult adoptees report their parents having used. Congruent with Galvin's (2006) typology, Docan-Morgan found that parents employed labeling, explaining, and defending to affirm identities. Moreover, Docan-Morgan's results extend Galvin's typology, arguing that parents used the previously unidentified external boundary management practice of joking as means to discursively affirm adoptive family identities.

## Call for Future Research on External Boundary Management

Overall, adoptive family external boundary management is less-studied as compared to internal boundary management. Although studies to date have focused on visibly different transracial, international adoptive families, much research is still needed within this context. Most importantly, more research is needed on the adoptee perspective.

The results of Docan-Morgan's (2010) study suggest several directions for future research. Docan-Morgan's results are based on retrospective accounts of Korean adult adoptees ranging from 18 to 40 years of age, with an average age of 26 years. Research suggests that by the time children are elementary-school aged, a great number of outsider remarks on family difference are being directly targeted toward the children. As such, future researchers should consider ways to recruit and elicit the perspectives of younger adoptees on these interactions. Such research might be able to flesh out if there are differences between adult adoptees' retrospective reports and young adoptees' current lived experiences with these intrusive and identity-challenging interactions. It stands to reason that adult adoptees' reported accounts might have benefited from years of sense-making. How might younger adoptees, who have not had the luxury of years of sense-making, report on these negative interactions? Might communication research on younger adoptees' experiences then be effectively translated in ways to facilitate younger adoptees' processes of sense-making? Moreover, how might these encounters have changed across time? The Korean adult adoptees surveyed by Docan-Morgan were reporting on interactions that occurred approximately between the years of 1970 and 1992. In what ways might have the discourses, dynamics, or identities involved in these interactions shifted or stayed the same in ways that might aggravate or alleviate the negative identity implications?

Furthermore, Docan-Morgan's (2010) second research question elicited information on the external boundary management strategies that Korean adult adoptees remember their parents employing. Future research on younger adoptees, in the midst of these experiences, might usefully explore the external boundary management strategies that the adoptees themselves report using in these interactions. Moreover, the perspective of the White, non-adopted sibling begs for study. Presumably, these siblings are present for many of these interactions. How might the White, non-adopted siblings in these families make sense of these interactions? How are their identities positioned? In what ways might they discursively respond?

To date, external boundary management has not been studied in the domestic adoptive context. Communication research is needed to redress this gap. How might these interactions and boundary management processes be similar to or depart from the knowledge to date? The racial distribution of both parents and children varies by type of adoption (U.S. Department of Health and Human Services, henceforth DHHS, 2009). Children adopted internationally are least likely to be White (19 percent) whereas their adoptive parents are the most likely to be White (92 percent). Children adopted privately from the United States are most likely to be White (50 percent) and 71 percent of their parents are also White. Children adopted from foster-care are most likely to be Black (35 percent) and whereas a sizeable portion of these children also have Black parents (27 percent), 63% of children adopted from foster-care have White parents (DHHS, 2009). Thus, it remains possible that the previously reported experiences with outsider remarks, parental responses, and identity positioning in the transracial, international context might be very similar in both the foster-adoptive and private domestic adoptive contexts. At the same time, it remains possible that these experiences and interactions might depart significantly, in part due to the viability of a relationship with the third side of the adoption triangle—the birth mother. Future research is warranted on how birth mother relations might alter the dynamics, discourses, and identity positionings in the domestic adoptive context.

# Narrative

Thus far, this chapter has discussed discursive practices within Galvin's (2006) two previously identified categories of internal and external boundary management processes. This last section addresses the newly proposed third category of narrative. The narrative category reconceptualizes narrating as no longer solely an internal boundary management process as initially proposed by Galvin, but also as an external boundary management process and a border work process in an effort to capture the work narratives does both within and across familial internal and external borders.

## Narrative as Internal Boundary Management Process

Some research on narrative processes and the adoptive family form reifies that narrating does indeed function as an internal boundary management process as initially theorized. Given that coherent autobiographical narratives are fundamental building blocks for the development of positive identities in adopted children (Pryor & Pettinelli, 2011), important research has focused on parental entrance narratives—the story of how and why the child entered the adoptive family. To date, two thematic analyses have illuminated the content of adoptive parents' entrance narratives. Krusiewicz and Wood (2001) identified the themes of dialectical tensions between personal feelings of joy and biological parents' sadness and loss, destiny, compelling connection, rescue, and legitimacy. Pryor and Pettinelli (2011) identified: loss and choice, emotion-based and logic-based processes, history and heritage, becoming a family, and accentuating the positive and eliminating the negative. These stories are told in varying ways (e.g., oral storytelling, original song, fairytale, Lifebook) and often become interactive, evolving speech events between parent and child (Harrigan, 2010).

Research finds that these stories promote positive identity development both for adoptees and their parents. Narrating helps build adoptee individual identity by offering positive reinforcement, breeding familiarity, building a complete history, and preventing fantasy (Harrigan, 2010). Narrating promotes parents' sense of family identity by affirming their families and the legitimacy of adoption (Krusiewicz & Wood, 2001) thereby redressing the cultural meaning of adoptive families as inferior to biogenetically formed families (Suter et al., 2011a).

However, recent research troubles these findings, suggesting that the relationship between entrance narratives and adoptee positive identity development might be more complicated than initially reported. Kranstuber and Koenig Kellas (2011) investigated the relationship between story content and adoptees' self-concept, finding that while adoptees whose stories focused on the theme of being the chosen child reported higher levels of self-esteem, adoptees whose entrance narratives focused on the theme of negative reconnection with their birthparents reported lower levels of self-esteem. As such, the identity-building properties of entrance narratives beg for more study.

## Narrative as External Boundary Management Process

Recent work on narrating and adoption demonstrates that narrating functions not only as an internal boundary management process, as initially conceptualized by Galvin (2006), but also as an external boundary management process.

Recently, Baxter, Norwood, Asbury, and Sharp (2014) interrogated the adoption back story—narratives told by adoptive parents to others interested in adoption about the events of be(com)ing a family. Parental narratives functioned as counter stories, resisting the prior cultural narrative that positions adoption as second best to biological reproduction. Through the dialogic practices of negating and countering (Baxter, 2011), parental narratives resisted the discourses of biogenetics and adoption as a stigmatized family form to present a view of adoption as worth the effort and adoptive relations as pre-destined. Through the dialogic practice of transformative hybridization (Baxter, 2011), parental narratives constructed a new conception of family that simultaneously honors both biological and nonbiological relations.

Two recent studies (Baxter, Suter, Thomas, & Seurer, in press; Suter, Baxter, Seurer, & Thomas, 2014) took seriously the call to study families in relation to larger societal contexts (Socha & Stamp, 2009) and in so doing demonstrate the discursive work narratives perform at adoptive families' external borders. Both studies examined parental meaning making in relation to the external institutional constraints of the U.S. foster-care system. Baxter et al. (in press) analyzed parental discursive constructions of the meaning of "adoption" in online foster adoption narratives. They identified two discourses, one that constructed adoption as a second-best pathway to parenting and the other that constructed adoption as a source of redemptive care for the foster adoptive child. Both competed to be centered by referencing the alternative discourse simply as a means to refute its legitimacy. A subset of narratives was able to suspend this discursive competition by constructing a hybrid meaning of adoption that positioned meeting child and parent interests as mutually rewarding. Suter et al. (2014) analyzed parental discursive constructions of the meaning of "family" in online foster adoption narratives, finding biogenetic and non-biogenetic discourses both in competition and at play with one another. Whereas some parental stories reified the cultural and foster-care system biogenetic bias towards biologically related families, other narratives resisted by maintaining that family legitimacy is established through enacted behaviors and shared affection rather than through shared genetics. Through the dialogic processes of negating, countering, and entertaining (Baxter, 2011), biogenetic and non-biogenetic discourses competed for the centered rather than marginalized position.

## Narrative as Border Work Process

Whereas recent work on narrating and adoptive families demonstrates a needed extension of Galvin's initial (2006) typology to include the external properties of narratives, a second modification is also warranted. Not only do narratives work within familial interior borders and at their exterior borders, but narratives transcend these borders, working not only within and at, but also across. Narrative as border work captures the work narratives do across internal and external borders.

Studies focusing on the least studied member of the adoption triad—the birthmother—demonstrate narrative border work. As discussed above, adoptions vary in terms of whether they are open or closed. Moreover, with open adoptions these arrangements exist on a continuum of degree of information disclosure and amount of contact (Seigel, 2013). Yet regardless of the specific arrangements, consideration of the birthmother complicates a tidy internal/external distinction given her positionality as both insider and outsider.

An initial study (Wahl, McBride, & Schrodt, 2005) considered how parents pursuing domestic, private adoption discursively construct themselves in online advertisements to prospective birthmothers. Parents' narratives fashioned themselves as worthy parents by characterizing themselves as an idealized suburban family, appealing to property, commodities, and income as indicators of their worthiness. Meanwhile, parental narratives constructed the adoptive child as a commodity to be traded between birthparent and adoptive parent.

Norwood and Baxter (2011) shifted the focus to the genre of Dear Birth Mother (DBM) Letters, which differ from ads in that in DBM letters adoptive parents explicitly address the prospective birthmother. Norwood and Baxter examined the competing discourses (Baxter, 2011) in DBM letters and how the interplay of those discourses works to construct the meaning(s) of adoption. Norwood and Baxter identified four discursive struggles: adoption as gain versus adoption as loss; adoption as desirable parenting versus adoption as last resort; birthmother as good parent versus bad parent; birthmother autonomy versus interdependence. Moreover, Norwood and Baxter found that DBM letters worked to silence accepted cultural discourses surrounding adoption and birthmothers that position adoption as second-best and birthmothers as lesser moms.

Baxter, Scharp, Asbury, Jannusch, and Norwood (2012) explicitly examined the birthmother perspective. Baxter et al.'s dialogic analysis of birthmothers' online adoption narratives found that birthmothers' narratives countered the dominant discourse of intensive mothering, an ideology that positions the mother as a married self-sacrificing primary caretaker who unconditionally loves her child. Birthmothers' narratives resisted this ideology by repositioning themselves as either good mothers or as agentic and self-fulfilling non-mothers.

Baxter, Norwood, Asbury, Jannusch, and Scharp (2012) extended this research by comparing the relative coherence of online adoption narratives from the three members of the adoption triad—adoptive parent, birthparent, adoptee—along the five dimensions of: sequential organization (degree to which the story contains a recognizable plot structure); orientation (degree of contextualizing); causal explanation (degree that reasons for actions are displayed); congruence of affect with content (degree of consistency between emotion and story content); and sense-making (degree of meaning-making display (e.g., moral or conclusion of the story). Overall, when comparing narratives across the triad, Baxter et al. found more incoherence than coherence, which might signal adjustment challenges across the triad. Whereas adoptive parents scored highest on sequential organization, orientation, and casual explanation, birthmothers scored highest on congruence of affect with content.

## Call for Future Research on Narratives

In the face of previous research on the internal properties of narratives that reports a positive association between entrance narratives and the identities of both adoptees and their parents, the results of Kranstuber and Koenig Kellas (2011) are surprising and warrant additional study. These findings are based on survey data from 105 adult adoptees. The study, however, did not distinguish between international or domestic adoptees. It remains possible that the negative identity findings associated with the theme of negative birthparent reconnection is only relevant to domestic adoptees. Story content in an *entrance* narrative about any type of reconnection with a birthparent in an international adoption is highly unlikely. International adoptions are mediated between birth countries and U.S. adoption agencies, not between adoptive parents and birthparents. Indeed, some international adoptees are able to search for and reconnect with their birthparents, but when this occurs it is typically later in an adoptee's life, far removed from the entrance narrative speech event. So, is it that internationally adoptive parents' entrance narratives tend to focus on the positive theme of chosen child and, as such, do indeed promote positive identity development? By contrast, do domestically adoptive parents tend to integrate the negative theme of negative reconnection and, as such, do they inadvertently negatively impact their child's growing sense of self-esteem? These are just two of the questions that future research that distinguishes between storytelling in domestic and international adoptive families might be able to answer.

Research on narrative border work integrates the birthmother, both family insider and outsider, a previously understudied member of the adoptive triad. While a pressing need continues for research on narratives directed toward and emanating from birthmothers, as vital is the need to study narrating and birthfathers. If the move to the online medium has opened up the study of domestic birthmothers, might this medium be successful in eliciting narratives from domestic birthfathers? Given the near cultural invisibility of birthfathers in adoption conversations, it is possible that birthfathers might not feel their narrative is desired or legitimated. As such, birthfathers might be the most resistant member to publicly post their story. Accordingly, future researchers might need to do work to elicit these narratives, providing perhaps a targeted online forum or other means of access. Analysis of birthfather narratives offers tremendous potential to offer insight into heretofore unreported issues. Perhaps the most important of these, when working with Galvin's (2006) constructs, is the issue of how birthfathers make sense of and position both themselves and adoption as a family-building event. Moreover, how might their meaning-making compare to or depart from birthmothers? Future research is needed.

## Conclusion

Knowledge on communicative processes in the adoptive family has increased significantly since the 2003 publication of Galvin's research agenda for communicative research on adoptive family communication and her 2006 articulation of internal and external boundary management processes. Using Galvin's (2006) framework, this chapter both reviewed the extant research on internal and external boundary management in the adoptive family form as well as extended her initial framework to accommodate the border work properties of narratives both within and across familial borders. Indeed, to date, Galvin's 2003 and 2006 publications have stimulated a number of important communicative studies on adoptive family communication. However, as the directions for future research outlined in this chapter indicate, there is still a great need for continuing communication research on the discursive accomplishment of identity in the adoptive family form, both with regard to internal, external, and border work relations, and both within the domestic and international adoptive context.

# CHAPTER TEN

# Discourse Dependence, Relational Ambivalence, and the Social Construction of Stepfamily Relationships

PAUL SCHRODT

*Yeah, 'stepfather,' I didn't know what that meant. I don't think I knew anyone with a 'step.' I probably didn't know how I was supposed to react to him. That was what was scary. I knew I couldn't call him 'Dad.' I didn't know how to deal with it.*

YOUNG ADULT STEPSON
(BRAITHWAITE, OLSON, GOLISH, SOUKUP, & TURMAN, 2001, P. 236)

*When I went into the marriage, I was still trying to recreate a nuclear family ... always trying to control everything, make everything okay. If everything could be okay, then there wouldn't be any conflict ... I don't know what nuclear family is, but those were my delusions.*

MOTHER FROM A STEPFAMILY
(WEAVER & COLEMAN, 2010, P. 318)

*Whenever I talk about them with people it's always my stepdad, my stepmom, stepsister, and now Kendra, I always [say] half-sister, so it's just I always put those terms in there because I do have a biological, real sister and so I guess, I try to help people out because obviously my family's really confusing so I just use it to help people out.*

YOUNG ADULT STEPSON
(KOENIG KELLAS, LECLAIR-UNDERBERG, & NORMAND, 2008, P. 251)

As illustrated by these accounts, the stepfamily is an exemplar of what it means to be a discourse-dependent family. From making sense of the uncertainty and confusion that often characterizes remarriages, to the frustrations associated with re-negotiating family schedules and routines across multiple households, to the ambivalence stepchildren experience as they use various address terms to explain their family relationships to others, stepfamilies involve an array of personal relationships that are created, sustained, and altered through discourse. Broadly defined as a family in which "at least one of the adults has a child (or children) from a previous relationship" (Ganong & Coleman, 2004, p. 2), stepfamilies represent one of the more fascinating and frustrating family forms to study. This is due, in part, to the difficulties associated with defining who is included in a study of stepfamilies. For instance, 2010 census data suggest that 4.2 million stepchildren live in the United States (U.S. Census Bureau, 2012, April). These estimates represent underestimates, however, because the census relies on a household definition that is based on co-residence, one that ignores the intricacies of stepfamily systems and the relationships they include (Teachman & Tedrow, 2008). Correcting for this definitional limitation, as of 2000, stepfamilies represented 13% of all families in the U.S. (Teachman & Tedrow, 2008), and 15% of children under the age of 18 reside in a married stepfamily (Stewart, 2007). More important than the sheer prevalence of stepfamilies, however, are the unique challenges and opportunities that stepfamilies create for the members who live in them, particularly as they make sense of and talk about their stepfamily experiences. Consequently, communication scholars have devoted the better part of two decades investigating the communication processes that characterize stepfamily development (for a recent review, see Braithwaite & Schrodt, 2012).

All families form and negotiate expectations and identities via interaction and are thus discourse dependent (Galvin, 2006). Families that depart from cultural norms (e.g., stepfamilies), however, are even more dependent on interaction to define and legitimate themselves as family as they negotiate boundaries and expectations for those inside and outside of the family. In her treatise on discourse and family identity, Galvin (2006) identified a number of communication behaviors that enable discourse-dependent families to manage both external and internal boundaries. In this chapter, I review what scholars have revealed thus far about the discourse-dependent nature of stepfamily relationships. My primary goal is not to provide a comprehensive and exhaustive review of the stepfamily literature that exists elsewhere (e.g., Braithwaite & Schrodt, 2012; Sweeney, 2010), but to identify the contributions that family scholars have made to our understanding of the *communication challenges and activities* that characterize stepfamily development. Scholars with a central focus on stepfamily communication are advancing research that centers communication as the primary, constitutive social process by which relationships are formed and enacted (cf. Baxter, 2004, 2011). With this in mind, I begin my review by identifying three sources of discourse dependence in stepfamilies that vary in terms of their theoretical and pragmatic scope: developmental changes and adaptation, dialectical tensions, and feeling caught. I then review three sites of discourse dependence in stepfamilies: stepfamily rituals and narratives, stepfamily roles, and coparenting relationships. Although these sources and sites of discourse-dependency are neither mutually exclusive nor exhaustive, they provide a preliminary scheme useful for differentiating the factors that prompt discourse dependency from the domains where such dependency is enacted. Finally, I conclude this chapter by unearthing a common theme that ties both the sources and sites of discourse dependence in stepfamilies together, namely, relational ambivalence.

## Sources of Discourse Dependence in Stepfamilies

Over three decades ago, Cherlin (1978) identified the stepfamily as an incomplete institution, given the lack of relational history among family members, the absence of relational norms to guide communication and relational development, and ambiguous family boundaries:

> Family members, especially those in first marriages, rely on a wide range of habitualized behaviors to assist them in solving the common problems of family life. We take these behavioral patterns for granted until their absence forces us to create solutions on our own. (pp. 636–637)

Indeed, one of the more common misunderstandings about stepfamilies, both for the individuals who live in them and the scholars who study them, is that they should function like first-marriage families. Historically, researchers investigating stepfamily relationships have typically done so using a "deficit-comparison" approach (Ganong & Coleman, 2004). This approach relies on a model of the conventional, nuclear family as the theoretical framework against which the stepfamily is found to be deficient and problematic. In other words, family scholars have had a tendency in the past to examine the behaviors and processes that are problematic in stepfamilies by comparing such processes to those found in first-marriage families. This is oftentimes done at the expense of examining the behaviors that promote growth and resilience in stepfamilies (Afifi, 2008).

Despite the deficit-comparison approach, many stepfamilies adapt to their changing environment and develop new ways of communicating that help facilitate healthy stepfamily relationships. Rather than viewing stepfamilies as incomplete institutions, focusing on stepfamily deficits, and indirectly stigmatizing them as "less than" first-marriage families, Pryor (2008) argued that scholars should instead focus on the sources of strength and resiliency that characterize adaptive and well-functioning stepfamilies. Consequently, family communication scholars have largely abandoned the deficit-comparison approach and expanded our understanding of how stepfamilies are discourse dependent by elucidating how stepfamily members communicate to create, sustain, and alter their family relationships. In what follows, I identify three sources of discourse dependence in stepfamilies, beginning with broader theoretical concerns about stepfamily development and change before focusing more specifically on the dialectical tensions and loyalty binds that animate communication processes in stepfamilies.

## Developmental Changes and Adaptation in Stepfamilies

One of the more pressing concerns for stepfamily members, and the practitioners who work with them, is how best to communicate during times of transition, and adapt to the changes in relationships and routines that occur when a stepfamily forms. As Coleman, Ganong, and Fine (2004) so eloquently put it, trying to answer the question of when a stepfamily begins is like "beginning a novel in the middle of the book" (p. 216). In the early 1990s, family clinicians advanced stage models in an effort to describe the stages that stepfamilies go through as they become a "new" family (e.g., Papernow, 1993). These models tended to depict the process as a unitary model of chronological stages or phases, providing prescriptive suggestions for how stepfamilies "should" develop. As Baxter, Braithwaite, and Nicholson (1999) observed, however, such models oversimplify relational development as a linear process. They neglect the possibility of multiple pathways to development, and they fail to capture the complex and dynamic nature of stepfamily interaction and relational development.

In response to these limitations, and in an effort to approach stepfamilies on their own terms rather than adopt a deficit-comparison approach, Baxter et al. (1999) interviewed stepfamily members about key turning points that produced important changes in "feeling like a family" during the first four years of stepfamily development. Their analysis revealed 15 primary types of turning points that produced either positive or negative changes in feeling like a family, ranging from physical events such as changes in household configurations and holiday/special events, to more interactional turning points such as conflict, spending quality time together, and overcoming family crises, to name a few. Baxter et al. then identified five developmental pathways found in the first four years of stepfamily development: (a) accelerated pathways (i.e., a pattern of quick movement toward 100% feeling like a family), (b) prolonged pathways (i.e., stepfamilies that progressed to higher levels of feeling like a family, although not as quickly as accelerated pathways),

(c) stagnant pathways (i.e., stepfamilies that "never took off"), (d) declining pathways (i.e., stepfamilies that began with a high level of feeling like a family, then declined to zero), and (e) high-amplitude turbulent pathways (i.e., stepfamilies who experienced dramatic up and down shifts in feeling like a family). Each of the developmental pathways differed in terms of the frequency of different types of turning points, as well as in reported levels of feeling like a family. Thus, Baxter et al.'s findings provided an initial glimpse into the various ways in which stepfamilies develop as a function of social interaction.

As a follow-up to Baxter et al.'s (1999) research, Braithwaite, Olson, Golish, Soukup, and Turman (2001) investigated how stepfamily members in the five trajectories interact and adapt during the process of becoming a family. They found that issues of boundary management, solidarity, and adaptation were central to the enactment of the different pathways of becoming a family. For instance, shared custody arrangements and/or extended family relationships often necessitated the negotiation of visitations and schedule changes. With respect to solidarity, most of the participants expressed a sense of optimism about becoming a family and wanting to feel like a family, even though many of them also expressed a sense of loss regarding their "old" family. Most notably, Braithwaite et al.'s results underscored the omnipresent nature of change in stepfamilies. They found that struggles often ensued when family members attempted to replicate traditional family roles and norms, in effect, attempting to live the myth of "instant family." Consequently, Braithwaite et al. concluded that stepfamily roles and identity take time to develop through periods of change as family members communicate in ways that facilitate flexibility and encourage solidarity.

In addition to the developmental pathways that stepfamilies take, researchers have also devoted attention to the various communication processes that facilitate coping and resiliency in stepfamilies. For instance, Tamara Afifi (formerly Golish) has advanced a program of research identifying the communication strengths that differentiate strong stepfamilies from those struggling with the developmental process (Afifi & Keith, 2004; Afifi, 2008; Golish, 2003). First, she identified seven primary challenges facing stepfamilies regardless of their strength: (1) "feeling caught," (2) regulating boundaries with a noncustodial family, (3) ambiguity of parental roles, (4) "traumatic bonding," (5) vying for resources, (6) discrepancies in conflict management styles, and (7) building solidarity as a family unit (Golish, 2003). In order to manage these challenges, however, strong stepfamilies were more likely than struggling stepfamilies to use a variety of communication behaviors, including more everyday talk among family members, greater levels of disclosure and openness, communicating clear rules and boundaries, engaging in family problem solving, spending time together as a family, and promoting a positive image of the noncustodial parent.

To further explore these issues, Afifi and Keith (2004) interviewed 81 stepfamily members to examine the ambiguous loss they experienced as members of postdivorce stepfamilies. "Ambiguous loss refers to a unique kind of loss where a loved one is technically present but functionally absent, creating a lack of closure and clarity" (Afifi & Keith, p. 67). As is often the case with divorce and remarriage, the status of relationships and the emotional connections that family members have with one another can become unclear. Afifi and Keith identified three types of ambiguous loss in postdivorce stepfamilies: (a) the loss of one's previous family form and the traditional nuclear family ideal, (b) the loss of a single-parent bond after the stepparent entered the household, and (c) the loss of intimacy and trust between noncustodial parents (primarily fathers) and their children. They then developed a risk and resiliency model of ambiguous loss in postdivorce stepfamilies that included a number of adaptive responses to the loss, such as continual contact with the noncustodial parent, everyday talk, positive coparental communication, and distancing from societal role prescriptions.

Collectively, then, researchers have identified the various turning points, boundary management processes, and communication strengths that enable stepfamily members to adapt to the changes that ensue during the process of becoming a family. In many ways, this corpus of research underscores the discourse dependency of stepfamily development, as family members depend on a variety of communication behaviors and activities to make sense of, and adjust to, a dynamic and complex family environment. Inherent to the developmental process is the ongoing experience of change and tension. Thus, a second source of discourse dependency in stepfamilies is the dialectical tensions that individuals enact as they (re)construct and (re)negotiate their stepfamily relationships.

## Dialectical Tensions in Stepfamily Relationships

Relational dialectics theory (RDT) views relating as a dialogic process: a communicative process characterized by the intersection of oppositional discourses that constitute a relationship (Baxter, 2004, 2011). From this perspective, scholars can better understand how family members relate to each other by identifying the primary discursive struggles and contradictions that animate their communication. Researchers using this theory focus on the constitutive nature of communication and the joint communicative actions of relating parties as they co-create both the relationship and themselves (Baxter, 2004; Braithwaite, Toller, Daas, Durham, & Jones, 2008). For example, RDT approaches the stepparent-stepchild relationship not from an "either-or" perspective (e.g., more close versus less close or that family members should reveal or not reveal their feelings to each other), but from a dialogic of "both-and," for example, to understand how stepparents and children enact discursive struggles over what children need to know. "From this dialogic standpoint, the stepparent-stepchild relationship is viewed as a system of substantial complexity, characterized by both satisfaction and dissatisfaction, both conflict and cooperation, both closeness and distance, and so forth" (Baxter, Braithwaite, Bryant, & Wagner, 2004, p. 449). Thus, communication scholars have found RDT to be a fruitful theory for understanding the complex, multivocal interactions of stepfamilies, interactions that further illustrate the discourse-dependent nature of stepfamilies.

To date, relational dialectics research on stepfamily relationships has coalesced around identifying the contradictions that animate: (a) marital and parental relationships, (b) stepparent-stepchild relationships, and (c) nonresidential parents' relationships with their children. For instance, Cissna, Cox, and Bochner (1990) conducted the first investigation of stepfamily relationships from a communication perspective, one that revealed a "relationship dialectic" between the voluntary remarriage relationship and the involuntary stepparent relationship. In an effort to manage the tension between their marital and parental roles, Cissna et al. found that remarried couples attempted to accomplish two relational tasks: (1) establish the solidarity of the marriage in the minds of their children, in essence, communicating a "unified front" to the kids, and (2) use the marital solidarity to establish the credibility of the stepparent as an authority in relationship with the stepchildren. As Cissna et al. noted:

> These two relational tasks are interactive and must be negotiated simultaneously. ... As long as the marriage is not accepted, the stepparent will not be accepted. As long as the stepparent is not accepted as a viable parent, the marriage is to some degree invalid in the eyes of the stepchildren. (p. 51)

Consequently, their results provided preliminary insight into the relational tensions that animated the remarried couples' discourse, as couples sought to (re)negotiate their relationships with each other and with their (step)children in an effort to build family solidarity.

In more contemporary research using RDT, Baxter et al. (2004) explored the dialectical tensions that permeated the discourse of stepparent-stepchild relationships and identified three underlying contradictions. First, stepchildren wanted emotional closeness and a relationship with their stepparent. At the same time, their discourse reflected the desire for emotional distance out of feelings of loyalty to their old family, particularly the nonresidential parent. Second, stepchildren wanted communication that reflected openness with the stepparent and, at the same time, they eschewed such open communication. Third, stepchildren's discourse revealed a dialectical tension of desiring parental authority to rest only in the residential parent, yet at the same time, they often wanted discipline from their stepparent as well. Consequently, these competing discourses created tremendous ambivalence in the stepchild-stepparent relationship (Baxter et al., 2004).

Communication scholars have also used RDT to enlighten the relationships and interactions of nonresidential parents and their children. For instance, Braithwaite and Baxter (2006) interviewed young adult stepchildren and identified interrelated discourses of parenting and nonparenting, coupled with openness and closedness. Although it seems reasonable to expect that most children would want a close parent-child relationship with their nonresidential parent (usually a father), the children in their sample were quite ambivalent when their nonresidential father or mother tried to parent them. At times, they perceived that the nonresidential parent did not have the experience or background in the child's daily life to be helpful to them. Moreover, stepchildren's discourse reflected the desire for intimate and open communication with their nonresidential parent, while at the same time they often found openness difficult.

These are but a few of the studies employing RDT to examine the discourses that reflect dialectical tensions in stepfamily relationships. Taken together, they further illustrate the idea that dialectical tensions animate communication processes in stepfamilies and, thus, constitute an important source of discourse dependency in this complex family form. Dialectical tensions are not the only kind of tensions experienced in stepfamilies, however, as researchers have also examined the tension of triangulation in stepfamilies. Thus, a third source of discourse dependency in stepfamilies is the loyalty binds and feelings of being caught between family members that often ensue as a result of remarriage and stepfamily development.

## Feeling Caught in Stepfamilies

Most of the communication research on triangulation and loyalty binds in stepfamilies has relied on the general principles of family systems theory (Minuchin, 1974). For instance, Baxter, Braithwaite, and Bryant (2006) identified four different types of communication triads that young adult stepchildren perceived in their stepfamilies. In the most frequently occurring triad among the four, the *linked triad*, stepchildren wanted their residential parent to function as an intermediary between themselves and the stepparent, fulfilling the roles of transmitter, interpreter, advocate, and/or protector. Likewise, stepchildren who experienced the *outsider triad* reported feeling very close to their residential parent, yet unlike those in the linked triad, they recognized only limited interdependence with the stepparent. In essence, the stepparent was an absent presence—physically present but relationally irrelevant to the stepchild's everyday life. In the *adult-coalition triad*, stepchildren perceived that their relationship with the residential parent had been compromised due to the parent's loyalty to his/her spouse. As a result, communication with the residential parent was characterized by suspicion and a fear that the parent would "side with" the stepparent. The fourth and final triadic communication structure was the *completed triad*. Although this triad included functional, positive relationships among all three members (i.e., stepchild, stepparent, residential parent) and a sense of "real family" with open communication, it appeared least frequently in Baxter et al.'s (2006) data.

Wanting to better understand the triangulation, stress, and coping that often occurs in stepfamily systems, Afifi and Schrodt (Afifi & Schrodt, 2003; Schrodt & Afifi, 2007; Schrodt & Ledbetter, 2007, 2012) conducted a series of studies identifying the antecedents and outcomes associated with "feeling caught" in stepfamilies. Children who feel caught between their parents often feel "put in the middle," "torn," or forced to defend their loyalty to each of their parents (Afifi, 2003; Amato & Afifi, 2006). Such feelings typically emerge when children become privy to their parents' disputes, are the recipients of negative or inappropriate disclosures, and when they become messengers or mediators of information between their parents (Afifi, 2003).

Remarriages occur and are maintained under the watchful eyes of third parties who hold a vested interest in the quality and stability of the stepfamily system, namely children from prior relationships and former spouses (Ganong, Coleman, & Hans, 2006). Consequently, feeling caught typically induces a level of stress that reduces mental health and well-being. For instance, Schrodt and Afifi (2007) found that interparental aggression, demand/withdraw patterns, and negative disclosures all positively predicted young adults' feelings of being caught between their parents, which in turn negatively predicted family satisfaction and mental health. Likewise, Schrodt and Ledbetter (2007, 2012) found that young adult children from divorced families (many of whom were members of stepfamilies) reported higher levels of stress, lower levels of self-esteem, reduced mental health, and lower levels of family satisfaction when they felt caught between their parents. However, some evidence suggests that parents can help buffer their children from the deleterious effects of feeling caught by strengthening their individual relationships with each child and communicating with them in a confirming manner (Schrodt & Ledbetter, 2012).

Of course, family systems theory is not the only lens useful for understanding how discourse activates and animates feelings of being caught in stepfamily relationships. Case in point, Braithwaite et al. (2008) conducted focus-group discussions with young adult stepchildren on what it meant to feel caught between parents. These scholars heard competing discourses wherein children wanted to be centered in the attention of their parents, and at the same time wanted to avoid being caught in the middle, as illustrated by one young adult stepchild who talked about feeling "like a bone between two dogs." Using RDT, Braithwaite et al. argued that stepchildren's desires to be centered were animated by managing two interrelated dialectical tensions of freedom-constraint and openness-closedness. Stepchildren struggled with communication from one or both parents that constrained the possibility of being centered without being caught, for example, when one parent critiqued the other in front of the child. This was tied to the second contradiction of openness-closedness, as children wanted enough information from their parents to be able to know what was going on, and at the same time desired closeness from their parents, not wanting to hear information that made them feel uncomfortable.

In sum, communication scholars have illuminated what it means to feel caught and the degree to which feeling caught is associated with other communication behaviors, though admittedly, the bulk of this research has focused primarily on the loyalty binds that stepchildren experience. When coupled with the developmental changes and dialectical tensions that emerge during the process of becoming a "family," however, feeling caught constitutes a third source of discourse dependency in stepfamily relationships. Of course, these are by no means the only factors that prompt discourse in stepfamily relationships. Nevertheless, they are the factors that have received the lion's share of scholarly attention to date. In the next section of this chapter, I turn my attention to three relational domains, or sites, where discourse dependence is enacted in stepfamilies.

## Sites of Discourse Dependence in Stepfamilies

One of the fundamental questions to emerge from the growing body of scholarship on stepfamilies is whether or not stepfamily relationships are qualitatively distinct from first-marriage (or "traditional, nuclear") family relationships (Schrodt & Braithwaite, 2010). Given the purpose of this anthology and the degree to which stepfamilies defy cultural norms and expectations of what it means to be a family, however, this question is in many ways ironic. At the same time, one of the fundamental conclusions to emerge from this body of work is that many of the challenges facing members of stepfamilies revolve around the roles of different family members and, particularly, the stepparent (Fine, Coleman, & Ganong, 1998; Schrodt, 2006a). Consequently, it should come as no surprise that stepfamily rituals and narratives, stepfamily roles, and coparenting relationships represent important sites of stepfamily life where discourse dependence is enacted.

## Family Rituals and Narratives in Stepfamilies

According to Bright (1990), rituals assist families in "resolving conflicts and resentments, negotiating relational boundaries, and developing new shared meanings about their ongoing life together" (p. 24). Defined as communicative events that pay homage to an object that is sacred (Goffman, 1967), rituals help provide a sense of family identity and typically consist of family celebrations (e.g., Christmas reunions), traditions (e.g., anniversaries), and/or patterned interactions (e.g., children's bedtime routines) (Wolin & Bennett, 1984). Given the developmental changes and adjustments that stepfamily members often experience, researchers have examined rituals as one important communication activity where stepfamily life is (re)created, (re)negotiated, and sustained. For example, Braithwaite, Baxter, and Harper (1998) interviewed 53 members of stepfamilies about their successful and unsuccessful ritual enactments. They identified a dialectical opposition between the "old family" and the "new family," such that the most productive ritual enactments were those that enabled stepfamily members to embrace their new family while still valuing what was important from their old family. In fact, Braithwaite et al. discovered that the adaptive nature of rituals demonstrated the process of adjusting to the loss of the old family and to living in the new stepfamily.

In more recent research, Baxter et al. (2009) explored stepchildren's perceptions of the remarriage ceremony. They identified six types of ritual enactments, five of which celebrated the couple's marriage and just one which paid homage to the new stepfamily as a whole. More importantly, they found three factors that led stepchildren to find the remarriage ceremony empty, that is, not positive or meaningful for them. First, stepchildren described the remarriage as empty if it included a ritual form that was either too traditional (e.g., a white wedding) or not traditional enough. In other words, they expressed a desire for the remarriage ceremony to have some elements of a traditional wedding, but not too many. Second, stepchildren perceived the remarriage as an empty ritual when they themselves found it difficult to legitimate the remarriage. In fact, most of the stepchildren in Baxter et al.'s study were not supportive of the remarriage, which undermined its legitimacy and furthered its "emptiness." Third, the meaningfulness of the remarriage ceremony was contingent upon the type and extent of involvement that stepchildren experienced prior to, and during, the ceremony itself. Baxter et al. found that a fully meaningful remarriage ritual allowed stepchildren to participate in a way that paid homage to their role as a member of the new stepfamily without de-legitimizing their family of origin. Their results further confirmed Braithwaite et al.'s (1998) finding that the most productive ritual enactments were oriented to the management of the dialectical struggles between the "old" and the "new" experienced by family members.

In addition to family rituals, family narratives also enable people to make sense of and cope with difficult family experiences (Trees & Koenig Kellas, 2009), as well as create, reinforce, and communicate individual and family identities (Thompson et al., 2009). For instance, Koenig Kellas and her colleagues (2014) adopted a narrative perspective to examine the content of 80 stepchildren's stories on the beginnings of their stepfamilies. They identified five themes to these stepfamily origin stories: (1) *sudden* stories were those that described the formation of the stepfamily as rushed, spontaneous, and involving very little planning and communication about the couple's courtship and marriage; (2) *dark-sided* stories described stepfamily origins that were overwhelmingly complicated and/or scandalous, typically as a result of gossip and secrecy, conflict, alcoholism, infidelity, drug abuse, physical abuse, and/or money problems; (3) *ambivalent* stories characterized the beginning of the stepfamily as a "mixed bag" of emotions and experiences that were simultaneously positive and negative; (4) *idealized* stories described a relatively easy transition to becoming a stepfamily, as participants talked about their stepfamily origin without a great deal of complication and with references to feeling like a "real family"; and (5) *incremental* stories represented the opposite of sudden stories, as participants described the process of beginning the family as organized, planned, and involving open communication with little to no mystery. Importantly, Koenig Kellas and her associates reported significant differences in family satisfaction based on the type of origin stories that were told, such that participants who told idealized stories were more satisfied with their stepfamilies than those who told sudden or dark-sided stories.

Taken together, family rituals and narratives represent key communication activities that enable stepfamily members to create, negotiate, and sustain family identity. Embedded within each of these activities, however, are the roles that family members perform as they pay homage to their stepfamily relationships and make sense of their stepfamily experiences.

## Roles and Labels in Stepfamily Relationships

Although the developmental transition that occurs in new stepfamilies represents a period of change for all family members, perhaps the most important and challenging task during the transition involves negotiating the role of the stepparent (Fine et al., 1998; Ganong, Coleman, Fine, & Martin, 1999; Schrodt, 2006a; Schrodt, Soliz, & Braithwaite, 2008). As Ganong and Coleman (2004) noted, the stepparent-stepchild relationship is typically considered to be the most challenging and stressful relationship in stepfamilies. Contrary to other personal relationships that are freely chosen by relational partners, step-relationships are often involuntary, leaving very little motivation for stepchildren and stepparents to develop close bonds (Ganong et al., 1999).

Some scholars contend that the stepparent should do no more than try to build a friendship with the stepchild(ren), whereas others (e.g., Hetherington, 1999) have found that the long-term benefits of having the stepparent act as a parent outweigh the short-term benefits of having the stepparent simply act as a friend. In their research, Fine et al. (1998) found different perceptions of the stepparent role between adults and children in the stepfamily system. Children were more likely than parents or stepparents to indicate that they preferred the stepparent to act as a friend rather than as a parental figure. However, adults were generally more likely to discuss the stepparent role with each other than they were to discuss this role with their stepchildren. This, in turn, led to little consistency in perceptions of parenting behaviors (i.e., warmth and control behaviors) for stepparents among family members, an unfortunate consequence given that consistency in perceptions of the stepparent role was positively associated with stepfamily members' interpersonal adjustment (Fine et al., 1998).

Schrodt (2006a) recently argued that viewing the stepparent relationship in terms of the positive regard that stepparents establish with their stepchildren, the parental authority that stepchildren grant their stepparents (if at all), and the degree to which stepparents and stepchildren discuss their feelings and their relationships with each other may be more useful in the long run than trying to fit the stepparent into some pre-existing role or label, such as "parent" or "friend." Likewise, researchers have identified a form of role ambivalence that often occurs for stepparents, one that centers around issues of biological "ownness" (i.e., the entitlements and responsibilities associated with biological parent-child relationships in families), and the absence of a societal script for how to be a good "stepparent" (Schrodt, 2006a). This ambivalence often varies as a function of whether or not the stepparent is a stepmother or a stepfather. For example, Schmeeckle (2007) found that stepmothers often act as meaningful gatekeepers to their husband's biological children, although they are still seen by stepchildren as investing more energy into their relationships with their own biological children. In fact, one of the most common pop culture references to stepfamilies is the "wicked stepmother" myth, a "stigma that places a significant strain on a stepmother's self-esteem and role enactment" (Christian, 2005, p. 28). As a result of such stigmatization, stepmothers often face greater challenges in developing satisfying stepparent-stepchild bonds than stepfathers, with such challenges emerging as particularly salient for nonresidential stepmothers (Weaver & Coleman, 2010). As Schrodt (2008) reported, stepchildren who identified a stepmother as their primary stepparent (i.e., the stepparent they either lived with the longest or had known the longest) reported more stepfamily dissension and avoidance, and less stepfamily involvement, expressiveness, and flexibility than stepchildren who identified a stepfather as their primary stepparent.

Although the stepparent role has received the lion's share of scholarly attention, the issue of whether or not the stepparent should function as a "parent" is not the only issue facing stepfamily members. (Non)residential parents and (step)children must also navigate their own role uncertainties, ambiguities, and ambivalence during the process of becoming a stepfamily. For instance, Coleman, Fine, Ganong, Downs, and Pauk (2001) found that residential parents (e.g., residential mothers) often wrestle with a "guard and protect" ideology with their new spouse or partner, in which the biological parent errs on the side of guarding and protecting their children's interests in any disputes that may arise with the stepparent. Likewise, nonresidential parents often experience tension and ambivalence as they negotiate access and coordinate visitations with their ex-spouses and their ex-spouses' new partners (i.e., the stepparents). As Braithwaite and Baxter (2006) found, stepchildren experience tremendous ambivalence and contradictions in relationships with their nonresidential parents. Such tensions and contradictions may constitute a primary source of the distancing that often occurs between nonresidential parents and their children in stepfamilies, as stepchildren attempt to reconcile loyalty divides (cf. Amato & Afifi, 2006).

Finally, (step)children may also be navigating tremendous role ambiguity and ambivalence in their relationships with other members of the family system, including stepparents, nonresidential parents, and/or stepsiblings. For instance, Ganong, Coleman, and Jamison (2011) recently interviewed emerging adult stepchildren about their relationship-building and maintaining behaviors with their stepparents. They developed a grounded theory of stepchild-stepparent relationship development that includes six different trajectories: (a) accepting as a parent, (b) liking from the start, (c) accepting with ambivalence, (d) changing trajectory, (e) rejecting, and (f) coexisting. Not only do their results lend further evidence to the ambivalence that often characterizes stepfamily relationships (cf. Schrodt & Braithwaite, 2010), but they further illustrate how communication and structural features of stepfamilies work in concert to shape the relational identities of stepchildren and stepparents.

A common, yet taken for granted, symbolic activity that holds tremendous implications for the individual and relational identities of stepfamily members is the use of address terms. Koenig Kellas, LeClair-Underberg, and Normand (2008) found that nearly two-thirds of the stepchildren in their sample varied the terms of address they used to identify their stepfamily members depending on context, audience, and/or relationship. Whether using *formal* address terms that defined the person in reference to a third party (e.g., "my dad's wife"), *familiar* terms that included stepparents' first names or included the word "step" in reference to the parent or sibling, or *familial* terms that dropped the prefix "step" (e.g., using "mom" instead of "stepmom"), stepchildren engaged in both internal and external code-switching. Such code-switching functioned to communicate solidarity at times, to communicate separateness at other times, and to manage the balance of stepfamily life. Intriguingly, Koenig Kellas and her colleagues found communicative ambivalence in stepchildren's use of address terms, as address terms were both important and unimportant; sometimes they mattered and sometimes they didn't.

In general, then, researchers have examined the role ambiguities and ambivalence that characterize stepfamily relationships, further illustrating the various ways in which family members are dependent upon discourse to label, negotiate, and enact their roles within the stepfamily system. That said, role expectations and performances have meaning only within the context of relationships, and thus, the final section of this chapter briefly reviews the discourse-dependent nature of coparenting relationships in stepfamilies.

## Coparenting Relationships in Stepfamilies

In her most recent treatise on communication in stepfamilies, Afifi (2008) argued that "the stepfamily consists of a web of relationships, with communication serving as the means through which family members relate to each other" (p. 312). Although the stepfamily is not unique in that other family forms are also comprised of a web of relationships, the relationships that comprise the stepfamily system may vary more so as a function of the unique challenges facing its members and the unique communication patterns that emerge as a result. Among a myriad of stepfamily relationships that depend largely upon social interaction, perhaps no other relationship is simultaneously more rewarding, more challenging, and more critical to the successful adaptation of the stepfamily system than the coparenting relationship. A coparenting relationship exists "when at least two individuals are expected by mutual agreement or societal norms to have conjoint responsibility for a particular child's well-being" (Van Egeren & Hawkins, 2004, p. 166). Coparental communication, in turn, refers not to the individual attempts of a parent to guide and direct the behaviors and activities of his or her child, but to the interaction patterns that emerge as one coparent supports and/or undermines the parenting attempts of his or her partner. Coparenting in stepfamilies presents its own unique set of challenges given that the coparental relationship between parents and their new partners co-occurs and even, at times, precedes the development of the remarried relationship.

Recently, Schrodt, Braithwaite, and their colleagues conducted a series of investigations examining coparenting relationships in stepfamilies. In one report (Braithwaite, McBride, & Schrodt, 2003), they used diaries to record the frequency and content of interactions among coparents over a typical two-week period. Not surprisingly, they found that most of the interactions that occurred between ex-spouses and between parents and their ex-spouse's new partner (i.e., the stepparent) were very brief, very business-like, and focused almost exclusively on the welfare of the children.

In a follow-up study using the same sample, Schrodt, Baxter, McBride, Braithwaite, and Fine (2006) employed structuration theory (Giddens, 1984) to examine the various ways in which coparents, through their interpersonal communication patterns, negotiated the praxis of their coparenting relationships in the "shadows" of the legal divorce decree. Specifically, these researchers identified two structures of signification, the first of which involved framing the decree as a legal document that dictated the rights and responsibilities of parenting (e.g., child access and financial issues), and the second of which involved framing the decree as a negotiating guide against which coparents employed more informal coparental decision-making processes. Throughout their discourse, Schrodt et al.'s participants evidenced a sense of ambivalence as they discussed how both of these structures of signification (i.e., decree as legal contract vs. decree as guide) enabled and constrained their coparenting relationships with the other adults in the stepfamily system. For example, several coparents discussed how the decree provided a guide for informal coparenting decisions and cooperation unless (or until) one of the parents perceived that the other parent was taking advantage of their goodwill, at which point the decree was invoked as a more formal, legal resolution to their parenting disputes. Thus, several coparents reported mixed emotions about the divorce decree as their coparenting communication patterns oscillated back and forth between the decree as "guide" and the decree as "legal contract."

One limitation to these initial investigations was their reliance upon individual parents as the unit of analysis. Responding to this limitation, Schrodt and Braithwaite (2011) surveyed coparenting dyads and found that residential parents' and stepparents' coparental communication quality (i.e., supportive and non-hostile) positively predicted their own (but not their partners') satisfaction and mental health. Couples' relational satisfaction, in turn, mediated the effects of parents' and stepparents' supportive coparental communication on their own mental health symptoms. In fact, after controlling for relational satisfaction, a suppressor effect emerged whereby parents' coparental communication with their partners produced an *inverse*, partner effect on stepparents' mental health. In one sense, being called upon to act as a parent may help a residential stepparent feel more like a member of the family, and yet in a completely different sense, such reliance on the stepparent in raising the (step)children may foster a heightened sense of stress and ambivalence as he or she navigates role uncertainties and expectations.

Not only must residential parents and stepparents navigate the challenges associated with coparenting children, but they often must do so under the watchful eyes of the nonresidential parent (Ganong, Coleman, & Hans, 2006). Hence, Schrodt (2010) examined couples' coparental communication with nonresidential parents as a predictor of residential parents' and stepparents' satisfaction and mental health. His results revealed that stepparents' coparental communication (i.e., supportive and cooperative) with nonresidential parents positively predicted their satisfaction with their current partners (i.e., with residential parents). Likewise, stepparents' coparental communication with nonresidential parents reduced their own mental health symptoms, but *positively* predicted their partner's mental health symptoms (i.e., indicating poorer mental health for residential parents). These results highlight the stress and ambivalence that residential parents might experience as they manage the tensions associated with having their current relational partner coparent with their ex-spouse.

Having discovered the ambivalence that both residential parents and stepparents feel as they coparent together, as well as with the nonresidential parent, Schrodt, Miller, and Braithwaite (2011) tested the effects of supportive and antagonistic coparental communication on ex-spouses' relational satisfaction in stepfamilies. Consistent with their first two reports, Schrodt and his associates found that ex-spouses' supportive and antagonistic coparental communication predicted their own (but not their ex-spouse's) relational satisfaction. More importantly, nonresidential parents' supportive and antagonistic coparental communication with the residential stepparent predicted their own satisfaction with their ex-spouse, as well as their ex-spouses' satisfaction with them. In essence, their findings further demonstrate the interdependence of coparenting relationships in stepfamilies, as supportive coparental communication between nonresidential parents and their ex-spouse's new partner (i.e., the stepparent) predicted meaningful variance in relational satisfaction for both ex-spouses.

Finally, Schrodt (2011) investigated coparental communication and relational satisfaction in residential stepparent/nonresidential parent dyads. He found that although some stepparents and nonresidential parents may avoid contact altogether when it comes to the children, those who do communicate with each other in ways that are understanding and supportive of each other's parenting attempts are likely to enhance the satisfaction that both adults feel in their coparenting relationship. More importantly, Schrodt discovered that nonresidential parents' coparental communication with their ex-spouses (i.e., with residential parents) predicted meaningful variance in stepparents' satisfaction with the nonresidential parent. To the extent that stepparents and nonresidential parents learn to cooperate with each other and work together with the residential parent in childrearing activities, such efforts may ease the stress and anxiety that comes from enacting a new role with a former (or current) partner's new (or former) partner.

Taken together, these investigations illustrate the discourse-dependent nature of coparental relationships in stepfamilies, as well as the interdependence that exists among various adult dyads within the stepfamily system.

## A Discourse-Dependent Conclusion

In their recent review of stepfamily research, Schrodt and Braithwaite (2010) argued that one of the defining characteristics that distinguishes stepfamilies from other family forms is the (dys)functional ambivalence inherent to stepfamily life. Consistent with their claim, each body of research reviewed within this chapter underscores the ambivalence that stepfamily members experience as they label, explain, legitimize, and defend their stepfamily relationships to those outside of the family, as well as name, discuss, narrate, and ritualize their relationships within the family. From the developmental changes and stress that stepfamily members cope with, to the discourses that animate dialectical tensions and feelings of being caught, to the various rituals, narratives, roles, and relationships where their discourse constructs their individual and familial identities, a recurring theme of ambivalence emerges. Ironically, each manifestation of ambivalence signals an opportunity for stepfamily members to craft their own unique relationships independent of what society deems as normal or functional. In other words, the relational ambivalence that distinguishes the stepfamily from other family forms is inherently discourse dependent. It can contribute to the fluidity and creativity of stepfamily members to create something unique, relationships that often lead different stepfamilies down different developmental pathways (e.g., Baxter et al., 1999; Schrodt, 2006b). This view of stepfamilies encourages researchers and practitioners to view stepfamilies in their own right, rather than as a "lesser cousin" to the traditional nuclear family form. In essence, such a move recognizes that stepfamilies possess both the opportunity and the burden that other discourse-dependent families have (Galvin, 2006), namely that they must create and legitimate their identity, roles, and expectations via family interaction.

# CHAPTER ELEVEN

# "He became like my other son"

## Discursively Constructing Voluntary Kin

DAWN O. BRAITHWAITE AND REBECCA DIVERNIERO

In this chapter we center our attention on voluntary (fictive, chosen) kin, "those persons perceived to be family, but who are not related by blood or law" (Braithwaite, Bach, Baxter et al., 2010, p. 390). These are relationships that are self-identified by the actors themselves and meet emotional and/or instrumental (practical) needs (Allen, Blieszner, & Roberto, 2011). Most of the families represented in this current volume are partially established through claims to biology or law. For example, stepfamilies formed through marriage contain some combination of biological and legal relationships, in addition to nonbiological relationships. Of all of the family types included in this present volume, we would argue that voluntary kinship is perhaps the "poster child" for discourse-dependent families, in that this kinship form is most often created outside of biology and law and thus faces the greatest discursive burden in its absence of ready access to claims of biological or legal ties.

The voluntary-kin family form can be particularly challenging as relational parties seek to legitimate themselves as real and worthy of acceptance. Scholars are working to illuminate the constitutive role of communication in voluntary-kin relationships, as "How people 'talk' about their everyday lives—how they constitute their worlds by language in interaction—reveals how they construct family" (Allen et al., 2011, p. 1157). Studying how members of voluntary-kin relationships communicate and enact this family form in everyday life presents researchers with the opportunity to understand this important family form. In this essay we discuss the boundaries of voluntary kin as discourse-dependent family relationships and explore challenges to understanding and legitimizing this family form. We end by posing still unanswered questions for researchers and voluntary kin members as they work to better understand and enact these relationships.

## Boundaries of Voluntary Kin

The study of voluntary kin is not new to family scholars. Scholars have long studied what are called "fictive families" across cultures and contexts. For example, Gallagher and Gerstel (1993) called for studies of "friend keeping" in order to examine how friendships might provide support and, in some cases, substitute for blood or legal kin in an increasingly mobile culture where people do not live near their family of origin. Nelson (2014) analyzed over 600 articles that referenced fictive kinship. Conceived broadly, most voluntary-kin relationships develop and exist outside of biology and law, yet these relationships function as family for those involved (Braithwaite, Bach, Baxter et al., 2010; Coontz, 1999a; Nelson, 2014).

What we are labeling "voluntary kin" has been called by various names and has an array of definitions and boundaries, leading to increased conceptual confusion over what these families entail (Nelson, 2014). The most common label has been fictive kin (e.g., Allen et al., 2011; Chatters, Taylor & Jayakody, 1994; Ebaugh & Curry, 2000; Ibsen & Klobus, 1972; Karner, 1998; Mac Rae, 1992; Muraco, 2006; Tierney & Venegas, 2006). Other labels include chosen kin (Johnson, 2000; Weston, 1991), intentional families or kin (e.g., Muraco, 2006; Nelson, 2014), self-ascribed kin (Galvin, 2006), informal kin (Galvin, 2006), urban tribes (Watters, 2003), kin-keepers or friend-keepers (Gallagher & Gerstel, 1993; Leach & Braithwaite, 1996), othermothers (Collins, 2000), and ritual kin (Ebaugh & Curry, 2000).

As Braithwaite, Bach, Baxter, and colleagues (2010) examined the literature they noticed that voluntary kin were most often defined by what they were not, rather than what they were. For instance, Floyd and Morman (2006) defined them as "family-like relationships that are neither genetically nor legally bound" (xii), and Galvin (2006) discussed them as families formed without biological and legal ties. In our own research we have been seeking to better understand what these self-identified kin are to one another and how, through talk, they legitimize and navigate what being family means to them. Nelson (2013) attempted to summarize what different scholars' approaches have in common: "With whatever population they are used, all of these terms basically refer to similar phenomena—instances when an individual designates some non-kin individual (or individuals) in their social worlds as being 'like' family or, even occasionally, as being 'family'" (p. 260).

The title of this chapter suggests a preference for referring to these relationships as "voluntary kin." For us, the label "fictive kin," which is most common in the literature, seems to connote that the relationship is not real (Weston, 1991). In fact, when Braithwaite, Bach, Baxter, and colleagues (2010) started interviewing people who self-identified as having fictive kin, the informants reacted to the term "fictive" very negatively. Thus we searched for a label that accurately identified the characteristics of these families while also capturing the emotional connections those who experienced them felt. We considered using Weston's (1991) label of "chosen kin"; however, this term is most often used to describe LGBT relationships specifically, and we wanted to account for these relationships as broadly as possible. We noted that the term "chosen" also "positions members of these alternative families as objects of selection" (Braithwaite, Bach, Baxter et al., 2010, p. 390), which did not suit our purposes either. In the end, we adopted the label "voluntary kin" to capture the breadth of these family relationships and to stress our perspective that these relationships are created and enacted in interaction. Although this term works well for our purposes, Nelson (2014) cautioned against thinking that one term fits all voluntary families and stressed the negative discursive consequences of doing so. These relationships appear in a wide variety of cultural and structural contexts, and scholars need to understand and take this into account.

As we attempt to understand the discursive legitimation and defense of voluntary kin, four challenges come to light that we will discuss: (a) developing and legitimizing voluntary kin, (b) labeling voluntary kin, (c) understanding cultural contexts of voluntary kin, and (d) navigating challenges to voluntary-kin relationships.

## Developing and Legitimizing Voluntary Kin

As we consider how voluntary kin discursively create, understand and defend their relationships, it is useful to understand different types of voluntary-kin relationships. Scholars have generated typologies of voluntary-kin relationships to understand better how these families are defined and function. For example, Nelson's (2013) excellent analysis of the broad landscape of available research resulted in her developing a "descriptive typology" (p. 261) of three broad categories of fictive kin. First, situational kin evolve from different sets of circumstances in which the blood or legal family is physically or otherwise absent or irrelevant; for instance, when the blood and legal family lives far away or do not or cannot provide caregiving in later life. Second, ritual kin involve cultural or customary practices, for example, naming someone as a godparent for a child. Third, intentional kin are those persons who are thought of and treated as family. Nelson (2013) stressed her preference for the *intentional kin* term over *voluntary* or *chosen* because she wanted to highlight that these relationships happen by choice over chance and, at some point in time, do not feel voluntary, an issue we will return to later in this chapter.

Braithwaite, Bach, Baxter et al. (2010) created a typology of voluntary kin in interviews with 110 persons who self-identified as having these relationships in their lives. We will discuss this typology in some detail, as the researchers generated the categories from participant discursive constructions of these families and descriptions of how each type is legitimated through communication. From their analysis of the perspectives of the voluntary-kin member themselves, the researchers identified four types of voluntary-kin relationships: (a) substitute kin, (b) supplemental kin, (c) convenience kin, and (d) extended kin, all expanded in the remainder of this section. Two issues stood out in the talk of these voluntary kin. First, three of the four types (substitute, supplemental, convenience) formed due to perceived deficits in the biological or legal family (what we'll call the *family of origin*). Second, the self-ascribed voluntary kin legitimated this family using the terminology for traditional families, such as "she is like a mother to me."

In the first type, substitute kin, voluntary kin stood in for or replaced the biological or legal family of origin in situations of death or complete estrangement (Braithwaite, Bach, Baxter et al., 2010). One woman described how the best friend of her biological son stayed in her life and "became just like my other son" after her biological son passed away. She asked this young man if she would lose him, too, now that his friend (her son) had died. He responded, "Mom I would never let you lose two sons that way—I am your son forever" (pp. 396–397). For others, voluntary kin replaced family of origin when the member was estranged from his or her family, for instance, following coming-out disclosures by LGBT individuals. LaSala (2000) also described this from clinical cases of lesbians and gay men who were cut off by their family of origin. One young man Braithwaite and her colleagues interviewed had come out as gay and was subsequently cut off by his family. He formed a non-romantic voluntary-kin relationship with a man he referred to as his brother and this took the place of the estranged family. Braithwaite and colleagues (2010) pointed out that the substitute voluntary-kin relationship was created and legitimized from a perceived deficiency in the family of origin. In the case of the death of a family member, the deficiency was in the form of absence, and in other cases, the family of origin or the individuals themselves rejected the relationship. Interestingly, complete estrangement, or no contact with the family or origin, was relatively rare, and only a handful of voluntary kin families represented in the program of research by Braithwaite and colleagues (Braithwaite, Bach, Baxter et al. 2010; Braithwaite, Bach, Wilder, Kranstuber, & Sato Mumm, 2010) have resulted from no contact whatsoever with the family of origin.

In the second type, supplemental kin, voluntary family members functioned as an addition to the family of origin, fulfilling needs unmet by the family of origin or stepping in when there was a geographic distance. This was the voluntary family type that appeared most in the interviews (Braithwaite, Bach, Baxter et al., 2010), and in a second data collection that was coded to this typology, supplemental kin represented 69% of the voluntary-kin relationships (Braithwaite, Bach, Wilder et al., 2010). In one supplemental family example, the informant explained, "I hate to say this but I'm not always as happy around my immediate family. I think there's more pressure to act and talk and think in a certain way and with Dan I feel more comfortable and I can be myself" (Braithwaite, Bach, Baxter et al., 2010, p. 398). In the case of geographic distance, a woman in her 60s was the self-appointed "grandfriend" (a term she created) of some children whose biological grandparents lived far away. In the supplemental family type, the voluntary family grew out of needs that were unmet in the family of origin due to differing values, roles that were underperformed, or physical distances that made meaningful contact impossible.

In the third type, convenience kin, the family relationships existed around a specific time period (e.g., going through drug rehabilitation together) or context (e.g., membership on a team). The voluntary kin were described as family-like relationships with fraternity brothers during the college years or a workplace as a second family. Braithwaite, Bach, Baxter, and colleagues (2010) noted that it was often challenging to understand how these convenience kin were different than close friendships that occur at a certain stage of life. The researchers also noted that informants had limited expectations for these relationships, and most indicated they counted on their family of origin to meet important instrumental needs. Yet, like the substitute and supplemental kin, convenience kin were legitimated on deficits in the family of origin, either because of unmet emotional needs, physical absence, or the absence of a particular shared experience the informant had with the convenience kin, such as the experience of going through rehabilitation.

The fourth type, extended kin, was different in that it was not constituted on a deficit of the family of origin; this voluntary kin type was created from a coming together of both biological or legal family members with non-related others (Braithwaite, Bach, Baxter et al., 2010). In one example a voluntary kin member described the family that was created with close neighbors who had lived near each other for many years:

Our parents were really close...my earliest memories are when her mom would... babysit me and I would always, I mean I always just assumed Ann was my sister. I mean I don't remember how the relationship developed, but she's been in my life as long as I can remember. Like her brother, I'm close with too, my mom is his godmother, so we're all kind of like intertwined. (p. 402)

Although extended voluntary kin did not form due to a deficit in the family of origin as in the other three types, they were still legitimated through using terminology from the traditional family as voluntary family members were added on to the family of origin.

In all four of these voluntary kin types, the members are challenged to communicatively construct and validate the voluntary family both internally within the relationship and externally to others, including their family of origin. Although voluntary kin are a departure from families formed via biology or law, members still invoke the traditional family model and use traditional family labels as they create, understand, and legitimize this new family form. As Nelson (2014) noted, "Whereas kin relationships produced through blood, marriage, adoption or the state—'real' kin—are, de facto, both significant and meaningful, other relationships have to *prove* that they are, indeed, both significant and meaningful" (p. 216). Braithwaite and her colleagues (Braithwaite, Bach, Baxter et al., 2010; Braithwaite, Bach, Wilder et al., 2010) found that members of voluntary families regularly turned to comparisons with the traditional family to accomplish this proof, as they conceptualized the voluntary kin in relation to roles they would enact in their family of origin. Voluntary-kin members are aided in this effort, as in most instances these families are created due to perceived deficits in the family of origin. In essence, the voluntary kin are stepping into existing roles that are missing or underperformed. In the case of the extended kin type, voluntary kin members reframe the traditional family boundary to include the voluntary kin as part of the family of origin.

Even though members of voluntary-kin relationships identify and discursively legitimize these voluntary-kin relations as family relationships, we need to ask how they understand and demarcate the boundaries of these relationships. What about these relationships render them understandable as family versus close friendships? Rawlins (1992) described close adult friendships that compensate for the absence or loss of close family, yet for voluntary kin there is more to it than that, evident from participants' explanations of their relationships. Braithwaite, Bach, Baxter, and colleagues (2010) attempted to garner descriptions of how participants perceived voluntary kin to be different than close or best friends, but participants expressed difficulty establishing a clear boundary between these relationship types. Participants clearly regarded the people they identified as "family," but most often they had not articulated how these relationships were different from friendship; they "just are family." As a follow-up, Braithwaite, Bach, Wilder, and colleagues (2010) again posed this question to voluntary kin members and asked them to explain how these relationships were different than best or close friends. The researchers concluded that voluntary kin considered these persons to be family because (a) they were relationships that persisted over time, (b) they represented a high level of closeness, (c) they had expectations of self and other that surpassed what they expected of close friends. This can be seen in examples such as, "Umm, because she is too special for a best friend. I feel like she is more than that now. I mean, she has been more than that for a while," and "I know that if I needed a kidney, she'd give me one" (Braithwaite, Bach, Wilder et al., 2010, p. 6). One interviewee in the Braithwaite, Bach, Wilder et al. (2010) study explained:

> I don't even know when I started calling her my family, but when I talk about her [to others], I call her my best friend. And Arleen and I consider each other as something different, so, I mean, I would talk about my other best friends, and she would talk about her best friend, and we would know it has nothing to do with us, because we just know we are different. I have considered her as my sister for a very long time. I mean, I don't have a sister... my brother and I don't get along....It's hard to explain, but I tell people that if I don't get along with my real family, I want the family I choose. (p. 5)

The perception of voluntary kin as family fits postmodern definitions of "family" (Stacey, 1999) that stretch the boundaries of family to include bonds of affection and long-term commitment along with biology or law (e.g., Baxter & Braithwaite, 2006b; Young, 1997). In essence, members of these families "define themselves for themselves with respect to their family identity as they interact with outsiders and even with one another" (Galvin & Braithwaite, 2014, p. 103).

This concept of family evolved from friendship also appeared in a study by Allen et al. (2011), wherein they interviewed women and men over the age of 55 who indicated they had fictive kin. Among the types of kin identified in the study, Allen and colleagues noted what they called *nonkin conversion*, relationships that were created out of close friendships which "enriched affective bonds and extended the utility of their kin network" (p. 1159). Because these researchers did not limit the data collection to nonfamily members, they were able to describe additional categories of fictive kin types that involved altering the status and expectations of relatives. They created the label *kin promotion* to describe a family wherein a more distant relative was promoted to a more primary one after a significant life change such as a death in the family, divorce, or an illness (p. 1164) as they would "adapt the normative ideology of kinship as a practical response to family change" (p. 1172). For example, participants might come to redefine and regard a distant cousin like a brother. In other conditions that the researchers labeled as *kin exchange*, the person would move kin from one place in the generational structure of the family to another, for example, coming to redefine and regard a sister as fulfilling a mother role in their lives.

One question we have wrestled with is how to understand the role of convenience kin, those considered to be family at a particular life stage or place, such as a therapy group or members of a sorority. Although convenience kin have been labeled "family" from the native's point of view, they seem to fall outside traditional family definitions in that these relationships do not persist over long periods of time or anticipate a future, at least in the same form. Thus, while one could stay friends with convenience kin, the characteristics that resulted in labeling the other(s) family tend not to persist over time. If they do persist, we would consider them another type of voluntary family, in most cases, as supplemental kin. Thus a roommate identified as family for a period of time would, if the perceived family relationship persisted, become supplemental kin. To examine the temporality of convenience kin, Braithwaite, Bach, Wilder, and colleagues (2010) interviewed 52 self-identified voluntary kin who were past emerging adulthood (over the age of 25) and coded each interview as representing one of the four voluntary kin types discussed above. In this particular set of informants at least, the convenience kin type dropped out completely. From this finding, we suspect that convenience kin might often be comprised of relationships in emerging adult stages of life, although we recognize that exceptions do occur, for example, being part of workplace or support group contexts that feel like family. We also suspect that when these relationships persist they become supplemental kin. These are issues researchers need to examine more fully.

No matter which type of voluntary kin is identified, what they all have in common is that they are created and legitimized on the back of conventional family models that are accepted as authentic. Nelson (2014) explained, "So even as research on fictive kin …says yes, these *are* important relationships, the language reinforces the naturalness, the rock-solid reality, the essential nature of 'real' kinship. *It cannot do otherwise*" (p. 216). The implication here is that voluntary families are always compared to "real family" leaving voluntary kin, like other discourse-dependent families, with the discursive burden of establishing their existence and value (Galvin, 2006).

## Labeling Voluntary Kin

A second discursive task voluntary kin face is how to label and talk about these relationships for self and others. Galvin (2006) argued that the process of labeling in discourse-dependent families serves to establish expectations for the relationship, helping the family and relevant outsiders develop an understanding of the relational functions and emotional ties for those individuals. One important aspect of understanding voluntary-kin relationships is the discursive representations of these relationships as reflected in their choice and use of address terms. Address terms are barometers of relational life that give insight to the existence and quality of relationships (Koenig Kellas, LeClair-Underberg, & Normand, 2008). Researchers who have interviewed voluntary kin about their experiences heard address terms used that most often reflected traditional family roles such as sister, grandparent, or parent (Allen et al., 2011; Braithwaite, Bach, Wilder et al., 2010). Braithwaite, Bach, Wilder et al. (2010) found that the address terms of voluntary kin members were most often expressed in qualified language or similes, for example, labeling the other as "like family to me," "like an older brother," or "as an older sister type." Allen et al. (2011) highlighted another discursive move was to use a modifier of a family-of-origin term, such as including "step" as a modifier; for example, a young female neighbor who is perceived to be family might be termed a "stepdaughter" rather than a daughter even in the absence of what we normally think of as a step-family structure (see Chapter Ten).

In all of the cases we have encountered in our data, the address terms reflect traditional gender and generational roles. Thus a woman would label a female voluntary kin around her age as a sister, and an older female as a mother, aunt, or grandmother, bringing with them some of the same behavioral expectations we would have of these roles in a traditional family structure, such as expecting nurturing from a voluntary mother or aunt or expecting to provide caregiving to an elderly man thought of as "like a grandfather." These linguistic moves reflect the creation and legitimation of voluntary relationships both internally to the voluntary kin and externally to the broader social network, including family of origin, yet at the same time, the modifiers of "like a sister" demarcate them as different than the family of origin.

Discourse-dependent families have the discursive task of internal and external boundary management (Galvin, 2006; Galvin & Braithwaite, 2014). On an internal level, they have the task of creating and perpetuating family identity among the family members themselves. To this end, using traditional family address terms might help voluntary-kin members understand and internalize the status of their relationships with one another. For instance, in an interview for the Braithwaite, Bach, Wilder et al. (2010) study, an informant explained that it was not until she heard herself saying the family address term out loud that she herself came to the realization that her relationship with a married couple, Vance and Karen, was one of family:

> We [informant and sister] went on a little weekend vacation with my Dad and with Vance. And we, we just referred to them as, you know, "I'm going with our two dads," and that's when it sort of struck me that we have a really strong relationship with, with Vance and Karen. (p. 13)

On an external level, communicating using family address terms is a way that voluntary kin announce, reflect, and legitimize the relationship to others (Gubrium

& Holstein (1990). However, Braithwaite, Bach, Baxter, and colleagues (2010) found that some voluntary kin chose to avoid the family term if it caused undue confusion or discomfort, especially for their family of origin. In this instance, some created and used a family-like label (e.g., "grandfriend") or added a modifier (e.g., "my pseudo-mom") to signify the relationship as an addition to, but not replacement of, the family of origin. The latter speaks to the complex and potentially challenging relationship between the voluntary and biological/legal family that we will discuss later in this chapter.

# Understanding the Diversity of Voluntary Kin

The diversity of voluntary-kin family relationships presents a third challenge associated with understanding the complexity of this family type. Voluntary-kin relationships exist across a wide variety of social groups: among immigrants (e.g., Chatters et al., 1994; Ebaugh & Curry, 2000); among low income or homeless persons (e.g., McCarthy, Hagan, & Martin, 2002; Prangnell & Mate, 2011); and also across racial or ethnic groups, such as African Americans or Latinos. This variation demonstrates the pervasiveness of voluntary kin, but it also poses challenges to understanding discourses through which the relationship is constructed and enacted. Although we cannot review all of the different variations of voluntary kin in this chapter, we focus on African Americans, Latinos, LGBT individuals, and the elderly to demonstrate variations that influence how these relationships are legitimated and enacted.

## Voluntary Kin among African Americans

A significant portion of the literature on voluntary kinship has been dedicated to understanding voluntary kin in the African American community (Nelson, 2014). Although scholars often criticize that nonwhite populations are underrepresented in research, in the case of voluntary kin it is not uncommon in the literature to see scholars claim that voluntary kin are more common and accepted among African Americans (e.g., Chatters et al., 1994; Johnson, 1999, 2000) as compared to White Americans. Voluntary-kin relationships have a long legacy in African American scholarship, beginning with ethnographic work on inner-city African American communities by Stack (1974). Chatters et al. (1994) found that one-third of their African American respondents reported having voluntary kin and noted that their respondents represented a wide spectrum of socioeconomic statuses. Although the incidence of voluntary kin might be higher among African Americans, Nelson

(2014) cautioned against assuming that a greater incidence of voluntary kin adds up to stronger voluntary relationships.

Researchers often combine the extended biological and legal kin and voluntary-kin networks of African Americans under the label of *extended kin network*, illustrating the cultural norm of subsuming voluntary kin members into the African American family. Scholars have traced the roots of extended kin networks in part back to African Americans' need to bond together for support during slavery (Chatters et al., 1994). Voluntary kin are reinforced as African American children are taught to address their elders with traditional family address terms such as "aunt" or "uncle" and to refer to each other as "brother" and "sister" despite their lack of blood and legal ties (Dilworth-Anderson, 1992; Stack, 1974). In a private conversation with the first author, an African American woman discussed both biological and non-biological children with whom she had resided, "If we'd called our brothers and sisters 'step brother' or 'step sister' we would have gotten into big trouble. They were our brothers and sisters and that was it." Dilworth-Anderson (1992) explained that this discursive practice of inclusion "emerged out of the idea of survival in a hostile and oppressive society where blacks viewed themselves as 'making it' only through the concerted efforts of groups of people" (p. 29).

Scholars have documented open household boundaries among African Americans, especially those families that are economically disadvantaged. Economically deprived African American women, for instance, often live with a variety of immediate, extended, and voluntary kin (Miller-Cribbs & Farber, 2008). Despite the potential strain on day-to-day needs in these overcrowded homes, large extended family and voluntary-kin networks provide a variety of functions, including providing instrumental support such as child care and sharing housing expenses. This reduces the need to depend on biological family, relieving them of some of the need to reciprocate support (Miller-Cribbs & Farber, 2008). In addition, extended kin networks in the African American community can provide assistance to children in need who find themselves neglected or emotionally abused (Hall, 2008). Hall (2008) found that for African American children with parents who were drug addicted, extended kin networks contributed in positive ways to the children's psychological well-being by spending time with them and offering advice and emotional support.

## Voluntary Kin among Latinos

In Latino culture, a system of supportive fictive kin relationships called *compadrazgo* is enacted throughout Mexico, Latin America, and in Latino immigrant populations in both rural and urban communities (Gill-Hopple & Brage-Hudson, 2012; Kemper, 1982). Although relatives can enact this role, more common are nonkin fictive ties. Ponzetti (2003) explained compadrazgo as "an elaboration of the Catholic concept of baptismal sponsorship blended with precolonial religious beliefs" (p. 672). It is a godparent-like relationship created most often during Catholic baptism (Mintz & Wolf, 1950), although these relationships are also established via other rituals associated with the lifecycle that are celebrated in the Catholic Church such as first communion or marriage (Kemper, 1982).

Mintz and Wolf (1950) stressed the importance of the relationship between the child and godparent and also the importance of establishing the relationship of "compadre" between the sponsor and the parents as "co-parents" of the child, thereby creating a "durable social, economic and religious institution" (p. 341). Although compadres can be of the same social and economic status, often they are combinations of higher and lower status persons to create symbolic commitments and to raise the social status of the family and thereby create upward mobility for the child (Ebaugh & Curry, 2000; Kemper, 1982; Ponzetti, 2003). Edbaugh and Curry (2000) described variations of the compadrazgo across a number of cultures including Spain, Eastern Turkey, Italy, Yugoslavia, and Greece, hence even this type of voluntary kinship cannot necessarily be generalized across cultures.

## Voluntary Kin among LGBT Persons

LGBT individuals have relied on communicatively constructed voluntary-kin relationships through both choice and default (Shapiro, 2010; Weston, 1991). These relationships fulfill familial functions, such as providing physical, emotional, and instrumental support (D'Augelli, Grossman, & Starks, 2008; Muraco, 2006; Weston, 1991). Given the stigma surrounding LGBT relationships in some circles, these voluntary-kin families must exhibit high degrees of commitment, resilience (Oswald, 2002), and fluid boundaries that can include both LGBT and heterosexual members (Muraco, 2006; Weston, 1991). Muraco (2006) focused specifically on voluntary kin among gays/lesbians and heterosexual persons self-identified as family, described as "deep and enduring relationships" (p. 1316). In more than half the cases for the respondents, these relationships superseded the family of origin. As with other voluntary-kin relationships, for LGBT persons these family relationships provided both instrumental and emotional support. Other researchers have found that the voluntary kin of LGBT persons need not replace the family of origin but instead can function as extensions of it in the form of supplemental kin (Braithwaite, Bach, Baxter et al., 2010; Braithwaite, Bach, Wilder et al., 2010).

For LGBT persons who cannot legally marry or choose not to marry, relationships with life partners are also families of choice (Weston, 1991). One question we've asked is whether LGBT chosen families are the same as voluntary kin. This issue came to light for Braithwaite, Bach, Baxter, and colleagues (2010) when they were seeking self-identified voluntary kin to interview. Some of the LGBT persons who participated in the interviews included their romantic partner as voluntary kin and completed the interview about their partner. However, other LGBT persons did not include their romantic partner as voluntary kin, but rather identified them as family, whether or not they could legally marry in their state of residence. One gay man who cohabited with his long-time partner stated quite strongly that his partner, Nathan, was his *family* and *not* voluntary kin, referencing a woman he had considered voluntary kin for over 30 years. As different U.S. states debate marriage and laws change in the years to come, understanding the communication surrounding marriage vs. voluntary kinship in the LGBT community will remain salient.

## Voluntary Kin among Elderly Persons

The later years in life present a time when many persons experience voluntary-kin relationships, even if they have not done so at other life stages. Older adults have more opportunities, and often necessity, for voluntary-kin relationships following the departure of children, divorce, death of a partner, and death of other members of their family of origin (Allen et al., 2011). During the later years of life, persons might reinterpret and redefine what "family" means to them (Allen et al., 2011) and turn to voluntary-kin networks to provide physical and psychological benefits (Johnson, 1999).

Many older adults find it necessary to expand and legitimize relationships beyond the traditional definition of family, a definition that they likely employed throughout their earlier lives. Older adults often find themselves dealing with family networks that are both expanding (by descendants' marriages, remarriages, childbearing, adoptions) and contracting (due to divorce, death, and other losses in their lives). Allen et al. (2011) found that older adults expanded the list of people they considered family by reinterpreting normative kinship structures. They explained that it was not uncommon for older adults to mark voluntary-kin relationships by modifying traditional family address terms, for example, "'she is *like* a daughter to me' to convey the meaning of an important relationship that would otherwise have no commonly understood ideological code" (p. 1163).

Professional caregivers could become a source of kinship for older adults who have at-home care or who live in a nursing home (Piercy, 2001). Scholars discovered that elderly persons often look for social and emotional connections with their caregivers (Kaye, 1986), particularly when the elderly individual's own family is under- or uninvolved in the person's life (Karner, 1998). Piercy (2000) discovered that some caregivers themselves also invoked traditional family address to describe elderly persons, referring to them as "grandparents," and they exchanged gifts during the holidays or watched television with them after work hours. This might be especially true for immigrants who are care workers for the elderly. Researchers have argued that these relationships can develop into voluntary kinships due to the cultural background and ideals of the immigrant care worker, reinforcing the ideal of family caretaking (Richter, 2008). Richter (2008) pointed out that the addition of familial ties could give "the homecare worker a means to negotiate the devaluation and lack of status of her employment" (p. 80). However, of the different voluntary kin types we have featured here, the relationship between persons who are elderly and caregivers might include the greatest amount of mismatch regarding the mutuality of the voluntary-kin relationship. Although some elderly persons do define some caregivers as family, the relationship is not always reciprocated (Piercy, 2000).

Clearly scholars need to resist a "one size fits all" approach to voluntary kin as they attempt to account for the role of culture in the formation, legitimation, and enactment of voluntary kin. For example, Nelson (2014) argued that different terminology for different cultural groups (e.g., "fictive kin" for African Americans, "chosen kin" for LGBT persons, and "voluntary kin" for largely White populations) confuses the issue and potentially plays up these relationships as functional in one culture and problematic in others. Beyond labels, scholars need to pay attention to the different motivations for forming voluntary-kin relationships (e.g., to meet financial exigencies, to address emotional needs, or to create family through the only available route). In short, scholars need to flesh out both cultural similarities and differences in the experience of voluntary kinship.

## Navigating Internal and External Challenges to Voluntary Kin

Voluntary-kin relationships contribute benefits to relational members as they create ways to give and receive emotional and instrumental support and overcome limitations that exist in families of origin. Voluntary-kin members wax poetic about the value added from these relationships in their lives. Pahl and Spencer (2010) described both liberation and functional benefits of these relationships. In the liberation view of voluntary kin, members are not tied to what families should be, but rather they are able to enact the freedom to create family in ways that best meet their needs. In the functional view of voluntary kin, those who act like family are family. In fact, the voluntary nature of these family relationships is one of their greatest benefits (Baxter, Braithwaite & Bach, 2009; Nelson, 2013).

Although voluntary kin do provide positive benefits, parties in these relationships often experience internal and external threats to the relationship, which is the fourth challenge we'll discuss in this chapter. Nelson (2013) lamented that scholars "rarely describe how fictive kin relationships might also create the kinds of complications (of disappointment from unfulfilled responsibility, unwanted interference, and outright conflict) that routinely emerge in kin relations" (p. 262). Galvin (2006) reflected on the need for discourse-dependent families to legitimize and defend their family, and this is especially true for voluntary kin, as there are no biological or legal structures that lend relational validity. The lack of consistent and culturally recognized labels, expectations, and rules for these relationships can make it difficult for members to explain and legitimize them in interaction with others.

Internal to the relationship, scholars need to understand better how voluntary-kin relationships form and whether they are always mutual. For example, what happens when one member perceives another as family but that perception is not reciprocated? Those who are in mutually agreed-upon voluntary-kin relationships must also navigate the obligations and expectations that are implied by the label "family" without sufficient cultural models to assist them (Pahl & Spencer, 2010). Baxter et al. (2009) analyzed interviews with self-identified voluntary kin and found that participants reported that at times they struggled with the perceptions of obligation to provide support to the other, and the work required to maintain the relationship. As one woman described:

> We got a message on our phone at home from her son that [her husband] had been taken to the hospital. So it was challenging in a sense to try to figure out how do I drop everything that I am doing and run there to the hospital, because she did that for me. … Or you know, I've got a kid here in school and this, and I've got a job and they don't, and so on and so forth. (p. 12)

Voluntary kin experience challenges as they navigate obligations to be responsive to the needs of these family members as life circumstances alter with illness, advancing age, or other relational changes. In addition, scholars need to better understand how voluntary-kin members negotiate situations in which expectations for the relationships are divergent between the voluntary-kin members.

On an external level, voluntary kin must validate and manage the relationship as they interact with members of their social network, especially the family of origin. Using relational dialectics theory (Baxter, 2011) to interpret their findings, Baxter et al. (2009) identified a dialectic of navigating integration and separation, observing that "Some [informants] felt that their voluntary-kin relationships were insufficiently independent from blood and legal kin dynamics. Others felt that their voluntary-kin relationships were inadequately integrated with those immediate family members" (p. 29). These challenges included not wanting the family of origin to know about the voluntary ties for fear of hurting them or inciting jealously, and fearing that the existence of the voluntary family itself would be seen as a critique or rejection of the family of origin. In addition, voluntary kin faced the challenges that come with embedding voluntary kin in their family of origin, which were often fraught with their own baggage (hence the need to supplement these relationships with voluntary kin in the first place). Some informants expressed concerns about entangling voluntary kin into dysfunctions of their family of origin. In other cases, they experienced challenges navigating their own relationship with the voluntary-kin member's family.

To better understand how voluntary kin manage the challenges of the relationship between voluntary kin and family of origin, Braithwaite, Stephenson Abetz, Moore, and Brockhage (2014) analyzed a set of interviews with supplemental kin concerning how voluntary kin navigate interaction and the relationship between voluntary and family origin. The researchers focused on the supplemental kin type because relationships are maintained with the family of origin as well as with the voluntary kin. The researchers observed that many of the voluntary kin effectively knit the two groups together, describing close, cordial relationships between the family of origin and the voluntary kin:

> I would say that that my family's relationship with Sherry and Sherry's with my family is, is very cordial and, and, and friendly and they do things where I'm not involved, you know, if I'm not around [pauses]. It wouldn't be out of the question for Sherry to interact with my family without my being there. But, um, I would think of it as more of a friend relationship.

For this interviewee, her voluntary kin had a friendship with her family of origin. For others, the two groups become seamless, with the family of origin also regarding the voluntary kin as family or, at minimum, accepting the voluntary kin as an important person in the life of their family member as in this example, "My mother even considers [Missy] a second daughter…Missy will invite my mom up to, if she wants her to invite her up to redecorate her kitchen. She's invited her when I've not even been there several times."

In many instances, voluntary kin were open with their family of origin about the importance of the voluntary-kin relationship but kept the two groups separate all or most of the time. In some instances this was due to geographic distance from the family of origin. However, for many supplemental kin, the two groups did not share core values, which was the impetus for forming the voluntary-kin relationship in the first place. Indeed, the two groups together were not a good mix. In some cases informants perceived that the relationship with the voluntary kin posed a threat to the family of origin:

> There were a lot of issues at that time between me and my family and…I would prob-ably reference like a conversation I had with Nick or you know if I missed a holiday or something cause I went to visit him they will always, they'll come back and say "well you always, you'll drop everything, you know, for Nick, you know, like you'll go visit him, you won't care about us or any of that" so it kind of stems from that, like me kind of defending myself.

In other cases members of voluntary-kin relationships were concerned about the troubles of the family of origin, or their own relational challenges with that family, bleeding over into their voluntary-kin relationship. In situations like these, the voluntary-kin relationship was kept as separate as possible from the family of origin.

Due to the nature of the supplemental voluntary-kin relationship, many of the interviewees reported being much more open with the voluntary kin than with the family of origin. They indicated that, although their family of origin knew they had a close relationship with this person, most members were unaware of how close the relationship was or that it was considered a family relationship. Several described the relationship between voluntary kin and family-of-origin members as cordial, but certainly not close. Finally, there are examples wherein the voluntary kin disapproved of the blood and legal family and discouraged contact because they perceived that it was harmful. In this situation, a person could easily experi-ence difficulties associated with getting caught in the middle between two sets of relationships.

## Conclusions and Future Directions

Of all the discourse-dependent relationships included in the present volume, volun-tary kin include some unique challenges both for participants in these relationships and to scholars who seek to understand them. Although voluntary kin contribute many benefits to people's lives by their very nature as chosen relationships, members rely on traditional family models to define and create expectations for these relation-ships, potentially devaluing the relationship to themselves as well as outsiders. This might suffice when traditional family models fit the needs of relational parties but will provide poor guidance for others wishing to engage in these relationships. In the end, scholars still know very little about the day-to-day interactions of voluntary kin, in particular, how parties in these relationships interact and initiate voluntary-kin ties, negotiate expectations and rules, and maintain these relationships over time and through different stages of the life course. These limitations are compounded as these relationships are culturally and temporally bound, making comparisons difficult.

An additional limitation of the literature is that scholars have studied voluntary kin from the perspective of one interactant, our work included. Although calls to study multiple perspectives are so common in the literature that they ring rather hollow in our minds, in the case of voluntary kin we believe this work is strongly warranted. There are many unanswered questions regarding the jointly enacted communication through which parties negotiate their voluntary-kin relationships. Scholars need to attend to whether perceptions of communication are mutual and the implications when they are not. Scholars also need to examine the contributions and challenges of voluntary kin across the lifespan, focusing on how these relationships are negotiated and legitimated at different life stages, especially when significant changes occur (Allen et al., 2011). For example, we do not know how partners in voluntary-kin relationships interact and navigate changes such as when a partner remarries and the new spouse does not accept the voluntary relationship or when there is a serious illness that creates a need for increased caregiving.

Although interpretive and post-positivistic scholars have added much to the study of voluntary kin, we believe critical studies are warranted to help scholars better understand the discursive challenges of legitimating these relationships within cultural discourses of the traditional family that often marginalize family relationships existing outside of biology and law. Critical scholars are well positioned to interrogate the liminalities of voluntary relationships. This undertaking has practical value as voluntary kin confront legal implications of caregiving and medical decision-making. While voluntary-kin relationships are clearly important to many, the discourse of the traditional family and the primacy of biology and law challenge their legitimacy. Scholars need to concentrate more fully on how participants interact and legitimate voluntary kin within larger web of family relationships.

# PART FOUR

# Remaking "Family" beyond Shared Households

# CHAPTER TWELVE

# Military Families

## Remaking Shared Residence, Traditional Marriage, and Future Communication Research

ERIN SAHLSTEIN PARCELL

The American military family is one of the most visible family forms in the post-9/11 public sphere. The frequent media circulation of heart-warming reunion videos between military service members and their families (Cipriani, 2013), the consistent recognition during charity and sporting events (e.g., "NFL honors Veterans Day, Military with Salute to Service," 2013), and the significant support for military families offered by First Lady Michelle Obama and Dr. Jill Biden through their program "Joining Forces" (White House, n.d.) are a few examples of how the American military family is rarely far from view in American culture. Of course, the attention is not without merit.

Over two million service members have deployed in the Global War on Terror since 9/11 (Tan, 2009) and many have been through multiple deployments (Baiocchi, 2013). The U.S. Department of Defense (2014) reported the armed forces have suffered over 6,600 fatalities in their ranks across operations in Iraq and Afghanistan. Traumatic brain injuries (TBIs) in the military population are a significant concern for wounded service members given recent reports of over 225,000 TBI cases on record since 2001 (Curtain & Mirkin, 2012). The public also must address the mental health of deployed and returning military given estimates that 15% of service members and veterans are affected by posttraumatic stress disorder (PTSD) ("VA, DOD to Fund $100 Million PTSD and TBI Study," 2012). The trials of the American military family also trace through the economic downturn in the United

States with the cutting of military budgets and service member benefits (Wotapka, 2013), the troubling numbers of home foreclosures (Zoroya, 2008), and the rising spousal unemployment rate in the military population (Merica, 2012). Given the visibility of the military and the significant challenges faced by its members and their families, communication researchers have (e.g., Jeffords & Rabinovitz, 1994) and are taking notice (e.g., Sahlstein Parcell & Webb, in press).

The scholarly research concerning military families cuts across many disciplines and decades (see Castro, Adler, & Britt, 2006, and MacDermid-Wadsworth & Riggs, 2011, for extensive reviews of the research outside of communication) but recently has surged within family communication (see Knobloch & Wilson, in press; Maguire, in press). Family communication researchers have taken a keen interest in military families post-9/11 with Operation Iraqi Freedom, Operation Enduring Freedom, and Operation New Dawn, while focusing on such issues as topic avoidance (Frisby, Byrnes, Mansson, Booth-Butterfield, & Birmingham, 2011), protective buffering (Joseph & Afifi, 2010), relational turbulence (Knobloch & Theiss, 2011), relational maintenance (Merolla, 2010b), contradictions across deployment (Sahlstein, Maguire, & Timmerman, 2009), and post-deployment family program assessment (Wilson, Wilkum, Chernichky, MacDermid Wadsworth, & Broniarczyk, 2011).

The military family is an important and unique context for family communication research. Not only does research help address significant concerns in the military community, but in light of this collection, the military family context challenges, or remakes, certain cultural assumptions about family that are worthy of reflection. In the remainder of this chapter, I closely examine the published research within family communication and discuss two primary ways scholars should consider remaking future research in this area. First, I address the state of the military family communication research in terms of who gets included as "family" and compare that to the shifting demographics of this population. Second, I reflect on how scholars typically approach the study of military families and offer ideas for how to remake future research as discourse centered.

## Remaking Shared (and Stable) Residence: The Unique Context of the Military Family

When citizens join a branch of the U.S. military, they become members of an organization, like most civilian organizations, where certain expectations and cultural values are communicated to their employees and their families (Blanchard, 2012). Military life, for example, requires service members and their families to become fluent in a new language with many acronyms and strict procedures that must be followed as well as detailed knowledge of the organizational hierarchy, one's place within it, and how to move up the ranks (Blaisure, Saathoff-Wells, Pereira, MacDermid Wadsworth, & Dombro, 2012). Civilian organizations reflect these same qualities as the successful navigation within a company or institution requires becoming part of the organization's system of interaction, behaviors, and beliefs. It is important to note the specific context of the military because recognizing its unique features allows for a nuanced understanding of the communication processes within families (Maguire, 2012) and the discourses surrounding them (Sahlstein & Maguire, 2013).

The military places demands on service members and their families that are atypical in the civilian population. As Blanchard (2012) noted, "As a work organization, the military requires a range of personal and family sacrifices that dominate the lifestyles of military personnel and their families in accommodating to its work mission" (p. 84). As such, the military can be labeled a "greedy" institution where "members...must be so fully and totally committed to [the organization] that they become unavailable for alternative lines of action" (Coser, 1974, p. 8). The military requires that service members and their families constantly be "at the ready" and prepared for action:

> There are few civilian occupations that require such a high level of commitment and dedication from employees. ... The military requires many sacrifices by the personnel employed and their family including frequent relocations, extended separations and subservience of the needs of the family to the requirements and objectives of the military. (Blanchard, 2012, p. 84)

All of these qualities, but in particular the frequent relocations and extended separations required from the organization, make the military family a unique context for studying family communication processes.

All of the families addressed in this collection, including the military family, "remake" certain taken-for-granted qualities of dominant forms of relation. As Baxter notes in her introductory chapter, the case of the military family (past and present) challenges the assumption of a shared residence with the frequent separations due to trainings and deployments required of military life, which makes military families a type of long-distance relationship, albeit temporary ones. Stafford (2005) cited four commonly held assumptions about "the nature of communication, proximity, and close relationships" (p. 8) that long-distance relationships violate:

1. Frequent face-to-face communication is necessary for close relational ties;
2. Shared meaning is necessary for close relationships;

3. Geographic proximity is necessary for close relationships;
4. Family members, couples, and parents and young children are supposed to share a residence.

As long-distance relationships, military families violate all four of these assumptions at some point or another. For example, although participants in my research studies indicate that military family members can and do communicate relatively frequently during deployments and other types of separations even across several different time zones, they cannot communicate face-to-face as often as might be considered healthy or ideal, which affects their feelings of closeness within the family (Sahlstein et al., 2009). Although new technologies like FaceTime and Skype allow for partners to feel some level of presence with one another, family members might not consider these moments on par with the "real" thing. For example, an Army wife in a recent study reported feeling, "so connected, but not at all" to her husband during a recent deployment as the frequent emails she and her husband exchanged did not help her feel as strongly connected as she expected (Maguire, Heinemann, & Sahlstein, 2013).

As a result of unmet expectations for communication frequency and mode, military family members find (re)developing and maintaining a sense of shared meaning difficult when they live apart, for example, during deployment, as well as when they come back together (Sahlstein et al., 2009). While relating at a distance, family members must work on maintaining a sense of connection even though the service member is physically absent (Wiens & Boss, 2006). Family members use a variety of maintenance tactics during deployments, for example, in order to keep up a shared sense of the relationship (Maguire et al., 2013; Merolla, 2010b); however, physical presence does not always assuage the challenges of connectedness caused by separation. Even when a service member is home during pre-deployment, for example, family members bemoan the fact that the person is not "really there" given the psychological distance that is present as the service member prepares for departure (Wiens & Boss, 2006). Feelings of distance also occur during post-deployment (Wiens & Boss, 2006). Family members frequently report reintegration difficulties, which often is marked by not feeling "on the same page" with one another and increased relational uncertainty (Knobloch & Wilson, in press). New routines must be established and the renegotiation of roles must occur in order for families to feel their lives have returned to a normal level of interrelatedness (Doyle & Peterson, 2005; Norwood, Fullerton & Hagen, 1996). Although military families certainly violate the first two assumptions cited by Stafford (2005), their deviations from the second two (i.e., close relationships require geographic proximity and families should share a residence) are what most clearly define the military family context.

The branches of the U.S. military and military family life are characterized by the possibility of deployment (Wiens & Boss, 2006), and since 9/11 it has dominated their realities. Reports have indicated that with the extended commitments in the Middle East, thousands of U.S. service members deployed multiple times and their optempo (rate of deployment) has increased (Keller et al., 2005). The U.S. Army alone sent over 1.5 million troops to Iraq and Afghanistan between 2001 and 2011, and the amount of time soldiers have been deployed during their service has increased by 28% since 2008 (Baiocchi, 2013). Such numbers are not new to the U.S. military, however. Dating back to the revolutionary war, military families have faced deployments, and the military is a culture defined by predictable change; however, military families face other types of separation in addition to deployment. Permanent change of station (PCS), which occurs when a service member is transferred to a new duty station, is another standing feature of military life for active duty members that might cause separation (temporary or permanent; short or far) between service members and their families (Blaisure et al., 2012). Temporary duty (TDY) is a third type of separation common in the military. TDY includes when service members attend boot camp, training sessions, and even extended schooling (e.g., officer candidate school), and these are typically shorter than deployments (Blaisure et al., 2012). These three types of separations disrupt the continuity of physical presence (i.e., geographic proximity) within the family due to the temporary lack of a shared residence, which distinguishes military families from "normal" or civilian families.

The *stability* of a shared residence is also violated within the military family context given service members and their families relocate periodically due to changes in the needs of the organization. Although civilian families change residences across their lifespans, active duty military families relocate more often and across larger distances than civilian families (Booth, Wechsler Segal, & Bell, 2007). Moving every few years is not unheard of in the military; for example, active duty Army soldiers move every 2–3 years on average (Burrell, 2006). Military families might also relocate to other countries, likely situating them far away from extended families. These frequent separations and changes in familial location position military families as distinct from the norm and the ideal family form that has a stable, shared residence.

The real and perceived violations of, or deviations from, the cultural assumptions Stafford (2005) cited are what translate into some of the problems emerging within these relationships and in turn what family communication researchers choose to study. The topics addressed reflect where the concerns lie; stress and coping is a significant area within the field with scholars working to identify the stressors military family members experience as well as how they manage them (Jennings-Kelsall, Aloia, Solomon, Marshall, & Leifker, 2012; Maguire & Sahlstein, 2012; Rossetto, 2013). Questions of how military family members maintain their relationships in the face of separation (Maguire, 2007; Maguire et al., 2013; Merolla, 2010b) as well as how they manage conversational topics (Frisby et al., 2011; Joseph & Afifi, 2010; Knobloch, Ebata, McGlaughlin, & Theiss, 2013; Knobloch, Theiss, & Wehrman, in press; Sahlstein et al., 2009) are also common lines of research. Knobloch, Theiss, and colleagues have amassed numerous studies addressing relational turbulence in military relationships (Knobloch, Ebata, McGlaughlin, & Ogolsky, 2013; Knobloch & Theiss, 2011, 2012; Theiss & Knobloch, 2013, 2014). Relatedly, Sahlstein Parcell and Maguire (in press-b) have studied the turning points and relationship trajectories of military deployment, and Sahlstein and her colleagues (Sahlstein et al., 2009) have examined contradictions across deployment phases. Military youth are also receiving research attention for their unique communicative concerns connecting during and reconnecting post-deployment with their parents (Knobloch, Pusateri, Ebata, & McGlaughlin, in press; Knobloch, Pusateri, Ebata, & McGlaughlin, 2012; Wilson, Chernichky, Wilkum, & Owlett, 2014; Wilson et al., 2011), and military spouses are highlighted for their "battles" with relationships across deployment (Sahlstein Parcell & Maguire, in press-a; Villagran, Canzona, & Ledford, 2013).

Overall, the military family communication scholarship assumes these long-distance relationships are problematic, in need of information for improving military family "resilience" in the face of separations. Family communication scholars should be commended for such exciting and practical research emerging from the communication discipline. As I have argued in the past (Sahlstein, 2006), family communication researchers need to focus on military families given they are some of the most important and deserving long-distance relationships. The lines of inquiry reflected in this review should continue and expand. However, if family communication researchers want to rethink the military family, then they must take a closer look at what this scholarship "rethinks" time and time again, including the assumption that separations are negative and need to be overcome (Sahlstein, 2004). In the following sections I discuss two additional ways family communication scholars currently think about military families and present ideas for how they should "remake" the research in this area.

## Remaking Military Families: Beyond Traditional, Heterosexual Forms and Biological Ties

As discussed elsewhere (Sahlstein & Maguire, 2013), across the varied disciplines contributing to military family research, samples typically include traditionally defined marriages (i.e., marriages consisting of one man and one woman) that are legally sanctioned by the government. For example, many studies explicitly focus on military spouses (e.g., Sahlstein et al., 2009), military marriages (Huffman & Payne, 2006), or military parents and their biological children (e.g., Lincoln, Swift, & Shorteno-Fraser, 2008). The focus is almost expected given that the common definition of family is based in biogenetic characteristics (Floyd, Mikkelson, & Judd, 2006; Segrin & Flora, 2011), and in most states only opposite-sex couples may obtain marriage licenses per the legal definitions set by lawmakers (see Lannutti, this volume). Many military families reflect these demographics as over half of service members, active duty and reservists, are married, divorced, or remarried (U.S. Department of Defense, 2012). But what is the range of military family forms today? What kinds of military families have family communication scholars studied? Who should they focus on for future research?

## Who Do Military Family Communication Scholars Study?

My qualitative impression of the research within the field is that researchers have focused almost exclusively on traditional, legally sanctioned opposite-sex marriages and their offspring (Sahlstein & Maguire, 2013), but a closer review of the literature is warranted before I address how to remake the military family communication research focus beyond the traditional, heterosexual marriage and biological ties. Therefore, I conducted a detailed analysis of the published empirical studies on military relationships by communication scholars and within communication outlets with the initial purpose of answering the question, "Who do family communication scholars include in their studies of military relationships?" I located the sample of studies included in the analysis by searching scholarly (peer-reviewed) journal articles in the "Communication and Mass Media Complete" database using the search terms "Military families," "Military marriages," and "Military couples." I examined each article for relevance to the current chapter and included studies that addressed family relationships as opposed to studies of the military in the media or rhetoric. I also reviewed recent literature reviews of research (Knobloch & Wilson, in press; Maguire, in press) for additional studies not captured by the initial database search. After deleting one article from the database search results that was authored by scholars outside of communication and published in a family psychology journal (Allen, Rhoades, Stanley & Markman, 2010), as well as those that did not study family relationships (e.g., Desens & Hughes, 2013), the final sample consisted of twenty-five articles or chapters published or in press within communication journals or books and/or authored by communication scholars.

In the published studies on military family communication, traditional marital relationships and/or biological parent-child relationships were included 100% of the time and typically dominated the samples; however, some samples did include engaged partners or couples (e.g., Theiss & Knobloch, 2013), stepparents or step-families (e.g., Wilson et al., 2014), divorced parents or single-parent families (e.g., Wilson et al., 2011), and dating couples (i.e., casually dating, dating, seriously dating; see, for example, Knobloch, Ebata, McGlaughlin, & Ogolsky, 2013). In some cases, authors limited the sexual orientation of the participants to heterosexual (Knobloch, Ebata, McGlaughlin, & Theiss, 2013) or reported if partners cohabitated or not (Knobloch & Theiss, 2011). Several included exclusively military wives, fiancées, or girlfriends (e.g., Jennings-Kelsall et al., 2012; Joseph & Afifi, 2010; Nichols, Martindale-Adams, Graney, Zuber, & Burns, 2013; Sahlstein et al., 2009) or milspouses (i.e., husbands and wives who are married to someone in the military; Villagran et al., 2013). A few studies excluded dual-military couples (e.g., Theiss & Knobloch, 2014) while others included them in their studies (e.g., Wilson et al., 2011). When the information was collected and made available, authors reported the husbands/dads are typically the deployed family member (e.g., Sahlstein et al., 2009; Wilson et al. 2014; Wilson, et al., 2011), which reflects the traditional nature of these relationships where the husband is the one to go off to war. Only one study included a singleton (Clark-Hitt, Smith, & Broderick, 2012).

As this review reflects, military families and family members included in family communication research are more often than not traditional and certainly heterosexual. The military family, however, does not have one face. There are diverse military family forms thus numerous contexts for communication researchers to study as a result. Below I discuss each with the objective of sparking future family communication research for these demographics.

## Same-Sex Marriage

In one significant respect—the sexual orientation of service members—the military family is rapidly shifting. Since the early years of the U.S. military, homosexuals have served the country within an unaccepting environment. In 1778, the first service member was dismissed for sodomy under the orders of General Washington, and since then the military has had a complicated history of policy making regarding homosexuals ("Key dates in U.S. policy and law on gays in the military," n.d.). Selected other dates of importance include:

- In 1957 a U.S. Navy Board of Inquiry stated in a report that there was no evidence to support homosexuals posing a threat to operations;
- In 1981 (and reinstated again in 1982, 1993, and 2008) the U.S. Department of Defense Directive 1332.14 was issued, which stated that

homosexuality is discordant with military service, and being found guilty of engaging in homosexual activities would be met with mandatory discharge orders;

- Governor Bill Clinton campaigned on the promise that if elected he would allow gays to serve in the military; however, in 1993 President Clinton signed into law the "Don't Ask, Don't Tell" (DADT) policy prohibiting gays from serving in the military;
- DADT was recently repealed by Congress and signed by President Barack Obama on December 22, 2010. ("Key dates in U.S. policy and law on gays in the military," n.d.)

Given the historical repeal of DADT, coupled with the partial overturn of the Defense of Marriage Act (DOMA) on June 26, 2013 (in which the federal government now acknowledges same-sex marriages but does not require states to recognize marriages that took place in other states), the U.S. military family has and will noticeably change. The U.S. armed forces now officially acknowledges the unions of gay service members who marry in states that legally sanction them and recognizes same-sex spouses as dependents. The reversals in policy are translating into significant shifts in what is considered military family. An estimated 17,000 gay troops currently are serving in or retired from the military (Jordan, 2013), and the numbers will grow as additional service members (current and future recruits) identify as homosexual and/or get married. Family support services must appeal to and provide services for gay couples, spouses, and parents. For example, gay service members may apply for up to ten days of "marriage leave" if they are forced to travel to another state that legally recognizes same-sex marriages in order to obtain a marriage license, and they are also eligible for health care benefits for their spouses and children, housing allowances, and family separation pay (Tilghman, 2013). In fact, the partial overturn of DOMA initiated the implementation of over 100 benefits for spouses of gay troops, and:

> The VA can expect to see an increase in its budget for entitlements, which not only includes disability compensation for veterans, but dependency and indemnity compensation for surviving spouses and Post-9/11 GI Bill benefits, which also may be transferred to spouses. (Jordan, 2013, para. 11)

As the numbers of gay troops increase, the need for research concerning same-sex marriages and families will also increase. As I will discuss in the final section of this chapter, family communication scholars are uniquely positioned to address a range of important issues in this regard.

## Female Service Members' Families & Dual-Military Marriages

Recent reports show nearly half of all women actively serving in the armed forces are married, and with over 45% of them in dual-career marriages, 55% of female military service members are married to civilian spouses (U.S. Department of Defense, 2012). These numbers indicate that over 400,000 male civilians are married to women in the military. Over 70,000 women in the reserves are also in dual-military marriages, but approximately 782,000 female reservists are married to civilians (U.S. Department of Defense, 2012).

Family communication scholars should take note of these numbers as these unique family contexts are in need of study. Women in the military who are married to civilians must address a host of issues that married men in the military who are married to civilians do not (e.g., deploying and leaving their husbands at home; negotiating child care). These women likely fall into similar communicative circumstances as commuter wives, where they must account for their identities in ways that challenge their work/home balance (Bergen, 2010b; see also Chapter Thirteen). Although the perspective of female service members has been largely understudied (Kelley, Doane, & Pearson, 2011), research indicates there are unique stressors put on military mothers and their children (Goodman et al., 2013) and negative effects on children whose mothers deploy (e.g., Lieberman & Van Horn, 2013) and increased anxiety levels and uncertainties for deploying mothers versus fathers (Kelley, Herzog-Simmer, & Harris 1994). Additional research must be directed at the female military service member/spouse/parent. A related line of inquiry that also needs attention is that of the nontraditional military marriage in which the husband is the spouse:

> The information and resources [are] typically structured for nonactive duty mothers whose husbands [are] deployed and [do] not address issues that [apply] to other types of caregivers such as male spouse and grandparents. As one mother stated, "Everything is so focused on the guy going; on dad going, and the briefings are about what the female spouse does who stays behind." (Goodman et al., 2013, p. 730)

Although research is needed on military marriages in which the wives are serving in armed forces and the husbands are the stay-at-home spouses, the case of dual-military marriage comes with a myriad of communicative concerns not experienced within marriages in which only one spouse serves in the military. These couples must negotiate multiple and potentially overlapping deployments, conflicting work schedules, and deviations from traditional spousal norms (Huffman & Payne, 2006). Family communication research does include work on dual-career marriages and couples (e.g., Buzzanell, 1997; Rosenfeld & Welsh, 1985), but recent study is scant and does not specifically address dual-military marriage. Military research on this marital form is also limited with most research including them within larger studies of marriage without a distinct focus on dual-military couples (Huffman & Payne, 2006). This is yet another family form where family communication researchers could place their efforts in order to remake and refine what they consider family.

## Childless Families

The U.S. Department of Defense (2012) reported 16.2% of active duty and reserve service members are married with no children compared to 37% who are married with children. Although their percentage is not particularly high, over 366,000 service members are in childless marriages, and they deserve research attention given their unique characteristics. Many support services for military marriages are provided by the various branches of the military, but the visible participant-led groups (e.g., family support groups) might too frequently appear "family focused" (i.e., tailored for those married with children) (Sahlstein Parcell & Maguire, in press-a). For example, Sahlstein Parcell and Maguire (in press-a) interviewed Army wives who felt their family readiness groups (FRG) did not meet their needs as childless spouses and often scheduled events with child-focused activities (e.g., birthday parties, bowling, and barbeques). One wife, Ebony, reported it was a challenge to feel a part of her FRG because the Army and the group's focus was on military children. She said:

> It's hard when you don't have kids to get involved with FRG here. It's just, it's different because you know it's like leave the kids there together to do art projects you know, and leave the kids together to go out and have picnics and stuff. … I'm just uncomfortable. It's just that I don't have kids and I have nothing really in common with them.

Little is known about how being childless might affect the support married military couples receive and do not receive. Given that the military climate can be considered "pro-family," these couples likely experience some level of marginalization with respect to support, in particular during deployment, and researchers should dedicate attention to this family form.

## Single Parents

Although most military children have two-parent households, 6.9% of active duty and reserve service members are single parents (U.S. Department of Defense, 2012).

The demands of being a single parent are unique and taxing.

> Single military families face the dual challenges of military family life and single parenthood and may require complex strategies for balancing their military careers and family life. Notably absent from the literature, however, are studies examining the needs, concerns, and adjustments of single military parents and their families. (Kelley, 2006, p. 99)

Two related challenges for the single military parent are deployment and finding caregivers for their children (Blanchard, 2012). Although married couples typically entrust their nonmilitary spouses to care for their children, single military parents must seek out ex-partners, extended family members, or friends for this support (Kelley, 2006), and some risk their military careers when they cannot find suitable arrangements ("Mother Refuses Deployment," 2009). The displacement of the children into new homes during deployment can cause problems given they might be unfamiliar with their caregivers and/or their surroundings and be forced to make new friends and assimilate into new schools and routines (Kelley, 2006). The challenges might be more pronounced for military children with single mothers, who might also experience more anxiety related to their pending separations than single military fathers (Kelley et al., 2011). More research is called for in the area of single military parent families and in particular single mothers with custody.

## Military Stepfamilies

Since 2000, the percentage of divorces each year for active duty service members across all branches of the military has trended upwards and in 2011 fell between 3.5–4%; yet, in the reserve population, the year to year changes do not reflect as much change but show increases across the same period (U.S. Department of Defense, 2012). The overall number of service members who have experienced divorce is estimated at 20%, approximately 30% of all married service members are "in a remarriage either through their own marital history or their spouse's," and about a third of armed forces have nonresidential children (Adler-Baeder, Pittman, & Taylor, 2005, p. 101). Although the exact number of stepfamilies is difficult to extract from the published figures, "there are large numbers of children, spouses, and military members who are struggling as divorced, remarried, or stepfamily members" (Hall, 2008, p. 94), and stepfamilies might experience more problems with adapting to military life and relocation (Adler-Baeder et al., 2005).

A number of unique challenges are placed on military stepfamilies given the frequent deployments and relocations required of the service member, which likely produces additional stressors as well as higher levels of stress (Hall, 2008). For example, if the stepparent is also the service member, then military obligations might create a wedge within the stepparent-stepchild relationship as the child deals with possibly moving far away from the nonresidential parent as well as other family and friends. When the stepparent is the civilian and the parent is the service member, the stepparent-stepchild relationship might be put under considerable stress when the service member deploys or attends trainings leaving the stepparent and stepchild to manage at home (Hall, 2008). The research on military stepfamilies is quite limited as are programs and services specifically for divorced and/or remarried military service members and their families (Adler-Baeder et al., 2005). Only a few studies from within communication (Wilson et al., 2014; Wilson et al., 2011) include military stepfamily members in their research, and no studies focus exclusively on military stepfamilies. Given the unique characteristics of stepfamilies coupled with the military lifestyle requirements, future research from within family communication, as well as from other disciplines, would offer valuable insight into this family form.

There are several other military families and family members that deserve future research attention: spouses of injured service members, widowed spouses, extended military families, grandparents of military service members and/or military children, cohabitating couples, and voluntary kin (e.g., co-workers who feel like family, relationships between military spouses). Given the substantial opportunities for "remaking" the military family, family communication scholars can significantly contribute to the military family research and positively affect military families. In the next section, I address the research beyond context and suggest conceptual lines of future inquiry.

## Remaking Approaches to Military Family Communication

Although the military family research within communication is surging, it is useful to take stock of not only how family is defined in the inquiry but also how it is approached. The substance of the scholarship is without question theoretically interesting and valuable in application. Nevertheless, how do researchers treat military family communication?

At this point in the research, family communication scholars approach military family communication from a distance-as-context perspective (Sahlstein, 2010). In line with the trends in long-distance relationship research, military family communication research is dominated by studies examining communication *in* military family relationships. Even more accurately, the research is dominated by participant reports about communication within these families. The distance-as-context perspective corresponds to what Baxter (2004) termed container approaches to the study of relationships, which finds it "intelligible to discuss 'communication in relationships' predicated on the assumption that relationships have a separate existence apart from communication and that communication is one variable among many to be studied about relationships" (p. 3). As with most areas of interpersonal and family communication, researchers designate a particular relationship form and then study communication variables in relation to that context (Sahlstein, 2010). For example, Merolla (2010b) conducted a study of relational maintenance during deployment involving military wives. He asked his participants to report what type of maintenance strategies they used with their deployed husbands, and from the data he determined the relative frequencies of each tactic. His findings reflect the potential types of communicative activities that wives use to maintain their military marriages. Another example from past military family communication research is Knobloch et al.'s (in press) study regarding military youth and their experiences communicating with redeployed parents upon reunion. The researchers interviewed children with deployed parents (i.e., fathers, mothers, or stepfathers) about their perceived changes in their families, expectations for the reunion, and types of uncertainty emergent from the deployment. A final example of the container approach is Maguire and Sahlstein's (2012) examination of stressors and communicative coping strategies in military marriages. Army and Army reserve wives reported the stressful events they experienced before, during, and after their husbands' most recent deployment as well as how they communicatively managed their stress. All three examples reflect the container approach (i.e., studies of communication within a certain context). They also treat the participants' reports as transparent records of communicative activity. The military family research, albeit producing important and useful results using this framework, could diversify into alternative approaches that would look at the (a) talk within these relationships, (b) military families as discourse-dependent, and (c) military family discourses.

My first suggestion (i.e., that first-hand conversational data be collected) is common with respect to family communication research. Understanding perceptions of the communication within a given context is useful, but examining actual talk would allow a nuanced analysis of interaction between relationship partners. For example, instead of asking participants to report on how they communicate during deployment, scholars could collect records of their conversations (e.g., Skype chats, emails exchanges). I do not wish to belabor this point given it is consistently offered as a direction for future research in the discipline. Also, this type of research would still fall under the military-as-context, or container, approach.

The second suggestion draws from Galvin's (2006) notion of discourse-dependent families. Galvin argued that, "less traditionally formed families are more discourse dependent" and therefore engage "in recurring discursive processes to manage and maintain identity" (p. 3). In the case of military families, their challenges to the cultural assumptions of "the nature of communication, proximity, and close relationships" (Stafford, 2005, p. 8) render them discourse-dependent akin to commuter marriages (Bergen, 2010b; see also Chapter Thirteen). Galvin identified several speech activities that discourse-dependent families, such as military families, likely use to externally and internally manage their identities. For example, military spouses and children have reported to me that they are asked periodically to explain their family to friends, teachers, neighbors, and even extended family members in response to questions such as, "Where is your dad?" or "When do you get to talk to your mom?" Explaining involves "making a labeled family relationship understandable, giving reasons for it, or elaborating on how it works" (Galvin, p. 10), which likely occurs at some point for all military family members and in some cases quite frequently when talking to civilians. Another speech activity Galvin has identified is defending (i.e., fending off attacks to the relationships validity). My participants, both long-distance dating and military families, have reported that their relationships are challenged by others through questions such as, "Can that really work?" or claims such as, "Distance is never good for a relationship." In these moments they feel compelled to defend their relationships as manageable and/or how they can benefit from separations. A third type of discourse-dependent speech activity military family members report is ritualizing. Enacting rituals allows for family members to (re)construct intimacy within their relationships. For example, military couples might call each other on a weekly basis for the sole purpose of discussing a book they are mutually reading. Service member parents and their children might exchange certain personal items upon separation and return them upon reunion. Both of these activities help bond the family members together while being apart. Clearly Galvin's discourse-dependence framework for theorizing and studying family relationships could take the military family communication research into new directions that could increase the field's understanding of the lived experiences of this atypical family form. Military family members could benefit as a result by seeing how others communicatively manage their relationships and possibly put into practice new patterns of relating.

My third and final suggestion for remaking family communication approaches to military families is to look at military families-as-discourse (versus military families-as-context). A communication theory that facilitates a discursive approach to military families is relational dialectics theory (RDT; Baxter, 2011). A complete discussion of this approach is not possible within the scope of this chapter, but briefly, the latest iteration of RDT (Baxter, 2011) focuses on competing discourses that are reflected in relational talk. Grounded in Bakhtin's (1986) concept of the utterance chain, Baxter's theory calls for the careful examination of relational talk for dominant and marginalized discourses regarding, for example, the self, relationships, and culture. In the case of military families, Sahlstein and Maguire (2013) provided a concrete example of work framed from this approach. They examined discourses that dominated their participants' (Army wives) talk about military deployment. Results from their analyses reflected competing discourses for what these women considered a "good military wife" and "good military family communication." Taking a military-as-discourse approach could expand the military family communication research into many different directions, such as looking at how discourses of American masculinity, and in particular masculinity within the U.S. military, informs husband/father talk with family members. Researchers could also take a closer look at discourses regarding what it means to be a good military mother. In light of my discussion of how the face of the military family is changing (e.g., with respect to sexual orientation of marital partners), family communication researchers could examine conversations in the media as well as within military families for how the dominant discourse of the traditional family is evoked. Discourses privileging physical proximity, shared residence, and frequent face-to-face communication might emerge in talk about military families, as well.

Contemporary U.S. military families face many challenges in the years to come as troops continue to deploy and redeploy in service of American missions around the world. Family communication researchers must continue their work in this area but also diversify their lines of inquiry. Remaking who are considered military families as well as how they are studied are just two important ways they will add to the already important research produced in the discipline.

# CHAPTER THIRTEEN

# Discourse Dependence in the Commuter Family

KARLA BERGEN

Commuter families, in which one spouse works and lives at a geographical distance far enough from the family home to require a second residence, reuniting with family periodically rather than daily, are increasingly common in both the U.S. (Forsyth & Gramling, 1998; Glotzer & Federlein, 2007) and other countries world-wide (Bassani, 2007; Li, Roslan, Abdullah, & Abdullah, 2014; Turcotte, 2013). Over the past decade, I have focused my scholarly work on commuter families in the U.S. (Bergen, 2003, 2006, 2007, 2009, 2010a, 2010b; Bergen, Kirby, & McBride, 2007; McBride & Bergen, in press). During the same period, researchers around the world have investigated commuter families in Great Britain (Holmes, 2006), Japan (Bassani, 2007), Malaysia (Li et al., 2014), Labrador and Newfoundland (Walsh, 2012), Thailand (Schvaneveldt, Young, & Schvaneveldt, 2001), The Netherlands (Van der Klis & Karsten, 2009a, 2009b), Germany (Häfner, 2011), Canada (Turcotte, 2013), and among recent immigrants from Hong Kong and China to Canada (Man, 2011). Much of this research focuses on describing the frequency and nature of commuter marriage in a specific country, as well as the culture-specific reasons for deviation from the norm of the single-residence family. In many studies, participants acknowledge that it would be more desirable to have their nuclear family under one roof.

Stated simply, families are expected to live together (Stafford, 2005) and, in spite of recent attention to diverse family forms, not much seems to have changed in the collective imagination of ordinary people. In a recent study of American laypersons' conceptualizations of family (Baxter et al., 2009), researchers found that participants consider co-residence a primary component of defining families. Glotzer and Federlein (2007) asserted that "Being separated from one's spouse, children, and household, by choice puts the commuter on the far edge of conventionality" (para. 8). The goal of this chapter, then, is twofold: first, to assess what we know about how commuter families maintain their identity as a family in spite of spouses spending considerable time in separate residences; and second, to provide an agenda for further research.

My interviews with commuter wives (Bergen, 2006, 2007, 2009, 2010a, 2010b; McBride & Bergen, in press) suggest that although they and their spouses have two residences, they self-identify as families because of established marital relationships, the recognition of a primary residence, and shared concern for adult children, grandchildren, and elderly relatives. A dilemma arises, however, when commuters' social network members assume that the spouses live apart due to marital problems, rather than their employment in different geographic locations (Bergen, 2006, 2009, 2010a, 2010b; McBride & Bergen, in press). Commuter wives reported their perceptions that others did not understand commuter marriages and therefore participants reported feeling compelled to explain their situations in response to questions or expressions of sympathy about the commuting arrangement. These findings illustrate Galvin's (2006) concept of discourse-dependent families.

Galvin (2006) noted that the proliferation of diverse family forms in the U.S. has called attention to the communication processes that nonnormative families use to "manage and maintain" their family identities (p. 3). Given that commuter families represent a growing, yet nonnormative, family form, it seems important to understand what communicative practices help commuter families to construct and maintain both their internal and external family identities. Internal practices relate to family members' communicative efforts to create a shared family identity within the immediate family circle, whereas external practices capture family members' communicative efforts to create a legitimate family identity to outsiders.

Understanding how communication functions in commuter families can be useful to commuter families, social network members, professional counselors, and those contemplating a commuter family. To that end, I review the scholarly work on commuter families and evaluate how this work contributes to the discussion of discourse dependence in commuter families. Sociologists initiated the study of commuter relationships. Although sociologists have remained in the conversation, gradually other disciplinary fields have joined in, including higher education, family studies/family counseling, and psychology, with communication studies joining the scholarly conversation a little more than a decade ago. Most of the research is from U.S. universities. Little of the literature focuses directly on communicative process-es. Although researchers frequently acknowledge communication processes with spouses, children, and others in the social network, such processes are not the prima-ry focus of most studies. With the exception of my own work (Bergen, 2003, 2006, 2007, 2009, 2010a, 2010b; Bergen et al., 2007; McBride & Bergen, in press), scant research examines the communicative practices members of commuter families use to create and maintain their identities. Before describing the findings of previous research, however, it is important to establish a clear definition of commuter marriage.

## Defining Commuter Marriage

Researchers studying commuter marriage have often defined it as spending at least three or four nights a week away from the primary family residence and maintain-ing a second residence in another location (e.g., Gerstel & Gross, 1984; Rhodes, 2002; Stafford, 2005; Winfield, 1985). Commuter marriage involves more than spouses being apart for a certain number of days or nights in a given period of time; one spouse also has a second residence in a different geographic location due to employment in that location, distant from the family home (Rhodes, 2002). Thus, families with spouses who travel (for example, sales representatives, trainers, and auditors) are not considered commuters because they do not establish and maintain a second residence. In contrast, politicians or lobbyists having a second residence in Washington, D.C. would be considered to have a commuter marriage.

Reuniting with some regularity is also a defining characteristic of commuter families (i.e., at least one spouse "commutes" or goes back and forth between the primary residence and the second residence). Although some spouses might reunite each weekend, others reunite in a bi-weekly, monthly, or every-few-months pattern, or as often as they are able to manage logistically and financially (see Bergen, 2006, for a detailed review). The relative freedom to reunite as a family regularly and a second non-institutional residence are characteristics that differentiate commuter families from military families, who have typically not been included in commuter marriage research (Rhodes, 2002; Stafford, 2005). In addition, the unique cultural context surrounding the U.S. military warrants examining military families as a separate group (see the chapter by Sahlstein Parcell, this volume).

There are other challenges to defining commuter marriage. Some researchers (e.g., Anderson & Spruill, 1993) have limited their samples to dual-career fam-ilies. In these cases, families where one spouse commutes for a job and the other spouse is a stay-at-home parent are excluded. Another challenge is presented by the international literature in which one spouse migrates to another country to work and send money back to the rest of the family, visiting perhaps once or twice a year (e.g., Man, 2011). I favor a broad definition of commuter families, defining them simply as families where one spouse works and lives at a geographic distance great enough to warrant establishing a second (non-institutional) residence, reuniting with family members periodically. Bear in mind, however, that the definitions and delimitations used by previous researchers are responsible for the demographics of families discussed in the following section.

## Demographics of Commuting Families

To date, research on commuter families in the U.S. has been conducted on primarily middle to upper-middle class, well-educated, dual-career professionals (Glotzer & Federlein, 2007; Rhodes, 2002). My own scholarly work (Bergen, 2003, 2006, 2007, 2009, 2010a, 2010b; Bergen et al., 2007; McBride & Bergen, in press) is based on similar demographics. Researchers have conducted limited research among working class commuter families in the U.S. (e.g., Erwin's [1993] dissertation on two blue-collar couples who commuted in response to the unemployment of the breadwinning spouse), although international research has been less tied to dual-career and professional families (e.g., Schvaneveldt et al., 2001; Walsh, 2012). Research on commuter families in the U.S. presents the commuting arrangement primarily as a solution to the "two-body problem" of academics and other dual-career couples' inability to find desirable employment for both spouses in the same geographic location (Wolf-Wendel, Twombly, & Rice, 2004).

Statistics indicate that the number of commuter marriages in the U.S. has grown substantially over the past three decades. In the mid-1980s, Winfield (1985) estimated the number of commuter marriages at about 700,000. Rhodes (2002) estimated the number of commuter marriages at 1 million. The most recent published data suggest there could be more than 3.5 million commuter marriages in the U.S. (U.S. Census Bureau, 2010). Given the recent depressed job market in the U.S., it stands to reason that there are probably even more families with one spouse commuting to a job in a distant location while the other spouse (and perhaps children) remain in the family home. Researchers studying commuter families in some non-U.S. locations speculate that commuter families in their countries are on the rise, as well (Bassani, 2007; Forsyth & Gramling, 1998; Turcotte, 2013).

Growing numbers of women in the workplace over the past four decades are also probable contributors to the rising numbers of commuter marriages (Bergen,

2006; Forsyth & Gramling, 1998; Glotzer & Federlein, 2007). The National Center for Marriage and Family Research found that the proportion of U.S. women in commuter marriages increased from 2.3% of all married women to 2.8% in the two-year period between 2009 and 2011. This rise suggests that women's careers are an important factor in the increasing numbers of commuter marriages (National Center for Marriage and Family Research, 2012). This finding is interesting because research has found that women who initiate commuter marriages tend to receive more negative social judgment than their male counterparts due to gender norms prescribing that women should prioritize family over careers (see Bergen, 2006, for a review). Given the well-documented cultural norms that still hold women primarily responsible for the home and childcare (Bergen et al., 2007; Holmes, 2004; Kingston, 2004), it is important to ask how women can manage a home and family when they are commuting to a distant location for their careers. The demographics of commuter family life might provide some clues.

The majority of U.S. commuter families studied to date have a particular family profile in terms of the length of marriage and the presence and age of children. Gerstel and Gross (1984) reported the average length of marriage for their respondents was 13 years. Anderson and Spruill (1993) indicated more than half of their participants had been married for 9 or more years, and Jehn, Stroh, and Von Glinow (1997) reported the commuter couples in their study had been married "or involved in a serious relationship" for an average of 14 years. My own sample of fifty women in commuter marriages had been married an average of about 20 years (Bergen, 2006). The length of these marital relationships seems to suggest that established couples are more likely to undertake a commuter marriage arrangement, but this finding could also simply reflect a sampling bias.

The great majority of research participants with commuter families in the U.S. had either no children or older children. Forty-six percent of Gerstel and Gross's (1984) sample had no children, 13% had grown children, 17% had children over age 12, and only 24% had children age 12 or under; Winfield's (1985) typical commuter couple had three or fewer grown children. Jehn et al. (1997) reported only 18% of their international sample had children. Van der Klis and Karsten (2009a) also stated that commuter families with children at home were not frequent in The Netherlands. The finding that many commuter families have no children or grown children is not particularly surprising, as the presence of dependent children creates more responsibility for the parent with whom they live. Gerstel and Gross (1984) observed that commuter marriage seems to work best for either childfree or empty-nesters who have launched their families, and the findings of other U.S. researchers (e.g., Glotzer & Federstein, 2007; Harris, Lowery, & Arnold, 2002) support this view. Although this research suggests that families might wait to commute until children are older to avoid the complications that might come with having young children while commuting, there are likely many families around the world for whom commuting is economically driven who do not have the luxury of choice regarding timing.

With this background on commuter families, let me turn to the research to see what previous scholars have learned about communicative processes in commuter families, generally, and the discourse-dependence of commuter families more specifically. At the outset, I note that very little of the research on commuter marriage comes from the communication discipline; scholars in other disciplines, however, have explored various communication issues in the commuter family.

## Foundational Academic Research

Commuter marriage first piqued the interest of journalists and academic researchers in the late 1970s and early 1980s, not long after women in the U.S. started entering the work force in large numbers. The term "commuter marriage" marked the relational form as nonnormative. For many people, the term was an oxymoron (Jehn et al., 1997). Given the conventional wisdom that people married ought to live together, the idea that a married couple who was not contemplating divorce would *choose* to live apart was completely unintelligible. Perhaps because of this confusion and perhaps due to the flurry of attention to commuter marriage in the popular press (Gerstel & Gross, 1984), academics found it a promising line of research.

Although there was much "to-do" in the press about this "new" relational form, early researchers pointed out that *men* had frequently spent time away from their families to fulfill the breadwinning role for hundreds of years; the new part was that women were now more frequently initiating commuter marriage for their *own* careers. The earliest academic research on commuter marriage came from sociology (Farris, 1978; Gross, 1980; Kirschner & Walum, 1978), in keeping with the interest of sociologists in describing social structures and interaction. In addition, some early researchers writing on commuter marriage were female academics who had experienced, or anticipated, commuter marriage (e.g., Gross, 1980; Winfield, 1985). Thus, it is understandable that these academics would want to investigate the factors that were correlated with the success of commuter marriage.

In the mid-1980s sociologists Gerstel and Gross (1984) published their foundational work on commuter marriage, followed by Winfield in 1985. Both books focused primarily on describing the characteristics of commuter families, including spouses' interactions with each other and members of their social networks.

Although neither study was specifically focused on communicative processes, it is not surprising to communication scholars that the importance of communication emerged as a central issue, since we know that communication is the way that relationships are created, negotiated, and maintained (Baxter, 2004). Relevant to the discussion on the discourse-dependence of commuter families, Gerstel and Gross (1984) focused more on internal communication *between* spouses, whereas Winfield (1985) gave more attention to external communication between spouses and members of their social networks.

One interesting communication phenomenon Gerstel and Gross (1984) discovered was participants' tendency to describe the commuting arrangement as temporary, both to themselves and to others, even when there was no planned ending date. Subsequent researchers, including myself, have also found that participants described their commuter marriages as temporary, even participants who had been in a commuter marriage for ten, fifteen, or twenty years (e.g., Bergen, 2006; Bunker, Zubek, Vanderslice, & Rice, 1992; Magnuson & Norem, 1999; Rhodes, 2002). Gerstel and Gross (1984) speculated that viewing (and describing) the commuting arrangement as temporary helped spouses to deal with the stress of their marriages not fitting the social norm, as well as "fend[ing] off negative imputations about their marriage" from "family, friends, and colleagues" (p. 155). Characterizing the commuter marriage as temporary could be a strategy that couples use in order to cope with their deviance while simultaneously explaining their commuting arrangement to others (Galvin, 2006).

Winfield (1985) emphasized the social disapproval that commuters are likely to encounter from family, friends, coworkers, and employers. Winfield described how the women commuters in her study were criticized for *leaving* their husbands (and children), men were criticized for *allowing* their wives to commute, and both were criticized by family and friends for going against the norm of traditional marital relationships; however, analysis of communicative interactions was not her focus. Foundational research from sociologists set the stage for commuter marriage research in other disciplines.

## Commuter Marriage Research in Diverse Disciplines

As commuter marriage became an increasingly common way to resolve work-life issues in families, interest in the relational form as a subject of academic research spread to diverse disciplines. Although many academic areas acknowledge communication as key to a successful commuter family, communication is tangential in many studies. Scholars in higher education, family counseling, and psychology have contributed to knowledge about communicative processes in commuter families, as well as researchers in the areas of interpersonal and family communication in which communicative processes are the primary focus.

## Higher Education

Researchers in higher education took an interest in commuter marriage fairly early, likely due to the fact that dual-career academics comprise a large portion of those in commuter marriages. About half of Gerstel and Gross's (1984) sample were academics, almost identical to the proportion in Johnson's (1987) study of 100 commuting spouses. In my study of 50 women in commuter marriages (Bergen, 2006), a full 60% were involved in higher education as either faculty or administrators. Understandably, authors in higher education have focused on educating peers about characteristics of commuter marriage and offering advice from those who have experienced it to those who might be contemplating it.

Several articles in higher education journals were written specifically for a female audience. Johnson (1987) sought to shed light on how families make the decision to adopt a commuting arrangement and how commuting women could successfully balance their personal and professional commitments. The problem-solution format of the article ("dilemmas to resolve" and "coping strategies") was oriented to an audience that might need to make the decision of whether or not to engage in a commuting arrangement. Hileman's (1990) study similarly focused on women in higher education, emphasizing the social, financial, emotional, and physical costs of a commuter marriage and calling for increased societal and institutional support for women who are commuting spouses. Harris et al. (2002) were enthusiastic about the opportunities commuting could make possible for women educators to advance professionally but were realistic about the problems and sacrifices. Taken collectively, researchers in this field concentrated on the benefits and challenges of commuter marriages, presenting commuter marriage as a sometimes-necessary-but-less-than-optimal strategy for women's career advancement, but communication processes were not the focus.

## Family Studies/Family Counseling

The disciplines of family studies, human development, and family counseling have been a rich source of studies on commuter marriage. Although the interest probably stems from the nonnormative nature of commuter marriage and the perception of risk for marital and family problems, the cumulative body of work has made a contribution in emphasizing the importance of communication processes in commuter relationships. It is not always clear, however, if their recommendations are grounded in empirical research.

Much of the literature in family counseling consists of literature reviews (Magnuson & Norem, 1999; Rhodes, 2002; Rotter, Barnett, & Fawcett, 1998) rather than empirical research, but because the counseling perspective is rooted in family systems theory, the notion that communication can be used intentionally to construct and maintain family identity is primary. For example, Rotter and colleagues (1998) stated that an important contribution counselors could make was to "help couples and families... *maintain a sense of family* while pursuing their respective careers" (p. 48, italics added). The authors proposed that counselors could do this by helping with problem-solving skills and decision-making processes, as well as "communication skills to facilitate the partners in negotiation and expression of mutual support" (Rotter et al., p. 47). Anderson and Spruill (1993) investigated commuter families' decision-making processes and concluded that for the majority of their participant couples, the decision-making process had not received the careful attention it warrants. These researchers recommended counseling to ensure a systematic decision-making process and to provide support with coping strategies. Glotzer and Federlein (2007) made the same recommendation. Although the aforementioned scholars acknowledged the importance of effective communication strategies, Rhodes (2002) made specific recommendations: daily phone calls while apart, weekly family meetings, and rituals for leaving and reunions, similar to the relational maintenance strategies for all long-distance relationships identified by communication scholars (Stafford, 2005; Stafford & Merolla, 2007).

Jackson, Brown, and Patterson-Stewart (2000) also offered concrete suggestions for communication strategies to enhance family life for commuter families. Although Jackson et al. interviewed only four couples, they broke new ground in commuter family research by focusing their study on African American couples, their children, and their friends. Each couple was asked to recruit one child and one friend to participate in an interview about how they viewed the commuting arrangement and how it affected their relationship with the commuting couple. Somewhat predictably, children who had been in college at the time their parents were commuting did not feel that they had been affected much, although one adult child recalled feeling a bit neglected. Other children who had been in junior high or high school while their parents had a commuter marriage complained about the long-distance parent not being able to attend their games or other school events.

Jackson et al. (2000) made important contributions to understanding the discourse dependence of commuter families in their discussion of ways counselors might help commuter families on the intrapersonal, interpersonal, and organizational/institutional levels. They suggested counselors could help couples in developing dyadic goals, mutually supportive behaviors, and in "reframing" intimacy and time apart. They also explained how counselors could help families "create a new meaning of family" (p. 33) through family discussions of the advantages, disadvantages, and appreciation of unique opportunities provided by their family's living arrangement, as well as spending time at both parents' residences. This discussion of specific communicative strategies for increasing commuter families' sense of family provides a clear example of Galvin's (2006) internal communication practices.

Potential problems that children might encounter when parents have a commuter marriage were addressed by Glotzer and Federlein (2007) in their auto-ethnographic case study. These researchers had both experienced commuter families and described the negative effects their children experienced as preschoolers and as adolescents/young adults. Glotzer reported his young son asking, "Are you and mom getting reversed?" (p. 9). This question highlights the cultural norm of co-residence so strongly that even a preschooler suspected his parents of getting divorced when the father accepted a position that required commuting.

In sum, the contributions from the family studies/family counseling area moved commuter marriage research forward by including African American couples, children, and social network members. In addition, these contributions provided a clear focus on communication strategies to strengthen family relationships and internal family identity.

## Psychology/Organizational Behavior

Researchers in psychology and organizational behavior have also contributed significantly to the commuter family literature, particularly those from countries beyond the United States (e.g., Häfner, 2011; Rispens, Jehn, & Rexwinkel, 2010; Van der Klis & Karsten, 2009a, 2009b). One of the strengths of the research from psychologists has been the examination of differences between commuter couples and single-residence, dual-career couples. For example, Bunker et al. (1992) compared 90 commuting couples and 133 single-residence couples on five measures of satisfaction and two measures of stress. These researchers found that although commuter couples were less satisfied with their family life and partner relationships, they were more satisfied with their work lives and perceived less stress overall than single-residence couples. Given the frequent research finding (Forsyth & Gramling, 1998; Glotzer & Federstein, 2007; Rhodes, 2002) that one of the advantages of commuter marriage is the ability to compartmentalize work and family, these findings make sense.

Although one might think that the commuting spouse would be more stressed due to having to travel or that the parent at home might be more stressed and less satisfied with having to function as a single-parent to young children during the week, there were no significant differences in the Bunker et al. (1992) study with respect to either satisfaction or stress based on gender, or whether the participants were the traveling or non-traveling spouse. Communication with family or partners was not a variable in this study, but findings might suggest that because commuters are less satisfied with their family and partner relationships, maintaining cohesive family identities could be more problematic for commuters. In a similar study almost two decades later with an international sample of 40 commuter and 36 non-commuting dual-career couples, Rispens and colleagues (2010) also found that participants were less satisfied with their family lives and rated themselves lower on relational intimacy with their partners.

Findings from these comparative studies raise the issue of whether strategic use of Galvin's (2006) internal boundary management strategies (for example, explaining the reason for mom and dad living apart because of mom's job to young children or instituting a ritual of a pizza party on Friday nights when dad comes home) might be helpful in strengthening a sense of family identity among family members.

The results of these comparative studies might be partly explained by the findings of a study in the Netherlands. Van der Klis and Karsten (2009b) investigated commuting partners' "meanings of home." They found that although 80% of the commuting spouses in their study attempted to make their commuter residence home-like by re-decorating and surrounding themselves with personal artifacts such as family pictures and collectables, a majority of participants never quite considered the commuter residence "home." They concluded, "For most commuting partners, the home is clearly where the heart is, and the heart is in the family dwelling" (p. 244). From a communication perspective, we might say that the "family dwelling," the communal residence, is a symbol of family. Labeling it as "home" clearly communicates that even though commuters spend much time in their commuter residence, it is not "home."

## Interpersonal/Family Communication

In a disciplinary field whose researchers focus on how communication practices create and maintain relationships, very few have examined the communicative processes within commuter families or between commuting spouses and their social network members. Communication scholars are uniquely positioned to study the communicative construction of identity, given the widespread belief that individual, relational, and group identities are constituted in communication (Baxter, 2004; Bergen & Braithwaite, 2009). Even though the research on communicative processes in commuter families is limited, it holds great potential.

A primary focus of some interpersonal communication scholars has been how communication is used to maintain relationships (e.g., Canary & Dainton, 2002). Although relational maintenance is not synonymous with the communicative construction of identity, relational maintenance behaviors are inherently communicative and one way that families maintain relational identities. Research examining relational maintenance in long-distance relationships has sometimes included commuter marriage (i.e., Merolla, 2010a; Sahlstein, 2004; Stafford, 2005). Stafford (2005) synthesized relational maintenance research relating to nonresidential and geographically distant relationships, including commuter marriage as a subset of long-distance adult romantic relationships, which also included nonresidential marital relationships due to military service, civilian careers involving traveling, and incarceration.

The maintenance strategies Stafford (2005) described for long-distance adult romantic relationships in general included: (a) periodic face-to-face contact; (b) mediated communication (i.e., contact by telephone, letters, email, and video-conferencing); (c) symbolic connections that included artifacts and rituals that invoke positive thoughts and memories of the partner; (d) rituals for reunion and departure; and (e) shared activities during time together. My own multiple-case study (Bergen, 2003) of relational maintenance in commuter marriage found four maintenance strategies that closely parallel Stafford's (2005) summary: (a) planning discussions; (b) frequent communication while apart in the form of telephone conversations, email, instant messaging, letters, and gifts; (c) reunion rituals; and (d) spending "quality time" together when physically co-present. Taken together, this work presents clear evidence of what Galvin (2006) calls internal communication practices in which family members communicate between themselves to maintain a cohesive family identity.

Relational maintenance scholars have also provided insight into how new communication technologies can assist commuter families in cultivating internal communication practices via mediated technology. Dainton and Aylor (2002) found frequent telephone conversations for long-distance dating couples correlated with higher levels of relational satisfaction and commitment, two of the most important predictors of relational success. The same finding might be true for commuter families. The proliferation of technologies such as text-messaging, video-web cam programs (such as Skype), and social networking sites offers additional ways for commuter families to maintain ties. Researchers conducting a study of commuting families in The Netherlands described how "some [parents in their study] give each child a cell phone or email their children frequently. One father is even active in the son's MSN network and both have webcams" (Van der Klis & Karsten, 2009a, p. 349). Relational maintenance research focusing on commuter families could provide additional insight into how these families communicate to create and maintain their internal family identity.

Although cross-disciplinary research on commuter families has addressed internal communication practices, external communication practices have been virtually ignored. As far as I am aware, my work (Bergen, 2006, 2009, 2010a, 2010b) is the only effort to study how members of commuter families communicate with those outside the family. I focused on the types of messages commuter wives received from others that might affirm or threaten their family identities as well as how they might respond to such messages. I found that my participants, almost without exception, reported questions about their commuting arrangement from social network members, in addition to reporting expressions of emotion (primarily sympathy for husbands and children), nonverbal messages (primarily communicating others' negative emotions), and second-hand messages from others (most of which reflect social disapproval). Questions about the commuter arrangements were most frequently reported and the most salient type of message commuter wives receive from members of their social networks (Bergen, 2006, 2010b). The questions fell into three broad categories: (a) requests for general information, (b) questions about the reason for the commuting arrangement, and (c) questions implying negative evaluation and judgment of the commuter marriage. The second most frequently reported category was expressions of emotion, including expressions of concern and sympathy (for example, comments from others saying how hard the commuting arrangement must be on the commuter, but especially the spouse and children), and expressions of disapproval and criticism (for example, the speaker stating that they themselves could never tolerate a commuting arrangement). A third category, labeled nonverbal messages, consisted of facial expressions, vocal intonation, and silence that the commuting wives interpreted as negatively valenced messages. Many of the questions and messages, such as expressions of sympathy for the husband, call commuting wives' identities into question by implicitly, and sometimes explicitly, asking how the couple can maintain a good marriage and how the woman can perform the expected functions of wife and mother while living apart from spouse and family. A number of commuter wives that I interviewed described how other people thought that the commuting arrangement meant they were having marital difficulties or getting a divorce.

Although most of the participants in my research (Bergen, 2006) did not have children or were empty-nesters, a handful of women in commuter marriages discussed how their children, while young, had to deal with the perception that their parents had a troubled marriage. One participant who commuted to a neighboring state for a doctoral program reported that her eight-year-old son had asked her, "Are you and dad divorced?" because the kids at school had insisted that was the case and would not believe him when he said "no" (Bergen, 2007, p. 10). Another of my participants who worked two hours from her rural home to practice her law specialty in a metropolitan area reported that her teenage daughter came home from church saying that people had asked if her mother had "left them." Although the daughter and husband usually sang in the choir on Sunday, the participant told me that the following week "we all sat together as a family and made a big deal out of talking to everybody and shaking hands and all that" (Bergen, 2007, p. 8). This family decided to handle the rumors by publicly presenting themselves as a family, reminiscent of the strategy of "doing family" in Suter, Daas, and Bergen's (2008) study of lesbian families.

In contrast to the family who "did family," the majority of participants in my (Bergen, 2006) study chose to provide explanations, justifications, and excuses to others when their family identity was challenged (Galvin, 2006). Most commuter wives reported presenting factual, straightforward explanations in response to questions. A second smaller group of commuter wives acknowledged strategic accounts to others in the form of justifications and excuses, often to pre-empt anticipated questions or to legitimize their commuting arrangement. Many reported they felt compelled to account for why they were commuting and living apart from their husbands. One respondent observed, "You almost have to explain what the commute is and then how often you see one another because if you commute and you don't see one another, somehow that undoes the concept of marriage" (Bergen, 2006, p. 148). Thus, many commuter wives I interviewed chose to present themselves to others as happily and securely married.

In summary, scholars in many disciplines have studied commuter families; however, much existing research is descriptive demographics (by sociologists) and prescriptive advice (by educators and family counselors). We are still far from having a complete picture of how commuter families maintain their sense of *being* a family, both internally and externally, and how commuter families negotiate day-to-day work-life balance.

## Directions for Future Research

As it stands, existing research on commuter families is piecemeal and suffers from biases and underdeveloped areas that hamper our more complete insight into how commuter families construct and enact their family identities. Two of the most obvious biases that limit understanding include: (a) a bias toward U.S.-based research; and (b) a bias toward couple-centric adults. Let me provide an agenda for rectifying these biases and charting a course for future research.

## U.S. Bias

U.S. scholars rarely incorporate non-U.S.-based research in their work. Studies in this chapter from non-U.S. scholars demonstrate a growing quantity of international research that could inform U.S. scholars' work. This chapter aims to raise awareness of work on commuter families by scholars in other countries. Comparative studies and international collaborations between researchers would enrich the work of both U.S. and non-U.S. scholars. Our scholarly associations with international membership could do much to promote such collaboration.

## Bias toward Couple-Centric Adults

Although much research on commuter families has purported to include children's perspectives, in reality, children's perspectives have largely been represented through interviews with parents about their perceptions of their children's behaviors, adjustment, performance, and so forth. The single exception is the study by Jackson et al. (2000), in which children themselves were interviewed. Lack of attention to children's perspectives might be due to anticipated difficulties with Institutional Review Boards permitting children to participate in research. However, young adult participants who have attained majority age might be more desirable respondents than younger children in their ability to be reflective about their experiences in commuting families. Other important directions regarding parent-child relationships include study of how commuting parents maintain relationships with children, and how the frequent absence of one parent might affect the relationship of the child with the other parent.

In addition to including children in commuter family research, researchers should consider including others who are part of the commuter family. For example, grandparents, aunts, uncles, or cousins who help with childcare, household tasks, or who are cared for by the commuting family, would provide another perspective. Future research needs to incorporate other family members to obtain a multidimensional picture of how communicative practices are used by commuter families to construct internal and external family identity.

Beyond these areas of bias, other areas that need further research attention include: (a) examination of how work-life issues are negotiated on a daily basis;

(b) examination of the timing in the life cycle of the commuter family form; and (c) identification of additional discourse-based strategies for creating, maintaining, and strengthening internal and external commuter family identity.

## Work-Family Balance

Commuting families exist to enable individuals to fulfill responsibilities to both work and family, yet we still know surprisingly little about how commuter families negotiate the day-to-day challenges of work and family. Van der Klis and Karsten (2009a) provided important insight into how Dutch commuter families manage work, childcare, and household responsibilities. Similarly, Man (2011) described a transnational parenting practices among Hong Kong and Chinese immigrant families to Canada called "astronaut families," in which one spouse (usually the father) worked in Asia while the mother remained with the child(ren) in Canada. In the U.S., Bergen et al. (2007) examined the macro-strategies that commuter families use to meet caregiving needs within their families, but this research barely scratched the surface. How families negotiate the division of labor and family members' degree of satisfaction associated with various strategies remains an important question to be interrogated.

## Timing and Fluidity of Commuting

As observed earlier, a recurrent finding in much U.S. research is that commuter marriage is theorized as difficult for families with young children, especially where perceived choice is involved. The difficulties attendant with commuter families having young children has also been mentioned by researchers in other countries (e.g., Man, 2011; Schvaneveldt et al., 2007; Van der Klis & Karsten, 2009a). It seems that this would be a matter for empirical investigation. Do commuter families (or potential commuter families) make conscious family planning choices because of such anticipated difficulties? How might they negotiate a pregnancy or a multiple birth, knowing that one parent would be single-parenting much of the time? Might such decisions be different for families in collectivist cultures where it is more common to live with extended family who could be expected to help care for children?

Such questions implicitly assume that commuting families make a choice. How much choice do commuting families really feel that they have? What about countries in which jobs enabling a particular quality of family life are simply not available locally? Cross-cultural comparative studies could be enlightening.

Future research should also focus on long-term commuter families who have been successful in both duration and satisfaction with the commuting arrangement. Knowledge of how long-term, satisfied families have maintained strong family bonds could serve as a model to other commuting families who are uncertain about the viability of the family form.

## Building Up the Menu of Discursive Strategies

Existing research provides a starting point for examining the internal and external strategies that commuter families use to create, negotiate, maintain, and strengthen their family identities, but this work is still in its infancy. Preliminary research on relational maintenance in commuter families provides some insight into the internal communication practices that help to construct a sense of family identity among family members, but research should be extended to samples larger than Bergen's (2003) case study. There are several other promising lines of investigation.

First, the role of symbols in constructing, maintaining, and strengthening family identity should be examined. One common symbol involves labels or naming (Suter et al., 2008). How do commuter families identify themselves? How do family members identify the commuting parent? How do spouses and children identify the second residence? How family members talk about other family members, the commuting arrangement, and the second residence holds much potential for constructing family identity. Artifacts, also are symbols that help to construct family identity (Bergen, 2003). What artifacts might trigger memories and fond feelings for absent family members?

Second, how do commuter families "do family"? What everyday activities make family members feel like family or show others that they are family? Are there conscious efforts to promote or maintain family rituals that lead to a sense of family cohesion? What efforts are made to promote family togetherness when all family members are together? Are there activities that invoke a feeling of family even though family members might not be together?

Third, how are recent communication technologies being used by commuter families to maintain a sense of family identity? Which forms of technology and what practices are most effective in promoting relational closeness between family members?

Finally, family communication scholars need to work with scholars in other fields, both in the U.S. and abroad, to devise a typology of relational maintenance strategies that promote an internal sense of family for commuter families as well as a typology of ways that commuter families present their family identity to those outside the family.

As scholars continue to study the role of communication practices in constituting commuter families' and other diverse families' identities, we can refine and augment the strategies used by discourse-dependent families in light of emerging research and perhaps help other commuter families discursively navigate the terrain of this nonnormative family form.

# CHAPTER FOURTEEN

# "Is he my *real* uncle?"

## Re-constructing Family in the Diaspora

CHITRA AKKOOR

In the past decade, family communication scholars have directed their attention to different kinds of families, for example, adoptive families (e.g. Docan-Morgan, 2010; Galvin, 2003; Harrigan, 2010; Suter & Ballard, 2009), stepfamilies (e.g. Baxter, Braithwaite, Bryant & Wagner, 2004; Golish, 2003), same-sex families (e.g. Bergen, Suter & Daas, 2006), and families of different ethnicities/nationalities in the United States (Bylund, 2003; Moriizumi, 2011). They have studied challenges such as negotiating address terms for same-sex parents, blending and "becoming" a family in stepfamilies, and identity issues in adoptive families. However, one population that is still largely unexplored in the family communication literature is that of refugees who leave their homelands due to war, religious persecution, or political turmoil in their homelands, forming diasporas as they disperse around the world.

The term *diaspora* has been used to describe the dispersal of people from a common homeland to locations around the world. Although originally used to describe forced dispersal of the Jewish people from their homeland, the term is now used to describe both voluntary and involuntary migration. A substantial body of research in other disciplines, such as anthropology, sociology, and diaspora studies, has identified the many challenges of diasporic people in the land of settlement, some of which addresses familial relationships. Drawing upon this body of literature, and my own research on Afghan Hindus in Germany, this essay will focus on how "family" is defined and re-negotiated among involuntary migrants who move to countries with cultures very different from their own. I will conclude by proposing ways in which family communication scholars can fruitfully engage in studying the complexities of family in diasporic contexts.

## Forced to Leave the Homeland

According to the United Nations High Commission for Refugees (hereafter UNHCR, 2011) 42 million people were forcibly displaced as a result of conflict and persecution in their homeland in 2011; of these, 15.2 million were refugees, 26.4 million were internally displaced persons, and 895,000 people were seeking asylum. Uprooted suddenly from their homeland due to war, violence, and/or fear of persecution, refugees leave their homeland and seek shelter in bordering countries. Many end up in refugee camps that have the bare minimum necessities, are congested, and lack sanitation (Lindley, 2011; Mott, 2009). Some refugees are helped through remittances from family living in other countries; these fortunate few are able to refuse UNHCR assistance and leave the refugee camps to support themselves in nearby cities. Others, after protracted stays in the camps, are eager to be resettled (Horst, 2002). Often refugees spend anywhere from 5 to 15 or 20 years in these camps waiting for resettlement.

Refugee status is generally determined by the UNHCR, while participating resettlement countries decide on how many refugees will be granted asylum in any year. According to the UNHCR, "The operational sub-region, covering 36 countries in Northern, Western, Central and Southern Europe, remained a major region of asylum in 2012" (UNHCR, 2011), with France, Germany, and Sweden the top three receiving countries.

Voluntary agencies (VOLAGS) assist in the resettlement by finding sponsors to support financially new arrivals until they are able to find employment, providing training prior to arrival in the host country, and arranging for travel (Xu, 2007). Despite the preparation and eagerness of refugees to leave the camp, resettlement brings with it a host of other problems (Eisenbruch, de Jong, & Van de Put, 2004).

## Post-migration Stressors

A large body of literature on involuntary migration shows that refugees are afflicted by a number of stressors, both psychological and cultural, due to conditions under which the migration happens. A common stressor identified among refugees is severe PTSD (post-traumatic stress disorders), a "potentially disabling condition characterized by traumatic flashbacks, hyper-vigilance, and emotional numbing" (Fazel, Wheeler, & Danesh, 2005, p. 1312). PTSD occurs as a result of witnessing or having personally gone through violence, persecution, torture, death of loved ones, personal injury, rape, or other atrocities (Awwad, 2003; Lie, Sveass, & Eilertsen, 2004; Schweitzer, Brough, Vromans, & Asic-Kobe, 2011). Post-resettlement depression can also result from discrimination, racism, and worries about those left behind in refugee camps or in the homeland (Kokanovic, Dowerick, Butler, Herrman, & Gunn, 2008).

In addition to psychological problems, refugees face cultural barriers such as language difficulties, unfamiliarity with cultural norms, loss of status, and lack of social networks (Bush, Bohon, & Kim, 2005). Language proficiency is linked to employment, and lack of skills in the host country's language means unemployment or employment in low-paid jobs (Suárez-Orozco & Suárez-Orozco, 2001). Sometimes professionals find that their qualifications are not recognized in the host country (McGregor, 2008). In addition to posing economic difficulties, lack of employment has a profound impact on the self-esteem of adults. Young children, on the other hand, pick up the local language quickly, making adults rely on children for basic social functions such as reading official letters, dealing with government officials, banking, speaking to doctors, and so on, resulting in further loss of status for adults and, to some extent, parental authority (Candappa & Ibinigie, 2003; Puig, 2002). While most European countries that resettle refugees offer generous welfare, they simultaneously relegate recipients to lower social strata by disabling them from becoming earning members of society (Mesthenous & Ioannidi, 2002; Wren, 2003). In addition, the media creates negative images of asylum seekers in the minds of mainstream viewers, portraying them as criminals or as a drain on the system, which in turn fosters social discrimination (Dunkerley, Scourfield, Maegusuku-Hewett, & Smalley, 2006; Steimal, 2010).

A major source of stress for refugees is loss of social networks due to separation of family members. Separation occurs in different ways. In some cases parents, while still in the homeland, send their children out of the country to avoid recruitment into the military (Gilad, 1990; Sample, 2007); these children live with extended family members in other countries (McGregor, 2008). Families also get separated while fleeing for their lives (Mott, 2009). Extended families break up into smaller groups, leaving at different times to avoid detection (Keown-Bomar, 2004). Some members of the family get resettled, whereas others remain in refugee camps hoping to be reunited with their families (Franz & Ives, 2008; Gilad, 1990).

Finally, the very definition of family poses difficulties, becoming a reason for fragmentation of the family. Most refugees from developing nations are resettled in developed countries where the nuclear family is the norm (Jubilut & Carneiro, 2007). For example, in 2010, the majority of refugees to the United States came from Iraq, Burma, and Bhutan, all of which have cultures that define family in terms of large extended kin that favor strong mutual ties (Eby, Iverson, Smyers, & Kekic, 2011). These definitions play a crucial role in the resettlement process.

## The Ideal Family

What constitutes family is profoundly cultural. Extended families or large kinship-based households are considered the ideal type in a number of societies, and this type of family serves important support functions. For example, among Somalians, extended family provides social support and child-care (Boyle & Ali, 2010). In Yemen, the family is based on filial obligations in which sons and their wives and children are expected to take care of parents as they age (Stevenson, 1997). In cultures where the extended family is the norm, brothers are expected to live together with their wives and children; the sibling bond is sometimes considered even more important than the spousal bond (Haines, Rutherford, & Thomas, 2012). Similarly, Ong (2003) described the "matrilocal residence" (p. 34) in Cambodia, where women live close to the natal family, forming "sisterly networks" of protection.

The extended family is based on interdependence. Individual identity is tied to family and relationships. In Albanian culture, a person's identity is first and foremost linked with the family (Griffith et al., 2005). Child rearing and social-ization of children is not just the domain of the parents but the entire house-hold. In the Israeli kibbutz, for example, children are considered as belonging to the community, not just the biological parents (Lee, 1982). In the Dominican Republic, family can consist of three generations of siblings and first cousins all of whom contribute to socializing children, and multiple generations contribute to the well-being of the family (Garrison & Weiss, 1979). Commenting on the interdependence and family obligations of refugees from Laos, Bosnia, Iraq, Sudan, and Afghanistan, resettled in Nebraska, Pipher (2003) noted, "Their attitudes towards family put ours into perspective. An American might be in therapy complaining of an intrusive mother. An immigrant will be working three jobs so that she can bring her aunt to this country" (p. 22). Obligation to the family supersedes obligation to self. These ideals of what it means to be family is challenged post-migration, as refugees come into contact with different ideals of the family in Western countries.

# Re-configuring Family during Resettlement

Researchers of refugee diasporas have identified three ways in which the ideal of the extended family is placed in opposition to the normative nuclear family when refugees resettle in Western countries. First and foremost, the nuclear definition of family is applied when granting asylum to refugees, which precludes other kin that are deemed important by the refugees from getting asylum. Second, definition of marriage as a legal monogamous relationship poses problems for those who come from societies in which polygamy is normative. Finally, in a number of developed countries, refugees are dispersed across the country based on the nuclear family.

Grillo (2008) has argued that "while the right to live in a family is recognized in international conventions, immigration policies may circumscribe that right by defining what a family is or should be" (p. 16). Receiving countries find extended families and other collectivistic practices of other cultural groups problematic because they interfere with their efforts of integrating immigrants into mainstream society. As a result, in the Scandinavian welfare states of Denmark, Norway, and Sweden, family reunification applications are severely restricted, contributing to the transformation of refugee extended families into nuclear families (Hagelund, 2008). Fearing rejection of their applications, refugees often present themselves as a nuclear family (Mott, 2009).

Definitions of family determine the order in which family members are accepted for resettlement. Marriage is generally at the center of reunification in Western countries, thus first preference is given to spouses, then to dependent children under the age of 18 (Fonseca & Ormond, 2008). Older parents and older children are denied asylum. Other family members seeking reunification must prove that they were left alone, or are dependent on the person sponsoring; otherwise they must seek asylum individually or find other means to immigrate. Another issue related to marriage that complicates definition of family, is that some cultures such as the Hmong, and many Islamic communities, practice polygamy (Keown-Bomar, 2004). In Yemen, men who have many wives maintain many households. When migrating, only the wife with whom the man is currently living is recognized and granted permission, leaving the other wives and children stranded to fend for themselves (Stevenson, 1997).

Given the strength of extended family ties in the homeland, it is not surprising that the new immigrants are often drawn to locations where kith and kin reside (Chavez, Hubbell, Mishra, & Valdez, 1997; Halilovich, 2012). The extended family helps new immigrants find jobs, helps them get adapted to the new culture, and helps economically by pooling resources. New arrivals lacking a line of credit find it expedient to borrow money from family (Keown-Bomar, 2004).

Although family provides both financial and social capital that new immigrants draw upon (Sanders & Nee, 1996), a number of countries have refugee dispersal policies to distribute refugees throughout the country. Receiving countries must balance the need of the refugees on the one hand, with the ability of local communities to be able to absorb the newcomers in terms of employment and housing. For example, a 1999 asylum act in the U.K. implemented a no-choice rule to steer newcomers from settling in particular areas (Wren, 2007). Similarly, in the mid-1970s refugees from Vietnam were dispersed across the United States (Haines, 2010). Norway imposes penalties, such as loss of state assistance, if refugees move from their designated location within three years (Valenta & Bunar, 2010).

Generally refugees are moved to remote areas where that particular ethnic group is altogether absent or exists in small numbers (Valenta & Bunar, 2010). In the process, these populations lose contact with family and the benefits of kinship support. The effect is not simply psychological. In one study among refugees in the U.K., single males spoke about the loss of kinship ties in terms of not being able to find a marriage partner, since in their culture this was a function of the family; not only did they lose connections to their family of origin, they also did not have the means to create a family for themselves (Agar & Strang, 2008). Dispersal laws, thus, have a profound effect on redefining the meaning of family by forcing nuclear family configurations.

With the review of research on refugees as a background, I now present a case study of Hindu minority population from Afghanistan settled in Germany. This research was part of a larger dissertation project on Afghan Hindu culture and communication practices, conducted over 5 years using ethnographic methods of participant-observation and in-depth interviews, at social and family gatherings (Akkoor, 2011). The research question sought to understand how Afghan Hindus discursively constructed their migration experiences and resettlement in Germany and challenges associated with the migration. The interview protocol was designed to let the participants speak about what they thought were important aspects of their migration and resettlement. The importance of family and challenges of renegotiating the cultural meaning of family figured prominently in their discursive constructions of migration and resettlement in Germany.

## Afghan Hindus: A Case Study

Afghan Hindus were a relatively small ethnic/religious minority living in Afghanistan for many centuries. When the Mujahideen came to power in 1992 and later the Taliban in 1994, *shari'a* (Islamic) laws were instituted and violence escalated. Hindus, who had gradually begun leaving Afghanistan after the Soviet withdrawal in 1989, left in larger numbers. Most Afghan Hindus first went to India, via Pakistan, where they were given aid by the United Nations. However, unable to find employment or establish their businesses in India, they decided to look elsewhere for long-term settlement.

Germany was an attractive destination because of an established welfare system for refugees with generous aid. Prior to 1993, Article 16 of the Basic Law allowed people who were persecuted for political and religious reasons to seek asylum in Germany (Chin, 2007). Family members, who had left during the Soviet occupation of Afghanistan and had settled successfully in Germany, encouraged later emigrants to migrate, leading to chain migration.

Unlike many refugee populations, Afghan Hindus did not spend time in refugee camps; they nevertheless described many of the challenges experienced by refugee groups. Many had experienced post-traumatic stress disorders in the early years. They described economic difficulties during their sojourn in India. Upon arrival in Germany, they faced economic, linguistic, and cultural barriers. Over the years, many Afghan Hindus had successfully adapted to Germany, and expressed gratitude to the country for granting them asylum, however; many were concerned about loss of religion and their identity as a people due to cultural assimilation. The term *Afghan Hindu* was in fact coined in Germany to emphasize their ties to their homeland and their religion. Older adults attempted to inculcate this identity in the next generation, and family cohesion was an integral part of their cultural heritage. Like many other Eastern cultures, "family" was defined based on large kinship relationships.

## Importance of Family Ties

The emphasis on familial relationships rather than the individual was evident even in initial introductions. When someone was introduced he or she was referred to not by name, but by relationship to the person performing the introductions; for example, "*Yeh mera bhatija hai*" ("This is my nephew"), "*Yeh meri behan hai*" ("This is my sister"). Often, I learned their names only later as I heard them being referenced in conversation. Even something as mundane as introductions emphasized relationships rather than individual identities.

One of the research participants, Dr. Pyasa, a physician, spoke of strong family ties as a source of pride. The doctor and I were sitting in his backyard during a visit to interview him, when a neighbor waved to him across the hedge between their properties. Later in the interview Dr. Pyasa said:

> This relationship [with family] is very important in our culture. For example, this German neighbor asked me last week, "What happened? Is everything alright?" I said, "Yes, why do you ask?" And he said, "Well looks like you haven't had any visitors lately" [laughing], because he sees that we have family visiting constantly. ... Our neighbors see how strong family relationships are for us.

I had many opportunities to observe the veracity of Dr. Pyasa's words, both in his family and among other families I visited. The doctor and Mrs. Pyasa's son, daughter-in-law, and grandchildren all lived in one house. During my visit to their home, his niece and her children were visiting from the U.K. and an assortment of relatives came and went during the course of the day and evening. I observed this in other families, especially during weekends.

Those who were unable to live together or in close proximity visited the Afghan Hindu temples, where I did a number of observations and interviews as well. Extended families got together to sponsor a meal after the Sunday service, getting together at the temple and preparing a feast for the congregation. Others lingered after the meal to catch up with family members. Thus the temple served as not only a religious and social space, but also as a space for families to maintain connections.

## Who Counts as Family?

"Family" was a comprehensive term for Afghan Hindus that included all types of close and distant ties through blood, marriage, friendships, and long association. In Afghanistan, family was a multi-member, multi-generational household. "We had huge families," was a statement I heard frequently as my participants recalled their lives in Afghanistan, where parents, sons and their wives and children, uncles and aunts, and grandparents all lived in one household. Afghan Hindus used *ghar* to describe these large households. The elder of the family, generally the oldest male, was the head of the household and the family business; mostly, all male members in the family worked for the business. A common way of speaking about this arrangement was, "*ek kamata thaa sab khaate the*," meaning, "one person earned, and everyone ate [fed everyone]." For any individual, or married couple, to leave the family to live on their own was a matter of shame for the whole family.

Afghan Hindus also spoke about family in terms of spatial arrangements and camaraderie:

> Dr. Pyasa, for example, remarked: We had big houses, not like small ones here, and in one house everyone lived. Those who were married had their own rooms but the food was cooked in one common kitchen. We used to eat together. Then after dinner we would all sit and drink tea together. There was a lot of fellowship and closeness between family members.

This description emphasized the largeness of the physical space in terms of the size of the homes, the living arrangements of the people, and "fellowship" and "closeness" among members of the household. Even those who were not wealthy managed, as described by another Afghan Hindu, "Not everyone had huge houses but even in small houses, when sons got married they used to live together. When parents became old, children would take care of them. I mean, there was a spirit of sacrifice there." People did not mind sharing the limited space in the interest of living together. Family meant sharing space, small or large, spending time together, and taking care of elders involving "sacrifice" on the part of the individual for the collective good. A middle-aged woman, Mrs. Swami, talked about the vacations to "the orchards" that the entire family would take, staying in cabins for a week or more. Having fun meant enjoying with the entire family.

I asked younger people, who were either born in Germany, or were infants when they arrived, if their parents ever spoke to them about their past in Afghanistan. Rani, a 22-year-old woman who left Afghanistan as an infant, said:

> My father tells so much about his family how he grew up not with one father but three fathers [his uncles]. Um he tells about the family because he always has in mind that our family has to be together. **Always.** So he tells about the family, but not so much about Afghanistan.

This construction of "family," in which uncles are fathers, is indicative of the emphasis on relationships beyond those of the immediate family; an uncle is not "like a father" but "a father" with all the rights that go with fatherhood. Indeed another participant, Ashok, described these rights in this way, "Children were disciplined not just by their parents but anyone or everyone in the household. So if you misbehaved you got spankings from everyone (laughing)." Child-care and discipline were not the domain only of parents but of the entire household.

Gradually these meanings of family were changing, especially for the younger generation who came to Germany when they were infants or were born there. For example, I once commented to Mrs. Chabra how everyone in the Afghan Hindu community seemed to be related to everyone else. She laughed, saying how her 18-year-old granddaughter, Amita, who was born in Germany, faced the same dilemma, "Whenever my daughter introduces someone as *maama* (mother's brother) or *chaacha* (father's brother), Amita, asks her, 'First tell me is he my **real** (*sagge*) uncle?' [laughing], so you're not the only one who is confused. Children growing up here also find it confusing." Similarly, Rani, a young woman, who came to Germany when she was very young, also laughingly described how difficult it was for her to know who was family:

You see this all the time, like at a wedding, my parents will call me and say, "Come here, I want you to meet your *maasi* (mother's sister)", and I am thinking to myself, "My 13<sup>th</sup> *maasi*, how many more do I have?" Or my dad will say, "Meet your *chacha*" (father's younger brother), and so I say politely, "Hello *chachaji*", wondering where he had sprung from (laughing). … It is really awful [laughing] because I can't keep count of all the *mamas* (uncles) and *maasis* (aunts) and *chachas* (uncles) I have. It is quite ridiculous.

The younger generation's perplexity at having everyone named as family pointed to some of the changes that are occurring in the understanding of "family" in this community, post-migration. Amita found the number of people who were introduced to her as uncles perplexing, while Rani found it downright funny. However, each of these reactions shows that the next generation is clearly influenced by alternative meanings of what constitutes family, hinting at the change that is already taking place.

## Fragmentation of Family Due to Dispersal

Many older Afghan Hindus attributed at least some of the changes in the meaning of "family" to the refugee dispersal policy in Germany. When Afghan Hindus arrived in Germany seeking asylum, they were placed in homes in remote places and were moved around the country. While the Afghan Hindu ideal of the family was based on togetherness, both relationally and in terms of physical proximity, the German asylum law was based on the nuclear family. In Germany, each adult member was eligible for refugee aid. Thus anyone over the age of 18 was not considered a dependent. A family, according to this system, was defined as comprising one or two parents, and children below 18. Homes were allotted based on this definition, creating challenges for the newly arrived Afghan Hindus, who often had elderly parents with them.

The Swamis arrived in Germany with their three-year-old daughter and Dr. Swami's mother in 1985. Unlike many Afghan Hindus who either lacked a high school education, or had college education but could not pursue higher education in Germany because of financial constraints and language difficulties, Swami, a medical doctor in Afghanistan, was determined to get his license to practice in Germany. Mrs. Swami describes their experience of how their family was separated on arrival in Germany:

We were placed in Neuberg near Stuttgart. My husband was studying there. His degree from Afghanistan was not recognized and he had to start all over again. He needed these specific courses that were not available in Stuttgart and so we had to move to Hamburg. But the government would not allow my mother-in-law to move with us. They wanted her to live alone there. It was really difficult. She lived there by herself for 18 months and was miserable. Then somehow we hired a lawyer and brought her here. This is not just in our family; many families have members stuck in various places.

Although they acknowledged that large households were no longer viable in Germany because of small apartments, Afghan Hindus at least expected that elderly members would be able to live with one of their sons, as was customary in their culture. The German system did not allow this. While the Swamis had been able to hire a lawyer to bring Dr. Swami's mother to Hamburg, not everyone was able to accomplish this.

Kishan, a young man in his early thirties who was very active in the community and was aware of many of the legalities of the refugee system in Germany, stated:

I know a family, my grandmother's sister, who is living with her son and daughter-in-law; all three are in poor health. We have been trying so hard to bring them here close to us, or to Frankfurt where their two sons live, but the government says that if you are willing to completely take over their expenses then you can move them, otherwise not. But her sons cannot afford to do that. Their economic situation is not so strong.

Kishan brought up an important point when he spoke about "expenses" of caring for elders. If adult children brought the elderly to live with them, they were expected to take care of them financially. The elderly person would forfeit their allowance from the government. The German system of granting aid and homes to refugees was therefore forcing Afghan Hindus to reconstruct their understanding of family.

## Roles, Rules, Privacy, and Conflict

Despite these constraints, some Afghan Hindus did live together with at least their elderly parents. However, roles of the elderly and norms of communicative conduct between family members had changed, leading to conflict. In Afghanistan the oldest male member of the family exerted authority, and his word was obeyed unquestioningly. As one man, Kanha, described it, "This hierarchy made it easier to maintain control and harmony in the family." Afghan culture prescribed certain rules for women, such as covering the face in the presence of male members, dressing in the traditional dress, and not speaking back to the elders. However, in Germany, younger women challenged their elders, departing from cultural norms that were age-based and gender-based, leading to conflict. Dr. Pyasa explained the reasons for such conflicts as follows:

> The main problem is this. When some of these [Afghan Hindu] girls came to Germany they were one or two years old. They went to school here. They learn here to take care of their own life, to live for themselves, to eat on their own, this life is for oneself type of thing. The mother-in-law is still in the other world where she thinks the daughter-in-law should not speak directly to the father-in-law, she should cover her face [out of respect], and so on. She may comment on the daughter-in-law's clothes, expecting her not to wear pants in the house.

Traditional cultural norms were based on older men and women in the household exerting considerable authority. In Germany, the roles were reversed. The younger generation, who had completed most of their schooling in Germany, spoke the language and were more independent. As a result, the elderly were no longer in a position of power in the household. Rather they were dependent on their children, resulting in loss of status and crisis of role identities for many. In Afghanistan, there was a system in place that everyone followed, in which the boundaries were clear; in Germany that system no longer worked, and many older Afghan Hindus attributed this to a culture of individuality and "freedom" (*azadi*) of the larger society. Although I met many families where traditional rules, roles, and norms of appropriate communicative conduct were followed, these were generally families in which sons and daughters-in-law had migrated when they were in their 20s or older. Problems seemed to occur more often in families in which the sons and daughters-in-law had mainly grown up in Germany. This generation felt they were respectful enough, but that their parents were unwilling to change.

Another source of conflict was expectations of privacy by the younger generation. In the large households of Afghanistan, there had been little or no expectation of privacy. It was common for families to gather and enjoy events collectively. In Germany, married couples belonging to a younger generation of Afghan Hindus expected to have their private time away from the rest of the family members. Speaking about the issue of privacy, Ahuja, a middle-aged man, stated:

> The daughter-in-law wants to go to the beach with her husband. She wants to spend time alone with her husband, perhaps swim in the water. And in our culture there is one thing. Wherever we went when we were in Afghanistan we went together as a family. So [now] the daughter-in-law says, "We are going to the beach" and the father-in-law says, "Great. Let's all go." He doesn't understand that the couple wants their privacy. So that is one way problems begin.

Older women recalled with nostalgia their large households in Afghanistan, where they enjoyed the company of many women in the family, sharing household tasks and raising children collectively. In Germany, even those who lived with a son and daughter-in-law expressed dissatisfaction with their present lives, describing a sense of loneliness because of lack of companionship.

In summary, many of the challenges that Afghan Hindus faced in Germany were similar to those of other refugees; however, my research revealed interpersonal dynamics in the family that need further investigation. Although much of the research in other disciplines describes families structurally, a focus on communication is absent. With more than a decade of examining different kinds of nonnormative families, family communication scholars are ideally positioned to study communication in the context of refugee and other diasporic families. In the next section, I discuss suggestions for future directions.

## Directions for Future Research

I began this essay by citing the broad range of families studied by family communication researchers in the past decade, particularly as it relates to challenges of nonnormative families formed by adoption, divorce, and same-sex partnership. Family, among many refugee populations, becomes nonnormative as well, in the land of resettlement. Different ideals of what constitutes family pose a number of challenges for refugees. The very meaning of family must be re-negotiated, because of refugee policies, and because of cultural influences of the larger society. Traditional roles and rules within the family are contested in the family, leading to conflict.

One theory that can provide insight into the negotiations among family members is communication privacy management proposed by Petronio (2002). The theory is based on the regulation of privacy in the family. CPM theory presents five criteria that influence how rules of information management develop: (a) culture, (b) gender, (c) motivations, (d) context, and (e) risk-benefit ratio. Diasporic families emphasize the roles of culture and context, as old cultural norms come up against new ones. When the very definition of the boundary of who is inside and who is outside of the family is unclear, privacy management is likely to be challenging. For example, in Afghanistan, control was in the hands of a male elder who was the head of the family and laid down the rules for the family; women did not leave the house without a male escort. Few women worked outside the home. In Germany, most women had to work outside the home. The elderly became helpless because they lacked language proficiency and employment. All this could result in what CPM calls "boundary turbulence" (Petronio, p. 177). Some of this boundary turbulence could be caused by unintentional rule violations, mistakes, differences in boundary orientations, or "fuzzy boundaries" (p. 177). Those who lived much of their adult lives in the homeland likely have different boundary orientations than those who were infants or young children at the time of migration.

The issue of defining the family's identity-based boundaries deserves scholarly attention in its own right, above and beyond implications for privacy management. Galvin's (2006) work on discourse dependence has been applied almost exclusively with U.S. samples, and it could be productively applied in understanding diasporic families. For example, who counts as family brings up questions of address terms: what is the appropriate way to address someone who is not one's own uncle but an uncle of sorts? Clearly this is a dilemma for the younger generation. Address terms implicate both labeling and naming, as identified by Galvin, depending on whether the context is fellow family members or outsiders. Policies of the receiving nation also add to boundary ambiguity. Although prior research has noted many aspects of fragmentation of the family post-migration, there is not much research on the communicative aspects of these changes. What are the communicative challenges when family roles, rules, and boundaries of the homeland no longer work as well in the land of resettlement? How do families handle those challenges? These are some questions that need further research.

Another theory that fits this context is stress theory (Hill, 1949), which describes two types of stressors, *normative and nonnormative stressors*. A normative stressor is that which occurs as a result of anticipated and fairly predictable transitions in life such as infancy to childhood, and later to adolescence, and still later on to adulthood, middle age, and so on (McCubbin & Patterson, 1982). Typically these transitions lead to changes in roles, relationships, and structure of the family. Nonnormative stressors happen because of unanticipated events, often leaving no time for families to prepare for them. Common situations described by Hill (1958) are "accidental injury to a member, illness in the family, hospitalization of a family member, or loss of employment" (xii). Involuntary migration is a nonnormative stressor and, as discussed earlier, can take various forms. Stressors implicate coping mechanisms. Afifi and Nussbaum (2006) have argued that while the stress and coping literature deals with cognitive aspects of coping, communicative aspects need more attention. The same argument can be made about migration as a nonnormative stressor; although much of the research focuses on mental, socio-cultural, and political aspects of migration, communication, and, more specifically, family communication, is relatively unexamined in this context. Communication is likely to play a particularly important role in the ways in which families cope with stressors of migration. In addition, research shows that the refugee story is not just one of stress but also one of resilience. Diasporic populations, created through voluntary and involuntary migration, have been known to maintain a strong sense of transnational "reciprocity and solidarity" (Bauböck & Faist, 2010, p. 11). Describing the Hmong, who fled Laos to escape persecution at the hands of a communist government, Keown-Bomar (2004) noted:

Hmong have developed a recognized schema of relatedness that allows them to build a network of people on whom they can depend, even in the most trying of circumstances…. What I found in my study was that Hmong refugees seek to rebuild and recreate what they know to work and their schema of kinship seems resilient and flexible enough to accommodate contexts of change. (pp. 66–67)

Wronska-Friend (2004) provided a beautiful example of resilience in maintaining strong kinship in the Hmong refugee diaspora. One participant in her study, who lived in New Zealand, wanted a Hmong dress for a New Year's celebration. The dress was made by family members in refugee camps in Thailand, sent to France to her mother, who added decorations to it. Her sister sent Mexican fabric for a matching hat from California. The sash was made by the participant from local New Zealand fabric and with beads sent from Thailand.

Researchers have documented a variety of strategies to maintain familial relationships ranging from living in specific neighborhoods (Satzewick & Wong, 2006), to establishing local and transnational organizations that span multiple countries (Audebert & Dorai, 2010), to providing financial support by sending money home, investing in family businesses, and helping solve family problems (Helweg & Helweg, 1990). However, there is relatively less research on how communication functions in constructing the transnational family by maintaining kinship ties not only in the land of settlement, but with family in the homeland, and family re-settled in different parts of the world. This is another rich site for family communication scholars to explore.

Finally, relational dialectics theory (Baxter, 2011; Baxter & Montgomery, 1996) can also be employed to understand some of the struggles in refugee families. People who come from collectivistic cultures emphasize a discourse of family connectedness over the interests of the individual (Hofstede, 2001). Yet, when they arrive in individualistic countries where people are expected to be independent, pursue individual goals, and emphasize self-achievement, a struggle ensues, particularly for the younger generation who is caught between the cultural expectations of the family and those of the larger society. The autonomy-connection dialectic was apparent in comments by some youth who spoke of wanting to fulfill family obligations yet felt the need to fulfill their own goals. This dialectic was also evident when some participants described how the German laws granted complete autonomy to an individual at the age of 18 that contradicted their cultural expectation that adult children will remain in the household. A dialectical approach can provide further insight into some of the struggles posed by contradictory cultural norms.

## Conclusion

We live in an age of frequent border crossings, both voluntary and involuntary. As I have demonstrated in this essay, policy decisions based on cultural assumptions of the nuclear family have a profound influence on refugee lives, challenging their traditional notions of family, resulting in fragmentation. Roles, rules, and boundaries of family are challenged by new cultural norms. Simultaneously, these families also show remarkable resilience in coping with difficulties. The diaspora, therefore, offers a rich site for family communication scholars to examine how family is constituted, sustained, and re-negotiated as a result of migration.

# References

Adler-Baeder, F., Pittman, J. F., & Taylor, L. (2005). The prevalence of marital transitions in military families. *Journal of Divorce and Remarriage, 44,* 91–106. doi: 10.1300/J087v44n01_05

Adoption and Foster Care Analysis and Reporting System (2011, July). *AFCARS report: Preliminary FY 2010 estimates.* Retrieved from website of the U.S. Department of Health and Human Services, Administration for Children and Families, Administration on Children, Youth and Families, Children's Bureau: http://www.acf.hhs.gov/programs/cb

Afifi, T. D. (2003). "Feeling caught" in stepfamilies: Managing boundary turbulence through appropriate communication privacy rules. *Journal of Social and Personal Relationships, 20,* 729–755. doi: 10.1177/0265407503206002

Afifi, T. D. (2008). Communication in stepfamilies: Stressors and resilience. In J. Pryor (Ed.), *The international handbook of stepfamilies: Policy and practice in legal, research, and clinical environments* (pp. 299–320). Hoboken, NJ: Wiley.

Afifi, T. D., Hutchinson, S., & Krouse, S. (2006). Toward a theoretical model of communal coping in postdivorce families and other naturally occurring groups. *Communication Theory, 16,* 378–409. doi: 10.1111/j.1468-2885.2006.00275.x

Afifi, T. D., & Keith, S. (2004). A risk and resiliency model of ambiguous loss in postdivorce stepfamilies. *Journal of Family Communication, 4,* 65–98. doi: 10.1207/s15327698jfc0402_1

Afifi, T. D., & McManus, T. (2010). Divorce disclosures and adolescents' physical and mental health and parental relationship quality. *Journal of Divorce and Remarriage, 51,* 83–107. doi: 10.1080/10502550903455141

Afifi, T. D., & Nussbaum, J. (2006). Stress and adaptation theories: Families across the life span. In D. O. Braithwaite & L. A. Baxter (Eds.), *Engaging theories in family communication: Multiple perspectives* (pp. 276–292). Thousand Oaks, CA: Sage.

Afifi, T. D., & Schrodt, P. (2003). "Feeling caught" as a mediator of adolescents' and young adults' avoidance and satisfaction with their parents in divorced and non-divorced households. *Communication Monographs, 70,* 142–173. doi: 10.1080/0363775032000133791

Agar, A., & Strang, A. (2008). Understanding integration: A conceptual framework. *Journal of Refugee Studies, 21,* 167–191. doi: 10.1093/jrs/fen016

Agar, M. H. (1996). *The professional stranger: An informal introduction to ethnography.* San Diego, CA: Academic Press.

Akkoor, C. V. (2011). *Ways of speaking in the diaspora: Afghan Hindus in Germany* (Unpublished doctoral dissertation). University of Iowa, Iowa City, IA.

Alderson, K. G. (2004). A phenomenological investigation of same-sex marriage. *The Canadian Journal of Human Sexuality, 13,* 107–122. Retrieved from http://www.utpjournals.com/Canadian-Journal-of-Human-Sexuality

Alexander, P. C. (2003). Parent-child role reversal: Development of a measure and test of an attachment theory model. *Journal of Systemic Therapies, 22,* 31–43. doi: 10.1521/jsyt.22.2.31.23349

Allan, G. A. (2008). Flexibility, friendship and family. *Personal Relationships, 15,* 1–16. doi: 10.1111/j.1475-6811.2007.00181.x

Allen, E. S., Rhoades, G. K., Stanley, S., & Markman, H. J. (2010). Hitting home: Relationships between recent deployments, posttraumatic stress symptoms, and marital functioning for Army couples. *Journal of Family Psychology, 24,* 280–288. doi: 10.1037/a0019405

Allen, K. R., Blieszner, R, & Roberto, K. A. (2011). Perspective on extended family and fictive kin in the later years: Strategies and meanings of kin reinterpretation. *Journal of Family Issues, 32,* 1156–77. doi: 10.1177/0192513X11404335

Amatea, E. S., Smith-Adcock, S., & Villares, E. (2006). From family deficit to family strength: Viewing families' contributions to children/s learning from a family resilience perspective. *Professional School Counseling, 9,* 177–189. Retrieved from http://www.schoolcounselor.org/school-counselors-members/publications/professional-school-counseling-journal

Amato, P. R. (2000). The consequences of divorce for adults and children. *Journal of Marriage and the Family, 62,* 1269–1287. Retrieved from http://www.jstor.org/stable/1566735

Amato, P. R. (2001). Children of divorce in the 1990s: An update of the Amato and Keith (1991) meta-analysis. *Journal of Family Psychology, 15,* 355–370. doi: 10.1111/j.1741-3737.2000.01269.x

Amato, P. R. (2005). The impact of family formation change on the cognitive, social, and emotional well-being of the next generation. *The Future of Children, 15,* 75–96. Retrieved from http://futureofchildren.org/publications/journals/article/index.xml?journalid=37&articleid=107&sectionid=694

Amato, P. R., & Afifi, T. D. (2006). Feeling caught between parents: Adult children's relations with parents and subjective well-being. *Journal of Marriage and Family, 68,* 222–235. doi: 10.1111/j.1741-3737.2006.00243.x

Amato, P. R., & Keith, B. (1991). Parental divorce and the well-being of children: A meta-analysis. *Psychological Bulletin, 110,* 26–46. doi: 10.1093/sf/69.3.895

Anagnost, A. (2000). Scenes of misrecognition: Maternal citizenship in the age of transnational adoption. *Positions, 8,* 389–421. doi: 10.1215/10679847-8-2-389

Anderson, C. (2003). The diversity of strengths, and challenges in single parent households. In F. Walsh (Ed.), *Normal family processes: Growing diversity and complexity* (3rd ed., pp. 121–152). New York, NY: Guilford Press.

Anderson, E. A., & Spruill, J. W. (1993). The dual-career commuter family: A lifestyle on the move. *Marriage and Family Review, 19,* 131–147. doi: 10.1300/J002v19n01_08

Anderson, L. S. (2008). Predictors of parenting stress in a diverse sample of parents of early adolescents in high-risk communities. *Nursing Research, 57,* 340–350. doi: 10.1097/01. NNR.0000313502.92227.87

Annunziata, D., Hogue, A., Faw, L., & Liddle, H. A. (2006). Family functioning and school success in at-risk, inner-city adolescents. *Journal of Youth and Adolescence, 35,* 100–108. doi: 10.1007/s10964-005-9016-3

Anyan, S., & Pryor, J. (2002). What is in a family? Adolescent perceptions. *Children and Society, 16,* 1–12. doi: 10.1002/chi.716

Arm, J. R., Horne, S. G., & Levitt, H. M. (2009). Negotiating connection to GLBT experience: Family members' experience of anti-GLBT movements and policies. *Journal of Counseling Psychology, 56,* 82–96. doi: 10.1037/a0012813

Armstrong, M. I., Birnie-Lefcovitch, S., & Ungar, M. T. (2005). Pathways between social support, family well-being, quality of parenting, and child resilience: What we know. *Journal of Child and Family Studies, 14,* 269–281. doi: 10.1007/s10826-005-5054-4

Astone, N. M., & MacLanahan, S. S. (1991). Family structure, parental practices and high school completion. *American Sociological Review, 56,* 309–320. doi: 10.2307/2096106

Attar-Schwartz, S., Tan, J. P., Buchanan, A., Flouri, E., & Griggs, J. (2009). Grandparenting and adolescent adjustment in two-parent biological, lone-parent, and step-families. *Journal of Family Psychology, 23,* 67–73. doi: 10.1037/a0014383

Audebert, C., & Dorai, M. K. (2010). *Migration in a globalised world: New research issues and prospects.* Amsterdam, NLD: Amsterdam University Press.

Awwad, E. (2003). Broken lives: Loss and trauma in Palestinian-Israeli relations. *International Journal of Politics, Culture, and Society, 17,* 405–414. doi: 10.1023/B:IJPS. 0000019610.75356.0b

Backhouse, J., & Graham, A. (2012). Grandparents raising grandchildren: Negotiating the complexities of role-identity conflict. *Child and Family Social Work, 17,* 306–315. doi: 10.1111/j.1365-2206.2011.00781.x

Badgett, M.V. L. (2009). *When gay people get married: What happens when societies legalize same-sex marriage.* New York, NY: New York University Press.

Bailey, S. J., Letiecq, B. L., & Porterfield, F. (2009). Family coping and adaptation among grandparents rearing grandchildren. *Journal of Intergenerational Relationships, 7,* 144–158. doi: 10.1080/15350770902851072

Baiocchi, D. (2013). *Measuring army deployments to Iraq and Afghanistan* (RAND Corporation Research Report No. 145). Retrieved from http://www.rand.org/content/dam/rand/pubs/research_reports/RR100/RR145/RAND_RR145.pdf

Bakhtin, M. M. (1986). The problem of speech genres. In C. Emerson & M. Holquist (Eds.), *Speech genres and other late essays* (V. M. McGee, Trans., pp. 60–102). Austin, TX: University of Texas Press.

Ballard, R. L., & Ballard, S. J (2011). From narrative inheritance to narrative momentum: Past, present, and future stories in an international adoptive family. *Journal of Family Communication, 11*, 69–84. doi: 10.1080/15267431.2011.554618

Barrett, A. E., & Turner, R. J. (2005). Family structure and substance use problems in adolescence and early adulthood: Examining explanations for the relationship. *Addiction, 101*, 109–120. doi: 10.1111/j.1360-0443.2005.01296.x

Barton, P. E. (2006). The dropout problem: Losing ground. *Educational Leadership, 63*, 14–18. Retrieved from http://www.ascd.org/publications/educational-leadership/feb06/vol63/num05/The-Dropout-Problem@-Losing-Ground.aspx

Bassani, C. D. (2007). The Japanese *tanshin funin*: A neglected family type. *Community, Work and Family, 10*, 111–131. doi: 10.1080/13668800601110884

Bauböck, F. R., & Faist, T. (2010). *Diaspora and transnationalism: Concepts, theories and methods.* Amsterdam, NLD: Amsterdam University Press.

Baumeister, R. F. (2002). Ego depletion and self-control failure: An energy model of the self's executive function. *Self and Identity, 1*, 129–136. doi: 10.1080/152988602317319302

Baumeister, R. F., Brewer, L., Tice, D. M., & Twenge, J. M. (2007). Thwarting the need to belong: Understanding the interpersonal and inner effects of social exclusion. *Social and Personality Psychology Compass, 1*, 506–520. doi: 10.1111/j.1751–9004.2007.00020.x

Baxter, L. A. (2004). Relationships as dialogues. *Personal Relationships, 11*, 1–22. doi: 10.1111/j.1475-6811.2004.00068.x

Baxter, L. A. (2006). Relational dialectics theory: Multivocal dialogues of family communication. In D. O. Braithwaite & L. A. Baxter (Eds.), *Engaging theories in family communication: Multiple perspectives* (pp. 130–145). Thousand Oaks, CA: Sage.

Baxter, L. A. (2011). *Voicing relationships: A dialogic perspective.* Thousand Oaks, CA: Sage.

Baxter, L. A., & Asbury, B. (in press). Critical approaches to interpersonal communication: Charting a future. In D. O. Braithwaite & P. Schrodt (Eds.), *Engaging theories in interpersonal communication.* Los Angeles, CA: Sage.

Baxter, L. A., & Braithwaite, D. O. (2002). Performing marriage: The marriage renewal as cultural performance. *Southern Communication Journal, 67*, 94–109. doi: 10.1080/10417940209373223

Baxter, L.A., & Braithwaite, D. O. (2006a). Family rituals. In L. Turner & R. West (Eds.), *The family communication sourcebook* (pp. 259–280). Thousand Oaks, CA: Sage.

Baxter, L. A., & Braithwaite, D. O. (2006b). Introduction: Meta-theory and theory in family communication research. In D. O. Braithwaite & L. A. Baxter (Eds.), *Engaging theories in family communication: Multiple perspectives* (pp. 1–15). Thousand Oaks, CA: Sage.

Baxter, L. A., Braithwaite, D. O., & Bach, B. W. (2009, February). *Communication challenges of voluntary-kin relationships.* Paper presented at the annual meeting of the Western States Communication Association, Mesa, AZ.

Baxter, L. A., Braithwaite, D. O., & Bryant, L. E. (2006). Types of communication triads perceived by young-adult stepchildren in established stepfamilies. *Communication Studies, 57,* 381–400. doi: 10.1080/10510970600945923

Baxter, L. A., Braithwaite, D. O., Bryant, L. E., & Wagner, A. (2004). Stepchildren's perceptions of the contradictions in communication with stepparents. *Journal of Social and Personal Relationships, 21,* 447–467. doi: 10.1177/0265407504044841

Baxter, L. A., Braithwaite, D. O., Koenig Kellas, J., LeClair-Underberg, C., Lamb-Normand, E., Routsong, T., & Thatcher, M. (2009). Empty ritual: Young-adult stepchildren's perceptions of the remarriage ceremony. *Journal of Social and Personal Relationships, 26,* 467–487. doi: 10.1177/0265407509350872

Baxter, L. A., Braithwaite, D. O., & Nicholson, J. H. (1999). Turning points in the development of blended families. *Journal of Social and Personal Relationships, 16,* 291–313. doi: 10.1177/0265407599163002

Baxter, L. A., Henauw, C., Huisman, D., Livesay, C. B., Norwood, K. M., Su, H. … Young, B. (2009). Lay conceptions of "family": Replication and extension. *Journal of Family Communication, 9,* 170–189. doi: 10.1080/15267430902963342

Baxter, L. A., & Montgomery, B. M. (1996). *Relating: Dialogues and dialectics.* New York, NY: Guilford Press.

Baxter, L. A., Norwood, K. M., Asbury, B., Jannusch, A., & Scharp, K. M. (2012). Narrative coherence in online stories told by members of the adoption triad. *Journal of Family Communication, 12,* 265–283. doi: 10.1080/15267431.2012.686944

Baxter, L. A., Norwood, K. M., Asbury, B., & Scharp, K. M. (2014). Narrating adoption: Resisting adoption as "second best" in online stories of domestic adoption told by adoptive parents. *Journal of Family Communication, 14,* 1-16. doi: 10.1080/15267431.2013.864294

Baxter, L. A., Scharp, K. M., Asbury, B., Jannusch, A., & Norwood, K. M. (2012). "Birth mothers are not bad people": A dialogic analysis of online birth mother stories. *Qualitative Communication Research, 1,* 53–82. Retrieved from http://www.jstor.org/stable/10.1525/qcr.2012.1.1.53

Baxter, L. A., Suter, E. A., Thomas, L. J., & Seurer, L. M. (in press). The dialogic construction of "adoption" in online foster adoption narratives. *Journal of Family Communication.*

Becker, G. (1997). *Disrupted lives.* Berkeley, CA: University of California Press.

Bell, C. (1997). *Ritual: Perspectives and dimensions.* New York, NY: Oxford University Press.

Bergen, K. M. (2003). *Staying connected when you're apart: A multiple case study of communication in commuter marriage.* Unpublished manuscript.

Bergen, K. M. (2006). *Women's narratives about commuter marriage: How women in commuter marriages account for and negotiate identities with members of their social networks* (Unpublished doctoral dissertation). University of Nebraska–Lincoln, Lincoln, NE.

Bergen, K. M. (2007, November). *Long-distance mothering: When mother's place is not in the home.* Paper presented at the National Communication Association Convention, Chicago, IL.

Bergen, K. M. (2009). "How is *that* going to work?": Explaining commuter marriage to others. In E. Kirby & M. C. McBride (Eds.), *Gender actualized: Cases in gender communication* (pp. 123–129). Dubuque, IA: Kendall Hunt Publishers.

Bergen, K. M. (2010a). Accounting for difference: Commuter wives and the master narrative of marriage. *Journal of Applied Communication Research, 38,* 47–64. doi: 10.1080/00909880903483565

Bergen, K. M. (2010b). Negotiating a "questionable" identity: Commuter wives and social networks. *Southern Communication Journal, 75,* 35–56. doi: 10.1080/10417940902951816

Bergen, K. M., & Braithwaite, D. O. (2009). Communicatively constituting identity. In W. Eadie (Ed.), *21ˢᵗ century communication: A sourcebook* (pp. 165–173). Thousand Oaks, CA: Sage.

Bergen, K. M., Kirby, E., & McBride, M. C. (2007). "How do you get two houses cleaned?": Accomplishing family caregiving in commuter marriages. *Journal of Family Communication, 7,* 287–307. doi: 10.1080/15267430701392131

Bergen, K. M., Suter, E. A., & Daas, K. L., (2006). "About as solid as a fish net": Symbolic construction of a legitimate parental identity for nonbiological lesbian mothers. *Journal of Family Communication, 6,* 201–220. doi: 10.1207/s15327698jfc0603_3

Bernard, J. (1973). *The future of marriage.* New York, NY: Bantam Books.

Bernardes, J. (1999). We must not define "The family"! In S. K. Steinmetz & G. W. Peterson (Eds.), *Concepts and definitions of family for the 21ˢᵗ century* (pp. 21–41). New York, NY: The Haworth Press.

Bianchi, S. M. (2006). Mothers and daughters "do," fathers "don't do" family: Gender and generational bonds. *Journal of Marriage and Family, 68,* 812–816. doi: 10.1111/j.1741–3737.2006.00296.x

Biblarz, T. J., & Savci, E. (2010). Lesbian, gay, bisexual, and transgender families. *Journal of Marriage and Family, 72,* 480–497. doi: 10.111/j.1741–3737.2010.00174.x

Black, K., & Lobo, M. (2008). A conceptual review of family resilience factors. *Journal of Family Nursing, 14,* 33–55. doi: 10.1177/1074840707312237

Blaisure, K. R., Saathoff-Wells, T., Pereira, A., MacDermid Wadsworth, S. M., & Dombro, A. L. (2012). *Serving the military families in the 21st century.* New York, NY: Routledge.

Blanchard, S. E. (2012). Are the needs of single parents serving in the Air Force being met? *Advances in Social Work, 13,* 83–97. Retrieved from https://journals.iupui.edu/index.php/advancesinsocialwork/article/viewFile/1872/1966

Blau, M., & Fingerman, K. L. (2009). *Consequential strangers: The power of people who don't seem to matter…but really do.* New York, NY: W.W. Norton & Company.

Blumstein, P., & Schwartz, P. (1983). *American couples: Money, work, sex.* New York, NY: William Morrow and Company.

Booth, B., Wechsler Segal, M., & Bell, D. B. (2007). *What we know about Army families: 2007 Update* (Caliber Company Report to the U.S. Army Family and Morale, Welfare and Recreation Command). Retrieved from http://www.army.mil/fmwrc/documents/research/WhatWeKnow2007.pdf

Boss, P. (1999). *Ambiguous loss: Learning to live with unresolved grief.* Cambridge, MA: Harvard University.

Boss, P. (2010). The trauma and complicated grief of ambiguous loss. *Pastoral Psychology, 59,* 137–145. doi: 10.1007/s11089-009-0264-0

Bourdieu, P. (1996). On the family as a realized category. *Theory, Culture & Society, 13*, 19–26. doi: 10.1177/026327696013003002

Bowman, J., & Dollahite, D. C. (2013). "Why would such a person dream about heaven?": Family, faith, and happiness in arranged marriages in India. *Journal of Comparative Family Studies, 44*, 207–225. Retrieved from http://soci.ucalgary.ca/jcfs/

Boylan, J. (2013). *Stuck in the middle with you: A memoir of parenting in three genders.* New York. NY: Crown Publishers.

Boyle, E. H., & Ali, A. (2010). Culture, structure, and the refugee experience in Somali immigrant family transformation. *International Migration, 48*, 48–79. doi: 10.1111/j.1468-2435.2009.00512.x

Braithwaite, D. O., Bach, B. W., Baxter, L. A., DiVerniero, R., Hammonds, J., Hosek, A. ... Wolf, B. (2010). Constructing family: A typology of voluntary kin. *Journal of Social and Personal Relationships, 27*, 388–407. doi: 10.1177/0265407510361615

Braithwaite, D. O., Bach, B. W., Wilder, S. E., Kranstuber, H., Sato Mumm, S. (2010, November). *"She is like a sister to me": Discourses of voluntary kin as family.* Paper presented at the annual meeting of the National Communication Association, San Francisco, CA.

Braithwaite, D. O., & Baxter, L. A. (2006). "You're my parent but you're not": Dialectical tensions in stepchildren's perceptions about communicating with the nonresidential parent. *Journal of Applied Communication Research, 34*, 30–48. doi: 10.1080/00909880500420200

Braithwaite, D. O., Baxter, L. A., & Harper, A. M. (1998). The role of rituals in the management of dialectical tensions of "old" and "new" in blended families. *Communication Studies, 48*, 101–120. doi: 10.1080/10510979809368523

Braithwaite, D. O., McBride, M. C., & Schrodt, P. (2003). "Parent teams" and the everyday interactions of co-parenting in stepfamilies. *Communication Reports, 16*, 93–111. doi: 10.1080/08934210309384493

Braithwaite, D. O., Olson, L., Golish, T., Soukup, C., & Turman, P. (2001). Developmental communication patterns of blended families: Exploring the different trajectories of blended families. *Journal of Applied Communication Research, 29*, 221–247. doi: 10.1080/00909880128112

Braithwaite, D. O., & Schrodt, P. (2012). Stepfamily communication. In A. L. Vangelisti's (Ed.), *Routledge handbook of family communication* (2nd ed., pp. 161–175). New York, NY: Routledge.

Braithwaite, D. O., Stephenson Abetz, J., Moore, J., Brockhage, K. (2014, November). *Communication structures of supplemental voluntary kin relationships.* Paper submitted to the Family Communication Division at the annual meeting of the National Communication Association, Chicago, IL.

Braithwaite, D. O., Toller, P., Daas, K. L., Durham, W. T., & Jones, A. (2008). Centered but not caught in the middle: Stepchildren's perceptions of dialectical contradictions in the communication of co-parents. *Journal of Applied Communication Research, 36*, 33–55. doi: 10.1080/00909880701799337

Bright, M. A. (1990). Therapeutic ritual: Helping families to grow. *Journal of Psychosocial Nursing and Mental Health Services, 28*, 19–24. Retrieved from http://www.healio.com/journals/jpn

Brodsky, A. E., & De Vet, K. A. (2000). You have to be real strong. *Journal of Prevention & Intervention in the Community, 20*, 159–178. doi :10.1300/J005v20n01_11

Brown-Standridge, M. D., & Floyd, C. W. (2000). Healing bittersweet legacies: Revisiting contextual family therapy for grandparents raising grandchildren in crisis. *Journal of Marital and Family Therapy, 26*, 185–197. doi: 10.1111/j.1752-0606.2000.tb00288.x

Bulanda, J. R., & Brown, S. L. (2007). Race-ethnic differences in marital quality and divorce. *Social Science Research, 36*, 945–967. doi: 10.1016/j.ssresearch.2006.04.001

Bulcroft, R. A., Carmody, D., & Bulcroft, K. A. (1998). Family structure and patterns of independence giving to adolescents. *Journal of Family Issues, 19*, 404–435. doi: 10.1177/019251398019004003

Bullock, K. (2005). Grandfathers and the impact of raising grandchildren. *Journal of Sociology and Social Welfare, 32*, 43–59. Retrieved from http://www.wmich.edu/socialwork/journal/

Bumiller, E. (1990). *May you be the mother of 100 sons: A journey among the women of India.* New York, NY: Fawcett Columbine.

Bunker, B. B., Zubek, J. M., Vanderslice, V. J., & Rice, R. W. (1992). Quality of life in dual-career families: Commuting versus single-residence couples. *Journal of Marriage and the Family, 54*, 399–407. doi: 10.2307/353071

Burr, V. (2003). *Social constructionism* (2nd ed.). New York, NY: Routledge.

Burrell, L. M. (2006). Moving military families: The impact of relocation on family well-being, employment, and commitment to the military. In C. A. Castro, A. B. Adler, & T. W. Britt (Eds.), *Military life: The psychology of serving in peace and combat (Volume 3: The military family)* (pp. 39–63). Westport, CT: Praeger Security International.

Bush, K. R., Bohon, S. A., & Kim, H. K. (2005). Adaptation among immigrant families: Resources and barriers. In P. C. McKenry and S. J. Price (Eds.), *Families and change: Coping with stressful events and transitions* (3rd ed., pp. 307–332). Thousand Oaks, CA: Sage.

Bute, J. J., Harter, L. M., Kirby, E. L., & Thompson, M. (2010). Politicizing personal choices? The storying of age-related infertility in public discourses. In S. Hayden & D. L. O'Brien Hallstein (Eds.), *Contemplating maternity in an era of choice: Explorations into discourses of reproduction* (pp. 49–69). Lanham, MA: Lexington Books.

Butler, J. (1990). *Gender trouble: Feminism and the subversion of identity.* New York, NY: Routledge.

Butler, J. (2002). Is kinship always already heterosexual? *Differences: A journal of feminist cultural studies, 13*, 14–44. doi: 10.1215/10407391-13-1-14

Buzzanell, P. M. (1997). Toward an emotion-based feminist framework for research on dual-career couples. *Women & Language, 20*, 40–48. Retrieved from http://www.womenandlanguage.org/

Bylund, C. (2003). Ethnic diversity and family stories. *Journal of Family Communication, 3*, 215–237. doi: 10.1207/S15327698JFC0304_04

Callan, V. J. (1985). Perceptions of parents, the voluntarily and involuntarily childless: A multidimensional scaling analysis. *Journal of Marriage and the Family, 47*, 1045–1050. doi: 10.2307/352349

Canary, D. J., & Dainton, M. (Eds.). (2002). *Maintaining relationships through communication: Relational, contextual, and cultural variations.* Mahwah, NJ: Erlbaum.

Candappa, M., & Ibinigie, I. (2003). Everyday worlds of young refugees in London. *Feminist Review, 73*, 54–65. doi: 10.1057/palgrave.fr.9400074

Carey, J. (1988). *Communication as culture: Essays on media and society.* Boston, MA: Unwin Hyman.

Carlo, G., Koller, S., Raffaelli, M., & Guzman, M. R. (2007). Culture-related strengths among Latin American families. *Marriage and Family Review, 41*, 335–360. doi: 10.1300/J002v41n03_06

Carlson, M. J., & Corcoran, M.E. (2001). Family structure and children's behavioral and cognitive outcomes. *Journal of Marriage and Family, 63*, 779–792. doi: 10.1111/j.1741-3737.2001.00779.x

Carr, D., & Springer, K. (2010). Advances in families and health research in the 21st century. *Journal of Marriage and Family, 72*, 743–761. doi: 10.1111/j.1741-3737.2010.00728.x

Carrington, C. (1999). *No place like home: Relationships and family life among lesbians and gay men.* Chicago, IL: University of Chicago Press.

Casper, L. M., & Bryson, K. R. (1998, October 31). *Co-resident grandparents and their grandchildren: Grandparent maintained families.* (Populations Division Working Paper No. 26). Retrieved from http://www.census.gov/population/www/documentation/twps0026/twps0026.html

Castro, C. A., Adler, A. B., & Britt, T. W. (2006). The military family: Common themes and future directions. In C. A. Castro, A. B. Adler, & T. W. Britt (Eds.), *Military life: The psychology of serving in peace and combat (Volume 3: The military family)* (pp. 245–247). Westport, CT: Praeger Security International.

Chabot, J. M., & Ames, B. D. (2004). It wasn't "Let's get pregnant and go do it": Decision making in lesbian couples planning motherhood via donor insemination. *Family Relations, 53*, 348–356. doi: 10.1111/j.0197-6664.2004.00041.x

Chandra, A., Martinez, G. M., Mosher, W. D., Abma, J. C., & Jones, J. (2005, December 25). *Fertility, family planning, and reproductive health of US women: Data from the 2002 national survey of family growth* (Vital and Health Statistics, Series 23, No. 25). Retrieved from http://www.cdc.gov/nchs/products/series.htm

Chatters, L. M., Taylor, R. J., & Jayakody, R. (1994). Fictive kinship relations in black extended families. *Journal of Comparative Family Studies, 25*, 297–313. doi: 10.1177/0192513X11404335

Chavez, L. R, Hubbell, A. F., Mishra, S. I., & Valdez, R. B. (1997). Undocumented Latina immigrants in Orange County, California: A comparative analysis. *International Migration Review, 31*, 88–107. doi: 10.2307/2547259

Chawla, D. (2004). *Arranged selves: Role, identity, and social transformations among Indian women in Hindu arranged marriages* (Unpublished doctoral dissertation). Purdue University, West Lafayette, IN.

Chawla, D. (2007). "I will speak out": Narratives of resistance in contemporary Indian women's discourses in Hindu arranged marriages. *Women & Language, 30*, 5–19. Retrieved from http://www.womenandlanguage.org/

Chawla, D. (2008). Enacting conflict as resistance: Urban Indian women in Hindu arranged marriages. In L. B. Arnold (Ed.), *Family communication: Theory and research* (pp. 228–236). Boston, MA: Allyn & Bacon.

Cheong, P. H. (2006). Communication context, social cohesion and social capital building among Hispanic immigrant families. *Community, Work, and Family, 9*, 367–387. doi: 10.1080/13668800600743495

Cherlin, A. J. (1978). Remarriage as an incomplete institution. *American Journal of Sociology, 84*, 634–650. doi: 10.1086/226830

Cherlin, A. J. (2005). American marriage in the early twenty-first century. *The Future of Children, 15*, 33–55. Retrieved from http://futureofchildren.org/futureofchildren/publications/journals/

Cherlin, A. J. (2009a). *The marriage-go-round: The state of marriage and the family in America today*. New York, NY: Vintage Books.

Cherlin, A. J. (2009b). The origins of the ambivalent acceptance of divorce. *Journal of Marriage and Family, 71*, 226–229. doi: 10.1111/j.1741-3737.2009.00593.x

Chin, R. (2007). *The guest worker question in postwar Germany*. London, UK: Cambridge University Press.

Christian, A. (2005). Contesting the myth of the "wicked stepmother": Narrative analysis of an online support group. *Western Journal of Communication, 69*, 27–47. doi: 10.1080/10570310500034030

Ciabattari, T. (2007). Single mothers, social capital, and work-family conflict. *Journal of Family Issues, 28*, 34–60. doi: 10.1177/0192513X06292809

Cipriani, M. (2013, December 5). *Pennsylvania mom returns home in time for daughter's 2nd birthday*. Retrieved from http://www.kitv.com/news/entertainment/pa-mom-returns-from-deployment-in-time-for-daughters-2nd-birthday/-/8905032/23305154/-/etykas/-/index.html

Cissna, K. N., Cox, D. E., & Bochner, A. P. (1990). The dialectic of marital and parental relationships within the stepfamily. *Communication Monographs, 37*, 44–61. doi: 10.1080/03637759009376184

Clark-Hitt, R., Smith, S. W., & Broderick, J. S. (2012). Help a buddy take a knee: Creating persuasive messages for military service members to encourage others to seek mental health help. *Health Communication, 27*, 429–438. doi: 10.1080/10410236.2011.606525

Cohn, D., Passel, J., Wang, W., & Livingston, G. (2011, December 14). *Barely half of U.S. adults are married—a record low* (Pew Research Social & Demographic Trends Report). Retrieved from http://www.pewsocialtrends.org/files/2011/12/Marriage-Decline.pdf

Colaner, C. W., & Kranstuber, H. (2010). "Forever kind of wondering": Communicatively managing uncertainty in adoptive families. *Journal of Family Communication, 10*, 236–255. doi: 10.1080/15267431003682435

Coleman, M. H., Fine, M., Ganong, L. H., Downs, K., & Pauk, N. (2001). When you're not the Brady Bunch: Identifying perceived conflicts and resolution strategies in stepfamilies. *Personal Relationships, 8*, 55–73. doi: 10.1111/j.1475-6811.2001.tb00028.x

Coleman, M. H., Ganong, L. H., & Fine, M. (2004). Communication in stepfamilies. In A. L. Vangelisti (Ed.), *Handbook of family communication* (pp. 215–232). Mahwah, NJ: Erlbaum.

Collins, P. H. (2000). *Black feminist thought* (2nd ed.). New York, NY: Routledge.

Conger, R. D., & Conger, K. J. (2002). Resilience in Midwestern families: Selected findings from the first decade of a prospective, longitudinal study. *Journal of Marriage and Family, 64*, 361–373. doi: 10.1111/j.1741-3737.2002.00361.x

Connolly, C. M. (2006). A process of change: The intersection of the GLBT individual and his or her family of origin. In J. J. Bigner (Ed.), *An introduction to GLBT family studies* (pp. 5–21). Binghamton, NY: Haworth Press.

Coontz, S. (1992). *The way we never were: American families and the nostalgia trap.* New York, NY: Basic Books.

Coontz, S. (Ed.). (1999a). *American families: A multicultural reader.* New York, NY: Routledge.

Coontz, S. (1999b). Introduction. In S. Coontz, M. Parson, & G. Raley (Eds.), *American families: A multicultural reader* (pp. ix–xxxiii). New York, NY: Routledge.

Coontz, S. (2003). Diversity and communication values in the family. *Journal of Family Communication, 3,* 187–192. doi: 10.1207/S15327698JFC0304_2

Coontz, S. (2005). *Marriage, a history: From obedience to intimacy or how love conquered marriage.* New York, NY: Viking.

Copen, C. E., Daniels, K., Vespa, J., & Mosher, W. D. (2012, March 22). *First marriages in the United States: Data from the 2006–2010 national survey of family growth* (National Health Statistics Reports, No. 49). Retrieved from http://www.cdc.gov/nchs/data/nhsr/nhsr049.pdf

Coser, L. A. (1974). *Greedy institutions: Patterns of undivided commitment.* New York, NY: Free Press.

Cox, C. B. (2000). Why grandchildren are going to and staying at grandmother's house and what happens when they get there. In C.B. Cox (Ed.), *To grandmother's house we go and stay: Perspectives on custodial grandparenting* (pp. 3–19). New York, NY: Springer.

Crompton, R., & Lyonette, C. (2006). Work-life "balance" in Europe. *Acta Sociologica, 49,* 379–393. doi: 10.1177/0001699306071680

Crosnoe, R., Mistry, R. S., & Elder, G. H. (2002). Economic disadvantage, family dynamics, and adolescent enrollment in higher education. *Journal of Marriage and Family, 64,* 690–702. doi: 10.1111/j.1741-3737.2002.00690.x

Curtain, L., & Mirkin, M. (2012, February 10). Healing the injured brain: VA, DoD join forces on research to combat TBI, PTSD. *Force Health Protection & Readiness Current News.* Retrieved from http://home.fhpr.osd.mil/press-newsroom/fhpr-news/current_news/12-02-10/Healing_the_injured_brain_VA_DoD_join_forces_on_research_to_combat_TBI_PTSD.aspx

Dainton, M., & Aylor, B. (2002). Patterns of communication channel use in maintenance of long-distance relationships. *Communication Research Reports, 19,* 118–129. doi: 10.1080/08824090209384839

D'Augelli, A. R., Grossman, A. H., & Starks, M. T. (2008). Families of gay, lesbian, and bisexual youth: What do parents and siblings know and how do they react? *Journal of GLBT Studies, 4,* 95–115. doi: 10.1080/15504280802084506

Dave Thomas Foundation. (2007, November 1). *National foster care adoption attitudes survey.* Retrieved from http://www.davethomasfoundation.org/wp-content/uploads/2011/02/ExecSummary_NatlFosterCareAdoptionAttitudesSurvey.pdf

Davis, E. C., & Friel, L. V. (2001). Adolescent sexuality: Disentangling the effects of family structure and family context. *Journal of Marriage and Family, 63,* 669–681. doi: 10.1111/j.1741-3737.2001.00669.x

Deleire, T., & Kalil, A. (2002). Good things come in threes: Single-parent multigenerational family structure and adolescent adjustment. *Demography, 39*, 393–413. doi: 10.1353/dem.2002.0016

Denzin, N. K., & Lincoln, Y. S. (Eds.). (2011). *Handbook of qualitative research* (4th ed.). Thousand Oaks, CA: Sage Publications.

Desens, L. C., & Hughes, L. (2013). Entertainment-education and strategic communication: A case study of Sesame Workshop's "Talk, Listen, Connect" initiative for military families. *International Journal of Strategic Communication, 7*, 292–309. doi: 10.1080/1553118X.2013.777903

Dewaele, A., Cox, N., Van den Berghe, W., & Vincke, J. (2011). Families of choice? Exploring the supportive networks of lesbians, gay men, and bisexuals. *Journal of Applied Social Psychology, 41*, 312–331. doi: 10.1111/j.1559-1816.2010.00715.x

DeWall, C. N., & Baumeister, R. F. (2006). Alone but feeling no pain: Effects of social exclusion on physical pain tolerance and pain threshold, affective forecasting, and interpersonal empathy. *Journal of Personality and Social Psychology, 91*, 1–15. doi: 10.1037/0022-3514.91.1.1

Dilworth-Anderson, P. (1992). Extended kin networks in black families. *Generations, 16*, 29–33. doi: 10.1177/0022022110388564

Docan-Morgan, S. (2010). Korean adoptees' retrospective reports of intrusive interactions: Exploring boundary management in adoptive families. *Journal of Family Communication, 10*, 137–157. doi: 10.1080/15267431003699603

Docan-Morgan, S. (2011). "They don't know what it's like to be in my shoes": Topic avoidance about race in transracially adoptive families. *Journal of Social and Personal Relationships, 28*, 336–355. doi: 10.1177/0265407510382177

Dolbin-MacNab, M. L. (2006). Just like raising your own? Grandmothers' perceptions of parenting a second time around. *Family Relations, 55*, 564–575. doi: 10.1111/j.1741-3729.2006.00426.x.

Dolbin-MacNab, M. L., & Keiley, M. K. (2006). A systematic examination of grandparents' emotional closeness with their custodial grandchildren. *Research in Human Development, 3*, 59–71. doi: 10.1207/s15427617rhd0301_6

Dolbin-MacNab, M. L., & Keiley, M. K. (2009). Navigating interdependence: How adolescents raised solely by grandparents experience their family relationships. *Family Relations, 58*, 162–175. doi: 10.1111/j.1741-3729.2008.00544.x

Dolbin-MacNab, M. L, Rodgers, B. E., & Traylor, R. M. (2009). Bridging the generations: A retrospective examination of adults' relationships with their kinship caregivers. *Journal of Intergenerational Relationships, 7*, 159–176. doi: 10.1080/15350770902851197

Domar, A. D. (2002). *Conquering infertility*. New York, NY: Penguin.

Donati, T. (1995). Single parents and wider families in the new context of legitimacy. *Marriage & Family Review, 20*, 27–42. doi: 10.1300/J002v20n01_02

Dorow, S., & Swiffen, A. (2009). Blood and desire: The secret of heteronormativity in adoption narratives of culture. *American Ethnologist, 36*, 563–573. doi: 10.1111/j.1548-1425.2009.01179x

Doss, B. D., Rhoades, G. K., Stanley, S. M., & Markman, H. J. (2009). The effect of the transition to parenthood on relationship quality: An eight-year prospective study. *Journal of Personal and Social Psychology, 96*, 601–619. doi: 10.1037/a0013969

Doyle, M. E., & Peterson, K. A. (2005). Re-entry and reintegration: Returning home after combat. *Psychiatric Quarterly, 76,* 361–370. doi: 10.1007/s11126–005-4972-z

Dunkerley, D., Scourfield, J., Maegusuku-Hewett, T., & Smalley, N. (2006). Field report. *Journal of Refugee Studies, 19,* 488–508. doi: 10.1093/refuge/fel019

Durham, W. T. (2008). The rules-based process of revealing/concealing the family planning decisions of voluntarily child-free couples: A communication privacy management perspective. *Communication Studies, 59,* 132–147. doi: 10.1080/10510970802062451

Durham, W. T., & Braithwaite, D.O. (2009). Communication privacy management within the family planning trajectories of voluntarily childfree couples. *Journal of Family Communication, 9,* 43–65. doi: 10.1080/15267430802561600

Durkheim, E. (1965). *The elementary forms of the religious life* (J. W. Swain, Trans.). New York, NY: Free Press. (Original work published 1912)

Ebaugh, H. R., & Curry, M. (2000). Fictive kin as social capital in new immigrant communities. *Sociological Perspectives, 43,* 189–209. doi: 10.1177/0002764206289145

Eby, J., Iverson, E., Smyers, J., & Kekic, E. (2011). The faith community's role in refugee resettlement in the United States. *Journal of Refugee Studies, 24,* 586–605. doi: 10.1093/jrs/fer038

Edwards, A. P., & Graham, E. E. (2009). The relationship between individuals' definitions of family and implicit personal theories of communication. *Journal of Family Communication, 9,* 191–208. doi: 10.1080/15267430903070147

Edwards, O. W. (2001). Grandparents raising grandchildren. In M. J. Fine & S. W. Lee (Eds.), *Handbook of diversity in parent education: The changing face of parenting and parent education* (pp. 199–213). San Diego, CA: Academic Press.

Ehrle, G. M. (2001). Grandchildren as moderator variables in the family: Social, physiological, and intellectual development of grandparents who are raising them. In E. L. Grigorenko & R. J. Sternberg (Eds.), *Family development and intellectual functions: A lifespan perspective* (pp. 213–226). Mahwah, NJ: Erlbaum.

Ehrle, G. M., & Day, H. D. (1994). Adjustment and family functioning of grandmothers rearing their grandchildren. *Contemporary Family Therapy: An International Journal, 16,* 67–82. doi:10.1007/BF02197603

Einhorn, B. (2013, July 2). Why China is ordering adult children to visit their parents. *Bloomberg BusinessWeek: Global Economics.* Retrieved from http://www.businessweek.com/articles/2013-07-02/why-china-is-ordering-adult-children-to-visit-their-parents

Eisenbruch, M., de Jong, J. T. V. M., & Van de Put, W. (2004). Bringing order out of chaos: A culturally competent approach to managing the problems of refugees and victims of organized violence. *Journal of Traumatic Stress, 17,* 123–131. doi: 10.1023/B:JOTS.0000022618.65406.e8

Elliott, D. B., & Simmons, T. (2011, August). *Marital events of Americans: 2009* (American Community Survey Reports, ACS-13). Retrieved from http://www.census.gov/prod/2011/pubs/acs-13.pdf

Erbert, L. A., & Alemán, M. W. (2008). Taking the grand out of grandparent: Dialectical tensions in grandparent perceptions of surrogate parenting. *Journal of Social and Personal Relationships, 25,* 671–695. doi: 10.1177/0265407508093785

Erwin, N. B. (1993). An interpretive case study of commuter marriage as a response to unemployment. *Dissertation Abstracts International: Section A. Humanities and Social Sciences, 54,* 4375.

Eurostat. (2012, October). *Marriage and divorce statistics.* Retrieved from http://epp.eurostat.ec.europa.eu/statistics_explained/index.php/Marriage_and_divorce_statistics

Evans, G. W., Kim, P., Ting, A. H., Tesher, H. B., & Shannis, D. (2007). Cumulative risk, maternal responsiveness, and allostatic load among young adolescents. *Developmental Psychology, 43,* 341–351. doi: 10.1037/a0031808

Farris, A. (1978). Commuting. In R. Rapoport & R. N. Rapoport (Eds.), *Working couples* (pp. 100–107). New York, NY: Harper and Row.

Fazel, M., Wheeler, J, & Danesh, J. (2005). Prevalence of serious disorder in 7000 refugees resettled in Western countries: A systematic review. *Lancet, 365,* 1309–1314. doi: 10.1016/S0140-6736(05)61027-6

Ferguson, S., & Leoutsakas, D. (Eds.). (2013). *More than blood: Today's reality and tomorrow's vision of family.* Dubuque, IA: Kendall-Hunt.

Fine, M., Coleman, M. H., & Ganong, L. H. (1998). Consistency in perceptions of the step-parent role among step-parents, parents, and stepchildren. *Journal of Social and Personal Relationships, 15,* 811–829. doi: 10.1177/0265407598156006

Fineman, M. A. (1993). Our sacred institution: The ideal of the family in American law and society. *Utah Law Review,* 387–404. Retrieved from http://heinonline.org

Fingerman, K. L., & Hay, E. L. (2002). Searching under the streetlight? Age biases in the personal and family relationships literature. *Personal Relationships, 9,* 415–433. doi: 10.1111/1475-6811.09404

Fisher, A. (2003). Still "not quite as good as having your own"? Toward a sociology of adoption. *Annual Review of Sociology, 29,* 335–361. doi: 10.1146/annurev.soc.29.010202.100209

Fitzpatrick, M. A. (1998). Interpersonal communication on the Starship Enterprise: Resilience, stability, and change in relationships in the twenty-first century. In J. S. Trent (Ed.), *Communication: Views from the helm for the 21st century* (pp. 41–46). Boston, MA: Allyn and Bacon.

Fitzpatrick, M. A., & Vangelisti, A. L. (1995). Extending family boundaries. In M. A. Fitzpatrick and A. L. Vanglisti (Eds.), *Explaining family interactions* (pp. 253–255). Thousand Oaks, CA: Sage.

Floyd, K., Mikkelson, A. C., & Judd, J. (2006). Defining the family through relationships. In L. H. Turner & R. West (Eds.), *The family communication sourcebook* (pp. 21–39). Thousand Oaks, CA: Sage.

Floyd, K., & Morman, M. T. (2006). Introduction: On the breadth of the family experience. In K. Floyd & M. T. Morman (Eds.), *Widening the family circle: New research on family communication* (pp. xi–xvi). Thousand Oaks, CA: Sage.

Fonseca, M. L., & Ormond, M. (2008). Defining "family" and bringing it together: The ins and outs of family reunification in Portugal. In R. Grillo (Ed.), *Family in question: Immigrant and ethnic minorities in multicultural Europe* (pp. 89–111). Amsterdam, NLD: Amsterdam University Press.

Footlick, J. (1990). What happened to the family? *Newsweek* (Special edition), Winter/Spring, 8–13.

Ford, D. Y. (1994). An exploration of perceptions of alternative family structures among university students. *Family Relations, 43*, 68–73. doi: 10.2307/585144

Ford-Gilboe, M. (2000). Dispelling myths and creating opportunity: A comparison of the strengths of single-parent and two-parent families. *Advances in Nursing Science, 23*, 41–58. Retrieved from http://journals.lww.com/advancesinnursingscience/Pages/default.aspx

Forsyth, C. J., & Gramling, R. (1998). Socio-economic factors affecting the rise of commuter marriage. *International Journal of Sociology of the Family, 28*, 93–106. Retrieved from http://www.jstor.org/stable/23070667

Foucault, M. (1972). *The archaeology of knowledge*. New York, NY: Pantheon.

Foucault, M. (1977/1995). *Discipline and punishment: The birth of the prison*. New York, NY: Vintage Books.

Foucault, M. (1978). *The history of sexuality: Volume I*. New York, NY: Random House.

Franz, B., & Ives, N. (2008, March). *Wading through muddy water: Challenges to Liberian refugee family restoration in resettlement*. Paper presented at the annual meeting of the ISA's 49th Annual Convention: Bridging Multiple Divides, San Francisco, CA. Abstract retrieved from http://www.isanet.org/

Freeark, K., Rosenblum, K. L., Hus, V. H., & Root, B. L. (2008). Fathers, mothers and marriages: What shapes adoption conversations in families with young adopted children? *Adoption Quarterly, 11*, 1–23. doi: 10.1080/10926750802291393

Frisby, B. N., Byrnes, K., Mansson, D. H., Booth-Butterfield, M., & Birmingham, M. K. (2011). Topic avoidance, everyday talk, and stress in romantic military and non-military couples. *Communication Studies, 62*, 241–257. doi: 10.1080/10510974.2011.553982

Fuller-Thomson, E., & Minkler, M. (2000). America's grandparent caregivers: Who are they? In B. Hayslip, Jr. & R. Goldberg-Glen (Eds.), *Grandparents raising grandchildren* (pp. 3–21). New York, NY: Springer.

Fuller-Thomson, E., & Minkler, M. (2007). Central American grandparents raising grandchildren. *Hispanic Journal of Behavioral Sciences, 29*, 5–18. doi:10.1177/0739986306293680

Fuller-Thomson, E., Minkler, M., & Driver, D. (1997). A profile of grandparents raising grandchildren in the United States. *The Gerontologist, 37*, 406–411. doi:10.1093/geront/37.3.406

Gabrielson, M. L. (2011). "We have to create a family": Aging support issue and needs among older lesbians. *Journal of Gay & Lesbian Social Services, 23*, 322–334. doi: 10.1080/10538720.2011.562803

Gallagher, S. K., & Gerstel, N. (1993). Kinkeeping and friend keeping among older women: The effect of marriage. *The Gerontologist, 33*, 675–681. doi: 10.1177/0265407510361615

Galvin, K. M. (2003). International and transracial adoption: A communication research agenda. *Journal of Family Communication, 3*, 237–253. doi: 10.1207/S15327698JFC0304_5

Galvin, K. M. (2004). The family of the future: What do we face? In A. L. Vangelisti (Ed.), *Handbook of family communication* (pp. 675–697). Mahwah, NJ: Erlbaum.

Galvin, K. M. (2006). Diversity's impact on defining the family: Discourse-dependence and identity. In L. H. Turner & R. West (Eds.), *The family communication sourcebook* (pp. 3–20). Thousand Oaks, CA: Sage Publications.

Galvin, K. M. (2009, April). *Keynote speech for communication week: Discourse dependence and family identity*. Indiana University – Northwest. Gary, IN.

Galvin, K. M. (2013). On the threshold: Evotypical families talk themselves into being. In S. Marrow & D. Leoutsakas (Eds.), *More than blood: Today's reality & tomorrow's vision of family* (pp. 1–5). Dubuque, IA: Kendall Hunt.

Galvin, K. M., & Braithwaite, D. O. (2014). Family communication theory and research from the field of family communication: Discourses that constitute and reflect families. *Journal of Family Theory & Review, 6*, 97–111. doi:10.1111/jftr.12030

Ganong, L. H., & Coleman, M. H. (2004). *Stepfamily relationships: Development, dynamics, and interventions*. New York, NY: Kluwer Academic/Plenum.

Ganong, L. H., Coleman, M. H., Fine, M., & Martin, P. (1999). Stepparents' affinity-seeking and affinity-maintaining strategies with stepchildren. *Journal of Family Issues, 20*, 299–327. doi: 10.1177/019251399020003001

Ganong, L. H., Coleman, M. H., & Hans, J. (2006). Divorce as prelude to stepfamily living the consequences of redivorce. In M. A. Fine & J. H. Harvey (Eds.), *Handbook of divorce and relationship dissolution* (pp. 409–434). Mahwah, NJ: Erlbaum.

Ganong, L. H., Coleman, M. H., & Jamison, T. (2011). Patterns of stepchild-stepparent relationship development. *Journal of Marriage and Family, 73*, 396–413. doi: 10.1111/j.1741-3737.2010.00814.x

Garrison, V., & Weiss, C. I. (1979). Dominican family networks and United States immigration policy: A case study. *International Migration Review, 13*, 264–283. doi: 10.2307/2545032

Gates, G. J., & Newport, F. (2012, Oct 18). *Special report: 3.4% of U.S. adults identify as LGBT*. Retrieved from http://.www.gallup.com/poll/158-66/special-report-adults-identify-lgbt

Geiger, S. N. G. (1986). Women's life histories: Method and content. *Signs: Journal of Women in Culture and Society, 11*, 334–351. doi: 10.1086/494227

Gerstel, N., & Gross, H. (1984). *Commuter marriage: A study of work and family*. New York, NY: Guilford Press.

Giddens, A. (1984). *The constitution of society*. Berkeley, CA: University of California Press.

Giddens, A. (1993). *The transformation of intimacy: Sexuality, love and eroticism in modern societies*. Stanford, CA: Stanford University Press.

Gilad, L. (1990). Refugees in Newfoundland: Families after flight. *Journal of Comparative Family Studies, 21*, 379–396. Retrieved from http://www.soci.ucalgary.ca/jcfs/

Gilby, R. L., & Pederson, D. R. (1982). The development of the child's concept of the family. *Canadian Journal of Behavioural Science, 14*, 110–121. doi: 10.1037/h0081245

Gillespie, R. (2000). When no means no: Disbelief, disregard and deviance as discourses of voluntary childlessness. *Women's Studies International Forum, 23*, 223–234. doi: 10.1016/S0277-5395(00)00076-5

Gill-Hopple, K., & Brage-Hudson, D. (2012). Compadrazgo: A literature review. *Journal of Transcultural Nursing, 23*, 117–123. doi: 10.1177/1043659611433870

Gladstone, J. W., Brown, R. A., & Fitzgerald, K.-A. J. (2009). Grandparents raising their grandchildren: Tensions, service needs and involvement with child welfare agencies. *International Journal of Aging and Human Development, 69*, 55–78. doi: 10.2190/AG.69.1.d

Glass, J. C., Jr., & Huneycutt, T. L. (2002). Grandparents raising grandchildren: Extent of situation, issues involved, and educational implications. *Educational Gerontology, 28*, 139–161. doi: 10.1080/03601270252801391

Glotzer, R., & Federlein, A. C. (2007). Miles that bind: Commuter marriage and family strengths. *Michigan Family Review, 12*, 7–31. Retrieved from http://quod.lib.umich.edu/m/mfr/4919087.0012.102

Goffman, E. (1963). *Stigma: Notes on the management of spoiled identity.* New York, NY: Simon & Schuster.

Goffman, E. (1967). *Interaction ritual.* Garden City, NY: Anchor.

Goldberg, A. E., & Kuvalanka, K. A. (2012). Marriage (in)equality: The perspectives of adolescents and emerging adults with lesbian, gay, and bisexual parents. *Journal of Marriage and Family, 74*, 34–52. doi: 10.1111/j.1741-3737.2011.00876.x

Golish, T. (2003). Stepfamily communication strengths: Understanding the ties that bind. *Human Communication Research, 29*, 41–80. doi: 10.1111/j.1468-2958.2003.tb00831.x

Goltz, D. B., & Zingsheim, J. (2010). It's not a wedding, it's a gayla: Queer resistance and normative recuperation. *Text and Performance Quarterly, 30*, 290–312. doi: 10.1080/10462937.2010.483011

Gomel, J. N., Tinsley, B., Parke, R., & Clark, K. (1998). The effects of economic hardship on family relationships among African American, Latino, and Euro-American families. *Journal of Family Issues, 19*, 436–467. doi: 10.1177/019251398019004004

Goodall, H. L. (2006). *A need to know: The clandestine history of a C.I.A. family.* Walnut Creek, CA: Left Coast Press.

Goodman, C. C. (2003). Intergenerational triads in grandparent families. *Journal of Gerontology: Social Sciences, 54B*, S281–S296. doi: 10.1093/geronb/58.5.S281

Goodman, C. C., & Silverstein, M. (2001). Grandmothers who parent their grandchildren: An exploratory study of close relations across three generations. *Journal of Family Issues, 22*, 557–578. doi: 10.1177/019251301022005002

Goodman, C. C., & Silverstein, M. (2006). Grandmothers raising grandchildren: Ethnic and racial differences in well-being among custodial and co-parenting families. *Journal of Family Issues, 27*, 1605–1626. doi: 10.1177/0192513X06291435

Goodman, P., Turner, A., Agazio, J., Throop, M., Padden, D., Greiner, S., & Miller, S. L. (2013). Deployment of military mothers: Supportive and nonsupportive military programs, processes, and policies. *Military Medicine, 178*, 729–734. doi: 10.7205/MILMED-D-12-00460.

Gordon, C. (2009). *Making meanings, creating family: Intertextuality and framing in family interaction.* New York, NY: Oxford University Press.

Gore, M. S. (1968). *Urbanization and family change.* New York, NY: Humanities Press.

Grall, T. S. (2009, November). *Custodial mothers and fathers and their child support: 2007* (Current Population Reports, P60–237). Retrieved from http://www.census.gov/prod/2009pubs/p60-237.pdf

Greeff, A. P., & Ritman, I. N. (2005). Individual characteristics associated with resilience in single-parent families. *Psychological Reports, 96*, 36–42. doi: 10.2466/pr0.96.1.36–42

Greeff, A. P., & Van Der Merwe, S. (2004). Variables associated with resilience in divorced families. *Social Indicators Research, 68*, 59–75. doi: 10.1023/B:SOCI.0000025569.95499.b5

Greil, A. L., McQuillan, J., & Slauson-Blevins, K. (2011). The social construction of infertility. *Sociology Compass, 5*, 736–746. doi: 10.1111/j.1751-9020.2011.00397.x

Griffin, K., Botvin, G., Scheier, L., Diaz, T., & Miller, N. (2000). Parenting practices as predictors of substance use, delinquency, and aggression among urban minority youth: Moderating effects of family structure and gender. *Psychology of Addictive Behaviors, 14*, 174–184. doi: 10.1037//0893-164X.14.2.174

Griffith, J. L., Agani, F., Weine, S., Ukshini, S., Coffey, E., Ulaj, J., ... Kallaba, M. (2005). A family-based mental health program of recovery from state terror in Kosova. *Behavioral Sciences and the Law, 23*, 547–558. doi: 10.1002/bsl.650

Grillo, R. (2008). *Family in question: Immigrant and ethnic minorities in multicultural Europe.* Amsterdam, NLD: Amsterdam University Press.

Gross, H. (1980). Dual-career couples who live apart: Two types. *Journal of Marriage and the Family, 42*, 567–576. doi: 10.2307/351900

Gubrium, J. F., & Holstein, J. A. (1990). *What is family?* Mountain View, CA: Mayfield.

Gubrium, J. F., & Holstein, J. A. (1993). Family discourse, organizational embeddedness, and local enactment. *Journal of Family Issues, 14*, 66–81. doi: 10.1177/0192513X93014001006

Haas, S. M., & Stafford, L. (2005). Maintenance behaviors in same-sex and marital relationships: A matched sample comparison. *Journal of Family Communication, 5*, 43–60. doi: 10.1207/s15327698jfc0501_3

Häfner, S. (2011). Impact of commuting on partnership and family life. *Zeitschrift Für Psychosomatische Medizin Und Psychotherapie, 57*, 2, 185–201. Abstract retrieved from http://www.ncbi.nlm.nih.gov/pubmed/21626481

Hagelund, A. (2008). "For women and children!": The family and immigrant politics in Scandinavia. In R. Grillo (Ed.), *Family in question: Immigrant and ethnic minorities in multicultural Europe* (pp. 71–88). Amsterdam, NLD: Amsterdam University Press.

Haines, D. W. (2010). *Safe haven?: A history of refugees in America.* Sterling, VA: Kumarian Press.

Haines, D. W., Rutherford, D., & Thomas, P. (2012). Community among Vietnamese refugees. *International Migration Review, 15*, 310–319. doi: 10.2307/2545345

Halberstam, J. J. (2012). *Gaga feminism: Sex, gender, and the end of normal.* Boston, MA: Beacon Press.

Halilovich, H. (2012). Trans-local communities in the age of transnationalism: Bosnians in diaspora. *International Migration, 50*, 162–178. doi: 10.1111/j.1468-2435.2011.00721.x

Hall, G. (2005). "These are my parents": The experiences of children in same-sex parented families during the first year of marriage legalization in Massachusetts. In *What I did for love, or benefits, or...: Same-sex marriage in Massachusetts: Wellesley Centers for Women, Working Paper No. 422.* (pp. 35–45). Wellesley, MA: Wellesley Centers for Women.

Hall, J. C. (2008). The impact of kin and fictive kin relationships on the mental health of black adult children of alcoholics. *Health and Social Work, 33*, 259–266. doi: 10.1093/hsw/33.4.259

Hall, L. K. (2008). *Counseling military families: What mental health professionals need to know.* New York, NY: Routledge.

Hamilton, B. E., & Sutton, P. D. (2013, June 6). Recent trends in births and fertility rates through December 2012. *NCHS Health E-Stat.* Retrieved from http://www.cdc.gov/nchs/data/hestat/births_fertility_2012/Births_Fertility_December, 2012. pdf

Harrigan, M. M. (2009). The contradictions of identity-work for parents of visibly adopted children. *Journal of Social and Personal Relationships, 26,* 634–658. doi: 10.1177/0265407509353393

Harrigan, M. M. (2010). Exploring the narrative process: An analysis of the adoption stories mothers tell their internationally adopted children. *Journal of Family Communication, 10,* 24–39. doi: 10.1080/15267430903385875

Harrigan, M. M., & Braithwaite, D. O. (2010). Discursive struggles in families formed through visible adoptions: An exploration of dialectical unity. *Journal of Applied Communication Research, 38,* 127–144. doi: 10.1080/00909881003639536

Harrigan, M. M., Dieter, S., Leinwohl, J., & Martin, L. (2012, November). *"It's just who I am...I have brown hair. I have a mysterious father": An exploration of donor-conceived offspring's identity construction.* Paper presented at the National Communication Association Convention. Orlando, FL.

Harris, S., Lowery, S., & Arnold, M. (2002). When women educators are the commuters in commuter relationships. *Advancing Women in Leadership, 10 (Winter).* Retrieved from http://www.advancingwomen.com/awl/winter2002/harris.html

Hawkins, A., Beckett, C., Rutter, M., Castle, J., Colvert, E., Groothues, C. ... Sonuga-Barke, E. (2007). Communicative openness about adoption and interest in contact in a sample of domestic and intercountry adolescent adoptees. *Adoption Quarterly, 10,* 131–156. doi: 10.1080/10926750802163220

Hayslip, B., Jr., & Glover, R. J. (2008–2009). Custodial grandparenting: Perceptions of loss by non-custodial grandparent peers. *Omega: Journal of Death and Dying, 58,* 163–175. doi:10.2190/OM.58.3.a

Hayslip, B., Jr., & Goodman, C. C. (2007). Grandparents raising grandchildren: Benefits and drawbacks. *Journal of Intergenerational Relationships, 5,* 117–119. doi: 10.1300/J194v05n04_12

Hayslip, B., Jr., & Kaminski, P. L. (2005). Grandparents raising their caregivers: A review of the literature and suggestions for practice. *The Gerontologist, 45,* 262–269. doi: 10.1093/geront/45.2.262

Hayslip, B., Jr., Shore, R. J., Henderson, C. E., & Lambert, P. L. (1998). Custodial grandparenting and the impact of grandchildren with problems on role satisfaction and role meaning. *Journal of Gerontology, 53B,* S164–S173. doi: 10.1093/geronb/53B.3.S164

Helweg, A. W., & Helweg, U. M. (1990). *An immigrant success story: East Indians in America.* Philadelphia, PA: University of Pennsylvania Press.

Herman, D. (2009). *Basic elements of narrative.* Malden, MA: Wiley-Blackwell.

Hertz, R. (2006). Talking about "doing" family. *Journal of Marriage and Family, 68,* 796–799. doi: 10.1111/j.1741-3737.2006.00293.x

Hertz, R. (2009). Turning strangers into kin: Half siblings and anonymous donors. In M. K. Nelson & A. I. Garey (Eds.), *Who's watching?: Daily practices of surveillance among contemporary families* (pp. 156–174). Nashville, TN: Vanderbilt University Press.

Hess, J. A. (2003). Measuring distance in personal relationships: The relational distance index. *Personal Relationships, 10,* 197–215. doi: 10.1111/1475-6811.00046

Hetherington, E. M. (1989). Coping with family transitions: Winners, losers, and survivors. *Child Development, 60,* 1–14. doi: 10.1111/1467-8624.ep7250664

Hetherington, E. M. (1999a). Family functioning and the adjustment of adolescent siblings in diverse types of families. *Monographs of the Society for Research in Child Development, 64* (4, Serial No. 259), 1–25. doi: 10.1111/1540–5834.00045

Hetherington, E. M. (1999b). Should we stay together for the sake of the children? In E.M. Hetherington (Ed.), *Coping with divorce, single parenting, and remarriage: A risk and resiliency perspective* (pp. 93–116). Mahwah, NJ: Erlbaum.

Hewlett, S. A. (2002). *Creating a life: What every woman needs to know about having a baby and a career.* New York, NY: Hyperion.

Hileman, S. (1990). The "female-determined" relationship: Personal and professional needs of academic women in commuter marriages. In L. B. Welch (Ed.), *Women in higher education: Changes and challenges* (pp. 119–125). New York, NY: Praeger.

Hill, R. (1949). *Families under stress.* Westport, CT: Greenwood.

Hill, R. (1958). Social stresses on the family: Generic features of families under stress. *Social Casework, 39,* 139–150. Retrieved from http://www.alliance1.org/

Hofstede, G. (1991). *Cultures and organizations: Software of the mind.* London, UK: McGraw-Hill.

Hofstede, G. (2001). *Culture's consequences: Comparing values, behaviors, institutions, and organizations across nations* (2$^{nd}$ ed.). Thousand Oaks, CA: Sage.

Holmes, M. (2004). The precariousness of choice in the new sentimental order: A response to Bawin-Legros. *Current Sociology, 52,* 251–257. doi: 10.1177/0011392104041811

Holmes, M. (2006). Love lives at a distance: Distance relationships over the life course. *Sociological Research Online, 11*(3). Retrieved from http://www.socresonline.org.uk/11/3/holmes.html

Holstein, J. A., & Gubrium, J. F. (1999). "What is family?": Further thoughts on a social constructionist approach. In B. H. Settles, S. K. Steinmetz, G. W. Peterson, & M. B. Sussman (Eds.), *Concepts and definitions of family for the 21$^{st}$ century* (pp. 3–20). Philadelphia, PA: Haworth Press.

Holtzman, M. (2008). Defining family: Young adults' perceptions of the parent-child bond. *Journal of Family Communication, 8,* 167–185. doi: 10.1080/15267430701856887

Horne, S. G., Rostosky, S. S., & Riggle, E. D. B. (2011). Marriage restriction amendments and family members of lesbian, gay, bisexual individuals: A mixed-method approach. *Journal of Social Issues, 67,* 358–375. doi: 10.1111/j.1540–4560.2011.01702.x

Horst, C. (2002). Vital links in social security: Somali refugees in the Dadaab camps, Kenya. *Refugee Survey Quarterly, 21,* 242–259. doi: 10.1093/rsq/21.1_and_2.242

Huffman, A. H., & Payne, S. C. (2006). The challenges and benefits of dual-military marriage. In C. A. Castro, A. B. Adler, & T. W. Britt (Eds.), *Military life: The psychology of serving in peace and combat (Volume 3: The military family)* (pp. 138–166). Westport, CT: Praeger Security International.

Human Rights Campaign. (n.d.). *Marriage center.* Retrieved from http://www.hrc.org/issues/marriage.asp

Ibsen, C. A., & Klobus, P. (1972). Fictive kin term use in social relationships: Alternative interpretations. *Journal of Marriage and Family, 34,* 615–620. Retrieved from http://www.jstor.org/stable/350312

Jackson, A. P., Brown, R. P., & Patterson-Stewart, K. E. (2000). African Americans in dual career commuter marriages: An investigation of their experiences. *The Family Journal, 8,* 22–36. doi: 10.1177/1066480700081005

Jacobson, H. (2008). *Culture keeping: White mothers, international adoption, and the negotiation of family difference.* Nashville, TN: Vanderbilt University Press.

Jacobson, H. (2009). Interracial surveillance and biological privilege: Adoptive families in the public eye. In M. K. Nelson & A. I. Garey (Eds.), *Who's watching?: Daily practices of surveillance among contemporary families* (pp. 73–91). Nashville, TN: Vanderbilt University Press.

Jadva, V., Blake, L., Casey, P., & Golombok, S. (2012). Surrogacy families 10 years on: Relationship with the surrogate, decisions over disclosure and children's understanding of their surrogacy origins. *Human Reproduction, 27,* 3008–3014. doi: 10.1093/humrep/des273

Jeffords, S., & Rabinovitz, L. (Eds.). (1994). *Seeing through the media: The Persian Gulf War.* New Brunswick, NJ: Rutgers University Press.

Jehn, K., A., Stroh, L., & Von Glinow, M.A. (1997). The commuting couple: Oxymoron or career freedom? In Y. Altunex (Ed.), *Careers in the new millennium* (pp. 163–178). Brussels, Belgium: Academic Cooperative.

Jendrick, M. P. (1994). Grandparents who parent their grandchildren: Circumstances and decisions. *The Gerontologist, 34,* 206–216. doi: 10.1093/geront/34.2.206

Jennings-Kelsall, V., Aloia, L. S., Solomon, D. H., Marshall, A. D., & Leifker, F. R. (2012). Stressors experienced by women within Marine Corps families: A qualitative study. *Military Psychology, 24,* 363–381. doi: 10.1080/08995605.2012.695255

Jeynes, W. (2002). *Divorce, family structure, and the academic success of children.* Binghamton, NY: Haworth.

Johnson, C. L. (1999). Fictive kin among oldest old African Americans in the San Francisco Bay area. *Journal of Gerontology: Social Sciences, 54B,* S368–S375. doi: 10.1093/geronb/54B.6.S368

Johnson, C. L. (2000). Perspective on American kinship in the late 1990s. *Journal of Marriage and Family, 62,* 623–639. doi: 10.1111/j.1741-3737.2000.00623.x

Johnson, S. E. (1987). Weaving the threads: Equalizing professional and personal demands faced by commuting career couples. *Journal of the National Association for Women Deans, Administrators, & Counselors, 50,* 3–10. Retrieved from https://catalyst.library.jhu.edu/catalog/bib_406012

Jones, C., & Hackett, S. (2007). Communicative openness within adoptive families: Adoptive parents' narrative accounts of the challenges of adoption talk and the approaches used to manage these challenges. *Adoption Quarterly, 10,* 157–178. doi: 10.1080/10926750802163238

Jones, D. J., Forehand, R., Brody, G. H., & Armistead, L. (2002). Positive parenting and child psychosocial adjustment in inner-city single-parent African American families: The role of maternal optimism. *Behavior Modification, 26,* 464–481. doi: 10.1177/0145445502026004002

Jordan, B. (2013, July 3). DoD, VA calculate costs of post-DOMA military. *Military.com News.* Retrieved from http://www.military.com/daily-news/2013/07/03/dod-va-calculate-costs-of-post-doma-military.html

Joseph, A. L., & Afifi, T. D. (2010). Military wives' stressful disclosures to their deployed husbands: The role of protective buffering. *Journal of Applied Communication Research, 38,* 412–434. doi: 10.1080/00909882.2010.513997

Jubilut, L. L., & Carneiro, W. P. (2007). Resettlement in solidarity: A new regional approach towards a more humane durable solution. *Refugee Survey Quarterly, 30,* 63–86. doi: 10.1093/rsq/hdr010

Julien, D., Chartrand, E., Simard, M., Bouthillier, D., & Begin, J. (2003). Conflict, social support, and relationship quality: An observational study of heterosexual, gay male, and lesbian couples' communication. *Journal of Family Psychology, 17,* 419–428. doi: 10.1037/0893-3200.17.3.419

Jurkovic, G. J., Thirkeild, A., & Morrell, R. (2001). Parentification of adult children of divorce: A multidimensional analysis. *Journal of Youth and Adolescence, 30,* 245–258. doi: 10.4135/9781452220604.n5

Kapadia, K. M. (1958). *Marriage and family in India.* Calcutta, India: Oxford University Press.

Kapur, P. (1970). *Marriage and the working woman in India.* Delhi, India: Vikas Publications.

Karner, T. X. (1998). Professional caring: Homeworkers as fictive kin. *Journal of Aging Studies, 12,* 69–82. doi: 10.1177/0265407510361615

Kaye, L. W. (1986). Worker views of the intensity of affective expression during the delivery of home care services for the elderly. *Home Health Care Services Quarterly, 7,* 41–54. doi: 10.1300/J027v07n02_05

Keller, R. T., Greenberg, N., Bobo, W. V., Roberts, P., Jones, N., & Orman, D. T. (2005). Soldier peer mentoring care and support: Bringing psychological awareness to the front. *Military Medicine, 170,* 355–361. Abstract retrieved from: http://www.ncbi.nlm.nih.gov/pubmed/15974199

Kelley, M. L. (2006). Single military parents in the new millennium. In C. A. Castro, A. B. Adler, & T. W. Britt (Eds.), *Military life: The psychology of serving in peace and combat (Volume 3: The military family)* (pp. 93–114). Westport, CT: Praeger Security International.

Kelley, M. L., Doane, A. N., & Pearson, M. R. (2011). Single military mothers in the new millennium: Stresses, supports, and effects of deployment. In S. MacDermind Wadsworth & D. Riggs (Eds.), *Risk and resilience in U.S. military families* (pp. 343–364). New York, NY: Springer.

Kelley, M. L., Herzog-Simmer, P. A., & Harris, M. A. (1994). Effects of military-induced separation on the parenting stress and family functioning of deploying mothers. *Military Psychology, 6,* 125–138. doi: 10.1207/s15327876mp0602_4

Kelly, M. (2009). Women's involuntary childlessness: A radical rejection to motherhood. *Women's Studies Quarterly, 37,* 157–170. doi: 10.1353/wsq.0.0164

Kemper, R. V. (1982). The compadrazgo in urban Mexico. *Anthropological Quarterly, 55,* 17–30. doi: 10.2307/3317372

Kendall, S. (2007). Introduction: Family talk. In D. Tannen, S. Kendall, & C. Gordon (Eds.) *Family talk: Discourse and identity in four American families* (pp. 3–23). New York, NY: Oxford University Press.

Kendall-Tackett, K. A. (2001). *The hidden feelings of motherhood: Coping with mothering, stress, depression and burnout.* Oakland, CA: New Harbinger.

Keown-Bomar, J. (2004). *Kinship networks among Hmong-American refugees.* New York, NY: LFB Scholarly Publishing.

Kertzer, D. I. (1991). Household history and sociological theory. *Annual Review of Sociology, 17,* 155–179. doi: 10.1146/annurev.soc.17.1.155

Key dates in U.S. policy and law on gays in the military. (n.d.). Retrieved from http://www.usni.org/news-and-features/dont-ask-dont-tell/timeline

Kim, O. M., Reichwald, R., & Lee, R. (2012). Cultural socialization in families with adopted Korean adolescents: A mixed-method, multi-informant study. *Journal of Adolescent Research, 27*, 1–27. doi: 10.1177/0743558411432636

Kingston, A. (2004). *The meaning of wife.* New York, NY: Farrar, Straus, and Giroux.

Kirschner, B. F., & Walum, L. R. (1978). Two-location families. *Journal of Family and Economic Issues, 1*, 513–525. doi: 10.1007/BF01083436

Kiser, L. J., Baumgardner, B., & Dorado, J. (2010). Who are we, but for the stories we tell: Family stories and healing. *Psychological Trauma: Theory, Research, Practice, and Policy, 2*, 243–249. doi: 10.1037/a0019893

Kluger, M. P., & Aprea, D. M. (1999). Grandparents raising grandchildren: A description of the families and a special pilot program. *Journal of Gerontological Social Work, 32*, 5–17. doi: 10.1300/J083v32n01_02

Kluwer, E. (2010). From partnership to parenthood: A review of marital change across the transition to parenthood. *Journal of Family Theory, 2*, 105–125. doi: 10.1111/j.1756-2589.2010.00045.x

Knobloch, L. K., Ebata, A. T., McGlaughlin, P. C., & Ogolsky, B. (2013). Depressive symptoms, relational turbulence, and the reintegration difficulty of military couples following wartime deployment. *Health Communication, 28*, 754–766. doi: 10.1080/10410236.2013.800440

Knobloch, L. K., Ebata, A. T., McGlaughlin, P. C., & Theiss, J. A. (2013). Generalized anxiety and relational uncertainty as predictors of topic avoidance during reintegration following military deployment. *Communication Monographs, 80*, 452–477. doi: 10.1080/03637751.2013.828159

Knobloch, L. K., Pusateri, K. B., Ebata, A. T., & McGlaughlin, P. C. (in press). Communicative experiences of military youth during a parent's return home from deployment. *Journal of Family Communication.*

Knobloch, L. K., Pusateri, K. B., Ebata, A. T., & McGlaughlin, P. C. (2012). Experiences of military youth during a family member's deployment: Changes, challenges, and opportunities. *Youth & Society.* Advance online publication. doi: 10.1177/0044118X12462040

Knobloch, L. K., & Theiss, J. A. (2011). Depressive symptoms and mechanisms of relational turbulence as predictors of relationship satisfaction among returning service members. *Journal of Family Psychology, 25*, 470–478. doi: 10.1037/a0024063

Knobloch, L. K., & Theiss, J. A. (2012). Experiences of U.S. military couples during the post-deployment transition: Applying the relational turbulence model. *Journal of Social and Personal Relationships, 29*, 423–450. doi: 10.1177/0265407511431186

Knobloch, L. K., Theiss, J. A., & Wehrman, E. C. (in press). Communication of military couples during deployment: Topic avoidance and relational uncertainty. In E. Sahlstein Parcell & L. M. Webb (Eds.), *A communication perspective on the military: Messages, strategies, meanings.* New York, NY: Peter Lang.

Knobloch, L. K., & Wilson, S. R. (in press). Communication in military families across the deployment cycle. In L. H. Turner & R. West (Eds.), *The Sage handbook of family communication.* Thousand Oaks, CA: Sage.

Koenig Kellas, J. (2005). Family ties: Communicating identity through jointly told stories. *Communication Monographs, 72,* 365–389. doi: 10.1080/03637750500322453

Koenig Kellas, J., Baxter, L. A., Braithwaite, D. O., LeClair-Underberg, C., Lamb-Normand, E., Routsong, T., & Thatcher, M. (2014). Telling the story of stepfamily beginnings: The relationship between young-adult stepchildren's stepfamily origin stories and their satisfaction with the stepfamily. *Journal of Family Communication, 14,* 149–166. doi: 10.1080/15267431.2013.864294

Koenig Kellas, J., LeClair-Underberg, C., & Normand, E. L. (2008). Stepfamily address terms: "Sometimes they mean something and sometimes they don't." *Journal of Family Communication, 8,* 238–263. doi: 10.1080/15267430802397153

Koenig Kellas, J., & Manusov, V. (2003). What's in a story? *Journal of Social and Personal Relationships, 20,* 285–307. doi: 10.1177/0265407503020003002

Koenig Kellas, J., & Trees, A.R. (2006). Finding meaning in difficult family experiences: Sense making and interaction processes during joint family storytelling. *Journal of Family Communication, 6,* 49–76. doi: 10.1207/s15327698jfc0601_4

Koenig Kellas, J., & Suter, E. A. (in press). Accounting for lesbian-headed families: Lesbian mothers' responses to discursive challenges. *Communication Monographs, 14,* 149-166. doi: 10.1080/15267431.2013.864294

Koerner, A. F., & Fitzpatrick, M. A. (2013). Communication in intact families. In A. Vangelisti (Ed.), The *Routledge handbook of family communication* (2nd ed., pp. 129–144). New York, NY: Routledge.

Kokanovic, R., Dowerick, C., Butler, E., Herrman, H., & Gunn, J. (2008). Lay account of depression amongst Anglo-Australian residents and East African refugees. *Social Science & Medicine, 66,* 454–466. doi: 10.1016/j.socscimed.2007.08.019

Kotchick, B. A., Dorsey, S., Miller, K. S., & Forehand, R. (1999). Adolescent sexual risk-taking behavior in single-parent ethnic minority families. *Journal of Family Psychology, 13,* 93–102. doi: 10.1037//0893-3200.13.1.93

Kranstuber, H., & Koenig Kellas, J. (2011). "Instead of growing under her heart, I grew in it": The relationship between adoption entrance narratives and adoptees' self-concept. *Communication Quarterly, 59,* 179–199. doi: 10.1080/01463373.2011.563440

Krusiewicz, E. S., & Wood, J. T. (2001). "He was our child from the moment we walked in that room": Entrance stories of adoptive parents. *Journal of Social and Personal Relationships, 18,* 785–803. doi: 10.1177/0265407501186003

Kumar, P., & Dhyani, J. (1996). Marital adjustment: A study of some related factors. *Indian Journal of Clinical Psychology, 2,* 112–116. Retrieved from http://psycnet.apa.org/index.cfm?fa=search.displayRecord&id=0F669A09-DCD6-F4A8-A04C-A92F383C-863D&resultID=1&page=1&dbTab=all&search=true

Kuntsche, E. N., & Silbereisen, R. K. (2004). Parental closeness and adolescent substance use in single and two-parent families in Switzerland. *Swiss Journal Psychology, 63,* 85–92. doi: 10.1024/1421-0185.63.2.85

Kurdek, L. A. (2004). Are gay and lesbian cohabiting couples really different from heterosexual married couples? *Journal of Marriage and Family, 66,* 880–900. doi: 10.1111/j.0022-2445.2004.00060.x

Kurdek, L. A. (2005). What do we know about gay and lesbian couples? *Current Directions in Psychological Science, 21,* 251–254. doi: 10.1111/j.0963-7214.2005.00375.x

Landry-Meyer, L., & Newman, B. M. (2004). An exploration of the grandparent caregiver role. *Journal of Family Issues, 25,* 1005–1025. doi: 10.1177/0192513x04265955

Langellier, K. M. (1989). Personal narratives: Perspectives on theory and research. *Text and Performance Quarterly, 9,* 243–279. doi: 10.1080/10462938909365938

Langellier, K. M. (1999). Personal narrative, performance, performativity: Two or three things I know for sure. *Text and Performance Quarterly, 19,* 125–144. doi: 10.1080/10462939909366255

Langellier, K. M., & Peterson, E. E. (2004). *Storytelling in everyday life.* Philadelphia, PA: Temple University Press.

Langellier, K. M., & Peterson, E. E. (2006a). Family storytelling as communication practice. In L. H. Turner & R. West (Eds.), *The family communication sourcebook* (pp. 109–128). Thousand Oaks, CA: Sage.

Langellier, K. M., & Peterson, E. E. (2006b). Narrative performance theory: Telling stories, doing family. In D. O. Braithwaite & L. A. Baxter (Eds.), *Engaging theories in family communication: Multiple perspectives* (pp. 99–114). Thousand Oaks, CA: Sage.

Langosch, D. (2012). Grandparents parenting again: Challenges, strengths, and implications for practice. *Psychoanalytic Inquiry: A Topical Journal for Mental Health Professionals, 32,* 163–170. doi: 10.1080/07351690.2012.655637

Lannutti, P. J. (2005). For better or worse: Exploring the meanings of same-sex marriage within the lesbian, gay, bisexual and transgendered community. *Journal of Social and Personal Relationships, 22,* 5–18. doi: 10.1177/0265407505049319

Lannutti, P. J. (2007a). The influence of same-sex marriage on the understanding of same-sex relationships. *Journal of Homosexuality, 53,* 135–151. doi: 10.1300/J082v53n03_08

Lannutti, P. J. (2007b). "This is not a lesbian wedding": Examining same-sex marriage and bisexual-lesbian couples. *Journal of Bisexuality, 3–4,* 239–260. doi: 10.1080/15299710802171316

Lannutti, P. J. (2008). Attractions and obstacles while considering legally recognized same-sex marriage. *Journal of GLBT Family Studies, 4,* 245–264. doi: 10.1080/1550428080209691

Lannutti, P. J. (2011a). Examining communication about marriage amendments: Same-sex couples and their extended social networks. *Journal of Social Issues, 67,* 264–281. doi: 10.1111/j.1540-4560.2011.01697.x

Lannutti, P. J. (2011b). Security, recognition, and misgivings: Exploring older same-sex couples' experiences of legally recognized same-sex marriage. *Journal of Social and Personal Relationships, 28,* 64–82. doi: 10.1177/0265407510386136

Lannutti, P. J. (2012, July). *Why not? Examining the experiences of US same-sex couples who choose not to marry.* Paper presented at the biannual convention of the International Association for Relationship Research, Chicago, IL.

Lannutti, P. J. (2013). Same-sex marriage and privacy management: Examining couples' communication with family members. *Journal of Family Communication, 13,* 60–75. doi: 10.1080/15267431.2012.742088

Lansford, J. E., Ceballo, R., Abbey, A., & Stewart, A. J. (2001). Does family structure matter? A comparison of adoptive, two-parent biological, single-mother, stepfather, and

stepmother households. *Journal of Marriage and Family, 63*, 840–851. doi: 10.1111/
j.1741-3737.2001.00840.x

Lanza, S., Rhoades, B., Nix, R., & Greenberg, M. (2010). Modeling the interplay of multilevel
risk factors for future academic and behavior problems: A person-centered approach.
*Development and Psychopathology, 22*, 313–335. doi: 10.1017/S0954579410000088

LaSala, M. C. (2000). Lesbians, gay men, and their parents: Family therapy for the coming-out
crisis. *Family Process, 39*, 67–81. doi: 10.1111/j.1545-5300.2000.39108

Leach, M. A., & Braithwaite, D. O. (1996). A binding tie: Supportive communication
of family kinkeepers. *Journal of Applied Communication Research, 24*, 200–216. doi:
10.1080/00909889609365451

Lee, E., & Mock. M. R. (2005). Chinese families. In M. McGoldrick, J. Giordano, &
N. Garcia-Preto (Eds.), *Ethnicity and family therapy* (3rd ed., pp. 302–318). New York,
NY: The Guilford Press.

Lee, G. (1982). *Family structure and interaction: A comparative analysis.* Minneapolis, MN:
University of Minnesota Press.

Lee, J. H., Nam, S. K., Kim, A.-R., Kim, B., Lee, M. Y., & Lee, S. M. (2013). Resilience:
A meta-analytic approach. *Journal of Counseling & Development, 91*, 269–279.
doi: 10.1002/j.1556-6676.2013.00095.x

Lee, R. M., & The Minnesota International Adoption Project. (2010). Parental perceived
discrimination as a postadoption risk factor for internationally adopted children and
adolescents. *Cultural Diversity and Ethnic Minority Psychology, 16*, 493–500. doi: 10.1037/
a0020651

Lehmiller, J. J., & Agnew, C. R. (2006). Marginalized relationships: The impact of social disapproval on romantic relationship commitment. *Personality and Social Psychology Bulletin, 32*,
40–51. doi: 10.1177/0146167205278710

Le Mare, L., & Audet, K. (2011). Communicative openness in adoption, knowledge of culture
of origin, and adoption identity in adolescents adopted from Romania. *Adoption Quarterly,
14*, 199–217. doi: 10.1080/10926755.2011.608031

LeMastro, V. (2001). Childless by choice? Attributions and attitudes concerning family size.
*Social Behavior and Personality, 29*, 231–244. doi: 10.2224/sbp.2001.29.3.231

Le Poire, B. (2006). Commentary on Part C. In K. Floyd & M. A. Morman (Eds.), *Widening
the family circle: New research in family communication* (pp. 189–192). Thousand Oaks, CA:
Sage.

Letherby, G. (2002). Childless and bereft?: Stereotypes and realities in relation to "voluntary"
and "involuntary" childlessness and womanhood. *Sociological Inquiry, 72*, 7–20. doi: 10.1111/
1475-682X.00003

Letiecq, B. L., Bailey, S. J., & Dahlen, P. (2008). Ambivalence and coping among custodial
grandparents. In B. Hayslip, Jr. & P. Kaminski (Eds.), *Parenting the custodial grandchild:
Implications for clinical practice* (pp. 3–16). New York, NY: Springer.

Lever, K., & Wilson, J. J. (2005). Encore parenting: When grandparents fill the role of primary
caregiver. *The Family Journal: Counseling and Therapy for Couples and Families, 13*, 167–171.
doi: 10.1177/1066480704273093

Levine, K. A. (2009). Against all odds: Resilience in single mothers of children with disabilities. *Social Work in Health Care, 48*, 402–419. doi: 10.1080/00981380802605781

Lewin, E. (2009). *Gay fatherhood: Narratives of family and citizenship in America.* Chicago, IL: University of Chicago Press.

Lewin, K. (1951). *Field theory in social science: Selected theoretical papers* (D. Cartwright, Ed.). New York, NY: Harper & Row.

Li, S. Y., Roslan, S., Abdullah, M. C., & Abdullah, H. (2014). Parental readiness, parental care, and adolescent school performance among commuter families in Malaysia: A mediation model. *Journal of Economics, Business, and Management, 2*, 297–301. doi: 10.7763/JOEBM.2014.V2.142

Lie, B., Sveass, N., & Eilertsen, D. E. (2004). Family, activity, and stress reactions in exile. *Community, Work & Family, 7*, 327–350. doi: 10.1080/1366880042000295745

Lieberman, A. F., & Van Horn, P. (2013). Infants and young children in military families: A conceptual model for intervention. *Clinical Child Family Psychology Review, 16*, 282–293. doi: 10.1007/s10567-013-0140-4

Lincoln, A., Swift, E., & Shorteno-Fraser, M. (2008). Psychological adjustment and treatment of children and families with parents deployed in military combat. *Journal of Clinical Psychology, 64*, 984–992. doi: 10.1002/jclp.20520

Lindley, A. (2011). Between a protracted and a crisis situation: Policy responses to Somali refugees in Kenya. *Refugee Survey Quarterly, 30*, 14–49. doi: 10.1093/rsq/hdr013

Livingston, G., & Cohn, D. (2012, Nov 29). *U.S. birth rate falls to a record low; Decline is greatest among immigrants* (Pew Research Social & Demographic Trends). Retrieved from http://www.pewsocialtrends.org/2o12/11/29/u-s-birth-rate-fall

Lofquist, D., Lugaila, T., O'Connell, M., & Feliz, S. (2012, April). *Households and families: 2010* (2010 Census Briefs C2010BR-14). Retrieved from http://www.census.gov/prod/cen2010/briefs/c2010br-14.pdf

Lucas, K., & Buzzanell, P. M. (2012). Memorable messages of hard times: Constructing short- and long-term resiliencies through family communication. *Journal of Family Communication, 12*, 189–208. doi: 10.1080/15267431.2012.687196

Luther, S. S., Cicchetti, D., & Becker, B. (2000). The construct of resilience: A critical evaluation and guidelines for future work. *Child Development, 71*, 543–562. doi: 10.1111/1467-8624.00164

Lyons, R. F., Mickelson, K., Sullivan, J. L., & Coyne, J. C. (1998). Coping as a communal process. *Journal of Social and Personal Relationships, 15*, 579–607. doi: 10.1177/0265407598155001

MacCullum, F., Lycett, E., Murray, C., Jadva, V., & Golombok, S. (2003). Surrogacy: The experience of commissioning couples. *Human Reproduction, 18*, 1334–1342. doi: 10.1093/humrep/deg253

MacDermid Wadsworth, S. M., & Riggs, D. (Eds.). (2011). *Risk and resilience in U.S. military families.* New York, NY: Springer.

MacIntosh, H., Reissing, E. D., & Andruff, H. (2010). Same-sex marriage in Canada: The impact of legal marriage on the first cohort of gay and lesbian Canadians to wed. *Canadian Journal of Human Sexuality, 19*, 79–90. Retrieved from http://www.utpjournals.com/Canadian-Journal-of-Human-Sexuality

Mac Rae, H. (1992). Fictive kin as a component of the social networks of older people. *Research on Aging, 14,* 226–247. doi: 10.1177/0164027592142004

Madison, D. S., & Hamera, J. (2007). Performance studies at the intersections. In D. S. Madison and J. Hamera (Eds.), *The SAGE handbook of performance studies* (pp. xi–xxv). Thousand Oaks, CA: Sage.

Magnuson, S., & Norem, K. (1999). Challenges for higher education couples in commuter marriages: Insights for couples and counselors who work with them. *The Family Journal, 7,* 125–134. doi: 10.1177/1066480799072005

Maguire, K. C. (2007). Bridging the great divide: An examination of the relationship maintenance of couples separated during war. *Ohio Communication Journal, 45,* 131–158. Retrieved from http://web.ebscohost.com

Maguire, K. C. (2012). *Stress and coping in families.* Malden, MA: Polity Press.

Maguire, K. C. (in press). Military family communication: A review and synthesis of the research. In E. Sahlstein Parcell & L. Webb (Eds.), *A communicative perspective on the military: Messages, strategies, meanings.* New York, NY: Peter Lang.

Maguire, K. C., Heinemann, D., & Sahlstein, E. (2013). To be connected, yet not at all: Relational presence, absence, and maintenance in the context of a wartime deployment. *Western Journal of Communication, 77,* 249–271. doi: 10.1080/10570314.2012.75779

Maguire, K. C., & Sahlstein, E. (2012). In the line of fire: Family management of acute stress during wartime deployment. In F. C. Dickson & L. Webb (Eds.), *Communication for families in crisis: Theories, methods, strategies* (pp. 103–127). New York, NY: Peter Lang.

Maisel, N. C., & Fingerhut, A. W. (2011). California's ban on same-sex marriage: The campaign and its effects on gay, lesbian, and bisexual individuals. *Journal of Social Issues, 67,* 242–263. doi: 10.1177/0265407510376253

Man, G. C. (2011). Working and caring: Examining the transnational familial practices of work and family of recent Chinese immigrant women in Canada. *The International Journal of Social Interdisciplinary Sciences, 6,* 199–212. Retrieved from http://iji.cgpublisher.com/product/pub.88/prod.1414

Martinez, G. M., Daniels, K., & Chandra, A. (2012, April 12). *Fertility of men and women aged 15–44 years in the United States: National survey of family growth, 2006–2010* (National Health Statistics Reports No. 51). Retrieved from http://www.cdc.gov/nchs/data/nhsr/nhsr051.pdf

Marx, J., & Solomon, J. C. (2000). Physical health of custodial grandparents. In C. B. Cox (Ed.), *To grandmother's house we go and stay: Perspectives on custodial grandparents* (pp. 37–55). New York, NY: Springer.

Mathews, T. J., & Hamilton, B. E. (2009, August). *Delayed childbearing: More women are having their first child later in life* (NCHS Data Brief No. 21). Retrieved from http://www.cdc.gov/nchs/data/databriefs/db21.htm

McAdams, D. P. (1997). *The stories we live by.* New York, NY: Guilford Press.

McBride, M. C., & Bergen, K. M. (in press). Voices of women in commuter marriages: A site of discursive struggle. *Journal of Social and Personal Relationships.*

McCarthy, B., Hagan, A., & Martin, M. J. (2002). In and out of harm's way: Violent victimization and the social capital of fictive street families. *Criminology, 40*, 831–865. doi: 10.1111/j.1745-9125.2002.tb00975.x

McCubbin, H. I., & Patterson, J. M. (1982). Family adaptation to crisis. In H. I. McCubbin, A. E. Cauble, & J. M. Patterson (Eds.), *Family stress, coping, and social support* (pp. 26–47). Springfield, IL: Charles C. Thomas.

McCubbin, M., & McCubbin, H. I. (1996). Resiliency in families: A conceptual model of family adjustment and adaptation in response to stress and crisis. In H. I. McCubbin, A. Thompson, & M. McCubbin (Eds.), *Family assessment: Resiliency, coping and adaptation-inventories for research and practice* (pp. 1–64). Madison, WI: University of Wisconsin Press.

McGinnis, H., Smith, S. L., Ryan, S. D., & Howard, J. A. (2009, November). *Beyond culture camp: Promoting healthy identity formation in adoption.* Retrieved from Evan B. Donaldson website: http://www.adoptioninstitute.org/research/2009_11_culture_camp.php

McGowen, M. R., & Ladd, L. (2006). On-line assessment of grandmother experience in raising grandchildren. *Educational Gerontology, 32*, 669–684. doi: 10.1080/03601270500494048

McGregor, J. (2008). Children and African values: Zimbabwean professionals in Britain reconfiguring family life. *Environment and Planning Annual, 40*, 596–614. doi: 10.1068/a38334

McKerrow, R. E. (1989). Critical rhetoric: Theory and praxis. *Communication Monographs, 56*, 91–111. doi: 10.1080/03637758909390253

McLanahan, S., & Booth, K. (1989). Mother-only families: Problems, prospects, and politics. *Journal of Marriage and Family, 51*, 557–580. doi: 10.2307/352157

McQuillan, J., Greil, A. L., Shreffler, K. M., Wonch-Hill, P. A., Gentzler, K. C., & Hathcoat, J. D. (2012). Does the reason matter? Variations in childlessness concerns among US women. *Journal of Marriage and Family, 74*, 1166–1181. doi: 10.1111/j.1741-3737.2012.01015.x

Medved, C. E. (2004). The everyday accomplishment of work and family: Exploring practical actions in daily routines. *Communication Studies, 55*, 128–145. doi: 10.1080/10510970409388609

Meisenbach, R. J. (2010). Stigma management communication: A theory and agenda for applied research on how individuals manage moments of stigmatized identity. *Journal of Applied Communication Research, 38*, 268–92. doi: 10.1080/00909882.2010.490841

Merica, D. (2012, February 15). Report highlights employment burdens on military spouses. *CNN Politics.* Retrieved from http://www.cnn.com/2012/02/15/politics/military-jobs

Merolla, A. J. (2010a). Relational maintenance and noncopresence reconsidered: Conceptualizing geographic separation in close relationships. *Communication Theory, 20*, 169–193. doi: 10.1111/j.1468-2885.2010.01359.x

Merolla, A. J. (2010b). Relational maintenance during military deployment: Perspectives of wives of deployed U.S. soldiers. *Journal of Applied Communication Research, 38*, 4–26. doi: 10.1080/00909880903483557

Mesthenous, E., & Ioannidi, E. (2002). Obstacles to refugee integration in the European Union member states. *Journal of Refugee Studies, 15*, 304–320. doi: 10.1093/jrs/15.3.304

Miall, C. E. (1985). The stigma of involuntary childlessness. *Social Problems, 33*, 268–282. doi: 10.2307/800719

Miller-Cribbs, J. E., & Farber, N. B. (2008). Kin networks and poverty among African Americans: Past and present. *Social Work, 53*, 43–51. doi: 10.2202/1944-2858.1053

Minkler, M., Fuller-Thomson, E., Miller, D., & Driver, D. (2000). Grandparent caregiving and depression. In B. Hayslip Jr. & R. Goldberg-Glen (Eds.), *Grandparents raising grandchildren: Theoretical, empirical, and clinical perspectives* (pp. 207–219). New York, NY: Springer.

Mintz, S. W., & Wolf, E. R. (1950). An analysis of ritual co-parenthood (compadrazgo). *Southwestern Journal of Anthropology, 6*, 341–368. Retrieved from http://www.jstor.org/stable/3628562

Minuchin, S. (1974). *Families and family therapy.* Cambridge, MA: Harvard University Press.

Moriizumi, S. (2011). Exploring identity negotiations: An analysis of intercultural Japanese-U.S. American families living in the United States. *Journal of Family Communication, 11*, 85–104. doi: 10.1080/15267431.2011.554359

Morin, R. (2011, February 10). *The public renders a split verdict on changes in family structure* (Pew Research Social & Demographic Trends Report). Retrieved from http://www.pew-socialtrends.org/2011/02/16/the-public-renders-a-split-verdict-on-changes-in-family-structure/

Mother refuses deployment. (2009, November 17). *New York Times.* Retrieved from http://www.nytimes.com

Mott, T. (2009). *African refugee resettlement in the United States.* El Paso, Texas: LFB Scholarly Publishing.

Mueller, K. A., & Yoder, J. D. (1997). Gendered norms for family size, employment, and occupation: Are there personal costs for violating them? *Sex Roles, 36*, 207–220. doi: 10.1007/BF02766268

Mukherjee, P. (1978). *Hindu women.* New Delhi, India: Orient Longman.

Mullatti, L. (1995). Families in India: Beliefs and realities. *Journal of Comparative Family Studies, 26*, 11–25. Retrieved from http://www.jstor.org/stable/41602364

Muraco, A. (2006). Intentional families: Fictive kin ties between cross-gender, different sexual orientation friends. *Journal of Marriage and Family, 68*, 1313–1325. doi: 10.1111/j.1741-3737.2006.00330.x

Murry, V. M., & Brody, G. H. (2002). Racial socialization processes in single-mother families: Linking maternal racial identity, parenting, and racial socialization in rural, single-mother families with child self-worth and self-regulation. In H. P. McAdoo (Ed.), *Black children: Social, educational, and parental environments* (2nd ed., pp. 97–115). Thousand Oaks, CA: Sage.

Murry, V. M., Bynum, M. S., Brody, G. H., Willert, A., & Stephens, D. (2001). African American single mothers and children in context: A review of studies on risk and resilience. *Clinical Child and Family Psychology Review, 4*, 133–155. Retrieved from http://www.ncbi.nlm.nih.gov/pubmed/11771793

Musil, C. M., Schrader, S., & Mutikani, J. (2000). Social support, stress, and special coping tasks of grandmother caregivers. In C. B. Cox (Ed.), *To grandmother's house we go and stay: Perspectives on custodial grandparents* (pp. 56–70). New York, NY: Springer.

Musil, C. M., & Standing, T. (2005). Grandmothers' diaries: A glimpse at daily lives. *International Journal on Aging and Human Development, 60*, 317–329. doi:10.2190/LF1U-JA0X-W7F9-341K

Musil, C. M., Warner, C. B., McNamera, M., Rokoff, S., & Turek, D. (2008). Parenting concerns of grandparents raising grandchildren: An insider's picture. In B. Hayslip Jr. & P. Kaminski (Eds.), *Parenting the custodial grandchild: Implications for clinical practice* (pp. 101–114). New York, NY: Springer.

Naples, N. A. (2001). A member of the funeral: An introspective ethnography. In M. Bernstein & R. Reimann (Eds.), *Queer families, queer politics: Challenging culture and the state* (pp. 21–43). New York, NY: Columbia University Press.

National Center for Family and Marriage Research. (2012). Krista Payne, NCFMR social science data analyst, finds slight increase among number of women in commuter marriages. *Bowling Green State University NCFMR in the News 2012*. Retrieved from http://ncfmr. bgsu.edu/page86070.html

National Stepfamily Resource Center. (2013). *Stepfamily fact sheet*. Retrieved from http://www. stepfamilies.info/stepfamily-fact-sheet.php

Nelson, M. K. (2006). Single mothers "do" family. *Journal of Marriage and Family, 68*, 781–795. doi: 10.1111/j.1741-3737.2006.00292.x

Nelson, M. K. (2013). Fictive kin, families we choose, and voluntary kin: What does the discourse tell us? *Journal of Family Theory & Review, 5*, 259–281. doi: 10.1111/jftr.12019

Nelson, M. K. (2014). "Whither fictive kin? Or, what's in a name." *Journal of Family Issues, 35*, 201–222. doi: 10.1177/0192513X12470621

Nelson, M. K., & Garey, A. I. (Eds.). (2009). *Who's watching? Daily practices of surveillance among contemporary families*. Nashville, TN: Vanderbilt University Press.

Netting, N. S. (2010). Marital ideoscapes in 21st century India: Creative combinations of love and responsibility. *Journal of Family Issues, 31*, 709–726. doi: 10.1177/0192513X09357555

Newman, J. L., Roberts, L. R., & Syre, C. R. (1993). Concepts of family among children and adolescents: Effect of cognitive level, gender, and family structure. *Developmental Psychology, 29*, 951–962. doi: 10.1037/0012-1649.29.6.951

NFL Communications. (2013, November 7). *NFL honors Veterans Day, military with salute to service*. Retrieved from http://www.nfl.com

Nichols, L. O., Martindale-Adams, J., Graney, M. J., Zuber, J., & Burns, R. (2013). Easing reintegration: Telephone support groups for spouses of returning Iraq and Afghanistan service members. *Health Communication, 28*, 767–777. doi: 10.1080/10410236.2013.800439

Nixon, E., Greene, S., & Hogan, D. (2006). Concepts of family among children and young people in Ireland. *Irish Journal of Psychology, 27*, 79–87. doi: 10.1080/03033910.2006.10446330

Norwood, A. E., Fullerton, C. S., & Hagen, K. P. (1996). Those left behind: Military families. In R. J. Ursano & A. E. Norwood (Eds.), *Emotional aftermath of the Persian Gulf War: Veterans, families, communities, and nations* (pp. 163–197). Washington, DC: American Psychiatric Press, Inc.

Norwood, K. M., & Baxter, L. A. (2011). "Dear birth mother": Addressivity and meaning-making in online adoption-seeking letters. *Journal of Family Communication, 11*, 198–217. doi: 10.1080/15267431.2011.554751

Nussbaum, M. (2000). *Women and human development: A capabilities approach*. Cambridge, UK: Cambridge University Press.

O'Connor, T., Dunn, J., Jenkins, J., Pickering, K., & Rasbash, J. (2001). Family settings and children's adjustment: Differential adjustment within and across families. *British Journal of Psychiatry, 179,* 110–115. doi: 10.1192/bjp.179.2.110

Ong, A. (2003). *Buddha is hiding: Refugees, citizenship and the new America.* Berkeley, CA: University of California Press.

Orthner, D. K., Jones-Sanpei, H., & Williamson, S. (2004). The resilience and strengths of low income families. *Family Relations, 53,* 159–167. doi: 10.1111/j.0022-2445.2004.00006.x

Oswald, R. F. (2002). Resilience within the family networks of lesbians and gay men: Intentionality and redefinition. *Journal of Marriage and Family, 64,* 374–383. doi: 10.1111/j.1741-3737.2002.00374.x

Pahl, R. E., & Spencer, L. (2010). Family, friends and personal communities: Changing models-in-the-mind. *Journal of Family Theory & Review, 2,* 197–210. doi: 10.1111/j.1756-2589.2010.00053.x

Papernow, P. L. (1993). *Becoming a stepfamily: Patterns of development in remarried families.* San Francisco, CA: Jossey-Bass.

Park, K. (2002). Stigma management among the voluntarily childless. *Sociological Perspectives, 45,* 21–45. doi: 10.1525/sop.2002.45.1.21

Park, K. (2005). Choosing childlessness: Weber's typology of action and motives of the voluntarily childless. *Sociological Inquiry, 75,* 372–402. doi: 10.1111/j.1475-682X.2005.00127.x

Parke, M. (2003, May). *Are married parents really better for children? What research says about the effects of family structure on child well-being* (Center for Law and Social Policy: Policy Brief 3). Retrieved from http://www.clasp.org/resources-and-publications/archive/0128.pdf

Parrenas, R. S. (2001). Mothering from a distance: Emotions, gender, and intergenerational relations in Filipino transnational families. *Feminist Studies, 27,* 361–390. Retrieved from http://www.jstor.org/stable/3178765

Passel, J., Wang, W., & Taylor, P. (2010, June 15). *Marrying out* (Pew Research Social & Demographic Trends Report). Retrieved from http://www.pewsocialtrends.org/files/2010/10/755-marrying-out.pdf

Patterson, D. G., & Schwartz, P. (1994). The social construction of conflict in intimate relationships. In D. D. Cahn (Ed.), *Conflict in personal relationships* (pp. 3–36). Hillsdale, NJ: Erlbaum.

Patterson, J. M. (2002). Understanding family resilience. *Journal of Clinical Psychology, 58,* 233–246. doi: 10.1002/jclp.10019

Paul, P. (2001). Childless by choice. *American Demographics, 23,* 45–50. Retrieved from http://www.researchgate.net/journal/0163-4089_American_demographics

Peplau, L. A., & Fingerhut, A. W. (2007). The close relationships of lesbians and gay men. *Annual Review of Psychology, 58,* 405–424. doi: 10.1146/annurev.psych.58.110405.085701

Personal Narratives Group. (1989). *Interpreting women's lives: Feminist theory and personal narratives.* Bloomington, IN: Indiana University Press.

Pertman, A. (2011). *Adoption nation* (2nd ed.). Boston, MA: The Harvard Common Press.

Peterson, B. D., Newton, C. R., & Feingold, T. (2007). Anxiety and sexual stress in men and women undergoing infertility treatment. *Fertility and Sterility, 88,* 911–914. doi: 10.1016/j.fertnstert.2006.12.023

Peterson, E. E., & Langellier, K. M. (2006). The performance turn in narrative studies. *Narrative Inquiry, 16*, 173–180. doi:10.1075/ni.16.1.22pet

Petronio, S. (2002). *Boundaries of privacy: Dialectics of disclosure.* Albany, NY: SUNY Press.

Piercy, K. W. (2000). When it's more than a job: Close relationships between home health aides and older clients. *Journal of Aging and Health, 12*, 362–387. doi: 10.1177/089826430001200305

Piercy, K. W. (2001). "We couldn't do without them": The value of close relationships between older adults and their nonfamily caregivers. *Generations, 25*, 41–47. Retrieved from http://generations.metapress.com/content/120835/?k=Piercy&mode=allwords&sortorder=asc&v=expanded&Copyright=2001

Pipher, M. (2003). *Middle of everywhere: The world's refugees come to our town.* New York, NY: Harcourt.

Ponzetti, J. J., Jr. (Ed.). (2003). Fictive kin. In J. J. Ponzetti (Ed.), *International encyclopedia of marriage and family* (2nd ed., Vol. 2, pp. 671–673). San Francisco, CA: Thomson.

Porche, M. V., & Purvin, D. M. (2008). "Never in our lifetime": Legal marriage for same-sex couples in long-term relationships. *Family Relations, 57*, 144–159. doi: 10.1111/j.1741-3729.2008.00490.x

Porche, M. V., Purvin, D. M., & Waddell, J. M. (2005). *Tying the knot: The context of social change in Massachusetts.* Wellesley, MA: Wellesley Centers for Women.

Portes, A. (1998). Social capital: Its origins and applications in modern sociology. *Annual Review of Sociology, 24*, 1–24. doi: 10.1146/annurev.soc.24.1.1

Powell, J. A., Wiltcher, B. J., Wedemeyer, N. V., & Claypool, P. L. (1981). The child's developing concept of family. *Home Economics Research Journal, 10*, 137–149. doi: 10.1177/1077727X8101000204

Powell, K. A., & Afifi, T. D. (2005). Uncertainty management and adoptees' ambiguous loss of their birth parents. *Journal of Social and Personal Relationships, 22*, 129–151. doi: 10.1177/0265407505049325

Prangnell, J., & Mate, G. (2011). Kin, fictive kin and strategic movement: Working class heritage of the Upper Burnett. *International Journal of Heritage Studies, 17*, 318–330. doi: 10.1080/13527258.2011.577965

Pryor, C., & Pettinelli, J. D. (2011). A narrative inquiry of international adoption stories. *Journal of Ethnographic & Qualitative Research, 6*, 45–61. Retrieved from http://connection.ebscohost.com/c/articles/73170129/narrative-inquiry-international-adoption-stories

Pryor, J. (Ed.). (2008). *The international handbook of stepfamilies: Policy and practice in legal, research, and clinical environments.* Hoboken, NJ: Wiley.

Puig, M. E. (2002). The adultification of refugee children: Implications for cross-cultural social work practice. *Journal of Human Behavior in the Social Environment, 5*, 85–95. doi: 10.1300/J137v05n03_05

Quiroz, P. A. (2012). Cultural tourism in transnational adoption: "Staged authenticity" and its implications for adopted children. *Journal of Family Issues, 33*, 527–555. doi: 10.1177/0192513X11418179

Ramos, C., Goldberg, N. G., & Badgett, M. V. L. (2009). *The effects of marriage equality in Massachusetts: A survey of the experiences and impact of marriage on same-sex couples.* Los Angeles, CA: The Williams Institute, UCLA.

Randolph, T. H., & Holtzman, M. (2010). The role of heritage camps in identity development among Korean transnational adoptees: A relational dialectics approach. *Adoption Quarterly, 13*, 75–79. doi: 10.1080/10926755.2010.481038

Rao, V. V., & Rao, N. (1975). Arranged marriages: An assessment of the attitudes of college students. *Journal of Comparative Family Studies, 7*, 433–453. Retrieved from http://www.jstor.org/stable/41600976

Rawlins, W. K. (1992). *Friendship matters: Communication, dialectics, and the life course*. New York, NY: Aldine De Gruyter.

Reczek, C., Elliott, S., & Umberson, D. (2009). Commitment without marriage: Union formation among long-term same-sex couples. *Journal of Family Issues, 30*, 738–756. doi: 10.1177/0192513X09331574

Rehberg, J. (2009). Waking up American. In R. L. Ballard (Ed.), *Pieces of me, Who do I want to be?: Voices for and by adopted teens* (p. 132). Warren, NJ: EMK Press.

Reissman, C. K. (2008). *Narrative methods in the human sciences*. Thousand Oaks, CA: Sage.

Resolve. (n.d.). *Infertility overview*. Retrieved from http://www.resolve.org/infertility-overview/what-is-infertility/

Reynolds, B., & Variano, D. (2009). The kinship family portraits project. *Journal of Intergenerational Relationships, 7*, 328–333. doi: 10.1080/15350770902850975

Rhodes, A. (2002). Long-distance relationships in dual-career commuter couples: A review of counseling issues. *The Family Journal: Counseling and Therapy for Couples and Families, 10*, 398–404. doi: 10.1177/106648002236758

Riala, K., Isohanni, I., Jokelainen, J., Jones, P. B., & Isohanni, M. (2003). The relationship between childhood family background and educational performance, with special reference to single-parent families: A longitudinal study. *Social Psychology of Education, 6*, 349–365. Retrieved from http://link.springer.com/article/10.1023%2FA%3A1025608401292#page-1

Richards, L. (1989). The precarious survival and hard-won satisfactions of white single-parent families. *Family Relations, 38*, 396–403. doi :10.2307/585744

Richter, C. (2008, November). *My American grandma: Theorizing fictive kinship and affective visibility in the lives of immigrant elder care workers*. Paper presented at the annual meeting of the National Communication Association, San Diego, CA.

Rigg, A., & Pryor, J. (2007). Children's perceptions of families: What do they really think? *Children & Society, 21*, 17–30. doi: 10.1111/j.1099-0860.2006.00028.x

Riggle, E. D. B., Rostosky, S. S., & Horne, S. G. (2009). Marriage amendments and lesbian, gay, and bisexual individuals in the 2006 election. *Sexuality Research & Social Policy, 6*, 80–89. doi: 10.1525/srsp.2009.6.1.80

Riggle, E. D. B., Rostosky, S. S., & Prather, R. A. (2006). Advance planning by same-sex couples. *Journal of Family Issues, 27*, 758–776. doi: 10.1177/0192513X05285730

Riley, N. E., & Van Vleet, K. E. (2012). *Making families through adoption*. Los Angeles, CA: Sage.

Rispens, S., Jehn, K. A., & Rexwinkel, R. B. (2010, May). *Asymmetry in dual career and commuting couples*. Paper presented to the International Association of Conflict Management, Boston, MA. doi: 10.2139/ssrn.1612891

Rodriguez, A., & Chawla, D. (2010). *Intercultural communication: An ecological approach.* Minneapolis, MN: Kendall Hunt.

Rolfe, A., & Peel, E. (2011). "It's a double-edged thing": The paradox of civil partnership and why some couples are choosing not to have one. *Feminism & Psychology, 21,* 317–335. doi: 10.1177/0959353511408059

Rosenfeld, L. B., & Welsh, S. M. (1985). Differences in self-disclosure in dual-career and single-career marriages. *Communication Monographs, 52,* 253–263. doi: 10.1080/03637758509376109

Ross, A. D. (1961). *The Hindu family in the urban setting.* Bombay, India: Oxford University Press.

Rossetto, K. R. (2013). Relational coping during deployment: Managing communication and connection in relationships. *Personal Relationships, 20,* 568–586. Advance online publication. doi: 10.1111/pere.12000

Rostosky, S. S., Riggle, E. D. B., Horne, S. G., Denton, F. N., & Huellemeier, J. D. (2010). Lesbian, gay, and bisexual individuals' psychological reactions to amendments denying access to civil marriage. *American Journal of Orthopsychiatry, 80,* 302–310. doi: 10.1111/j.1939-0025.2010.01033.x

Rostosky, S. S., Riggle, E. D. B., Horne, S. G., & Miller, A. D. (2009). Marriage amendments and psychological distress in lesbian, gay, and bisexual (LGB) adults. *Journal of Counseling Psychology, 56,* 56–66. doi: 10.1037/a0013609

Rothblum, E. D., Balsam, K. F., & Solomon, S. E. (2011). The longest "legal" U.S. same-sex couples reflect on their relationships. *Journal of Social Issues, 67,* 302–315. doi: 10.1111/j.1540-4560.2011.01699.x

Rotter, J. C., Barnett, D. E., & Fawcett, M. L. (1998). On the road again: Dual-career commuter relationships. *The Family Journal: Counseling and Therapy for Couples and Families, 6,* 46–48. doi: 10.1177/1066480798061009

Rowley, C. T. (2002). The maternal socialization of Black adolescent mothers. *Race, Gender, & Class, 9,* 168. Retrieved from http://www.jstor.org/stable/41675012

Russell, G. M. (2000). *Voted out: The psychological consequences of anti-gay politics.* New York, NY: New York University Press.

Sahlstein, E. (2004). Relating at a distance: Negotiating being together and being apart in long-distance relationships. *Journal of Social and Personal Relationships, 21,* 689–702. doi: 10.1177/0265407504046115

Sahlstein, E. (2006). The trouble with distance. In D. Kirkpatrick, S. Duck, & M. K. Foley (Eds.), *Relating difficulty: The processes of constructing and managing difficult interaction* (pp. 119–140). Mahwah, NJ: Erlbaum.

Sahlstein, E. (2010). Communication and distance: The present and future interpreted through the past. *Journal of Applied Communication Research, 38,* 106–114. doi: 10.1080/00909880903483615

Sahlstein, E., & Maguire, K. C. (2013). Family relationships as more than blood: Military families as dialectics and discourses. In S. Marrow & D. Leoutsakas (Eds.), *More than blood: Today's reality and tomorrow's vision of family* (pp. 174–182). Dubuque, IA: Kendall-Hunt.

Sahlstein, E., Maguire, K. C., & Timmerman, L. (2009). Contradictions and praxis contextualized by wartime deployment: Wives' perspectives revealed through relational dialectics. *Communication Monographs, 76,* 421–442. doi: 10.1080/03637750903300239

Sahlstein Parcell, E. (2013). Trajectories research in family communication: Toward the identification of alternative pathways for inquiry. *Journal of Family Communication, 13,* 167–177. doi: 10.1080/15267431.2013.799027

Sahlstein Parcell, E., & Maguire, K. C. (in press-a). Comfort, cliques, and clashes: Family readiness groups as dilemmatic sites of relating during wartime. *Journal of Social and Personal Relationships.*

Sahlstein Parcell, E., & Maguire, K. C. (in press-b). Turning points and trajectories of military deployment. *Journal of Family Communication.*

Sahlstein Parcell, E., & Webb, L. M. (Eds.). (in press). *A communicative perspective on the military: Messages, strategies, meanings.* New York, NY: Peter Lang.

Sample, E. (2007). State practice and the family unity of Africa refugees. *Forced Migration Review, 2008, 28,* 50–52. Retrieved from http://fmreview.nonuniv.ox.ac.uk/FMRpdfs/FMR28/28.pdf

Sanders, J. M., & Nee, V. (1996). Immigrant self-employment: The family as social capital and the family of human capital. *American Sociological Review, 61,* 231–249. doi: 10.2307/2096333

Sarkisian, N. (2006). "Doing family ambivalence": Nuclear and extended families in single mothers' lives. *Journal of Marriage and Family, 68,* 804–811. doi: 10.1111/j.1741-3737.2006.00295.x

Sarkisian, N., & Gerstel, N. (2004). Kin support among blacks and whites: Race and family organization. *American Sociological Review, 69,* 812–837. doi :10.1177/000312240406900604

Sastri, H. C. (1972). *The social background of the forms of marriage in ancient India (Vol. I).* Calcutta, India: Sanskrit Pustak Bhandar.

Sastri, H. C. (1974). *The social background of the forms of marriage in ancient India (Vol. II).* Calcutta, India: Sanskrit Pustak Bhandar.

Satzewick, V., & Wong, L. (2006). *Transnational identities and practices in Canada.* Vancouver, Canada: UBC Press.

Scharp, K. (2014). *(De)constructing family: Exploring communicative practices in establishing and maintaining estrangement between adult children and their parents.* (Unpublished doctoral dissertation). University of Iowa, Iowa City, IA.

Schecter, E., Tracy, A. J., Page, K. V., & Luong, G. (2008). Shall we marry? Legal marriage as a commitment event in same-sex relationships. *Journal of Homosexuality, 54,* 400–422. doi: 10.1080/00918360801991422

Scherman, R. M. (2006). *Intercountry adoption of Eastern European children in New Zealand: Issues of culture* (Doctoral dissertation). Available from ProQuest Dissertations and Theses database. (UMI No. 3214157)

Schmeeckle, M. (2007). Gender dynamics in stepfamilies: Adult stepchildren's views. *Journal of Marriage and Family, 69,* 174–189. doi: 10.1111/j.1741-3737.2006.00352.x

Schneider, D. M. (1980). *American kinship: A cultural account* (2nd ed.). Chicago, IL: The University of Chicago Press.

Schrodt, P. (2006a). The stepparent relationship index: Development, validation, and associations with stepchildren's perceptions of stepparent communication competence and closeness. *Personal Relationships, 13,* 167–182. doi: 10.1111/j.1475-6811.2006.00111.x

Schrodt, P. (2006b). A typological examination of communication competence and mental health in stepchildren. *Communication Monographs, 73,* 309–333. doi: 10.1080/03637750600873728

Schrodt, P. (2008). Sex differences in stepchildren's reports of stepfamily functioning. *Communication Reports, 21,* 46–58. doi: 10.1080/08934210802019462

Schrodt, P. (2010). Coparental communication with nonresidential parents as a predictor of couples' relational satisfaction and mental health in stepfamilies. *Western Journal of Communication, 74,* 484–503. doi: 10.1080/10570314.2010.512282

Schrodt, P. (2011). Stepparents' and nonresidential parents' relational satisfaction as a function of coparental communication in stepfamilies. *Journal of Social and Personal Relationships, 28,* 983–1004. doi: 10.1177/0265407510397990

Schrodt, P., & Afifi, T. D. (2007). Communication processes that predict young adults' feelings of being caught and their associations with mental health and family satisfaction. *Communication Monographs, 74,* 200–228. doi: 10.1080/03637750701390085

Schrodt, P., Baxter, L. A., McBride, M. C., Braithwaite, D. O., & Fine, M. (2006). The divorce decree, communication, and the structuration of co-parenting relationships in stepfamilies. *Journal of Social and Personal Relationships, 23,* 741–759. doi: 10.1177/0265407506068261

Schrodt, P., & Braithwaite, D. O. (2010). Dark clouds with silver linings: The (dys)functional ambivalence of stepfamily relationships. In W. R. Cupach & B. H. Spitzberg (Eds.), *The dark side of close relationships II* (pp. 243–268). New York, NY: Routledge.

Schrodt, P., & Braithwaite, D. O. (2011). Coparental communication, relational satisfaction, and mental health in stepfamilies. *Personal Relationships, 18,* 352–369. doi: 10.1111/j.1475-6811.2010.01295.x

Schrodt, P., & Ledbetter, A. M. (2007). Communication processes that mediate family communication patterns and mental well-being: A mean and covariance structures analysis of young adults from divorced and non-divorced families. *Human Communication Research, 33,* 330–356. doi: 10.1111/j.1468-2958.2007.00302.x

Schrodt, P., & Ledbetter, A. M. (2012). Parental confirmation as a mitigator of feeling caught and family satisfaction. *Personal Relationships, 19,* 146–161. doi: 10.1111/j.1475-6811.2010.01345.x

Schrodt, P., Miller, A. E., & Braithwaite, D. O. (2011). Ex-spouses' relational satisfaction as a function of coparental communication in stepfamilies. *Communication Studies, 62,* 272–290. doi: 10.1080/10510974.2011.563453

Schrodt, P., Soliz, J., & Braithwaite, D. O. (2008). A social relations model of everyday talk and relational satisfaction in stepfamilies. *Communication Monographs, 75,* 190–217. doi: 10.1080/03637750802256318

Schulman, J. L., Gotta, G., & Green, R. (2012). Will marriage matter? Effects of marriage anticipated by same-sex couples. *Journal of Family Issues, 33,* 158–181. doi: 10.1177/0192513X11406228

Schvaneveldt, P. L., Young, M. H., & Schvaneveldt, J. D. (2001). Dual-resident marriages in Thailand: A comparison of two cultural groups of women. *Journal of Comparative Family Studies, 32*, 347–360. Retrieved from http://www.jstor.org/stable/41603757

Schweitzer, R. D., Brough, M., Vromans, L., & Asic-Kobe, M. (2011). Mental health of newly arrived Burmese refugees in Australia: Contributions of pre-migration and post-migration experiences. *Australian and New Zealand Journal of Psychiatry, 45,* 299–307. doi: 10.3109/00048674.2010.543412

Scott, L. S. (2009). *Two is enough.* Berkeley, CA: Seal Press.

Seccombe, K. (2002). "Beating the odds" versus "changing the odds": Poverty, resilience, and family policy. *Journal of Marriage and Family, 64,* 384–394. doi:10.1111/j.1741-3737.2002.00384.x

Segrin, C., & Flora, J. (2011). *Family communication* (2nd ed.). New York, NY: Routledge.

Seigel, D. H. (2013). Open adoption: Adoptive parents' reactions two decades later. *Social Work, 58,* 43–52. doi: 10.1093/sw/sws053

Shapiro, W. (2010). The old kinship studies confront gay kinship: A critique of Kath Weston. *Anthropological Forum, 20,* 1–18. doi: 10.1080/00664670903524178

Sharma, K. L. (1997). *Social stratification in India: Issues and themes.* New Delhi, India: Sage.

Shastri, S. R. (1969). *Women in the Vedic age.* Bombay, India: Bharati Vidya Bhavan.

Shattuck, C. (1999). *Hinduism.* Upper Saddle River, NJ: Prentice Hall.

Shattuck, R. M., & Kreider, R. M. (2013, May). *Social and economic characteristics of currently unmarried women with a recent birth: 2011* (American Community Survey Reports ACS-21). Retrieved from http://www.census.gov/prod/2013pubs/acs-21.pdf

Shore, R. J., & Hayslip, B., Jr. (1994). Custodial grandparenting: Implications for children's development. In A. Gottfried & A. Gottfried (Eds.), *Redefining family: Implications for children's development* (pp. 171–218). New York, NY: Plenum.

Shorter, E. (1975). *The making of the modern family.* New York, NY: Basic Books.

Sigman, S. (1995). Toward study of the consequentiality (not consequences) of communication. In S. Sigman (Ed.), *The consequentiality of communication* (pp. 1–14). Hillsdale, NJ: Erlbaum.

Simons, L., Chen, Y. F., Simons, R. L., Brody, G., & Cutrona, C. (2006). Parenting practices and child adjustment in different types of households: A study of African American families. *Journal of Family Issues, 27,* 803–825. doi: 10.1177/0192513X05285447

Skinner-Drawz, B. A., Wrobel, G. M., Grotevant, H. D., & Von Korff, L. (2011). The role of adoption communicative openness in information seeking among adoptees from adolescence to emerging adulthood. *Journal of Family Communication, 11,* 181–197. doi: 10.1080/15267431003656587

Smart, C. (2007). Same sex couples and marriage: Negotiating relational landscapes with families and friends. *The Sociological Review, 55,* 671–686. doi: 10.1111/j.1467-954X.2007. 00747.x

Smith, C. J., Beltran, A., Butts, D. M., & Kingson, E. R. (2000). Grandparents raising grandchildren: Emerging program and policy issues for the 21st century. *Journal of Gerontological Social Work, 34,* 81–94. doi: 10.1300/J083v34n01_06

Smith, D. T., Juarez, B. G., & Jacobson, C. K. (2011). White on Black: Can White parents teach Black adoptive children how to understand and cope with racism? *Journal of Black Studies*, *42*, 1195–1230. doi: 10.1177/0021934711404237

Smith, G. C., Palmieri, P. A., Hancock, G. R., & Richardson, R. A. (2008). Custodial grandmothers' psychological distress, dysfunctional parenting, and grandchildren's adjustment. *International Journal of Aging and Human Development*, *67*, 327–357. doi: 10.2190/AG.67.4.c

Smith, R. A. (2007). Language of the lost: An explication of stigma communication. *Communication Theory*, *17*, 462–485. doi: 10.1111/j.1468-2885.2007.00307.x

Smith, R. A., & Hipper, T. J. (2010). Label management: Investigating how confidants encourage the use of communication strategies to avoid stigmatization. *Health Communication*, *25*, 410–422. doi: 10.1080/10410236.2010.483335

Socha, T. J., & Stamp, G. (Eds.). (2009). *Parents and children communicating with society: Managing relationships outside the home*. New York, NY: Routledge.

Solantaus, T., Leinonen, J., & Punamaki, R. (2004). Children's mental health in times of economic recession: Replication and extension of the family economic stress model in Finland. *Developmental Psychology*, *40*, 412–429. Retrieved from http://www.ncbi.nlm.nih.gov/pubmed/15122967

Solomon, S. E., Rothblum, E. D., & Balsam, K. F. (2004). Pioneers in partnership: Lesbian and gay male couples in civil unions compared with those not in civil unions and marred heterosexual siblings. *Journal of Family Psychology*, *18*, 275–286. doi: 10.1037/0893-3200.18.2.275

Spencer, L., & Pahl, R. E. (2006). *Rethinking friendship: Hidden solidarities today*. Princeton, NJ: Princeton University Press.

Sprecher, S., & Chandak, R. (1992). Attitudes about arranged marriages and dating among men and women from India. *Free Inquiry in Creative Sociology*, *20*, 59–69. Retrieved from http://search.proquest.com/docview/61278926?accountid=14663

Stacey, J. (1990). *Brave new families: Stories of domestic upheaval in late twentieth century America*. New York, NY: Basic Books.

Stacey, J. (1996). *In the name of the family: Rethinking family values in the postmodern age*. Boston, MA: Beacon Press.

Stacey, J. (1999). Gay and lesbian families are here; all our families are queer; let's get used to it! In S. Coontz (Ed.), *American families: A multicultural reader* (pp. 327–405). New York, NY: Routledge.

Stacey, J. (2011). *Unhitched: Love, marriage, and family values from West Hollywood to Western China*. New York, NY: New York University Press.

Stack, C. (1974). *All our kin: Strategies for survival in a black community*. New York, NY: Basic Books.

Stafford, L. (2005). *Maintaining long-distance and cross-residential relationships*. Mahwah, NJ: Erlbaum.

Stafford, L., & Merolla, A. J. (2007). Idealization, reunions, and stability in long-distance dating relationships. *Journal of Social and Personal Relationships*, *24*, 37–54. doi: 10.1177/0265407507072578

Stamp, G., & Shue, C. K. (2013). Twenty years of family research published in communication journals: A review of the perspectives, theories, concepts, and contexts. In A. Vangelisti (Ed.), *The Routledge handbook of family communication* (2nd ed., pp. 11–28). New York, NY: Routledge.

Steimal, S. J. (2010). Refugees as people: The portrayal of refugees in American human interest stories. *Journal of Refugee Studies, 23*, 219–237. doi: 10.1093/jrs/feq019

Steuber, K. R. (2013). *Filling the void: Qualitative support gaps in women coping with infertility.* Unpublished manuscript.

Steuber, K. R., & Solomon, D. H. (2008). Relational uncertainty, partner interference, and infertility: A qualitative study of discourse within online forums. *Journal of Social and Personal Relationships, 25*, 831–855. doi: 10.1177/0265407508096698

Steuber, K. R., & Solomon, D. H. (2011a). Factors that predict married partners' disclosures about infertility to social network members. *Journal of Applied Communication Research, 39*, 250–270. doi: 10.1080/00909882.2011.585401

Steuber, K. R, & Solomon, D. H. (2011b). "So, when are you two having a baby?" Managing information with social network members during infertility. In M. Miller-Day (Ed.), *Family communication, connections, and health transitions* (pp. 297–322). New York, NY: Peter Lang.

Steuber, K. R., & Solomon, D. H. (2012). Relational uncertainty, partner interference, and privacy boundary turbulence: Explaining discrepancies in spouses' infertility disclosures. *Journal of Social and Personal Relationships, 29*, 3–27. doi: 10.1177/0265407511406896

Stevenson, T. B. (1997). Migration, family, and household in highland Yemen: The impact of socio-economic and political change and cultural ideals on domestic organization. *Journal of Comparative Family Studies*, 15–53. Retrieved from http://www.jstor.org/stable/41603503

Stewart, S. D. (2007). *Brave new stepfamilies: Diverse paths toward stepfamily living.* Thousand Oaks, CA: Sage.

Stiers, G. A. (1999). *From this day forward: Commitment, marriage, and family in lesbian and gay relationships.* New York, NY: St. Martin's Press.

Stone, E. (1988/2008). *Black sheep and kissing cousins: How our family stories shape us.* New Brunswick, NJ: Transaction Press.

Suárez-Orozco, C., & Suárez-Orozco, M. (2001). *Children of immigrants.* Cambridge, MA: Harvard University Press.

Suizzo, M. A., Robinson, C., & Pahlke, E. (2008). African American mothers' socialization beliefs and goals with young children: Themes of history, education, and collective independence. *Journal of Family Issues, 29*, 287–316. doi: 10.1177/0192513X07308368

Sur, A. K. (1973). *Sex and marriage in India.* Bombay, India: Allied Publishers.

Suter, E. A. (2008). Discursive negotiation of family identity: A study of U.S. families with adopted children from China. *Journal of Family Communication, 8*, 126–147. doi: 10.1080/15267430701857406

Suter, E. A. (2012). Negotiating identity and pragmatism: Parental treatment of international adoptees birth culture names. *Journal of Family Communication, 12*, 209–226. doi: 10.1080/15267431.2012.686940

Suter, E. A., & Ballard, R. L. (2009). "How much did you pay for her?": Decision-making criteria underlying adoptive parents' responses to inappropriate remarks. *Journal of Family Communication, 9,* 107–125. doi: 10.1080/15267430902773253

Suter, E. A., Baxter, L. A., Seurer, L. M., & Thomas, L. J. (2014). Discursive constructions of the meaning of "family" in online narratives of foster adoptive parents. *Communication Monographs, 81,* 59–78. doi: 10.1080/03637751.2014.880791

Suter, E. A., Daas, K. L., & Bergen, K. M. (2008). Negotiating lesbian family identity via symbols and rituals. *Family Issues, 29,* 26–47. doi: 10.1177/0192513X07305752

Suter, E. A., Morr Serewicz, M. C., Hanna, M. D., & Strasser, D. (2013). *Communication privacy management of parents in transracial, international adoptive families: Rule attributes and rule structures.* Manuscript in preparation.

Suter, E. A., Reyes, K. L., & Ballard, R. L. (2011a). Adoptive parents' framing of laypersons' conceptions of family. *Qualitative Research Reports in Communication, 12,* 43–50. doi: 10.1080/17459435.2011.601524

Suter, E. A., Reyes, K. L., & Ballard, R. L. (2011b). Parental management of adoptive identities during challenging encounters: Adoptive parents as "protectors" and "educators." *Journal of Social and Personal Relationships, 28,* 242–261. doi: 10.1177/0265407510384419

Sweeney, M. M. (2010). Remarriage and stepfamilies: Strategic sites for family scholarship in the 21st century. *Journal of Marriage and Family, 72,* 667–684. doi: 10.1111/j.1741-3737.2010.00724.x

Tan, M. (2009, December 18). 2 million troops have deployed since 9/11. *MarineCorps Times.* Retrieved from http://www.marinecorpstimes.com/news/2009/12/military_deployments_121809w/

Tannen, D. (2001). *I only say this because I love you.* New York, NY: Random House.

Tannen, D. (2007). Power maneuvers and connection maneuvers in family interaction. In D. Tannen, S. Kendall, & C. Gordon (Eds.), *Family talk: Discourse and identity in four American families* (pp. 27–48). New York, NY: Oxford University Press.

Tannen, D., Kendall, S., & Gordon, C. (Eds.). (2007). *Family talk: Discourse and identity: Discourse and identity in four families.* New York, NY: Oxford University Press.

Taylor, S. E., Way, B. M., & Seeman, T. E. (2011). Early adversity and adult health outcomes. *Development and Psychopathology, 23,* 939–954. doi: 10.1017/S0954579411000411

Teachman, J., & Tedrow, L. (2008). The demography of stepfamilies in the United States. In J. Pryor (Ed.), *The international handbook of stepfamilies: Policy and practice in legal, research, and clinical environments* (pp. 3–29). Hoboken, NJ: Wiley.

Theiss, J. A., & Knobloch, L. K. (2013). A relational turbulence model of military service members' relational communication during reintegration. *Journal of Communication, 63,* 1109–1129. doi: 10.1111/jcom.12059

Theiss, J. A., & Knobloch, L. K. (2014). Relational turbulence and the post-deployment transition: Self, partner, and relationship focused turbulence. *Communication Research, 41,* 27–51. doi: 10.1177/0093650211429285

Thomas, A. J., & King, C. (2007). Gendered racial socialization of African American mothers and daughters. *The Family Journal, 15,* 137–142. doi: 10.1177/1066480706297853

Thompson, B., Koenig Kellas, J., Soliz, J., Thompson, J., Epp, A., & Schrodt, P. (2009). Family legacies: Constructing individual and familial identity through intergenerational storytelling. *Narrative Inquiry, 19,* 106–134. doi: 10.1075/ni.19.1.07tho

Thornton, A. (2009). Framework for interpreting long-term trends in values and beliefs concerning single parent families. *Journal of Marriage and Family, 71,* 230–234. doi: 10.1111/j.1741-3737.2009.00594.x

Thornton, A., & DeMarco-Young, L. (2001). Four decades of trends in attitudes toward family issues in the United States: The 1960s through the 1990s. *Journal of Marriage and Family, 63,* 1009–1037. doi: 10.1111/j.1741-3737.2001.01009.x

Tierney, W. G., & Venegas, K. M. (2006). Fictive kin and social capital: The role of peer groups in applying and paying for college. *American Behavioral Scientist, 49,* 1687–1702. doi: 10.1177/0002764206289145

Tilghman, A. (2013, August 14). Some gay troops to get extra "marriage leave." *Army Times.* Retrieved from http://www.armytimes.com/article/20130814/BENEFITS/308140021/Some-gay-troops-get-extra-marriage-leave-

To have and to hold: The trend giving homosexuals full marriage rights is gaining momentum (2012, November 17). *The Economist.* Retrieved from http://www.economist.com/news/international/21566626-trend-toward-giving-homosexuals-full-marriage-rights-gaining-momentum-have-and

Tracey, K. (2002). *Everyday talk: Building and reflecting identities.* New York, NY: Guilford Press.

Trees, A. R., & Koenig Kellas, J. (2009). Telling tales: Enacting family relationships in joint storytelling about difficult family experiences. *Western Journal of Communication, 73,* 91–111. doi: 10.1080/10570310802635021

Troll, L. E. (1983). Grandparents: The family watchdogs. In T. H. Brubaker (Ed.), *Family relationships in later life* (pp. 63–74). Beverly Hills, CA: Sage.

Trost, J. (1990). Do we mean the same by the concept of family? *Communication Research, 17,* 431–443. doi: 10.1177/009365090017004002

Trujillo, N. (2004). *In search of Naunny's grave: Age, class, gender and ethnicity in an American family.* Walnut Creek, CA: Alta Mira Press.

Turcotte, M. (2013). Living apart together. *Insights on Canadian Society.* Retrieved from http://www.statcan.gc.ca/pub/75-006-x/2013001/article/11771-eng.pdf

Turner, J. H. (1986). *The structure of sociological theory* (4th ed.). Chicago, IL: The Dorsey Press.

Turner, L. H. (2006). Diversity's impact on defining the family. In L. H. Turner & R. West (Eds.), *The family communication sourcebook* (pp. 3–20). Thousand Oaks, CA: Sage.

Turner, L. H., & West, R. (2011). "Sustaining the dialogue": National culture and family communication. *Journal of Family Communication, 11,* 67–68. doi: 10.1080/15267431.2011.554490

Turner, V. (1969). *The ritual process: Structure and anti-structure.* Ithaca, NY: Cornell University Press.

Turner, V. (1974). *Dramas, fields, and metaphors: Symbolic action in human society.* Ithaca, NY: Cornell University Press.

Uberoi, P. (1993). *Family, kinship, and marriage in India.* Delhi, India: Oxford University Press.

Uberoi, P. (Ed.). (1996). *Social reform, sexuality, and the state.* Delhi, India: Sage.

U.S. Bureau of the Census. (1992). Marriage, divorce, and remarriage in the 1990's. *Current Population Reports* (pp. 23–180). U.S. Government Printing Office: Washington, D.C.

U.S. Census Bureau. (2010a). *American fact finder*. Retrieved from http://factfinder2.census.gov/faces/tableservices/jsf/pages/productview.xhtml?pid=ACS_11_1YR_B10001&prodType=table

U.S. Census Bureau. (2010b). *America's families and living arrangements, 2010*. Retrieved from http://www.census.gov/population/www.socdemo/hh-fam/cps2010.htm

U.S. Census Bureau. (2012, April). *Households and families: 2010* (2010 Census Briefs, C2010BR-14). Retrieved from http://www.census.gob/prod/cen2010/briefs/C2010br-14.pdf

U.S. Census Bureau. (2012, October 25). *Census Bureau Releases 2009–2011 American Community Survey Estimates*. Retrieved from http://www.census.gov/newsroom/releases/archives/american_community_survey_acs/cb12-204.html

U.S. Department of Defense. (2012, November). *2011 demographics: Profile of the military community updated November 2012*. Retrieved from http://www.militaryonesource.mil/12038/MOS/Reports/2011_Demographics_Report.pdf

U.S. Department of Defense. (2014). *Casualty status*. Retrieved from http://www.defense.gov/news/casualty.pdf

U.S. Department of Health and Human Services. (2009). *Adoption USA: A chartbook based on the 2007 national survey of adoptive parents*. Retrieved from http://aspe.hhs.gov/hsp/09/NSAP/chartbook/chartbook.cfm?id=65

United Nations High Commission for Refugees. (2011). *Global trends*. (UNHCR A Year of Crises: 2011). Retrieved from http://www.unhcr.org/4fd6f87f9.html

Usdansky, M. L. (2009). A weak embrace: Popular and scholarly depictions of single-parent families, 1900–1998. *Journal of Marriage and Family, 71*, 209–225. doi: 10.1111/j.1741-3737.2009.00592.x

Usdansky, M. L., & Wolf, D. A. (2008). When child care breaks down. *Journal of Family Issues, 29*, 1185–1210. doi: 10.1177/0192513X08317045

VA, DOD to fund $100 million PTSD and TBI study. (2012, September 19). *Department of Veterans Affairs Office of Public and Intergovernmental Affairs News Release*. Retrieved from http://www.defense.gov/news/newsarticle.aspx?id=117933

Valenta, M., & Bunar, N. (2010). State assisted integration: Refugee integration policies in Scandinavian welfare states: The Swedish and Norwegian experience. *Journal of Refugee Studies, 23*, 463–483. doi: 10.1093/jrs/feq028

Van der Klis, M., & Karsten, L. (2009a). The commuter family as a geographical adaptive strategy for the work-family balance. *Community, Work, & Family, 12*, 330–354. doi: 10.1080/13668800902966372

Van der Klis, M., & Karsten, L. (2009b). Stories of belonging: Commuting partners, dual residences, and the meaning of home. *Journal of Environmental Psychology, 29*, 235–245. doi: 10.1016/j.jenvp.2008.11.002

Van Egeren, L. A., & Hawkins, D. P. (2004). Coming to terms with coparenting: Implications of definition and measurement. *Journal of Adult Development, 11*, 165–178. doi: 10.1023/B:JADE.0000035625.746720b

Villagran, M., Canzona, M. R., & Ledford, C. J. W. (2013). The milspouse battle rhythm: Communicating resilience throughout the deployment cycle. *Health Communication, 28,* 778–788. doi: 10.1080/10410236.2013.800441

Vinson, C., Mollen, D., & Smith, N. G. (2010). Perceptions of childfree women: The role of perceivers' and targets' ethnicity. *Journal of Community & Applied Social Psychology, 20,* 426–432. doi: 10.1002/casp.1049 10.1002/casp.1049

Wagner, K., Ritt-Olson, A., Chou, C., Pokhrel, P., Duan, L., Baezconde-Garbanati, L., ... Unger, J. (2010). Associations between family structure, family functioning, and substance use among Hispanic/Latino adolescents. *Psychology of Addictive Behavior, 24,* 98–108. doi: 10.1037/a0018497

Wahl, S. T., McBride, M. C., & Schrodt, P. (2005). Becoming "point and click" parents: A case study of communication and online adoption. *Journal of Family Communication, 5,* 279–294. doi: 10.1207/s15327698jfc0504_3

Waites, C. (2009). Building on strengths: Intergenerational practice with African American families. *Social Work, 54,* 278–287. doi: 10.1093/sw/54.3.278

Waldrop, D. P., & Weber, J. A. (2001). From grandparent to caregiver: The stress and satisfaction of raising grandchildren. *Families in Society: The Journal of Contemporary Human Services, 82,* 461–472. doi: 10.1606/1044-3894.177

Walker, L. J., & Hennig, K. H. (1997). Parent/child relationships in single-parent families. *Canadian Journal of Behavioural Science, 29,* 63–75. doi: 10.1037/0008-400X.29.1.63

Walsh, D. (2012). Using mobility to gain stability: Rural household strategies and outcomes in long-distance labour mobility. *Journal of Rural and Community Development, 7,* 123–143. Retrieved from http://jrcd.ca/include/getdoc.php?id=1468&article=677&mode=pdf

Walsh, F. (1996). The concept of family resilience: Crisis and challenge. *Family Process, 35,* 261–281. doi: 10.1111/j.1545-5300.1996.00261.x

Walsh, F. (2002). A family resilience framework: Innovative practice applications. *Family Relations, 51,* 130–137. doi: 10.1111/j.1741-3729.2002.00130.x

Walsh, F. (2003). Family resilience: A framework for clinical practice. *Family Process, 41,* 1–18. doi: 10.1111/j.1545-5300.2003.00001.x

Walsh, F. (2009). Human-animal bonds II: The role of pets in family systems and family therapy. *Family Process, 48,* 481–499. doi: 10.1111/j.1545-5300.2009.01297.x

Wamboldt, F., & Reiss, D. (1989). Task performance and the social construction of meaning: Juxtaposing normality with contemporary family research. In D. Offer & M. Sabshin (Eds.), *Normality: Context and theory* (pp. 2–40). New York, NY: Basic Books.

Watters, E. (2003). *Urban tribes: A generation redefines friendship, family, commitment.* New York, NY: Bloomsbury.

Weaver, S. E., & Coleman, M. H.(2010). Caught in the middle: Mothers in stepfamilies. *Journal of Social and Personal Relationships, 27,* 305–326. doi: 10.1177/0265407510361729

West, C., & Zimmerman, D. H. (1987). Doing gender. *Gender and Society, 1,* 125–151. doi: 10.1177/0891243287001002002

Weston, K. (1991). *Families we choose: Lesbians, gays, kinship.* New York, NY: Columbia University Press.

Whitchurch, G. G., & Dickson, F. C. (1999). Family communication. In M. Sussman, S. K. Steinmetz, & G. S. Peterson (Eds.), *Handbook of marriage and the family* (2nd ed., pp. 687–704). New York, NY: Plenum.

White House. (n.d.). *Joining forces.* Retrieved from http://www.whitehouse.gov/joiningforces

Widmar, E. D. (2006). Who are my family members? Bridging and binding social capital in family configurations. *Journal of Social and Personal Relationships, 23,* 979–998. doi: 10.1177/0265407506070482

Wiens, T. W., & Boss, P. (2006). Maintaining family resiliency before, during and after military separation. In C. A. Castro, A. B. Adler, & T. W. Britt (Eds.), *Military life: The psychology of serving in peace and combat (Volume 3: The military family)* (pp. 12–38). Westport, CT: Praeger Security International.

Wilcox, W. B. (2009). *The state of our unions: Marriage in America.* Retrieved from http://www.stateofourunions.org

Williamson, J., Softas-Nall, B., & Miller, J. (2003). Grandmothers raising grandchildren: An exploration of their experiences and emotions. *The Family Journal: Counseling and Therapy for Couples and Families, 11,* 23–32. doi: 10.1177/1066480702238468

Wilson, S. R., Chernichky, S. M., Wilkum, K., & Owlett, J. S. (2014). Do family communication patterns buffer children from difficulties associated with a parent's military deployment? Examining deployed and at-home parents' perspectives. *Journal of Family Communication, 14,* 32–51. doi: 10.1080/15267431.2013.857325

Wilson, S. R., Wilkum, K., Chernichky, S. M., MacDermid Wadsworth, S. M., & Broniarczyk, K. M. (2011). Passport toward success: Description and evaluation of a program designed to help children and families reconnect after a military deployment. *Journal of Applied Communication Research, 39,* 223–249. doi: 10.1080/00909882.2011.585399

Winfield, F. E. (1985). *Commuter marriage: Living together, apart.* New York, NY: Columbia University Press.

Wolf-Wendel, L., Twombly, S. B., & Rice, S. (2004). *The two-body problem: Dual-career-couple hiring practices in higher education.* Baltimore, MD: Johns Hopkins University Press.

Wolin, S. J., & Bennett, L. A. (1984). Family rituals. *Family Process, 23,* 401–420. doi: 10.1111/j.1545-5300.1984.00401.x

Wood, J. T. (in press). Critical feminist theories. In D. O. Braithwaite & P. Schrodt (Eds.), *Engaging theories in interpersonal communication* (2nd ed.). Los Angeles, CA: Sage.

Wooley, M. E., & Grogan-Kaylor, A. (2006). Protective family factors in the context of neighborhood: Promoting positive school outcomes. *Family Relations, 55,* 93–104. Retrieved from http://www.uncssp.org/publications/Woolley%20%282006%29%20Protective%20Family%20Factors%20FR.pdf

Wotapka, D. (2013, November 7). Military families fear housing allowance is at risk. *The Wall Street Journal.* Retrieved from http://online.wsj.com/news/articles/SB10001424052702304682504579157740669179908

Wren, K. (2003). Refugee dispersal in Denmark: From macro to micro-scale analysis. *International Journal of Population Geography, 9,* 1–19. doi: 10.1002/ijpg.273

Wren, K. (2007). Supporting asylum seekers and refugees in Glasgow: The role of multi-agency networks. *Journal of Refugee Studies, 20,* 391–413. doi: 10.1093/jrs/fem006

Wronska-Friend, M. (2004). Globalised threads: Costumes of the Hmong community in North Queensland. In N. Tapp & G. Y. Lee (Eds.), *The Hmong of Australia culture and diaspora* (pp. 25–58). Canberra, Australia: Pandanus Books.

Wydra, M., O'Brien, K. M., Merson, E. S. (2012). In their own words: Adopted persons' experiences of adoption disclosure and discussion in their families. *Journal of Family Social Work, 15,* 62–77. doi: 10.1080/10522158.2012.642616

Xu, Q. (2007). A child-centered refugee settlement program in the United States. *Journal of Immigrant & Refugee Studies, 5,* 37–59. doi: 10.1300/J500v05n03_03

Young, I. M. (1997). *Intersecting voices: Dilemmas of gender, political philosophy, and policy.* Princeton, N.J.: Princeton University Press.

Zoroya, G. (2008, April 25). More U.S. troops battle foreclosure. *USA Today.* Retrieved from http://usatoday30.usatoday.com/news/military/2008-04-24-foreclosure_N.htm

# About the Contributors

**Tamara D. Afifi** (Ph.D., University of Nebraska-Lincoln) is a Professor in the Department of Communication Studies at the University of Iowa. Her research focuses on communication patterns that foster risk and resiliency in families and in other interpersonal relationships, with particular emphasis on: (1) information regulation (privacy, secrets, disclosures, avoidance) and (2) communication processes related to stress, conflict, uncertainty, social support, strength, and communal coping.

**Chitra Akkoor** (Ph.D., University of Iowa) is Assistant Professor at Keene State College. Her research interests include the study of culture, communication, and interpersonal relationships among diasporic populations. Her teaching interests include courses in intercultural communication, family communication, ethnography, and diaspora. She is passionate about travelling in search of new cultural experiences.

**Melissa W. Alemán** (Ph.D., University of Iowa) is the Associate Dean of The Graduate School and Professor of Communication Studies at James Madison University. She examines discursive and narrative understandings of communication in families, particularly aging families, including explorations of communication in long-term marriages, accounts of custodial grandparents, and dialectics of caregiving in later life. Her scholarship informs her engagement, outreach and advocacy with practitioners who work with aging families.

**Leslie A. Baxter** (Ph.D., University of Oregon) is a Professor of Communication Studies and a Collegiate Fellow in the College of Liberal Arts & Sciences, where she was also named F. Wendell Miller Distinguished Professor. She is interested in the competing discourses through which meanings are made, especially in family relationships. She has published over 160 books, chapters, and research articles and is the recipient of several disciplinary awards for her scholarship, including from the NCA, the Distinguished Scholar Award, the Mark L. Knapp Interpersonal Communication Award, and the Bernard J. Brommel Family Communication Award.

**Karla Mason Bergen** (Ph.D., University of Nebraska-Lincoln) is Associate Professor at the College of Saint Mary. A dual background in Family Communication and Women's Studies led to her scholarly agenda of investigating questions related to women's communicative construction of identity. Her scholarly work on the communicative dynamics of commuter marriage has been published in outlets including *Journal of Applied Communication, Journal of Family Communication,* and *Journal of Social and Personal Relationships.*

**Dawn O. Braithwaite** (Ph.D., University of Minnesota) is a Willa Cather Professor of Communication and Chairperson at University of Nebraska-Lincoln. She examines how those in personal and family relationships communicate during transitions and challenge, studying rituals, relational dialectics, and supportive communication. She has published over 95 articles and five books. Braithwaite received the National Communication Association's Brommel Award in Family Communication. She is Past President of the Western States of Communication Association and of the National Communication Association.

**Devika Chawla** (Ph.D., Purdue University) is Associate Professor in the School of Communication Studies at Ohio University. She is interested in narrative and performative approaches to family identity. Alongside numerous essays, she is the author of two books (with Amardo Rodriguez)—*Liminal Traces: Storying, Performing, and Embodying Postcoloniality* (Sense Publishers) and *Intercultural Communication: An Ecological Approach* (Kendall Hunt). Her new book-length monograph, *Home, Uprooted: Oral Histories of India's Partition*, is forthcoming with Fordham University Press.

**Shardé Davis** (M.A., University of California-Santa Barbara) is a doctoral student in the Department of Communication Studies at the University of Iowa. Her interdisciplinary research program uses theories and approaches from Communication,

Feminist Studies, and Ethnic Studies to investigate how ethnicity and gender shape relational dynamics and communication processes.

**Rebecca DiVerniero** (Ph.D., University of Nebraska-Lincoln) is an Assistant Professor of Communication at Dixie State University. She investigates the communication in and around family and interpersonal relationships during times of stress and change, with a particular focus on uncertainty management, accommodation, and privacy management in transitional periods. She was named National States Advisory Council's 2013 "Scholar of the Year" for her research on turning points in new stepfamily and extended kin relationships.

**Kathleen M. Galvin** (Ph.D., Northwestern University) is Professor of Communication Studies at Northwestern University. Her scholarly interests include how members of families formed beyond biology and law construct and maintain their identities through communication practices and how families make decisions when a child faces major health crises. She has co-authored or edited nine books, as well as multiple chapters and articles. She is the senior author of *Family Communication: Cohesion and Change*, the first textbook in family communication.

**Pamela J. Lannutti** (Ph.D., University of Georgia) is Associate Professor of Communication and Director of the Graduate Program in Professional and Business Communication at La Salle University. She studies communication in personal relationships, especially in same-sex relationships. She has published her research on same-sex marriage in various journals including *Journal of Family Communication, Journal of Social and Personal Relationships,* and *Journal of Homosexuality.*

**Anne Merrill** (M.A., University of California-Santa Barbara) is a doctoral candidate in the Department of Communication at the University of California-Santa Barbara. Her research interests are in interpersonal, relational, and family communication, focusing on processes such as information regulation (i.e., topic avoidance, disclosure, secrecy, and privacy), conflict, uncertainty, stress, and coping within close relationships.

**Erin Sahlstein Parcell** (Ph.D., University of Iowa) is an Associate Professor in the Department of Communication at the University of Wisconsin, Milwaukee. She studies communication within and about personal relationships, most recently military families and deployment. She has published in outlets such as the *Journal of Applied Communication Research, Communication Monographs,* and the *Journal of Family Communication.* She is currently co-editing a collection for Peter Lang on military research in the communication discipline (*A Communicative Perspective on the Military: Messages, Strategies, Meanings*).

**Paul Schrodt** (Ph.D., University of Nebraska-Lincoln) is the Philip J. & Cheryl C. Burguières Professor, Graduate Director, and Professor of Communication Studies at Texas Christian University. He studies communication behaviors that facilitate family functioning, with a particular interest in stepfamily relationships. He has published over 80 articles and book chapters and was the 2012 recipient of the Brommel Award for Outstanding Scholarship in Family Communication from the National Communication Association.

**Keli Ryan Steuber** (Ph.D., Pennsylvania State University) is an Assistant Professor of Communication Studies at the College of New Jersey. Her work examines how individuals and spouses manage information within their social networks during health and relational transitions, most recently within the context of infertility. Her research is published in outlets such as *Communication Monographs, Journal of Social and Personal Relationships*, and *Journal of Applied Communication Research*.

**Elizabeth A. Suter** (Ph.D., University of Illinois at Urbana-Champaign) is an Associate Professor in the Department of Communication Studies at the University of Denver. Her scholarship examines issues of identity, sexuality, and race in families with a particular focus on lesbian families and adoptive families. To pursue her program of research, she takes a qualitative social-scientific approach. Most recently, she was awarded the Monograph of the Year Award from the National Communication Association's GLBTQ Division and Caucus.

# Subject Index

# Cited Author Index

# J

Jackson, A. P., 219, 225, 265
Jacobson, C. K., 141, 283
Jacobson, H., 26, 143, 145, 146, 265
Jadva, V., 136, 265, 271
Jamison, T., 170, 260
Jannusch, A., 40, 153, 249
Jayakody, R., 176, 253
Jeffords, S., 196, 265
Jehn, K., A., 215, 216, 220, 265, 278
Jendrick, M. P., 86, 265
Jenkins, J., 71, 276
Jennings-Kelsall, V., 200, 202, 265
Jeynes, W., 71, 265
Johnson, C. L., 176, 184, 187, 265
Johnson, S. E., 218, 265
Jokelainen, J., 71, 278
Jones, A., 162, 251
Jones, C., 141, 265
Jones, D. J., 79, 265
Jones, J., 122, 253
Jones, N., 266
Jones, P. B., 71, 278
Jones-Sanpei, H., 78, 276
Jordan, B., 203, 265
Joseph, A. L., 196, 200, 202, 265
Juarez, B. G., 141, 283
Jubilut, L. L., 232, 266
Judd, J., 201, 258
Julien, D., 52, 266
Jurkovic, G. J., 80, 266

# K

Kalil, A., 82, 256
Kallaba, M., 262
Kaminski, P. L., 86, 263
Kapadia, K. M., 104-106, 110, 266
Kapur, P., 104, 106, 107, 266
Karner, T. X., 176, 188, 266
Karsten, L., 211, 215, 220, 221, 223, 226, 287

Kaye, L. W., 187, 266
Keiley, M. K., 99, 101, 256
Keith, B., 74, 247
Keith, S., 161, 162, 245
Kekic, E., 232, 257
Keller, R. T., 199, 266
Kelley, M. L., 204, 206, 266
Kelly, M., 126, 266
Kemper, R. V., 186, 266
Kendall, S., 27, 266, 285
Kendall-Tackett, K. A., 20, 266
Keown-Bomar, J., 231, 233, 242, 266
Kertzer, D. I., 4, 266
Kim, A.-R., 45, 270
Kim, B., 45, 270
Kim, H. K., 231, 252
Kim, O. M., 141, 142, 267
Kim, P., 73, 258
King, C., 75, 285
Kingson, E. R., 87, 282
Kingston, A., 215, 267
Kirby, E., 211, 250
Kirby, E. L., 129, 252
Kirschner, B. F., 216, 267
Kiser, L. J., 91, 267
Klobus, P., 176, 264
Kluger, M. P., 100, 267
Kluwer, E., 123, 267
Knobloch, L. K., 196, 198, 200-202, 208, 267, 285
Koenig Kellas, J., 40, 61, 84, 91, 151, 154, 157, 168, 170, 171, 182, 249, 268, 286
Koerner, A. F., 11, 268
Kokanovic, R., 231, 268
Koller, S., 76, 253
Kotchick, B. A., 78, 268
Kranstuber, H., 141, 143, 144, 151, 154, 178, 251, 254, 268
Kreider, R. M., 69, 70, 282
Krouse, S., 81, 245
Krusiewicz, E. S., 150, 151, 268
Kumar, P., 106, 107, 268
Kuntsche, E. N., 77, 78, 268

# LIFESPAN
## COMMUNICATION
*Children, Families, and Aging*

Thomas J. Socha, *General Editor*

From first words to final conversations, communication plays an integral and significant role in all aspects of human development and everyday living. The Lifespan Communication: Children, Families, and Aging series seeks to publish authored and edited scholarly volumes that focus on relational and group communication as they develop over the lifespan (infancy through later life). The series will include volumes on the communication development of children and adolescents, family communication, peer-group communication (among age cohorts), intergenerational communication, and later-life communication, as well as longitudinal studies of lifespan communication development, communication during lifespan transitions, and lifespan communication research methods. The series includes college textbooks as well as books for use in upper-level undergraduate and graduate courses.

Thomas J. Socha, Series Editor | *tsocha@odu.edu*
Mary Savigar, Acquisitions Editor | *mary.savigar@plang.com*

To order other books in this series, please contact our Customer Service Department at:

(800) 770-LANG (within the U.S.)
(212) 647-7706 (outside the U.S.)
(212) 647-7707 FAX

Or browse online by series at www.peterlang.com